Virtual Freedoms, Terrorism and the Law

AF757918

Edited by
Giovanna De Minico and Oreste Pollicino

Virtual Freedoms, Terrorism and the Law

Routledge
Taylor & Francis Group
LONDON AND NEW YORK

G. Giappichelli Editore

First published 2021
by Routledge
2 Park Square, Milton Park, Abingdon, Oxon OX14 4RN

and by Routledge
605 Third Avenue, New York, NY 10158

Routledge is an imprint of the Taylor & Francis Group, an informa business

© 2021 selection and editorial matter, Giovanna De Minico and Oreste Pollicino; individual chapters, the contributors

The right of Giovanna De Minico and Oreste Pollicino to be identified as authors of the editorial material, and of the authors for their individual chapters, has been asserted in accordance with sections 77 and 78 of the Copyright, Designs and Patents Act 1988.

All rights reserved. No part of this book may be reprinted or reproduced or utilised in any form or by any electronic, mechanical, or other means, now known or hereafter invented, including photocopying and recording, or in any information storage or retrieval system, without permission in writing from the publishers.

Trademark notice: Product or corporate names may be trademarks or registered trademarks, and are used only for identification and explanation without intent to infringe.

British Library Cataloguing-in-Publication Data
A catalogue record for this book is available from the British Library

Library of Congress Cataloging-in-Publication Data
A catalog record has been requested for this book

ISBN: 978-0-367-48670-9 (hbk-Routledge)
ISBN: 978-0-367-55017-2 (pbk)
ISBN: 978-88-921-3024-1 (hbk-Giappichelli)
ISBN: 978-1-003-09156-1 (ebk-Routledge)

Typeset in Simoncini Garamond
by G. Giappichelli Editore, Turin, Italy

The manuscript has been subjected to the double blind peer review process prior to publication.

This book has been published with the contribution of Ermes – European research centre on media for e-society (director Prof. Giovanna De Minico).

The co-editors wish to thank Giovanni De Gregorio and Miriam Viggiano for their help in our editorial project.

Giovanna and Oreste

Contents

List of Contributors

Abbondante Fulvia, Researcher of Public Law, Professor of Information and Communication Law at University of Naples Federico II (Italy)

De Gregorio Giovanni, PhD candidate in Constitutional Law at University of Milano-Bicocca (Italy)

De Minico Giovanna, Full Professor of Constitutional Law, University of Naples Federico II (Italy). Director of the European Research Centre on Media for e-Society (www.ermes.unina.it)

de Oliveira Santos Colnago Cláudio, PhD in Fundamental Rights and Guarantees at Law Faculty of de Vitória (Brazil)

De Tullio Maria Francesca, PhD in "Human Rights. Theory, History, Practice" at University of Naples Federico II (Italy), Post-doc researcher at University of Antwerp (Belgium)

Orefice Maria, PhD in Constitutional Law at University of Naples Federico II (Italy)

Pollicino Oreste, Full Professor of Constitutional Law at Bocconi University, Milan (Italy). Member of the Executive Board, European Agency for Fundamental Rights, Vienna (Austria)

Reisel Mary, Cultural Anthropologist at Rikkyo University of Tokyo (Japan)

Serra Cristóbal Rosario, Full Professor of Constitutional Law at University of Valencia (Spain)

Shcherbovich Andrey A., PhD, Associate Professor at Department of Constitutional Law of National Research University Higher School of Economics of Moscow (Russia)

Teruel Lozano Germán M., Assistant Professor in Constitutional Law at University of Murcia (Spain)

Viggiano Miriam, Lawyer, Officer at Italian Data Protection Authority, PhD in National and European Public Law at Second University of Naples (Italy)

Introduction

Today's terrorism has changed from an isolated and extra-ordinary event to an endemic and normally expected situation, even if it is unforeseeable when, where and how the new explosion of violence will take place. Thus, it is no longer an event encompassed in a definite time frame, after which a legal order will resume its normal course. It tends, rather, to last *sine die*, affecting individuals' daily life. Summing up, it can be defined as an ordinary time terrorism.

In this volume a group of international scholars, members of the International Association of Constitutional Law research group "Constitutions in the Age of the Internet", has devoted special attention to the following questions: What are the characteristics of ordinary time terrorism in normal circumstances? What risks imperil the Internet, which is put under stress by this kind of terrorism? What was – and what will be – the supranational lawmakers' reaction to this challenge in a state of law? What is the role of judges?

The Internet, challenged in the face of this new terrorism, has shown a dual, unprecedented and contradictory identity: a place for the exercise of all kinds of freedom, but also a field for terrorism-related crimes. This role involuntarily helps terror strategies, thus undermining the rights and freedoms of individuals online.

This Janus-faced situation has led to a two-edged regulatory response: promoting, on the one hand, and undermining, on the other hand, individuals' fundamental rights. The legislation of different countries affected by the various interventions looks schizophrenic: it states everything and its opposite. Indeed, the Internet as multiplier of the liberties has called for a regulation expanding rights and freedoms. Whereas the aptitude of the Internet to technically facilitate the commission of crimes, compared to what would happen in the material reality, has led, at the national and supranational level, to the adoption of regulation restraining the aforementioned spaces of freedom. One could consider the terrorists' recruitment, whose border with the right of association is very weak, because the crime is built on the model of crimes of "abstract danger". The latter term means a crime where the existence of the danger is merely assumed, while the infringement of security is not verified.

In the case of Internet the response of national and European lawmakers, as shown in several chapters in the book, favours security, by generally restricting fundamental freedoms, in violation of the precautionary and proportionality principles. These two principles constitute the legitimacy tests with which the model of the 'laws of fear' shall comply to protect the rule of law by avoiding an atypical regime of constant emergency.

Finally, it is worth emphasising the way the Internet is tailored by the creative role played by the European Court of Justice (ECJ) and the European Court of Human Rights (ECHR) in reviewing the controversial relationship between the protection of personal data and the safeguarding of national security, drawn by the legislator. The symbolic cases, Digital Rights Ireland and Schrems, show how the ECJ broadly interpreted the scope of protection of the fundamental rights of privacy and data protection. In addition to this, Schrems gives the opportunity to discuss the new compromise resulting from the Privacy Shield. Its implementation does not seem to have resolved the uncertainties related to the level of protection provided by the US legal order and most notably by the Safe Harbor principles. We wish to clarify that this part of the discussion will basically be focused on the possible evolution of the digital privacy enforcement and on the exploration of the relevant constitutional issues raised in line with the supranational constitutional framework.

We have chosen a completely new bottom-up method. This is due to the specific theme – the new rights and the new forms of protection in the age of the Internet – which is a rapidly evolving field, and as such is susceptible to change day by day.

These are, thus, our scientific contributions to the development of Internet in a time of ordinary terrorism.

Giovanna and Oreste

Every Day's Terrorism

Giovanna De Minico

1. *The New Face of Terrorism*

The latest generation of terrorism can assume the threatening face of a foreign fighter or that, apparently innocent, of a neighbour totally committed to his daily routines. It may be imported from distant grounds of violence or grow hidden in the social desert of a *banlieue*. It can target the traditional symbols of established powers or hit with irrational cruelty any moment of civil gatherings. It is a changing and polymorphic phenomenon, difficult to prevent and repress, that injects fear in everybody's mind due to the expectation that it can come back time and again.

Today's terrorism mutates its nature from an isolated and extra-ordinary event to an endemic and normally expected one, even if it is unforeseeable when, where, and how the new explosion of violence will take place. Thus, it is no longer an event encompassed in a definite time frame, after which a legal order resumes its normal course. It tends, rather, to last *sine die*, hanging over the daily life of the people.

Summing up, it can be defined as an ordinary time terrorism.

The recurrent nature of this event affects the work of the emergency legislator, which has to dwell upon the probability of the terrorist act happening on the basis of an *ex ante* prognosis. The legislator has to assess in advance what the chances are that the feared event may actually take place, in order to provide proper remedies for removing or reducing the citizens' fear.

It is precisely this fear that is at the origin of the "law of fear" expression, which is not a law generically aimed at preventing and repressing ordinary violence. It is, rather, a law generated by the special fear caused by the latest generation of terrorism: a fear that exerts a pervasive effect over the daily life of each person and that gives rise to a collective social alert.

The legislator has to face problems, which may even be old, but certainly require a completely new approach. The regulation to be laid down in order to determine and prevent the terrorist event in advance cannot be based on a fact that has already occurred or on the *id quod plerumque accidit* criterion. The legislator must perform a probabilistic assessment of the risk of it taking place in the future.

In this chapter, which should serve as a general framework to the volume, we will focus on the basic issue posed by terrorism: to what extent can an emergency situation depart from the fundamental principles of the rule of law without compromising a return to the normal institutional order?

Our *iter procedendi* will be the following: the first step considers the model of the "law of fear", as sketched by American doctrine and now accepted also by the European legal culture. The second step entails an analysis of the Directive of the European Parliament and the Council 2017/541 'on combating terrorism', as well as of the French law 2017 'renforçant la sécurité intérieure et la lute contre le terrorisme'. The last step sets out our evaluation of the paradigm of the law of fear in respect of both its European legitimacy profile and its effectiveness. In this way our reasoning will come to a circular conclusion.

2. *The Law of Fear Today*

Let us have a closer look at the "law of fear" model. It owes its construction to Cass R. Sunstein. [1] In his opinion, this paradigm is utilized when the policy-maker intends to anticipate a dangerous event that is likely to happen, but is not certain. The aim thus pursued is to prevent the danger of a future event being converted into a reality.

Here, the legislator must move on the slippery slope of risk, involving both verifying and assessing the probability of it taking place. In this context, his task requires the mediation between opposing values: on the one side, there are the fundamental rights – freedom of speech, personal liberty, privacy, and so on – that may be legally squeezed in order to preserve the security of citizens. [2] On the other side, the opposite value is represented by the security of citizens, [3] which requires the prevention of the risk of terrorism. Indeed, the legislator is normally expected to balance constitutionally relevant and equivalent goods; but here these values are misaligned because of the different time of their coming into effect. In fact, a present and certain damage occurs to the fundamental freedoms, which are being compressed; by contrast, a future

[1] Cass R Sunstein, *The Laws of Fear* (Cambridge University Press 2005), in particular chapters 1-–2.

[2] Arianna Vedaschi and Gabriele Marino Noberasco, 'From DRD to PNR: Looking for a New Balance between Privacy and Security', in David D Cole, Federico Fabbrini, and Stephen Schulhofer (eds), *Surveillance, Privacy and Trans-Atlantic Relations* (Hart Publishing 2017), 67-–87.

[3] See: Stephen Sedley, 'Terrorism and Security: Back to the Future?', in David D Cole, Federico Fabbrini, and Arianna Vedaschi (eds), *Secrecy, National Security and the Vindication of Constitutional Law* (Edward Elgar Publishing 2013), 13, and Federico Fabbrini, 'Privacy and National Security in the Digital Age. European and Comparative Constitutional Perspectives' (2015) 20 Tilburg Law Review, 5-–13.

and hypothetical advantage is expected with reference to security, which is strengthened. So the damage suffered by the holder of the right to privacy (to indicate just one of the rights in question) should be more than compensated for by the future (though uncertain) advantage provided to the holders of the right to security.

The legal decision concerning the risk, which is at the root of the "law of fear", appears to be a classic example of a political issue that entails an assessment without certainty and incontestability. In fact, if the evaluation parameter is modified, a decision contrary to the initial one would probably be reached.

This being the case, the evaluation of the risk is usually subjected to legal criteria, but a non-eliminable political discretion remains.

In the light of the above, chief judges – national and supranational, from the Supreme Court of the United States[4] to the European Court of Justice[5] – have been narrowing the discretion of the policy-maker in accordance with the precautionality and proportionality principles, which should guarantee a balanced coexistence between competing values.

3. *About the Precautionality Principle*

The legislator has to assess what the actual chances are that the risk will happen. It is an *ex ante* prognosis judgment of the threatened danger which is far from being a mathematical test. [6] In fact, the answer to this question depends on the level on the

---

[4] Just to quote the leading case: the US Supreme Court has clearly stated that emergency powers cannot be conceived as unlimited; *ex parte* Milligan (1866), 71 U.S. 2, Wall. 2 2; Korematsu v. United States (1944), No. 22, 323 U.S. 214. Moreover, it has elaborated a proportionality test to balance public interest with the individual freedom: Mathews v. Eldridge (1976) 424 U. S. 319; United States v. Salerno (1987) 481 U. S. 739, 746; Schall v. Martin (1984) 467 U. S. 253, 274-275, quoted in Hamdi et al. v. Rumsfeld, secretary of defense, et al. (2004), No. 03-6696.

[5] Court of Justice, Joined Cases C-293/12 and C-594/12 [2014] Digital Rights Ireland Ltd v. Minister for Communications, Marine and Natural Resources, Minister for Justice, Equality and Law Reform, The Commissioner of the Garda Síochána, Ireland and the Attorney General and Kärntner Landesregierung, Michael Seitlinger, Christof Tschohl and Others (hereinafter: Digital Rights Ireland), [2014]OJ C175/6; Id., Case C-362/14 [2015] Maximillian Schrems v. Data Protection Commissioner, see in particular para. 33.

[6] Here we cannot summarize American literature which is an incomparable reference in this subject. We mention only those Authors who have described different features of this criterion. For the comparison of values misaligned in time, see: David E Adelman, 'Harmonizing Methods of Scientific Inference with the Precautionary Principle: Opportunities and Constraints' (2004) 34 Environmental Law Reporter, 10133. On the relativity of the criterion affected by the political perspective of the legislator, see: Daniel Bodansky, 'Deconstructing the Precautionary Principle', in David D Caro and Harry N Scheiber (eds), *Bringing New Law To Ocean Waters* (Martinus Nijhoff/Brill 2004), 381 ss.; Gregory N Mandel and James T Gathii, 'Cost-benefit Analysis Versus the Precautionary Principle: Beyond Cass Sunstein's Laws of Fear' (2006) 5 University of Illinois Law Review, 1037–1079; Oren Perez, 'Precautionary Governance and the Limits of Scientific Knowledge: A Democratic Framework for Regulating Nanotech-

ladder of risk at which the legislator has chosen to stop: what is the danger that he is prepared to take?

Such a decision will be influenced by two factors: the time and the social target of the decision. As to the first factor, one may assume that the lawmaker is more prone to meet a security demand when an electoral vote is imminent than in the absence of any such event. Restrictive measures may be adopted in this case in order to acquire the *electoris favor,* independently of the existence of an effective risk of a terroristic attack.

Passing to the second factor, i.e. the social target selected, the outcome of the decision is different depending on the category of persons whose interests are given priority. Rich people are inclined to accept higher security risks because they are unwilling to lose their liberties. In fact, not only are they the formal holders of these rights, they are also those who may effectively exercise them.

The reverse applies to poor people, who only enjoy a formal right to these liberties. Thus, they have little to lose in case of restrictive measures, demanding instead, and at least, that their security be assured.[7]

It is clear, therefore, that the time and the social target of the decision affect the position on the ladder of risk selected by the lawmaker. In turn, this will result in a different appreciation of the precautionality principle and a different balance between liberties and security.

The foregoing remarks lead to the conclusion that the outcome of the precautionality assessment is disputable, i.e. it is controversial.

In accordance with the precautionality principle, the legislator should lay down criminal offences based on danger, that is conducts whose realization doesn't require the actual happening of the criminal event: clearly, when the terrorist attack occurs, it would be too late and useless to intervene. It is equally true that the mere criminal intention isn't *per se* to be punished, when no protected value has been actually and concretely affected. Here the double principles of materiality and offensiveness are brought to the concept of the attempted crime. The latter must not be fully completed in every material element, but it should consist at least in fragments of material behaviour capable of offending the protected value, to put it at risk of being compromised.

Having said that, the first corollary coming from the precautionality principle implies that the legislator should abstain from typical legal assessments, namely he must not assume the existence of a risk regardless of its concrete evaluation. He should rather check by an *ex ante* prognosis the reasonable occurrence of the feared event. One con-

---

nology' (2010) Bar Ilan University Pub Law Working Paper; also Noah Sachs, 'Rescuing the Strong Precautionary Principle from its Critics' (2011) 4 University of Illinois Law Review, 1285–1338. For a helpful discussion on the precautionary principle in the European context, see: Cristopher Hodd, Henry Rothstein, and Robert Baldwin, *The Government of Risk* (Oxford University Press 2004), in particular chapter 7.

[7] Conor Gearty, *Liberty and Security* (Polity Press 2013), 20-21 and 74.

sequence of this is that the *periculum* must be an imminent, serious, and great danger.

At this point the question is: which symptoms would be able to reveal the risk to the legislator? Or, in other words, which is the right moment for the legislator to act, without punishing the mere criminal intention? This issue will be dealt with when we analyse the concrete examples of criminal laws of fear.

4. *About the Proportionality Principle*

Given the insufficiency of the precautionality criterion, the legislator had to supplement it by means of the proportionality parameter. Pursuant to the proportionality principle, the cost suffered by a freedom that would be compressed must be compared with the benefits provided to security, the opposite value that would be favoured.[8]

The difference in weight between costs and benefits should suggest that judges set the proportionality not in the usual terms of equivalence, but in those of reasonable inequality: the advantage to the protected value (security), because of its uncertainty, must exceed the certain damage caused to the compressed right (the right to the freedom being attacked).[9] This asymmetrical balance can be clearly perceived if one considers that the compared goods are not aligned on the same temporal dimension: individual freedom, for example privacy, suffers damage here and now, while security will receive a future and uncertain advantage, depending on the occurrence of the feared event. So let's see if this 'asymmetrical balance' between the competing values has been respected in a key act of prevention against terrorism: the Data Retention Directive 2006/24.[10]

---

[8] See, for instance: Gregory Mandel and James T Gathii, *Cost-Benefit Analysis versus the Precautionary Principle: Beyond Cass Sunstein's Laws of Fear,* 1044–1045 '[t]he difficulties inherent in application of cost-benefit analysis are now well described. A considerable literature (including some of Sunstein's own work) demonstrates that substantial challenges regarding (a) uncertainty, (b) valuation, and (c) temporal concerns render even rough application of cost-benefit analysis often impossible'. Opinion also of: Mark Geistfeld, 'Implementing the Precautionary Principle?' (2001) 31 Environmental Law Reporter, 11326–11333; David E Adelman, 'Harmonizing Methods of Scientific Inference with the Precautionary Principle: Opportunities and Constraints', 10131–10140; Matthias J Borgers and Elies van Sliedregt, 'The Meaning of the Precautionary Principle for the Assessment of Criminal Measures in the Fight Against Terrorism' (2009) 2(2) Erasmus Law Review, 171 ss. and Sidney A Shapiro, Elizabeth C Fisher, and Wendy E Wagner, 'The Enlightenment of Administrative Law: Looking Inside the Agency for Legitimacy' (2012) 3 Wake Forest Law Review, 463 ss.

[9] On some of the complexities here, see: Kent Roach, *The 9/11 Effect. Comparative Counter-terrorism* (Cambridge University Press 2011), 426; Robert Alexy, *Teoria dei diritti fondamentali* (Il Mulino 2011), 651-653.

[10] Directive 2006/24/EC of the European Parliament and of the Council of 15 March 2006 on the retention of data generated or processed in connection with the provision of publicly available electronic communications services or of public communications networks and amending Directive 2002/58/EC [2006] OJ L 105/54.

In brief, the basic philosophy of the Directive has been to change the negative duty imposed on the Internet Service Provider (ISP) and the communications operators. The previous prohibition to retain extrinsic data of phone conversations or Internet communications has been converted into the opposite obligation to store all data of any consumers for a long time in order to prevent future criminal offences.

This is the hard core of the rule.

The Court of Justice [11] declared invalid this regulation essentially for breaching the proportionality principle (Art. 52 of the EU Charter of Fundamental Rights).

The decision is particularly significant for our purposes for two reasons: firstly, it states in clear words which is the *minimum status* of the privacy; secondly, it admits that, without prejudice of such *minimum*, this fundamental right can be downgraded to account for the need for security, provided however that the fair balance between these two competing values is assured.

Let's follow the reasoning of the Supreme Judge. [12]

For what concerns the *mimimum*, the above right is deemed to be characterized by an indefectible content that may not be lowered for security reasons. Thus, the privacy cannot be compressed to such an extent to *de facto* result in a complete denial of the right. But this has been exactly what happened with the Directive, which in requesting the collection of all the extrinsic data of each citizen has created a permanent eye on the life of the entire European population. [13]

Hence security must not infringe a first essential feature: the adopted regulation may not affect the generality but only defined subjects.

The same request for specificity applies to the object and the methods of the collection process, which may concern only identified data, otherwise it is a trawling mechanism, and may be implemented only by means of well identified tools. The Directive, instead, was drawing the data from all means of electronic communication, the use of which is widespread and of growing importance in people's everyday lives.

Furthermore, privacy can be sacrificed in the presence of a serious and imminent threat to security, certainly not just because of a generic repression of organized crime. This feature is strictly connected to the judgment of the *ex ante* prognosis, as discussed above; the judge requests that the data collected belong only to persons who have a link, even if indirect, to terrorism. Instead, the Directive weakens the effective risk of terrorism to an extent that does not entail stretching the data collection to include everyone, even those above suspicion. Certainly Directive 2006/24 'contributes to the fight against serious crime', but 'does not require any relationship between the data whose retention is provided for and a threat to public security' and, as the European Court of Justice has noted, the retention is not restricted 'in relation

---

[11] Digital Rights Ireland.

[12] Among several scholars, see: Orla Lynskey, *The Foundations of EU Data Protection Law* (Oxford University Press 2015) 163–169, with wide references to jurisprudence.

[13] Digital Rights Ireland, para. 56.

'to data pertaining to a particular time period and/or a particular geographical zone and/or to a circle of particular persons likely to be involved, in one way or another, in a serious crime', or 'to persons who could, for other reasons, contribute, by the retention of their data, to the prevention, detection, or prosecution of serious offences'. [14]

Last but not least, privacy also requires that access to data is allowed only to certain public subjects that offer a guarantee of impartiality, the judge, and independent authorities. Whereas, the Directive has opened up generalized access also on the side of the beneficiary. [15]

In a comparative perspective the Directive went way beyond the American Foreign Intelligence Surveillance Act, [16] which has conditioned this bulk collection to three guarantees: the facts have to evidence that there are reasonable grounds for a person to be suspected of being a terrorist; these meta data have to be 'relevant' to the investigation, and, finally, the order in favour of the NSA's access is taken by a judge, even if a special one (the Intelligence Surveillance Court of Review).

Well, even these three *minimum* guarantees, [17] however insufficient, have not been inserted in the Directive in question.

Thus, the final step of the reasoning is completed when the judge links the minimum status to proportionality, considering it satisfied only when the progress of security to the detriment of privacy stops in front of the essential requirements of the latter.

To conclude, the European judge has stated that – in order to fight terrorism – a fundamental right, here privacy, can be limited only if its injury is equivalent to the benefits provided to security and in so far as the restrictive measures are strictly necessary. Therefore, the collection and storage of all kinds of data, on an ongoing basis, from each electronic device, and what is worse, referred to every person, i.e. also those not suspected of terrorist offences, are considered to be a massive and unreasonable intrusion into the private life of each European citizen.

We can fairly conclude, then, that the Court has found a deep disproportion in the Data Retention Directive, since no balance could be established between the right to privacy – erased, rather than merely limited – and the need for security, which was favoured even when not actually threatened.

Indeed, this approach is in stark contrast with the indifference that the European legislator has shown in Directive 2017/541, that will be analysed later.

---

[14] Digital Rights Ireland, para. 59.

[15] Digital Rights Ireland, para. 62.

[16] 'Each application under this section [...] shall include [...] a statement of facts showing that there are reasonable grounds to believe that the tangible things sought are relevant to an authorized investigation (other than a threat assessment) conducted in accordance with subsection (a)(2) to obtain foreign intelligence information not concerning a United States person or to protect against international terrorism or clandestine intelligence activities': 50 USC. § 1861(b)(2)(A), in http://www.law.cornell.edu/uscode/text/50/1861.

[17] John C Yoo, 'The Legality of the National Security Agency's Bulk Data Surveillance Programs', UC Berkeley Public Law Research Paper No. 2369192, http://ssrn.com/abstract=2369192, 3–4.

An answer, although a partial one, to the lack of proportionality, can be found in Directive 2016/680 [18] which regulates several fields; it provides stricter rules with regard to the purpose of data processing (Art. 1) and to the rights of data subjects (Art. 12), both elements have gained in determination: personal data have to be 'adequate and relevant for the purposes for which they are processed' and, in particular, 'not excessive and not kept longer than is necessary for the purpose for which they are processed', as well as 'processed only if the purpose of the processing could not reasonably be fulfilled by other means'. [19]

At the same time the Directive presents the same vices as the previous one: not limiting the time of data storage, not precisely identifying the substantial consistence of the authorities' right to access data, and not creating a binding link between data collection and a reasonable suspicion.

Moreover, it requires that data can only be transferred to countries that ensure an adequate level of protection (adequacy that has to be intended as equivalence, since the Court's Schrems decision). [20] It must be observed, however, that the Directive while apparently complying with the proportionality criterion set aside the adequacy requirement by introducing a broad exception to the latter, in case of 'the prevention of an immediate and serious threat to public security of a Member State or a third country'.

5. *The Exceptional and Temporary Nature of the Law*

After the preceding discussion on the precautionality and proportionality principles, we can proceed now to analyse two identity features of the "law of fear": the exceptional and temporary nature of its rules.

The former attribute implies that the discipline is authorized to derogate to the constitutional order without infringing the rule of law, provided that these derogations don't compromise the basis of the constitutional architecture.

The deviation from the constitutional order can touch the fundamental rights or the principle of the separation of powers; the discipline of the European Directive 2017/541 entails significant examples of derogation to the fundamental rights, while the French counter terrorism laws offer examples also in regard of the separation of powers.

---

[18] Directive (EU) 2016/680 of the European Parliament and of the Council of 27 April 2016 on the protection of natural persons with regard to the processing of personal data by competent authorities for the purposes of the prevention, investigation, detection, or prosecution of criminal offences or the execution of criminal penalties, and on the free movement of such data, and repealing Council Framework Decision 2008/977/JHA.

[19] Directive 2016/680, Recital 26.

[20] Maximillian Schrems v. Data Protection Commissioner. See: Chapter 2 of Oreste Pollicino in this book for doctrine and bibliography.

The rules in question, being an exception to general principles, must be strictly interpreted and, above all, have default validity over time. So, when the state of emergency ends, the special regime comes to an end and the ordinary course of events is resumed.

The law of fear entails a temporary discipline, whose validity lasts for the time strictly necessary to face an extraordinary situation so that, when the urgency ceases, the institutional order can go back to its original status.

This means that, after the entering into effect of the sunset clause, the emergency law should not be extended except in extreme cases.

The temporary nature of the law is so relevant that the Italian Constitutional Court[21] – like other Supreme Courts, such as the French Conseil constitutionnel and the Supreme Court of the United States – has deemed it fit to admit heavy restrictions to liberties precisely on the grounds of their short duration in time. Thus, serious offences to protected rights have been tolerated, although they were not mere derogations, if the Court had defined them in such terms in order to overcome cases of patent constitutional illegality.

Nothing else has justified the lenient attitude shown in such cases but the brevity of the compression of the involved rights.

Actually, our Court, while duly finding the existence of constitutional breaches, has failed to sanction them in its ruling, reserving the right to do so in case of future *sine die* extensions of the restrictive measures.[22]

The question then arises as to whether the amnesty granted to otherwise illegal measures would still apply in situations of danger of an ongoing nature. Would it still be admissible to impose on the citizens a continuous sacrifice of their liberties, without knowing if and when it would come to an end?

It is our opinion that the time element may not be upgraded from a circumstance mitigating the sanction to a factor making legal an *ab initio* illegal rule, especially if a constitutional breach is involved.

Furthermore, if what is temporary becomes definitive, if the terrorism risk turns into a stable connotation of our daily life, then a law limited in time is *de facto* converted into a permanent regime.

In view of this situation, it should not be possible for the Courts to actually suspend an unconstitutionality decision using a variety of legal devices offered by their respective national systems: the infringement of the Constitution should be immediately declared, with the ensuing annulment of the vitiated law.[23]

---

[21] See Italian Constitutional Court, 1 February 1982, n. 15, which is the symbol decision of the announced illegitimacy but not ordered. Its critical comment can be found in (1982) *Giur. cost.*, I, 82 ss.

[22] The above quoted decision states that: 'l'emergenza, nella sua accezione più propria, è una condizione certamente anomala e grave ma anche essenzialmente temporanea. Ne consegue che essa legittima sì misure insolite, ma che queste perdono legittimità se ingiustificatamente protratte nel tempo'.

[23] A more in-depth analysis of this subject can be found in Giovanna De Minico, *Costituzione, Emergenza e Terrorismo* (Jovene 2016), 182-186.

The exception would, otherwise, replace the general rule and the compression of freedom pursuing an uncertain advantage in the future would no longer be compensated by the temporary nature of an unbalanced regulation.

6. *The European Law of Fear*

Our analysis can now proceed considering whether and to what extent the European legislator has complied with the precautionality and proportionality principles: in particular, our attention will be focused on Directive 2017/541.[24] This Directive does not mark year zero with respect to crimes having terrorist objectives. The regulatory process started with the Framework Decisions of 2002 and 2008,[25] but Directive 2017/541 may not be equated to them in view of the different criminal policy pursued. In the two preceding acts, the balance between security and liberty did not entail unreasonable sacrifices from either of the two competing values; by contrast, in our opinion the same does not apply in the case of Directive 2017/541.

In comparison to the above Decisions, Directive 2017/541 is the expression of a counter terrorism policy that is security oriented even if security is not effectively threatened, it is insensitive to the principle of non-discrimination on grounds of race and religious belief, and pays scarce attention to the specificity, exhaustivity, and materiality requirements laid down by European law in regard to criminal conduct. We explain the reasons on which this opinion is based in the following remarks.

The Directive aims to strengthen the fight against terrorism through criminal legislation. So, it has sketched new criminal offences, such as public provocation to commit a terrorist offence (Art. 5), recruitment for terrorism (Art. 6), travelling for the purpose of terrorism (Art. 9), terrorism financing (Art. 11): just to recall some of the new crimes.

That said, we observe that the act presents three different aspects of doubtful European legitimacy.

a) The conduct relating to the new offences is not described in such a way as to clarify exactly what the forbidden behaviours are, because the Legislator utilizes the purpose of the conduct to distinguish a legal action from an illegal one; moreover, he abstains from properly typifying such purpose, as exemplified by Art. 3, para. 2, Let. c).

---

[24] Directive (EU) 2017/541 of the European Parliament and of the Council of 15 March 2017 on Combating Terrorism and Replacing Council Framework Decision 2002/475/JHA and Amending Council Decision 2005/671/JHA, O.J. L 88/6, 31.3.2017 https://eur-lex.europa.eu/legal-content/EN/TXT/PDF/?uri=CELEX:32017L0541&from=IT.

[25] Council Framework Decision of 13 June 2002 on Combating Terrorism (2002/475/JHA) (O. J. *L* 164/3, 22.6.2002), https://eur-lex.europa.eu/legal-content/EN/TXT/PDF/?uri=CELEX:32002F0475&from=IT, modified by Council Framework Decision 2008/919/JHA of 28 November 2008 Amending Framework Decision 2002/475/JHA on Combating Terrorism (OJ *L* 330,21, 9.12.2008) https://eur-lex.europa.eu/legal-content/EN/TXT/PDF/?uri=CELEX:32008F0919&from=IT.

Thus, a conduct described in generic terms is followed by an equally unspecified purpose of the conduct, which may lead to untenable results; for instance, the Directive could permit the punishment of 'people who attacked the military infrastructure of dictatorial regimes even if in the interest of preserving or restoring [...] democratic values'.[26]

The Directive appears, therefore, to be both deficient and excessive[27] at the same time. Indeed, on the one hand, it omits to typify the conduct and, on the other hand, it dilutes the terrorist purpose to such an extent that an acceptable conduct could be punished as a crime.

b) The situation of illegality becomes more acute when the European legislator makes recourse (actually with a certain levity) to the model of the offence based on the criminal intention, while the materiality principle of the European criminal law (Art. 49 Charter of Fundamental Rights of the European Union, hereinafter CFR)[28] would have required a "type" of offence based on the conduct. As a consequence of this choice, the Directive reserves a determining role for the emotional element, which becomes the qualifying factor of a conduct that otherwise could be deemed lawful or absorbed into a crime of a lesser gravity.[29]

One may think, for example, of a person who performs acts aimed at 'facilitating travelling for the purpose of terrorism' (Directive Art. 10). The illegality of this incriminating provision is of immediate evidence considering that the criminal purpose is confined to the mind of the presumed offender. As a matter of fact, the intention is not established here *per relationem*, i.e. it is not tied to concrete and current indications to be found in the real world; rather it remains confined to the inner life of the involved person. Save for the introductory remarks,[30] it does not seem that the Di-

---

[26] Meijers Committee, *Notes on an EU Proposal for a Directive on Combating Terrorism*, 16 March 2016, https://free-group.eu/2016/03/17/meijers-committee-notes-on-an-eu-proposal-for-adirectve-on-combatng-terrorism/.

[27] *Contra*: Eugenia Dumitriu, 'The E.U.'s Definition of Terrorism: The Council Framework Decision on Combating Terrorism' (2004) 5 German Law Journal, 602, offers a view in favour of the European legislator: 'The Framework Decision adopts a horizontal approach of terrorism and establishes synthetic and precise definitions satisfying the requirements of legal safety the European Union and its Member States must respect'. With regard to the preparatory work of the Directive see the detailed report of the FREE Group, *Terrorism: EDRI Recommendations for the EP Report on Terrorism*, 31 March 2016, https://freegroup.eu/2016/03/31/terrorism-edri-recommendations-for-the-ep-report-on-terrorism/.

[28] CFR [2012] OJ C 326/391.

[29] For a wide study see: Unione delle Camere Penali Italiane, *Osservatorio Europa, Osservazioni sulla Nuova Proposta di Direttiva per la Lotta al Terrorismo Com (2015)625 della Commissione europea del 2 dicembre 2015*, http://www.camerepenali.it/public/file/Documenti/Osservatorio%20Europa/2016-04-22---Doc-OssEuropa--Commento-proposta-direttiva-lotta-al-terrosismo.pdf.

[30] See European Commission, COM(2015) 625 final 2015/0281 (COD) Proposal for a Directive of the European Parliament and of the Council on Combating Terrorism and Replacing Council Framework Decision 2002/475/JHA on Combating Terrorism, http://ec.europa.eu/transparency/regdoc/rep/1/2015/EN/1-2015-625-EN-F1-1.PDF: 'The aim of the provision is to oblige a Member State to criminalize the act of travelling to another country, if it can be demonstrated that the intended purpose

rective requires concrete elements connecting a person to a terrorist plan or actual circumstances that evidence the terrorist purpose of the travelling. In the absence of such elements the conduct should be considered lacking in criminal relevance.

So, normal behaviours, such as taking a chemistry course or buying fertilizer, could become illegal in the light of the actor's *mens rea* (Art. 7 'Providing training for terrorism'); it follows that the person's alleged intention plays an even greater role in defining the *actus reus* and, what is worse, this intention is not deducible from material and objective elements. It follows that in the field of terrorism there is a great risk that the authorities may infer such an intention from ideologies and religious beliefs. In this way, the definition of criminal offences does not appear to be clearly delineated, as required by the European legality principle (Art. 49 CFR).

Thus, the Directive can be reasonably criticized [31] for surrendering to discriminatory temptations against Muslims. If the *mens rea* is what differentiates a legal conduct from an illegal one, the judge does not have factual elements from which to draw the criminal intention. An interpretative tendency does inevitably prevail towards the 'author's type' of crime, meaning that the existence of a crime is not inferred from facts, but rather from the presumed offender belonging to an ethnic group or professing a religious creed. In this way a dangerous trend is favoured towards the subjectivation of the type of crime. [32] Hence the same conduct can be classified in opposite terms, depending on the identity of its author; it will be considered generally legal, unless attributable to certain minorities which are presumed to be guilty on the ground of a hidden criminal intent: 'because the *actus reus* does not make the difference, the person's alleged intention (*mens rea*) plays an even greater role'. [33]

c) To carry on with the analysis of the Directive, we have to underline that the Directive not only prefers the attempted offence to the implemented offence (Art. 3 and following), but even anticipates the threshold of illegality to the planning phase of a conduct, going further than the normal criminal law has ever done. Indeed, the General Approach issued by the EU Council had stressed that 'criminalisation of conduct at an unwarrantably early stage should be avoided', [34] but the Directive didn't comply with this guideline.

---

of that travel is to commit, contribute to or participate in terrorist offences as defined in Article 3, or to provide or receive training for terrorism as defined in Articles 7 and 8'.

[31] Amnesty International, The International Commission of Jurists, The Open Society Justice Initiative and The Open Society European Policy Institute, *Joint submission regarding the European Commission's proposed draft Combatting Terrorism Directive*, February 2016 http://www.amnesty.org/en/documents/ior60/3470/2016/en/.

[32] See for helpful survey of the Italian doctrine: Giovanni Fiandaca and Enzo Musco, *Diritto penale. Parte generale* (Zanichelli 2014), 508.

[33] So the Meijers Committee, *Notes on an EU Proposal for a Directive on Combating Terrorism* (see footnote No. 26), 4.

[34] Council of the European Union, *Conclusions on Model Provisions, Guiding the Council's Criminal Law Deliberations, 2979th JHA Council Meeting*, 30 November 2009, http://www.consilium.europa.eu/uedocs/cms_Data/docs/pressdata/en/jha/111543.pdf.

It's worth noting that the Meijers Committee and the Council had requested the existence of a strict link between the conduct and a serious and immediate harm. In other words, the forbidden behaviours had to be capable of causing a real danger of potential terrorist offences.

The legislator has proved to have more respect for the materiality requirement of the conduct solely when describing the crime of 'Public provocation to commit a terrorist offence' (Art. 5), the final wording of which no longer shares that of the model of the crimes of presumed danger. Indeed, while the conduct envisaged in the original text merely consisted of divulging messages with a view to encouraging the commission of terrorist offences, without mentioning its likelihood of 'causing a danger that one or more such offences may be committed', the final wording precisely demands what was excluded by the original one. In fact, the provision requires a specific causality link between the spreading of an apologetic message and the actual promotion of a terrorist attack. Thus, the inseparable connection is recreated which must tie the provocation to commit a crime to the active push to commit it by the addressees of the message; this dispels the suspicion that the legislator is prepared to punish a mere criminal intention devoid of any offensive capability.

Nonetheless the original text of the proposal has only been partially corrected. The legislator has excluded that said conducts be held *per se* dangerous, since they require an *ex facto* assessment and cannot be the object of a typical legal evaluation; but the proposal has left still undefined the borderline distinguishing the freedom of speech from the apology of a terrorist crime. This last criminal conduct is described in a manner so vague that it becomes applicable even to the activity of a reporter excessively praising terrorist deeds. Similarly, the prohibition would also apply to the diffusion of messages that may be considered to denigrate the victims of terrorism, although involving words and images that could be censured only for offending the dignity of said victims: 'such messages and images may also include those denigrating victims of terrorism'.[35] Consequently, nothing would prevent a State from holding that such conducts are sufficient to materialize an apology crime, even in the absence of any concrete risk to security.[36] This is not a hypothetical risk because the European legislator has failed to request that the appreciative message be suitable to create a serious and current risk of repetition of the celebrated crime.

The amendment to the initial text has done little to set a clear border between the freedom of speech[37] and the provocation to commit a crime,[38] nor has the norm

---

[35] Meijers Committee, *Note on an EU Proposal for a Directive on Combating Terrorism* (see footnote No. 26), 5.

[36] One can consult the opposite proposal of the FREE GROUP, *Terrorism: EDRI Recommendations for the EP Report on Terrorism*, 31 March 2016 https://free-group.eu/2016/03/31/terrorism-edrirecommenda tions-for-the-ep-report-on-terrorism.

[37] We have to see the opposite opinions of Rosario Serra Cristóbal and Germán M. Teruel Lozano respectively in this book (chaper 3, page 45 anche capter 8, page 135).

[38] See the critical remarks of Stef Wittendorp, 'Incitement to Terrorism and the Regulation of Free

gained in specificity since the European legislator has deferred this task to the national level. Actually, during the parliamentary proceedings, and in particular within the European Parliament Committee on Civil Liberties, Justice and Home Affairs (LIBE) Commission, this wavering attitude has been the subject of critical remarks for its 'chilling effect on freedom of speech'.[39]

7. *The French Laws 'Relative à l'État d'Urgence'*

We turn now to examine, in general terms, the counter terrorism policy pursued in France, highlighting its doubtful compatibility with the principles of proportionality and precautionality which represent common values of modern constitutionalism.

Loi 2015/1501[40] has provided an opportunity not only to adapt the French policy to the changed nature of terrorism, but also to keep it in line with the times, bearing in mind that the Internet has replaced the communication tools traditionally used to spread terrorist strategies, as well as to incite and train to execute them.[41]

Let us note the formal features characterizing this law. It is an extra-ordinary law, as it is based on the state of emergency previously declared by a government decree;[42] an ordinary law, since according to the case law of the Conseil constitutionnel it did not need to be legitimated by a specific constitutional norm,[43] which has not pre-

Speech' (Explosivepolitics.com, 12 June 2016) http://explosivepolitics.com/blog/incitement-to-terrorism-and-theregulation-of-free-speech.

[39] LIBE Commission, whose words have been quoted in the draft of Meijers Committee, 'Notes on an EU Proposal for a Directive on Combating Terrorism' (see footnote No. 26), 5.

[40] Loi n° 2015-1501 du 20 novembre 2015 Prorogeant l'Application de la Loi n° 55-385 du 3 avril 1955 Relative à l'État d'Urgence et Renforçant l'Efficacité de Ses Dispositions, in JORF n° 0270 du 21 novembre 2015, Texte n° 1, http://www.legifrance.gouv.fr/eli/loi/2015/11/20/2015-1501/jo/texte.

[41] Marc Rees, 'Vers une nouvelle loi renseignement pour 2020, année de péremption des boîtes noires', (NextInpact.com, 2019) https://www.nextinpact.com/news/107819-vers-nouvelle-loi-renseignement-pour-2020-annee-peremption-boites-noires.htm.

[42] Décret n° 2015-1475 du 14 novembre 2015 Portant Application de la Loi n° 55-385 du 3 avril 1955', Journal officiel "Lois et Décrets" (JORF) n° 0264 du 14 novembre 2015, texte n° 44, https://www.legifrance.gouv.fr/eli/decret/2015/11/14/2015-1475/jo/texte.

[43] Conseil constitutionnel, Décision n° 1985-187 DC du 25 janvier 1985, http://www.conseil-constitutionnel.fr/conseil-constitutionnel/francais/les-decisions/acces-par-date/decisions-depuis-1959/1985/85-187-dc/decision-n-85-187-dc-du-25-janvier-1985.8162.html; more recently see: Décision n° 2015-527 QPC du 22 décembre 2015, http://www.conseil-constitutionnel.fr/conseil-constitutionnel/francais/les-decisions/acces-par-date/decisions-depuis-1959/2015/2015-527-qpc/decision-n-2015-527-qpc-du-22-decembre-2015.146719.html, in which the Supreme Judge stated that: '[c]onsidérant que la Constitution n'exclut pas la possibilité pour le législateur de prévoir un régime d'état d'urgence; qu'il lui appartient, dans ce cadre, d'assurer la conciliation entre, d'une part, la prévention des atteintes à l'ordre public et, d'autre part, le respect des droits et libertés reconnus à tous ceux qui résident sur le territoire de la République'.

vented the launch of an aborted revision of Art. 36 of the French Constitution during the Hollande Presidency;[44] a temporary law, as it was destined *ex lege* to last for a predetermined period of time; an exceptional law, because it derogated to the normal regime concerning the division of powers and the fundamental freedoms; finally (and again), an extra-ordinary law, because its ultimate goal was the return of the legal order to its normal institutional status as soon as possible after the emergency.[45]

While the law in question should have been in line with the above essential traits, one can easily see that things took a substantially different path: it has become a permanent law, being successively prorogated *sine die* and making normal and stable the emergency regime regardless of the existence of a real danger to be faced.

Let us see now how little its rules regarding the division of powers and liberties conform to the proportionality and precautionality principles. The two points will be examined jointly in order to provide the reader with a unitary picture.

Under Law 2015, as under that of 1955, the task of applying the restrictive measures is distributed between the top political authority, the Minister of the Interior, and its territorial administrative agent, the Prefect, to the detriment of the judiciary order. However, differing from the preceding model, it has extended the powers granted to them and reduced the procedural safeguards.

The Minister of the Interior is entitled to impose a forced residence on a person if he has 'raisons sérieuses de penser que son comportement constitue une menace pour la sécurité et l'ordre publics' (Art. 6, co. 1). Such a measure, which is adopted without hearing the interested party, is neither decided by a judge nor subject to review *ex post* in a proper judicial proceeding. Furthermore, with regard to the precautionary criterion, it is not founded on solid proofs, susceptible to be verified under objective parameters; the presence of vague indications may be sufficient for the Minister to assume that the behaviour of a person represents a serious and imminent threat to security. Thus, Law 2015 constitutes an attack on liberties, not so much because it introduces new restrictive measures, but because of its implementation modalities and for its disregard for the precautionality principle.

A confirmation of the above remarks is offered by the day and night searches, which may be decided by the Prefect without the previous authorization of the judge. They may concern also objects found during the search, for example a computer, the data contained in it (which can be copied), or that assembled in a cloud accessible through the computer.[46] These searches permit the acquisition of a full picture of a

---

[44] Projet de Loi Constitutionnelle de Protection de la Nation, n° 3381 du 23 décembre 2015, Leg. XIV http://www.assemblee-nationale.fr/14/projets/pl3381.asp.

[45] G Agamben, *Stato di eccezione* (Bollati Boringhieri 2003), 34.

[46] Copying data from a pc was declared unconstitutional by the Constitutional Council, Décision n° 2016-536 QPC du 19 février 2016, JORF n° 0044 du 21 février 2016, texte n° 27, http://www.conseil-constitutionnel.fr/conseil-constitutionnel/francais/les-decisions/acces-par-date/decisions-depuis-1959/2016/2016-536-qpc/decision-n-2016-536-qpc-du-19-fevrier-2016.146991.html. In its reasoning the Council, levelling this measure to a seizure, declared that a war-

person, looking into his personal and professional life, past and future, individual and family or social life; they may also involve someone who has been in contact with the presumed terrorist just by chance. This unrestricted day and night intrusion into the private life of a person not only concerns his usual residence, as would be appropriate, but also the properties occasionally attended by anyone whose conduct may raise a possible threat to security (Art. 11, para. 1).

At the expiry of the six month term, this law has been continuously prorogated – a mechanism converting *de facto* a temporary into a definitive act – up to Law 2016,[47] which has strengthened the apparatus of restrictions and formally upheld a theory sustained by the Conseil constitutionnel:[48] namely, the sufficiency of a mere 'lien opérationnel et fonctionnel'[49] between the restrictive measures and a generic situation of danger, not necessarily to be identified in the terrorist risk which was at the origin of the declaration of an emergency.

This theory is dangerous for democracy, as it may legitimate restrictions to liberties in order to prevent riots in no way connected with terrorism. Actually, the ultimate goal of the law appears to be to avoid the police, already heavily committed to counter terrorism, from being diverted from their primary task. Consequently, any social movements – be it groups of fans, ecologists, *sans papiers*, trade unionists – capable of increasing tensions or adversely affecting an already unstable situation had to be *a priori* prohibited, regardless of the existence of a conduct concretely offensive to the public order.

It is thus admitted that liberties can be sacrificed in a precautionary and anticipated way, as well as in respect of an undetermined mass of subjects, not necessarily suspected of terrorism,[50] just to avoid a deterioration of a public order situation.

---

rant instead of a simple administrative order was needed to access the data, in consideration that the independence and impartiality of the judge guarantee the lawfulness of this measure limiting a fundamental right. Only with the Loi n° 2017-1510 some significant guarantees were assured: the copy of the data or the seizure of the pc can happen in the presence of the judicial police; none can access data before a warrant is granted.

[47] Loi n° 2016-987 du 21 juillet 2016 Prorogeant l'Application de la Loi n° 55-385 du 3 avril 1955 Relative à l'État d'Urgence et Portant Mésures de Renforcement de la Lutte Antiterroriste, in JORF n°0169 du 22 juillet 2016, Texte n° 2, https://www.legifrance.gouv.fr/eli/loi/2016/7/21/INTX1620056L/jo/texte.

[48] Conseil constitutionnel, Décision n° 1985-187 DC du 25 janvier 1985, http://www.conseil-constitutionnel.fr/conseil-constitutionnel/francais/les-decisions/acces-par-date/decisions-depuis-1959/1985/85-187-dc/decision-n-85-187-dc-du-25-janvier-1985.8162.html; lastly, Décision n° 2015-527 QPC du 22 décembre 2015, cit.: '[c]onsidérant que la Constitution n'exclut pas la possibilité pour le législateur de prévoir un régime d'état d'urgence; qu'il lui appartient, dans ce cadre, d'assurer la conciliation entre, d'une part, la prévention des atteintes à l'ordre public et, d'autre part, le respect des droits et libertés reconnus à tous ceux qui résident sur le territoire de la République'.

[49] Xavier Domino, 'Conclusions du Rapporteur Public', audience du 11 décembre 2015 http://www.journaldujour.re/IMG/pdf/293083035-conclusions-rapporteur-public-audience11122015.pdf; Mélina Elshoud 'État d'Urgence & Juge Administratif' (2016), 1 Le Journal de Droit Administrative, http://www.journal-du-droit-administratif.fr/?p=511.

[50] Maria Francesca De Tullio, 'Internet and Non-nationals: Is the Net a Tool for Inclusion or Exclusion?', especially pp. 00, in this book.

Hence, operational needs contribute to the regression of the rule of law into a regime of terror, where the restriction of liberties changes from an exceptional rule to an ordinary one; the incrimination based on mere suspicion replaces the necessity for a robust apparatus of evidence; the presumption of abstract dangerousness prevails over the assessment of a concrete offensive conduct; the constitutional safeguards are frozen *sine die*; Parliament is kept out of any decisions on terror, which are concentrated in the hands of Government; and the latter enjoys immunity from the control of the ordinary judge, as a result of the reductive interpretation of Art. 66 of the French Constitution by the Conseil constitutionnel. [51]

Making normal and definitive a legal system initially qualified as exceptional and temporary: [52] this has been the effect of Law 2017/1510, [53] as we will see in the next section.

8. *The French Law 'Renforçant la Sécurité Intérieure et la Lutte contre le Terrorisme'*

In this section we will examine Loi 2017/1510, a normative model aimed, as the preceding laws, at strengthening 'la Securité Intérieure et la Lutte contre le Terrorisme'; however, unlike the emergency regulations previously considered, this law is characterized by the fact that it makes recourse not to extra-ordinary and temporary rules, but to ordinary and definitive ones.

Let's examine its ideological assumptions first and then delve into its content.

As far as its nature is concerned, the law is neither special nor temporary; rather, it is a common law *tout court*, thus designed to remain in force indefinitely. This radical shift of nature is only due to a political concern: to allow the State to return to institutional normality.

In this way, the law implements President Macron's promise [54] not to extend the

---

[51] Conseil constitutionnel, Décision n° 2015-527 QPC du 22 décembre 2015, http://www.conseil-constitutionnel.fr/conseil-constitutionnel/francais/les-decisions/acces-par-date/decisions-depuis-1959/2015/2015-527-qpc/decision-n-2015-527-qpc-du-22-decembre-2015.146719.html.

[52] Wanda Mastor and François Saint-Bonnet, 'De l'Inadaptation de l'État d'Urgence Face à la Menace Djihadiste' (2016) 3 Pouvoirs, 64; Stéphane Pierré-Caps, 'Constitutionnaliser l'état d'urgence?' (2016) 1 Civitas Europa, 150—153; Denis Salas, 'La Banalisation dangereuse de l'état d'urgence', (2016) 3 Études, 38-–39 and Mission Internationale d'Enquête, 'Mesures antiterroristes contraires aux droits humains. Quand l'Exception devient la règle' (2016) Rapport, https://www.fidh.org/IMG/pdf/rapportfrance-hd1_def.pdf, 27-–32.

[53] Loi 2017-1510 du 30 octobre 2017 Renforçant la Sécurité Intérieure et la Lutte contre le Terrorisme, JORF n° 0255 du 31 octobre 2017.

[54] Emmanuel Macron, 'Discours du Président de la République aux Préfets', 5 September 2017, http://www.prefectures-regions.gouv.fr/ile-de-france/content/download/36702/247580/file/05.09%20-%20Discours%20du%20Pr%C3%A9sident%20de%20la%20R%C3%A9publique%20aux%20Pr%C3%A9fets.pdf.

state of emergency, adopted for the first time in 2015 and extended six times since then. A central question arises though: has the President's promise to revoke the *état d'urgence* really been kept?

On the one hand, the law aims at identifying a proper balance between safety and fundamental rights. Consequently, it does not make the state of emergency a prerequisite, which is no longer renewed, unlike the previous law models. Rather, it acknowledges the existence of an *ordinary time* terrorism as a given fact.

The expression *ordinary time* terrorism is used here to stress the ordinary and permanent nature that terrorism has acquired, being no longer something exceptional or temporary. Indeed, terrorism cannot be seen as a separate and single event, but as a series of interlocking actions taking place through time and space. This is a fact and the law has grasped it perfectly. As a result, the French legislator has pragmatically avoided any *fictio iuris* (legal fiction) and has treated terrorism for what it really is: a current emergency, which therefore does not need to be declared by an extraordinary act of the Council of Ministers.

However, if the existence of terrorism is not denied – being indeed at the basis of the new law – what is under discussion is the choice of normalizing the state of emergency, turning its exceptional regulation into a general and ordinary discipline.

The fundamental rights of the citizens – already compressed by the previous laws – are once more flouted and restrained on the ground of fear. [55]

What emerges is far from being a promising scenario. The absence of time restrictions and the introduction of additional limitations on freedoms are bound to exacerbate tensions even more.

From now on, for instance, the law enables the closure of places of worship; and home detention measures – through changing their name into *individual surveillance measures* – remain in force substantially unchanged, if not worse.

New expressions are coined to replace old ones, as in the case of house searches now renamed 'visits' (Art. 4). The latter – which have nothing to do with doctors – are always conducted by a prefect, who is allowed to search places and houses or to seize computers and all their contents. And this is not based on the presence of strong evidence, but on merely vague allegations linked to terrorist acts by a weak connection.

We have to add another consideration: the expiry of the *état d'urgence* annuls the guarantee of its judicial review, which had as its object the formal declaration of the

---

[55] Marc Rees, 'Les nouvelles technologies dans le projet de loi anti-terroriste' (NextInpact.com, 18 September 2017), https://www.nextinpact.com/news/105186-les-nouvelles-technologies-dans-projet-loi-anti-terroriste.htm; Jean-Baptiste Jacquin and Julia Pascual, 'Le gouvernement choisit la surenchère sécuritaire pour sortir de l'état d'urgence' (LeMonde.fr, 25 September 2017, http://www.lemonde.fr/police-justice/article/2017/09/25/le-gouvernement-choisit-la-surenchere-securitaire-pour-sortir-de-l-etat-d-urgence_5190725_1653578.html; Julien Lausson, 'Terrorisme: la nouvelle loi française alarme des experts en droits de l'homme de l'ONU' (Numerama.com, 27 September 2017) http://www.numerama.com/politique/293193-terrorisme-la-nouvelle-loi-francaise-alarme-des-experts-en-droits-de-lhomme-de-lonu.html.

emergency, that is no longer present in this case, even if the restrictions to the fundamental rights were already in place.

This remark sheds light on the most controversial question of the law: the role of the judge. According to Art. 66 Fr. Const.,[56] any restrictions on fundamental freedoms should be submitted to the *ex ante* or *ex post* control of an ordinary judge, at least according to the Fathers of the Fifth French Republic:[57] in fact, the expression 'la liberté individuelle' was meant to encompass the entire category of fundamental rights.

By opting for a restrictive interpretation supported by the Conseil constitutionnel,[58] the 2017 Legislator has only given the ordinary judge control over personal freedom, while all other freedoms fall under the competence of the administrative judge. Clearly, because of its constitutional collocation, the ordinary judge offers greater guarantees of impartiality; by contrast, the administrative judge is less autonomous and independent from the Executive power and therefore a less suitable candidate to accomplish this judicial review.

Consequently, while the decision to revoke the endless state of emergency by normalizing it may be accepted, the above choice should have been supported by the softening of the restrictions to the fundamental freedoms, once justified by their temporary character. Thus, the new law was expected to ease measures limiting freedoms and to reinforce the guarantees of judicial review, yet none of this has taken place.

It is hard to avoid feeling that France, albeit in a surreptitious way, is acquiring the traits of a 'police state'. Ironically, the country of the *Revolution* is gradually moving away from modern constitutionalism, the first foundations of which model it laid.

Is it really the institutional normality President Macron had promised to restore?

9. *The Law of Fear Tomorrow*

It is now time to turn to some conclusive remarks.

In brief, it has emerged from the foregoing that the current standard of law of fear has opened the door to very significant breaches to the constitutional order. It is,

---

[56] Art. 66 para. 2: 'L'autorité judiciaire, gardienne de la liberté individuelle, assure le respect de ce principe dans les conditions prévues par la loi'.

[57] See the speech of Charles de Gaulle, 'Discours prononcé Place de la République à Paris', 4 septembre 1958, http://www.charles-de-gaulle.org/pages/l-homme/accueil/discours/le-president-de-la-cinquieme-republique-1958-1969/discours-prononce-place-de-la-republique-a-paris-4-septembre-1958.php.

[58] To analyse the whole *cursus* of the Conseil constitutionnel on Art. 66 Fr. Cost, read Bertrand Louvel, 'Auditions sur le projet de loi constitutionnelle n° 395 (2015–2016)', adoptée par l'Assemblée nationale, de protection de la Nation, mardi 1er mars 2016, Leg. XIV, http://www.senat.fr/compte-rendu-commissions/20160229/lois.html#toc2t.

To see a symbolic decision on a restrictive interpretation of Art. 66 see: Conseil constitutionnel, Décision n° 2015-527 QPC du 22 décembre 2015, quoted above.

therefore, worth considering if there are any remedies that could bring the emergency regimes back to legality without changing the constitutional framework.

a) *De iure condendo,* a valid remedy could be found by bringing the Legislator in Europe – both at the national and the EU level – back to respecting the principles of precautionality and proportionality, which should be taken into account especially in situations of danger to rights and democracy itself.

Any legislative innovation should comply with these principles. Apart from their political and ethical value, the principles of precautionality and proportionality can be already drawn from the existing Constitutions as well as from the EU Charter. In the contrary case, the regulation would be illegitimate, as widely illustrated above, but also ineffective because controlling everyone is like controlling no one. A preventive action could be truly effective if it is aimed and targeted at specific objectives.

b) Another remedy could consist of having the emergency regime periodically re-examined by the legislator; the prorogation of the regime could be made subject to progressively qualified and growing political majorities. This proposal, advanced by Ackerman [59] for the US system, could be applied in principle also to the European legal systems.

Scholars consider that a growing qualified majority rule in parallel to the progressive extensions of the state of emergency constitutes a guarantee against abuses of the emergency powers. Actually, the necessary consent of the minorities to prorogation proposals is amply justified by the importance of the decision to be taken. The aim of the said guarantee is to avoid that rule of law system from becoming 'un état de droit de necessité', [60] where temporary deviations from the ordinary legality tend to be converted over time into a stable extra-ordinary legality and lead to the introduction of a new political and legal order replacing the preceding one: a kind of atypical normality.

If the aim of the Executive is to stabilize the emergency, i.e. to make permanent what should remain temporary, the consent of the minorities is indispensable and its importance grows the more the emergency approximates to a definitive status. Thus, normalizing the state of emergency, which is in any case an event to be discouraged, requires a level of awareness and an aggregation of consents far greater than those sufficient to support a government.

Looking at the issue from a different point of view, it is reasonable also to assume

[59] Bruce Ackerman, *Before the Next Attack: Preserving Civil Liberties in an Age of Terrorism* (Yale University Press 2006), 116–121.

[60] Stéphane Pierré-Caps, 'Constitutionnaliser l'état d'urgence?' (2016) 31 Civitas Europa, 153. Also see: Dominique Dyzenhaus, 'L'état d'exception', in Michel Troper and Dominique Chagnollaud (eds), *Traité internanational de droit constitutionnel, Vol. II, Distribution des pouvoir* (Dalloz 2012), 751–752, where the Author says that: '… lorsque la menace est considérée d'une durée indéfinie, comme c'est le cas avec le terrorisme international à la Al-Qaed, il manque à la déclaration de l'état d'exception l'un de ses traits essentiels: l'anticipation de sa fin. Un état d'exception permanent semble être une contradiction dans les termes. Si les conditions sont telles que l'ordre politique et juridique doit être reconfiguré indéfiniment, c'est le nouveau normal, pas un état d'exception'.

that a public debate outside the secret rooms of government powers and voting within elected Assemblies would either strengthen the idea that the exceptional regime has to be maintained or unmask an attempt to establish a police state. This alternative is properly unravelled by means of a parliamentary debate and the extended involvement of the political-representative pluralism. Only large and growing majorities can ensure a correct decision over keeping or eliminating the state of emergency.[61] Nonetheless, Ackerman's proposal appears difficult to be implemented as it would require constitutional amendments to the legislative procedures laid down in the Member States' Constitutions.

c) In conformance with the principle of the division of powers, each political body should comply with its institutional mandate. On the legislative side the decision-maker should strictly observe the rule of law requirements – proportionality, precautionality, necessity, and due process – in writing the laws of fear.

Should the legislator fail to perform this task, national Supreme Courts should play an active role. Their excessive tolerance towards the Legislator has permitted temporary emergency regulations to be converted into a definitive model, legal derogations to rights to evolve into heavy breaches of the mandatory statute of fundamental rights, proportional and precautionary measures to be turned into unreasonable and discriminatory norms governed by absolute presumptions. From our perspective, in contrast, the Supreme national and supra-national Courts should conduct a strict judicial review of the laws of fear to make the above requirements effective. Otherwise, why would the legislator comply with these binding parameters if the Authority, entrusted with their enforcement, prefers a light control?

In general, the effectiveness of the constitutional order is based on the fact that derogatory measures do not subvert the core of such order. Here, our reasoning goes back to the starting point: the emergency legislator has been given a mandate to preserve the endangered legal system. This is the genetic limit of any derogatory laws, the overcoming of which entails the violation of the same legality which the emergency legislation has to defend. The extraordinary law has its own natural limit in bringing the system back into balance, which has been temporarily altered and threatened by the state of danger. In order to do so, the derogatory power has to be limited in time, so as to ensure the reversal to a normal state, avoiding the occurrence of irreversible breaches to the established order. Such breaches would alter the core of both the fundamental principles and the liberties of the constitutional order, preventing the system to resume its original identity.

It's time to sum up: the measures of prevention must not be *extra-ordinem* but compatible with the system. The emergency power, despite being exceptional, still remains a constituted power subject to the requirements of the rule of law. This

---

[61] Bruce Ackerman, *Before the Next Attack: Preserving Civil Liberties in an Age of Terrorism* (see footnote No. 59), 117.

power does not write on a blank blackboard, because there is a constitutional framework to be respected. The emergency must be kept within the boundaries of the rule of law, otherwise the introduction of an exceptional law would disguise a new legal-political order, aiming to illegally replace the existing one. [62]

In conclusion, the fundamental rights and the guarantees of democracy must be defended especially in times of crisis. Otherwise, when the crisis is over, there would be a return to an abnormal reality, achieved by the sacrifice of liberties and democracy. However, these two values represent the ultimate *ratio* of the emergency legislation.

---

[62] Clinton Rossiter, *Constitutional Dictatorship: Crisis Government in the Modern Democracies* (Princeton University Press 1948) 314, where the Author underlines that: 'No sacrifice is too great for our democracy, least of all the temporary sacrifice of democracy itself'.

Enforcement of the Right to Digital Privacy

Oreste Pollicino

SUMMARY: 1. Atoms, Bits, and Terrorism. – 2. Digital Rights Ireland. – 3. Google Spain. – 4. Schrems. – 5. Tele2 Sverige. – 6. Conclusions.

1. *Atoms, Bits, and Terrorism*

How has the coming of the Internet affected the exercise and the judicial protection of privacy and data protection in the framework of the European Union ('EU')? To what extent does the protection of privacy and data protection in the digital environment change the fight against terrorism? Responding to these research questions would require taking into account at least one factor: the role of the European Court of Justice ('ECJ'). Nowadays, the ECJ acts as a 'playmaker' in interpreting and solving issues deriving from interconnected legal regimes affecting the protection of fundamental rights. Its position and ability to dialogue are even more amplified in the digital age.

This is due to some peculiarities of the (digital) environment where, for example, the right to privacy and data protection are involved. The first peculiarity concerns the gap between law and technologies. Usually, legal reforms lag behind technological developments. As a result, the inertia of lawmakers in addressing this natural asymmetry weighs heavily on the shoulders of Courts. It should come as no surprise that Courts have played a key role in working out new solutions to new challenges generated by digital technologies.

The second reason for choosing to focus on privacy and data protection in the digital environment is connected to the jurisdictional issues brought about by the rise of the Web that resulted in crucial implications for the protection of fundamental rights. This second point is particularly relevant as Courts have been able to eradicate and establish jurisdiction successfully challenging the so-called anarchic nature of the Internet. This approach can be captured by looking at the beginning of the new millennium when national Courts started to reject the so-called 'futility argument', according to which laws based on geographic borders are not feasible on the Internet. Therefore, Courts have started to require a manipulation of the website architecture in order to reproduce territorial boundaries in the digital environment. In other words, the focus on relevant case law will show that geography and boundaries are crucial even for a global channel of communication like the Internet.

Returning to the research question mentioned above, the investigation of this chapter focuses on the approach of the ECJ to privacy and data protection online and the consequences for the fight against terrorism. This methodology is proper since the rise of the Internet has raised new challenges for the protection of fundamental rights. When addressing the digital environment, it is crucial to look at how privacy and data protection are perceived in the online dimension to understand how this influences the enforcement of these rights.

2. Digital Rights Ireland

The first case rendered by the ECJ in the field of digital privacy unveils the spirit of exploration of the European courts, most notably when it comes to new technologies. In *Digital Rights Ireland*,[1] the decision invalidated the data retention Directive. In this case, the ECJ, against its previous and well-established case law, on the one hand, seems to be more likely to consider as independent parameters the fundamental rights established by Articles 7 and 8 of the Charter. While, on the other hand, it draws a clear distinction between the profile relating to the violation of the essence of those rights by the Directive and the assessment of the proportionality of the measures provided by the Directive to achieve the objectives of protecting public order and preventing terrorism.[2]

The preliminary proceeding had been introduced by the references raised by the High Court of Ireland and the Austrian Constitutional Court. The High Court was facing a dispute involving Digital Rights Ireland and local authorities regarding the national measures provided for the retention of data related to electronic communications. Whereas, the Austrian Constitutional Court had received a number of constitutional complaints in which the applicants sought the annulment of the domestic provisions implementing the Directive 2006/24.[3]

---

[1] Joint cases C-293/12 and C-594/12 [2014] *Digital Rights Ireland Ltd v Minister for Communications, Marine and Natural Resources, Minister for Justice, Equality and Law Reform, The Commissioner of the Garda Síochána, Ireland and the Attorney General and Kärntner Landesregierung, Michael Seitlinger, Christof Tschohl and Others*, Court of Justice of the European Union.

[2] Ibid, paragraphs 39 and 40 of the judgment are very clear in this respect: 'So far as concerns the essence of the fundamental right to privacy and the other rights laid down in Article 7 of the Charter, it must be held that, even though the retention of data required by Directive 2006/24 constitutes a particularly serious interference with those rights, it is not such as to adversely affect the essence of those rights given that, as follows from Article 1(2), the Directive does not permit the acquisition of knowledge of the content of the electronic communications as such. Nor is that retention of data such as to adversely affect the essence of the fundamental right to the protection of personal data enshrined in Article 8 of the Charter, because Article 7 of Directive 2006/24 provides, in relation to data protection and data security, that, without prejudice to the provisions adopted pursuant to Directives 95/46 and 2002/58, certain principles of data protection and data security must be respected by providers of publicly available electronic communications services or of public communications networks. According to those principles, Member States are to ensure that appropriate technical and organisational measures are adopted against accidental or unlawful destruction, accidental loss or alteration of the data'.

[3] In particular, the first reference had been raised by the High Court of Ireland and questioned

The legal issues raised by the case originated from the fact that the Directive made it possible for national authorities to obtain very intrusive information about many aspects of the private life of subscribers to telecommunications service providers (such as the identity of the individuals, the place where the communications took place, and the time at which they were carried out). So that, taken as a whole, this information could provide very precise details on the private lives of the individuals whose data were subject to retention. Many claims had therefore arisen in respect of both Directive 2006/24 and the domestic provisions transposing the content of the latter, since the conditions under which the interference with the private lives of individuals could be justified were not set up in a clear and precise manner.

The Directive derives from the *securitization ethos* that was the immediate reaction to the attacks of 11 September 2001 as it finds its roots in the rise in the EU context of reasons connected to the protection of European security. This objective emerged, in the first instance, as a functional requirement for an efficient implementation of the four fundamental freedoms established by the Treaties, and then, as of the coming into force of the Treaty of Maastricht, as an independent *telos* of the EU. Such a Directive, so imbued with the logic of preventive control and widespread suspicion,[4] has carved out, as noted by the Advocate General in his Opinion,[5] some exceptions to the protection of the right to respect for private life set up by the Directives 95/46 ('Data Protection Directive') and 2002/58 with respect to the processing of personal data in electronic communications. In fact, these Directives aimed at ensuring confidentiality of communications and traffic data and, in order to do so, established the obligation for telecommunication operators to delete or make anonymous the data when no longer necessary for the transmission of a communication (unless it is necessary for billing purposes). Against this background, the Directive 2006/24,[6] in dero-

---

whether the provisions established by the Directive were compatible with the principle of proportionality provided for by Article 52 of the Charter and violated the right to respect for private life, the right to data protection, and the right to freedom of expression provided for by Articles 7, 8, and 11 of the Charter. Second, it was the Constitutional Court of Austria, to which 11,130 individual applications seeking constitutional protection and the annulment of the Directive had been filed, that raised a preliminary reference. The Austrian Court questioned whether the collection and retention of data were provided in a manner incompatible with the protection of the rights to private life, data protection, and freedom of expression. Also, the Constitutional Court sought clarification with respect to the application of Article 52, paragraph 1, of the Charter; particularly, it asked the Court of Justice whether the legal framework in force in the EU respected the essence of the fundamental right to data protection and whether the retention of data was compatible with the constitutional traditions of the Member States and with Article 8 of the European Convention on Human Rights.

[4] Joint cases C-293/12 and C-594/12, 37. According to the ECJ: 'as the Advocate General has pointed out in paragraphs 52 and 72 of his Opinion, the fact that data are retained and subsequently used without the subscriber or registered user being informed is likely to generate in the minds of the persons concerned the feeling that their private lives are the subject of constant surveillance'.

[5] Opinion of the Advocate General Cruz Villalòn paras. 39–40.

[6] Ibid, 46. According to the Advocate General in this case: 'Directive 2006/24 is characterized by its functional duality. It is, on the one hand, an entirely traditional directive which seeks to harmonize national laws that are disparate or likely to become so, and was adopted in the interests of the functioning

gation of the general principles above, has established that that Member States shall, 'for the purposes of the investigation, detection and prosecution of serious crime',[7] provide an obligation to retain data for a period of not less than six months nor more than two years.

The first of the two aspects that deserve special emphasis is given by the independent significance attributed, innovatively, to Articles 7 and 8 of the Charter. These provisions, in fact, have been construed so far as 'just' inseparable elements. In particular, the Advocate General Cruz Villalòn had drawn quite clearly in his opinion a distinction between the two profiles involved. The reasoning of the Advocate General aimed at bringing to light the fact that there may be cases in which legislation restricting the right to protection of personal data in accordance with Article 8 of the Charter may nevertheless be regarded as a disproportionate restriction to Article 7 of the same. And to achieve this, the Attorney General needs to draw a difference, to a certain degree artificial, between 'personal data' *per se* and data 'more than personal'.[8]

A second distinction emerges, instead, in the reasoning of the ECJ and constitutes an innovative step compared to its previous case law. It is the distinction based on the text of Article 52(1) of the Charter, between the profile of the assessment of a possible violation of the essence of the rights provided by Articles 7 and 8 of the Charter and the assessment of the proportionality of the measures specified by the Directive to achieve the objectives of safeguarding public order and preventing terrorism, considered to be legitimate by the Court.

Prior to the decision in question, the case law of the ECJ has been looking at the first paragraph of Article 52 of the Charter as a single block, without considering that a restriction of the fundamental rights at stake, although not affecting the essence of the latter, could nevertheless be found disproportionate with respect to the goals pursued by the relevant legislation. In the decision on the data retention Directive, on the contrary, finding that 'the interference caused by Directive 2006/24 with the fundamental rights laid down in Articles 7 and 8 of the Charter' is 'wide-ranging', the ECJ addresses separately the above-mentioned profiles of Article 52(1).

However, it is in relation to the assessment of the proportionality of the collection and storage of data as regulated by the Directive that the ECJ has found a breach of EU primary law.[9] Having ascertained the wide-ranging interference to the rights pro-

---

of the internal market and precisely calibrated for that purpose, as the Court ruled in Ireland v Parliament and Council. However, it is also, on the other hand, a directive which, even in its harmonising function, seeks to establish, where appropriate, obligations – in particular data retention obligations – which constitute, as I shall show later, serious interference with the enjoyment of the fundamental rights guaranteed to European citizens by the Charter, in particular the right to privacy and the right to the protection of personal data'.

[7] Directive 2006/24/EC, Article 1.

[8] Joint cases C-293/12 and C-594/12, 65.

[9] For general comments on the Directive 2006/24 see F Bignami, 'Protecting Privacy Against the Police in the European Union: The Data Retention Directive' (2007) 8 *Chicago Journal of International Law* 233; E Kosta, 'The Way to Luxembourg: National Court Decisions on the Compatibility of the

tected by Articles 7 and 8 of the Charter, the Court has focused, in fact, on the proportionality of such interference with regard to the objectives pursued by the Directive. Thus, the reasoning of the judges aims at analysing the existence of appropriate and necessary safeguards to justify the proposed limitations to the relevant fundamental rights guaranteed by the Charter.

Moving from this approach, the Court provides an in-depth analysis of the critical points of the Directive. The judges first note that the interference with the fundamental right to private life affects the entire European population, without any distinction. In this light, the Court has pointed out that the collection of data involves individuals who are not necessarily suspected to have committed a crime and, pursuant to the Directive, is carried out regardless of any direct or indirect connection with the commission of a serious crime. In other words, the collection of data is neither limited to a certain group of individuals, nor to a particular geographical area or a certain period of time.

The reference to the notion of 'serious crimes' has been found to be inaccurate and too generic by the Court, and, in any case, incompatible with the principle of proportionality. According to the Court, in fact, while allowing each Member State to set up its own definition of 'serious crimes', the Directive 2006/24 makes this notion unlikely to be properly defined.

The Court has also stressed the lack of any specific guarantee – from both a substantive and a procedural standpoint – concerning the access that domestic authorities of each Member State may have to data. The group of individuals that, within the respective authorities of each Member State, may have access to the data subject to retention is in turn undetermined. [10] Nor is the same access to data subject to any preliminary scrutiny by any judicial or independent administrative authority.

Also, the period of time for which data may be subject to retention is under scrutiny by the Court. In this respect, the critical issues stem from the absence of any distinction between the various categories of data and the relevant retention time. This period, in any case, should be limited to the necessary time for the purposes of the retention to be fulfilled.

On the basis of these grounds, the ECJ has declared that Directive 2006/24 does not establish provisions clear and specific enough to regulate in the appropriate manner the interference with the fundamental rights enshrined in Articles 7 and 8 of the Charter. Not even such a wide-ranging interference can find its legal basis in the principle of necessity, which is to a certain degree ancillary and integrative to the principle of proportionality. [11]

Data Retention Directive with the Right to Privacy and Data Protection' (2013) 10 *scritpted* 339, www.script-ed.org.

[10] C. Cocq and F. Galli, 'Comparative Paper on Data Retention Regulation in a Sample of EU Member States' (2013) *Surveille Project D4.3*, surveille.eui.eu.

[11] Joint cases C-293/12 and C-594/12, 65.

What is particularly important to stress is that such a decision constitutes not only the recognition of the high standard of the EU system in protecting fundamental rights of privacy and data protection, but also the starting point of the EU path towards digital privacy. This can be considered also the beginning of another phase of the 'constitutionalization process' of the right to data protection which, especially in this case, has been considered separately from the right to privacy as distinct references, in order to examine more precisely the actual impact of the measures provided for by the Directive on, respectively, the right to private life and the right to data protection, no longer considered as a unique parameter.

3. Google Spain

The path towards the recognition of a *digital right to privacy*, started by the ECJ with the decision invalidating the data retention Directive, has found its climax in the decision delivered a few weeks afterwards in the *Google Spain* case. [12]

In particular, the ECJ has further extended the consideration attached to Articles 7 and 8 of the Charter, by affording absolute protection to the right to privacy when it comes to the digital environment. The Court, in fact, has provided an interpretation of the relevant parameters (including, in addition to Articles 7 and 8, the relevant provisions of the Data Protection Directive) inspired by the purpose of granting the widest possible protection to the rights to privacy and data protection. Such an interpretation, quite similar in certain nuances to a very form of manipulation of the relevant legislation, has probably been fostered by the circumstance that the Data Protection Directive entered into force during the transition from the analogue to the digital environment, but was not drafted with the rise of the Internet in mind.

Generally speaking, by the preliminary reference raised by the Spanish *Audiencia Nacional* the ECJ has been asked to consider the relationship between the Data Protection Directive, which constitutes the legal framework in force on data protection, and the role of Internet service providers ('ISPs'), particularly of the search engine providers. In the national proceeding, the Spanish Data Protection Authority has ordered Google to remove some links that resulted from the use of the name of the plaintiff as a keyword. Specifically, the applicant claimed the removal of links to news published by a legal bulletin (which was obliged to publish this information) concerning a proceeding involving him which had ended many years before. Google refused to comply with the request of the applicant, by declaring that, as a US-based company, it was not subject to EU law (and, accordingly, to domestic legislation im-

[12] Case C-131/12 [2014] *Google Spain SL and Google Inc. v Agencia Española de Protectión de Datos (AEPD) and Mario Costeja Conzález.*

plementing the Data Protection Directive). In the view of Google, an injunction like that sought by the plaintiff would have most likely restricted the freedom of expression of the website owners. Rather, only an injunction against the websites concerned (and not the search engine) to delete specific content could remove any prejudicial effect for the plaintiff.

The *Audiencia Nacional*, in the course of the appeal proceedings against the injunction issued by the Spanish Data Protection Authority, raised a preliminary reference to the ECJ concerning, in a nutshell, the possibility of enforcing the individual's right to be forgotten (if any in EU law) against the Internet search engine services providers. [13]

It is worth noting the ECJ has found that the balance between the right to be forgotten, on the one hand, and, on the other hand, freedom of information can be struck on a case-by-case basis taking into account the relevant individual claims. The reasoning of the Court on this point has omitted to consider the consequences that such an obligation (or such a burden) is likely to raise having regard to the legal regime of the Internet services providers as defined by the Directive 2000/31 ('e-Commerce Directive'). In fact, the e-Commerce Directive exempts providers from a general obligation to monitor content transmitted by users. Moreover, the e-Commerce Directive exempts providers from liability in case of unlawful content or activities unless the provider has been notified of the same and has failed to take the necessary steps to remove the concerned content. The assumption behind this regime is that the provider does not exercise any editorial activity, acting as an intermediary offering services to third parties. Such a legal regime also reflects, thus, the business model of the ISP. Then, the question should be asked – among others – whether the ECJ has given appropriate consideration to these aspects when finding that search engine providers fall within the scope of controller pursuant to the Directive on data protection. It seems that, even in this respect, the ECJ has been inspired by the driving force of Articles 7 and 8 of the Charter.

It is important now to draw the attention to the choice made by the judges of Luxemburg to base the judgment almost exclusively on the parameters offered by Articles 7 and 8 of the Charter. Indeed, unlike the Advocate General, the Court has made no express mention of Article 11 and Article 16 of the Charter, which respectively protect freedom of expression and freedom to conduct business. In the Opinion delivered by Jääskinen, in fact, there is an almost equivalent reference to both Articles 7 and 8 and Articles 11 and 16. However, no reference appears in the judgment of the Court, where the floor is completely devoted to Articles 7 and 8. In particular, the ECJ has stressed this aspect when saying that, in the balance between the right to information and the right to privacy, the latter is generally assumed to prevail, apart from the cases where the removal of the information concerned may undermine the legitimate interest of Internet users to receive the same. In other words, the general

[13] Opinion of the Advocate General Jääskinen 25 June 2013.

rule would be the limitation of the right to have access to information for the sake of other rights relating to the private sphere and the personal data of users. The prevalence of the former over the latter would work only as an exception, under certain circumstances and on specific conditions.

Given that the emphasis granted to the role of Articles 7 and 8 of the Charter is crucial with respect to the approach of the Court to the balance between conflicting fundamental rights, no less importance is attached to the same parameters when it comes to applying the relevant provisions enshrined in the Data Protection Directive in the case. It is possible to find at least three points where the manipulative effects of the interpretation given by the judges of Luxembourg to the provisions of the Data Protection Directive in light of Articles 7 and 8 emerge: the relevance in the case of EU law; the definition of Internet search engine provider as controller in the context of data processing; the application of Article 12(b) of the Directive, concerning the right to obtain the erasure blocking and rectification of personal data.

With regard to the first point, it has to be noted that the opinion of the Advocate General had come to the same conclusion as the judgment of the Court as to the applicability of the Data Protection Directive to an Internet search engine service provider that has established a subsidiary acting as commercial agent in a Member State to promote, facilitate, and effect the sale of online advertising products and services to third parties and the marketing of that advertising. The ECJ, however, has gone beyond the justification provided by the Advocate General, in the view of the judges; an extensive interpretation must be given to the notion of 'context of the activities of an establishment', [14] provided by Article 4(a), in order to ensure effective and complete protection of the fundamental rights and freedoms of natural persons, and in particular their right to privacy, with respect to the processing of personal data, those words cannot be interpreted restrictively.

With regard to the definition of Google as controller, it has to be pointed out that the reason the Court drew such a conclusion was because it regarded Articles 7 and 8 as the exclusive relevant legal parameters. As the ECJ has noted, excluding 'the operator of a search engine from that definition on the ground that it does not exercise control over the personal data published on the web pages of third parties' is 'contrary not only to the clear wording of that provision but also to its objective – which is to ensure, through a broad definition of the concept of "controller", effective and complete protection of data subjects'. [15]

This statement raises some issues. In fact, the consequence of defining the search engine as controller is making it subject to some obligations which are laid down by the Directive and that, if applied to an ISP, are likely to conflict with the regime de-

---

[14] Article 4 of the Directive 95/46 provides: 'Each Member State shall apply the national provisions it adopts pursuant to this Directive to the processing of personal data where [...] the processing is carried out in the context of the activities of an establishment of the controller on the territory of the Member State'.

[15] Case C-131/12, 34.

signed by the e-Commerce Directive and, accordingly, the same business model of the operator of a search engine. The Court has noted that the processing of personal data carried out by the Internet search engine service provider is separate and autonomous from that operated by the owners of the websites from which information is retrieved and indexed. Then, the question that may arise is whether the search engine provider itself must obtain the consent of the data subject, at least while it assumes that the processing is carried out for business purposes.

With respect to the third of the points above, the Court, as noted, has been tasked with assessing whether Articles 12(b) and 14(1)(b) confer to the data subjects the rights to obtain from search engines the removal of search results including links to web pages containing personal data or information, without prior consultation of the website owner, and with no requirement that the information being processed is unlawful. Here the balance has to be struck between the freedom of expression of the website owners and the protection of personal data. It is relevant the construction given by the Court to Article 12(b) of the Directive, [16] in order to grant as much protection as possible to the right to digital privacy of the data subjects.

Pursuant to said provision, the data subject may ask for the erasure, rectification, or blocking of the data when the processing of the same does not respect the principles laid down by the Directive and, in particular, because of the inaccurate or incomplete nature of the data. The Court has construed this provision as not limited to but only including, among the others, the cases listed in Article 12. This way, the Court has established the grounds for making any breach of the general principles set forth by the Directive a cause for action for the data subject to enforce his rights against the controller. Therefore, the judgment of the Court has significantly extended the scope of application of the provision, by attaching relevance to the generic reference to Articles 6 and 7 of the Directive.

These being the most important outcomes of the manipulation made by the ECJ in light of Articles 7 and 8 of the Charter, there is, however, something paradoxical in the conclusions reached by the Court at the end of a very fundamental rights-based reasoning.

Having explored the reasoning of the ECJ in the decisions on the data retention Directive and in the *Google Spain* case, it should go without saying that the Court has taken seriously the protection of a new right to digital privacy. In particular, the Court has attempted to model to the characteristic of the digital world the right to privacy that Warren and Brandeis had depicted looking at the world of atoms. Additionally, one could also point out that in these judgments the ECJ has taken too seri-

---

[16] Even the interpretation that the Court of Justice gives to the right to objection provided for by Article 14(1)(b) of the Directive may be challenged. In fact, the data subject can object to the processing of personal data on compelling legitimate grounds relating to his particular situation. The Court of Justice has nevertheless extended the scope of this provision: according to the judges of Luxembourg, this provision permits the data subjects to attach relevance to any circumstance characterizing the peculiar situation with no specific limits.

ously the issue relating to the definition and protection of such a new right. So seriously that it neglects the consequences that are likely to arise from this approach, most likely inspired by the scandal raised by the NSA case.

Two particular negative consequences should be taken into account. The first one is underestimating the implications which arise from taking to an extreme degree the protection afforded to personal data on the protection of other values provided with constitutional grounds and ranked as fundamental rights, first of all, freedom of expression. Furthermore, there is a risk that such an extreme way of approaching personal data protection results in excess of Europeanization, connected to a balkanization of Internet regulation. With regard to the first risk, as it has been noted above, the absence of any express mention of Article 11 of the Charter in the whole judgement in the *Google Spain* case is only one of the various signals confirming that the balance made by the ECJ seems to be skewed towards the right to digital privacy. An additional consequence of this overbalancing is the lower degree of protection that is granted to freedom of expression on the Internet than the standard of protection that the ECJ is familiar with when it comes to the non-digital world.

4. Schrems

Even, the *Schrems* decision has given rise to strongly debated issues among lawyers and experts. [17] The judgment has been felt to have overwhelming consequences for organizations that process a huge amount of personal data every day, including collecting and transferring the same from Europe to the US.

As is well known, these worries have been ongoing for some time, initially they spread across Europe and then beyond, resulting in a domino effect that led some data protection authorities of non-EU countries (including Israel and Switzerland) to withdraw from the respective Safe Harbor Agreements in force with the US.

This fact confirms that the model of protection of fundamental rights in the EU is crucial not just from a political and non-legally binding perspective.

As it turns out, the consequences of the *Schrems* decision have proved to be quite limited, in so far as the invalidation of the Safe Harbor Agreement has led the EU and the US to revisit the conditions for effective protection to be ensured to personal data. This compromise resulted in the signature of the Privacy Shield, along with other minor acts to reduce threats to personal data when data are processed by law enforcement authorities.

The coming into being of the Privacy Shield does not seem to have resolved, *prima facie,* all the uncertainties surrounding the appropriateness of the level of protection provided by the US legal order and, most notably, by the safe harbor principles.

---

[17] Case C-362/14 [2015] *Maximillian Schrems v Data Protection Commissioner.*

The first assumption is that at the root of the decision of the ECJ is the goal of extending as much as possible the protection of data privacy, according to a manipulative approach that had already emerged in the *Digital Rights Ireland* and *Google Spain* judgments. More specifically, the judgment of the Court reflects this goal with the amplification of the right to privacy and data protection as well as the powers entrusted to national data protection authorities. In particular, one of the questions raised before the ECJ was whether national regulators have *marge de manoeuvre* to challenge the decision of the Commission, such as the one that was invalidated by the ECJ, assessing the adequacy of the level of protection ensured by third countries' legal systems. According to the ECJ, even though a decision adopted pursuant to Article 25 of the Data Protection Directive is binding on all the Member States, [18] the existence of such an act does not deprive individuals of the right to appeal before the competent authorities according to Article 28(4) for the protection of their fundamental rights. In this respect, it is Article 47 of the Charter that has to be taken into account, and given priority over Articles 7 and 8, by the ECJ. [19]

However, the Court underlines that the Decision of the Commission may not undermine the powers of the national regulatory authorities to protect individuals' rights.

In this respect, then, the grounds for a manipulation of the legal framework in force take their roots when the Court provides a broad interpretation of the powers of these authorities with a view to giving individuals appropriate means to seek the protection of their personal data. [20] Indeed, according to the Court, it would be contrary to the system set up by the Data Protection Directive and to the objective of Articles 25 and 28 thereof for a Commission decision adopted pursuant to Article 25(6) to have the effect of preventing a national supervisory authority from examining a person's claim concerning the protection of his rights and freedoms in regard to the processing of his personal data which has been or could be transferred from a Member State to the third country covered by that decision. [21] Then, by interpreting the legal framework in force in light of Article 47 of the Charter, the Court has effectively strengthened the individual's rights under Articles 7 and 8 and has opened the door to extending the degree of protection of data privacy.

The most important point that sheds light on the manipulative approach of the

---

[18] Ibid, 51.

[19] Ibid, 52. In particular: 'until such time as the Commission decision is declared invalid by the Court, the Member States and their organs, which include their independent supervisory authorities, admittedly cannot adopt measures contrary to that decision, such as acts intended to determine with binding effect that the third country covered by it does not ensure an adequate level of protection. Measures of the EU institutions are in principle presumed to be lawful and accordingly produce legal effects until such time as they are withdrawn, annulled in an action for annulment or declared invalid following a reference for a preliminary ruling or a plea of illegality'.

[20] Ibid, 54.

[21] Ibid, 56.

Court relates to the part of the judgment where it has questioned whether the conditions set forth by Article 25 of the Data Protection Directive, which requires an adequate level of protection for personal data to be transferred to third countries, were actually met by Decision 2000/520. In the same stage of the Decision, the Court shows its attitude to manipulate the content of the relevant EU law provisions when the right to private life and the right to data protection are at stake.

In particular, this review required the ECJ to determine first of all whether the US legal system, and notably the safe harbor principles, afforded the personal data of European residents 'an adequate level of protection'. Only if this requirement is fulfilled, the transfer of personal data to third countries is legitimate. The Court has pointed out that the Data Protection Directive assumed a relatively flexible notion of 'adequate level of protection'. A rather significant degree of ambiguity and vagueness then surrounds this parameter. Indeed, the adequacy of the level of protection afforded by a third country shall be assessed in the light of all the circumstances surrounding a data transfer operation or set of data transfer operations, and particular consideration shall be given to the nature of the data, the purpose and duration of the proposed processing operation or operations, the country of origin and country of final destination, the rules of law, both general and sectoral, in force in the third country in question, and the professional rules and security measures which are complied with in that country.

In order to reduce the said ambiguity and vagueness, the Data Protection Directive spells out some factors to be considered while assessing whether the level of protection offered by a third country is actually 'adequate'. Nonetheless, Article 25 does not clarify whether these parameters are binding and exhaustive, preventing any evaluation of relying on different ones. If a certain degree of uncertainty affects the crucial notion of 'adequate level of protection', then the ECJ can benefit from more space for speculation as well as interpretative manipulation therefrom.

On the one hand, the Court has pointed out that Article 25(6) of the Data Protection Directive requires that a third country 'ensures' an adequate level of protection by reason of its domestic law or its international commitments; on the other one, in the Court's view, the adequacy of the protection has to be assessed 'for the protection of the private lives and basic freedoms and rights of individuals'. So, that what is to be made is not a purely normative assessment, but – more demanding – a fundamental right-based one.

While the compatibility of the Decision on the safe harbor agreement with the Data Protection Directive is called into question, in fact, the ECJ acts as a fundamental rights adjudicator with a view to enforcing Article 7 and Article 8 of the Charter. But when the Court observes that the assessment of the adequacy of the level of protection is necessary for the protection of the fundamental rights at stake, it seems that while *prima facie* the judges aims to elaborate on that notion a little bit more, they eventually deprive the same of any specific and binding meaning.

In the following point of the judgment,[22] the Court provides arguments which confirm its fundamental right-oriented approach based on a strict interpretation of the notion of 'adequate level of protection', which converts this parameter, *de facto,* into a standard requiring equivalence between the compared legal orders. In this respect, in fact, the Court reflects on the objective of Article 25 of the Data Protection Directive, i.e. 'to ensure that the high level of that protection continues where personal data is transferred to a third country'. The reasoning behind the view taken by the ECJ, then, is the assumption that the level of adequacy referred to by Article 25 requires a geographical extension of the scope of application of the guarantees provided for by EU law.

Even though an adequate level of protection does not require third countries to adopt an identical standard, individuals may nevertheless enjoy a degree of protection that is 'substantially equivalent' to that offered by EU law.[23] The equivalency of the degree of protection is required, according to the Court, 'by virtue of an interpretation of the Data Protection Directive in light of the Charter'.

The Charter, then, becomes the legal device for the Court to raise the level of protection required by EU law through a manipulation of the parameter of 'adequacy'. This approach is everything but rhetorical, since the Court has actually taken inspiration from the coming into force of the Charter to revisit the provisions enshrined in the Data Protection Directive and rely on a renewed interpretation of the same. It turns out, then, that the meaning of the provisions of the Data Protection Directive has been affected and, accordingly, the level of protection provided to personal data is nowadays much broader than previously, when the Directive was adopted and the Charter was not yet in force.

Also, the judgment seems to pay attention to the dynamic nature of the level of protection, which may vary depending upon a number of factors. This is basically the reason why the Court urges the Commission to regularly carry out an assessment on whether the finding relating to the adequacy of the level of protection offered by third countries is still factually and legally justified. In addition to that, 'such a check is required, in any event, when evidence gives rise to a doubt in that regard'.[24]

---

22 Ibid, 72.

23 Opinion of the Advocate General Bot, 23 September 2015. In particular, para. 141 states: 'a third country ensures an adequate level of protection only where, following a global assessment of the law and practice in the third country in question, it is able to establish that that third country offers a level of protection that is essentially equivalent to that afforded by the Directive, even though the manner in which that protection is implemented may differ from that generally encountered within the European Union'. Therefore, initially it is up to the Advocate General to manipulate the interpretation of the Directive. Having taken this crucial step, however, he has pointed out that, at para. 142: 'Although the English word "adequate" may be understood, from a linguistic viewpoint, as designating a level of protection that is just satisfactory or sufficient, and thus as having a different semantic scope from the French word "adéquat" ("appropriate"), the only criterion that must guide the interpretation of that word is the objective of attaining a high level of protection of fundamental rights, as required by Directive 95/46'.

24 Case C-362/14, 78.

To this end, the European institutions should take into account all the factually and legally relevant circumstances that have occurred once the assessment has been carried out. This approach mirrors a revisited interpretation of the standard of adequacy according to which a kind of 'continuity' in the level of protection must be guaranteed not only from a geographical point of view but also over the period of time.[25]

So, the legitimacy of the Decision on the Safe Harbor principles no longer hinges solely on the Data Protection Directive. Indeed, the parameter that the Court has relied on in reviewing the decision of the Commission extends to the Charter, the coming into force of which has led to a change from a mainly market-oriented Europe to a fundamental right oriented one. This remark is crucial for the Court as it highlights that the measures taken by third countries must be effective in order to ensure protection substantially equivalent to the standard applied within the EU.

On the one hand, the Court has conceded that such an adequate level of protection can be reached through the implementation of measures that may not necessarily correspond to those practised within the EU and provided by Member States' domestic legislation. The Court seems to have taken a step back and adopted a restrained approach in which it recognizes that the goal of guaranteeing appropriate protection may be pursued by different means, tailored to the specific and relevant legal context. This step could apparently be the basis on which Court could declare itself incompetent to review the legal measures in force in countries other than the EU Member States according to the EU law standard.

On the other hand, the Court has gone down a different route and explored the merits of the legal instruments in force in the legal order of the US with a view to determining whether the same instruments are compatible with the purpose of granting personal data an adequate level of protection. The ECJ has challenged Decision 2000/520 by adopting a reasoning that is quite uncommon when it comes to protecting fundamental rights. In particular, the judgment is remarkable for its rather unambiguously pragmatic view, which is reflected in the efforts made by the Court

---

[25] Once again, this approach reflects the influence of the Advocate General's opinion, particularly at paras. 146–148: '[I]n order to ensure that Article 25(1) to (3) of Directive 95/46 is effective, account should be taken of the fact that the adequacy of the level of protection afforded by a third country involves a developing situation that may change with the passage of time, depending on a series of factors. The Member States and the Commission must therefore be constantly alert to any change of circumstances that may necessitate a reassessment of whether the level of protection afforded by a third country is adequate. An assessment of the adequacy of that level of protection cannot be fixed at a specific time and then be maintained indefinitely, irrespective of any change in circumstances showing that in reality the level of protection afforded is no longer adequate. The obligation for the third country to ensure an adequate level of protection is thus an ongoing obligation. While the assessment is made at a specific time, retention of the adequacy decision presupposes that no circumstance that has since arisen is such as to call into question the initial assessment made by the Commission. Indeed, it must not be forgotten that the objective of Article 25 of Directive 95/46 is to prevent personal data from being transferred to a third country that does not ensure an adequate level of protection, in breach of the fundamental right to protection of personal data guaranteed by Article 8 of the Charter'.

to determine if the objective of ensuring adequate protection has been actually met ('in practice' according to the text of the decision).

These remarks constitute the premise of the analysis that the Court has carried out on the compliance of the safe harbor principles with EU law. The judgment specifically explored the framework in force in the US to drew the conclusion that it does provide personal data with adequate protection compared to the EU standard. Even though the review was formally conducted by comparing the Data Protection Directive with the content of the Safe Harbor principles, from a substantial standpoint the decision of the ECJ has found, in the end, that the US legal system was not compatible with the protection of the fundamental rights enshrined in Article 7 and Article 8 of the Charter.

5. *Tele2 Sverige*

Previously, the ECJ had boldly recognized, in *Google Spain*, the right of the data subject to obtain delisting from search engines and decided, in the *Digital Rights Ireland* case, to annul Directive 2006/24. And it is precisely this latter, historical, and controversial decision and its narrative that is relevant to the ruling that the Grand Chamber of the ECJ delivered in the Tele2 *Sverige* case, [26] in which the compatibility with EU law on traffic data retention measures was at stake. The Court was faced with the need to revisit and clarify the interpretation of Directive 2002/58 so as to make it compatible with the content of the Charter and the same case law which had already applied it.

According to the Advocate General, 'If men were angels, no government would be necessary. If angels were to govern men, neither external nor internal controls on government would be necessary', consequently 'In framing a government which is to be administered by men over men, the great difficulty lies in this: you must first enable the government to control the governed; and in the next place oblige it to control itself'. [27]

This citation, if it is seriously considered, is particularly relevant because the difficulty identified by Madison lies at the root of the balancing activity of the ECJ in this case. The ECJ was called, in fact, to judge the compatibility with EU law of provisions of domestic law which obliged providers of electronic communications services to maintain traffic and location data for a certain period of time. In other words, the retention of communication data allows the government to control individuals, making available to the competent authorities' tools of investigation useful

[26] Case C-203/15 [2016] *Tele2 Sverige AB v Post- och telestyrelsen and Secretary of State for the Home Department v Tom Watson and Others.*

[27] Opinion of the Advocate General Saugmandsgaard Øe 19 July 2016.

for tackling serious crimes. However, the government needs to take into account the threats to the right to privacy resulting from the conservation and access to the stored data. At the root of such complexity is the question of how to find a balance between the protection of public safety, especially with reference to the need to prevent terrorist attacks, on the one hand, and protection of digital privacy.

In this scenario, the aforementioned *Digital Rights Ireland* case plays a crucial role since, as already stressed, that case dealt with the retention period of data envisaged for the purposes of protecting public order. The importance of this decision in relation to the resolution of the dilemma lies in the questions that the Swedish and British judges have put to the ECJ. Indeed, although, in this case, the subject of analysis of the Court was different since it regards Directive 2002/58, the national courts questioned whether national legislation which establishes a generalized and undifferentiated preservation of subscriber data relying on the margin of discretion provided by the Directive, was in contrast, *inter alia*, with the decision in *Digital Rights Ireland*.

The Court's response leaves no room for doubt. The margin of discretion that the Directive gives to the Member States, by incorporating a derogation from the ordinary regime of protection of confidentiality, must in fact be interpreted strictly. Thus, the Court has interpreted Directive 2002/58 guided not only by the EU constitutional framework of protection of fundamental rights, in particular, confidentiality and personal data, but also, and perhaps above all, by the case law of the same ECJ, starting with *Digital Rights Ireland.*[28] Put another way, although the ECJ's scope for action was formally delimited by Directive 2002/58, the decision has incorporated a genuine scrutiny of domestic legislation from the perspective of fundamental rights, in particular on the basis of Articles 7 and 8 of the Charter. Also, the ECJ's case law has become a parameter of judgment in this respect.

Moreover, if this ruling is analysed from a political perspective, the central question that emerges is whether such an interference with the right to privacy and data protection of individuals is still compatible with European law after the ruling that has annulled the Directive on data retention. What is certain is that the ECJ, in providing an interpretation of the scope of Directive 2002/58, in particular of the derogations provided for in the right to privacy, seems to have once again been exercising its constitutional role with respect to Articles 7 and 8 of the Charter, whose trace of such an approach had already been found in the *Digital Rights Ireland*, *Google Spain* and *Schrems*.

Digging deeper into the case in question, the preliminary reference was based on Article 15 of Directive 2002/58, adopted following the entry into force of the Data Protection Directive with the primary objective of adapting the EU privacy and data

---

[28] It is interesting to note that in the ruling the ECJ again merged the protection recognized by Articles 7 and 8 of the Charter, without examining separately the profiles inherent to each of the rights concerned, adopting a diametrically opposed perspective, instead, to that made its own, for the first time, in the decision *Digital Rights Ireland*.

protection framework with respect to the field of electronic communications. This provision allows Member States to derogate from the principle of confidentiality in order to adopt necessary, appropriate, and proportionate measures in a democratic society to safeguard certain interests, including the security of the state.

This is a provision that has a close link with Directive 2006/24. Evident, in fact, was the concern that, in the absence of unambiguous indications, each order could model in a very different way the sphere of interference legitimated by the law. These two questions, arising from the above two cases, have been brought together and brought before the Court.

Firstly, the ECJ was called to clarify whether this provision, read in light of the Charter, prevented Member States from introducing generalized and undifferentiated measures to store traffic data and data relating to the location of subscribers and users of electronic communications services. In one of the two main proceedings, in fact, the legitimacy of an injunction adopted by the Swedish communications authority on the basis of the national legislation, in which Tele2 was ordered to provide for the retention of data relating to electronic communications, was controversial. Secondly, the other main question was whether Article 15 prevented Member States from providing access to personal data by the competent national authorities without limiting such access to the purposes of combatting crime and without subjecting it to prior review by the judicial or administrative authority. In the second main proceedings, the power of the British Ministry of the Interior to impose data retention for electronic communications service providers for a maximum period of 12 months without any prior scrutiny by the competent authorities was challenged.

Against the background of both questions raised for a preliminary ruling, there is widespread uncertainty about the actual implications of the *Digital Rights Ireland* decision and the consequent annulment of the data retention Directive. Indeed, as already underlined, the above-mentioned case has played a crucial role in this case.

The Court firstly addressed a preliminary question observing whether the legislative measures adopted by the Member States pursuant to Article 15 fall within the scope of the Directive, as they concern the processing of personal data by providers of electronic communications services. However, it was not an obvious solution. Indeed, on the one hand, Article 1(3) of the Directive excludes matters of public security, defence, and public order from its scope; on the other hand, Article 15 authorizes Member States to adopt measures that restrict privacy, but refers to activities characteristic of States or State authorities that are unrelated to fields in which individuals are active.

Despite this provision, there is part of the act that regulates electronic communications services and the activities of their suppliers. According to the ECJ the only reading that preserves a useful effect of Article 15 is the one that recognizes that the legislative measures adopted by the Member States fall within the scope of the Directive. [29]

[29] Case C-203/15, 78–81.

Having solved this preliminary issue, the Court notes that the aforementioned provision constitutes an exception to the prohibition on storing traffic data without the consent of the users. It follows that, by allowing Member States to derogate from the principle requiring the confidentiality of communications and traffic data, Article 15 must be the subject of a restrictive interpretation. Within this framework, the Court notes that the measures taken under this provision should aim to safeguard national security defence, public security, and the prevention, investigation, detection, and prosecution of criminal offenses or of the unauthorized use of the electronic communication system. The Court clarified that this list should be considered exhaustive as it appears clear from a literal interpretation. It follows that the Member States cannot adopt measures that interfere with the confidentiality of individuals to pursue purposes other than those expressly mentioned in Article 15.[30]

The second crucial step consists of the reference to the general principles of EU law. Indeed, the Court emphasized the provisions established by Article 15 especially since the rule states the need to ensure that the legislative measures in question comply with the general principles of EU law, including fundamental rights. Here, the aim of the Court is clear and aimed at fostering the need for a constitutional interpretation based on the protection of fundamental rights and, therefore, *a fortiori*, on limitations of the public power to limit the privacy of individuals.[31]

At this point, the Court examined the criteria according to which it is possible to interfere with the fundamental rights protected by the Charter. The Court recalled, first of all, that Article 52 of the Charter recognizes that any limitation on the exercise of the rights and freedoms contained therein must be provided for by law and respect their essential content. On the other hand, the restrictions that are necessary and actually meet the general interest objectives or the protection of the rights of others can be justified in compliance with the principle of proportionality.

Moreover, the ECJ noted that the legislation in question which legitimizes a generalized and undifferentiated preservation, in a continuous and systematic manner, both of the traffic data and of the data on the location of subscribers, which is registered in relation to all electronic means of communication, recalls the measures provided for in Directive 2006/24. In particular, in view of the large amount and heterogeneity of the data that must be kept by the providers of electronic communications services, the legislation imposes a great interference with the right to privacy, which the Court considers particularly serious.

Moreover, the lack of a notification to the interested parties can generate the perception of continuous surveillance affecting not only the right to privacy and protection of personal data but also freedom of expression since the retention of traffic and location data could nonetheless have an effect on the use of means of electronic communication.

---

[30] Ibid, 89–90.

[31] Ibid, 91 *et seq*.

On this basis, the Court draws the conclusion that such a significant interference with the fundamental rights of individuals can only be justified by an equally important objective, in particular in the fight against serious crime. But this does not mean that in the presence of this objective, the other fundamental rights at stake do not deserve protection. According to the Court, even if this was the objective underlying the legislative measures adopted pursuant to Article 15, the provision of a generalized and undifferentiated preservation of traffic data should be considered unnecessary.

Indeed, as observed by the Court, on the one hand, in these circumstances, the measures that the Article 15 authorizes by way of exception would constitute the general rule, overturning the order of priority indicated by the European legislator. On the other hand, the Court observes that the measures provided for by the national legislation leave no room for any differentiation, limitation, or exception in relation to the objective pursued concerning all individuals destined to use electronic communications services regardless of the potentialities of such services to generate serious crimes.

Thus, no correlation is required between the data required for conservation and the existence of a threat to public security. Moreover, similarly to Directive 2006/24, limitations are not indicated, especially in relation to the period of time, the geographical scope, or the individuals to whom traffic data retention would be applicable without distinction.

Such considerations would be enough for the Court to declare that such legislation goes beyond the limits strictly necessary and cannot be justified by Article 15. On the contrary, this rule can justify the application of measures aimed at the targeted conservation of traffic data and location data, for the purposes of combating crime, where conservation is limited by necessity in relation to categories of data, means of communication, and interested individuals, as well as the duration of retention. Thus, the Court has defined guidelines on the conditions that legitimize the application of such measures. Firstly, national legislation should define, by means of clear and precise rules, the scope and application of retention measures, setting their requirements also in order to allow data subjects to be aware of and able to protect their data.

Secondly, with regard to the substantive conditions which the national legislation must satisfy, the Court states that, although they may vary according to the measures adopted, retention must meet objective criteria, on the basis of a relationship between the data to be kept and the objective pursued. [32]

Finally, the Court specifies that similar safeguards should also be applied when determining the potential recipients of the measures and the situations in which they apply. It is necessary that such measures are based on objective criteria or, rather, on procedures which allow the revelation of the connection with acts of serious crime or a serious risk to public security.

---

[32] Ibid, 110.

Moving to the second question raised by the British judge, the ECJ dedicates only some considerations.[33] First of all, regarding the objectives which can justify an interference with the confidentiality of electronic communications, the Court recalled the argument based on the exhaustive list of objectives indicated in Article 15. Indeed, no other objectives can justify retention measures, and in this case, given the gravity of the interference, only the fight against serious crime can be taken into account.

Secondly, the Court focused on the principle of proportionality, arguing that access to the data guaranteed to the competent national authorities should take place within the limits of what is strictly necessary and in the presence of clear and precise rules that identify the conditions. In this sense, the Court clarified the need for national legislation to be based on objective criteria, for example by restricting access to data based on combatting crime within a group of persons suspected of designing, committing, or having committed a serious infringement. Furthermore, the additional requirement is that the access of the national authorities to the stored data should be subject to prior checking by a court or administrative body on the basis of a request motivated by the procedural authority.

Similarly, emphasis is put on the need for authorities to inform interested parties of the adoption of measures, starting from the moment when the communication is not likely to jeopardize investigations. Lastly, the retention of personal data operated by providers of electronic communications services requires the use of appropriate technical and organizational measures to prevent abuse and alterations to data integrity and confidentiality. All these conditions should be considered within the framework of the national system in which an independent authority pursuant to Article 8(3) of the Charter exercises its control powers, overseeing the level of protection of the rights of natural persons.

As a result, for the Court, any measure aimed at the retention of traffic data ordered by the national authorities can be justified in EU law and does not constitute an infringement of the fundamental rights referred to in Articles 7, 8, and 11 of the Charter, where it respects the conditions described above that allow the application to be restricted within the limits of strict necessity.

6. *Conclusions*

At this point, it is necessary to ask whether the ECJ has provided a radically innovative interpretation or, as it seems, the decision in question should be considered only as the natural development of the path followed by the Court from *Digital Rights Ireland*.

The answer is clear. Recently, the ECJ has interpreted EU law and the national laws implementing EU secondary measures in the light of a high level of protection

[33] Ibid, 113–133.

of fundamental rights. The case of digital privacy is particularly significant. The first case was embodied in the 2014 ruling in which the Court had annulled a directive that sacrificed the protection of personal data in the name of the fight against international terrorism. The second occasion dates back to 2014 in the landmark decision *Google Spain* about the right to be forgotten online and the third decision was delivered in the autumn of 2015 with the *Schrems* ruling about the transfer of data belonging to EU citizens outside the territory of the Union. In this framework, the *Tele2 Sverige* case can be considered as the last extension of the relevance of digital privacy to the legislators of Member States.

The extensive interpretation of the scope of the right to privacy and data protection, when it comes to balancing these interests with other fundamental rights, does not represent a novelty in the case law of the European Courts, in particular, the ECJ. In light of the above, it turns out that the ECJ has revisited, beginning with the judgment on the invalidation of the Data Retention Directive, the status of data privacy within the European context. The reconstruction of the new digital right to privacy has been supported, as noted, by the emphatic enforcement of Articles 7 and 8 of the Charter.

However, this underestimation of the importance of economic freedoms resulting from this approach does not seem to be consistent with the Charter, which is inherently placing on the same level the various fundamental rights which fall within its scope on the same level. No difference as to the rank of fundamental rights, indeed, seems to emerge if one looks at the catalogue encapsulated by the Charter. Against this background, it goes without saying that fundamental rights may conflict with each other under certain circumstances: it is up to the Court, in such cases, to find a balance in order to ensure that the substantial essence of the rights at hand is in any case respected or, in any case, that the necessary restrictions are proportionate to the aim pursued. This new interpretation of the catalogue of fundamental rights protected by the Charter has indirectly paved the way for manipulating the standard of adequate protection of personal data in order to require a substantially equivalent one, as said above. To sum up, the decisions of the ECJ in this field have led the Union to be the fortress of personal data without considering the political and legal impact of this decision with regard, for example, to the relationship with third countries but also to other interests such as public security involving the fight against terrorism. Indeed, the high standard of protection online enjoyed by these two fundamental rights will increase the degree of complexity in addressing this cross-border threat.

In this scenario, it is worth asking how the scope of application of the Regulation (EU) 2016/679 (General Data Protection Regulation, hereinafter 'GDPR') will contribute to influence the aforementioned judicial approach. It is possible to observe how the GDPR scope of application codifies the attempts of the ECJ to ensure effective protection of the rights of EU citizen from a transnational perspective. In particular, Article 3(2) of the GDPR can be considered as the result of the high level of the standard of protection of privacy in the EU which, in the information society, can no longer be limited to the EU territory but needs to be ensured globally. The consequence of such a rule is two-fold. On the one hand, this provision involves jurisdiction. In particular, all the cases involving the processing of personal data and covered by the scope defined by Article 3(2) GDPR will be subject to the EU jurisdiction. This approach will overcome the doctrine of establishment developed by the ECJ in *Google Spain* since even those entities which are not established in the EU will be subject to this regulation.

Even, more importantly, from a substantive perspective, the primary consequence of such Regulation is to extend the EU privacy rules to the global context. This political choice of the EU can be read as an attempt to codify the right to *digital privacy* which the ECJ has contributed to defining in the last years starting with the *Digital Rights Ireland* case.

Processing Personal Data on EU Cross-Border Movements to Fight Terrorism*

Rosario Serra Cristóbal

SUMMARY: 1. Jihadist Terrorism as a Cross-Border Phenomenon. – 2. The Importance of the Sharing of Data on Cross-Border Movements within the Schengen Area. – 3. The New Directives on the Processing of Data and the Safeguarding of National Security. – 4. The Passenger Registry (Personal Name Record or PNR). – 5. When Data Crosses the External Border: Data Sharing with Non-EU Third Countries. – 6. Closing Remarks.

1. *Jihadist Terrorism as a Cross-Border Phenomenon*

Jihadist terrorism is a terrorism displaying new features: [1] a dispersed structure, a high degree of fanaticism and extraordinary power to cause damage. With these, it searches for fresh and vulnerable targets, using novel methods of recruitment, training and indoctrination in hatred, such as social media. [2] As has been pointed out, the threat of jihadist terrorism has existed in Western Europe since the early 1990s. However, the processes of radicalization and recruitment that are associated with that threat have never been as extensive and intense in European societies as they are today. [3]

Such terrorist groups have revealed wide-ranging skills in the management of telematic networks not only for the financing of their activities but also for the recruitment and indoctrination of followers of the jihadist cause. [4] This management is

---

* This chapter was written in the framework of the R+D 'Public Security, Private Security and Fundamental Rights' (Ref.: RTI2018-098405-B-100) supported by Ministry of Economy, Industry and Competitiveness and FEDER.

[1] As González Cussac states, 'since the attacks of September 11, the new terrorism is no longer analyzed as a purely criminal or national issue, but involves many other projections that the old terrorism never had. It is a terrorism that does not have clear regulation, whose strategic objective is to provoke the collapse of the civilian status quo. It is a terrorism which tries to take advantage of the potentialities of the enemy for its own benefit, and it abuses the freedoms in democratic societies to cover its illegal activities'. José Luis González, 'Servicios de inteligencia y contraterrorismo' in Guillermo Portilla Contreras and Ana Isabel Pérez Cepeda (Dirs.), *Terrorismo y contraterrorismo en el Siglo XXI. Un análisis penal y político crimininal* (Ratio Legis 2016) 117 and 120.

[2] Mario Losano, *La rete e lo stato islámico. Internet e i diritti delle donne nel fondamentalismo islamico* (Mimesis edizioni 2017).

[3] Fernando Reinares, 'Amenaza yihadista en Europa, ¿qué hacer?' (2016) 171 *Estudios de Política Exterior* 52.

[4] In this regard, see Manuel Torres Soriano, *La dimensión propagandística del terrorismo yihadista global* (Ministerio de Defensa 2009).

characterized by its aptitude for international expansion through charismatic leaders who spread their slogans through the Internet and especially through the use of social networks, calling on followers from all over the world to commit attacks. As a result, prosecution is difficult; this is an enemy which is not always apparent and can surface as an isolated cell in any corner of any city. Terrorists are increasingly difficult to identify. Jihadist terrorism constitutes a diffuse danger with a high potential for harm, which is why the phenomenon cannot be fought exclusively by the security forces as though it were an ordinary crime but must be treated as a global threat. Co-operation among State intelligence services and defence bodies is paramount.

One of the greatest concerns in recent times in the fight against jihadist terrorism and the safeguarding of national security has been the control and pursuit of so-called "foreign terrorist fighters", particularly following Resolution 2178 (2014) of the United Nations (UN) Security Council. These are individuals who travel and return to the West from countries such as Syria and Iraq after accumulating knowledge and experience in the handling of weapons and other technical expertise, with the intention of committing attacks. Society also faces the growing threat posed by individuals who, while remaining within Europe, receive inspiration or instructions from terrorist groups located abroad.

The problem of foreign terrorist fighters triggered changes in the criminal legislation of several Western countries. This was the primary subject matter of Directive 2017/541 of the European Parliament and the Council, of 15 March 2017, regarding the fight against terrorism. For instance, in Spain, new offences were introduced to criminalize behaviours that were previously not included in criminal legislation, such as leaving Spain for the purpose of joining groups that intend to commit terrorist attacks.

Yet the issue is not only to penalize but also to combat terrorism through prevention. Hence it is crucial, among many other things, to control the exit and entry of possible jihadist terrorists across European borders and it is here that cooperation becomes crucial. The UN called for a greater sharing of information among States with the aim of identifying these fighters, understanding their modes of displacement and disseminating empirical evaluation of the risk that they entail in order to prevent foreign terrorist fighters travelling from Western countries to jihadist-controlled territories. Thus, it was said:

> 'The Security Council reiterates, as expressed in Resolutions 2161 (2014) and 2178 (2014), its appeal to Member States to use INTERPOL databases and require that the airlines in their jurisdiction provide advance information on passengers to detect the departure, entry or transit through their territories of persons included in the list of sanctions against Al-Qaida and also encourages them to supply lists of passengers, where appropriate, to the competent national authorities'.

These statements promoted awareness of the usefulness of data sharing for the prosecution of terrorism, as well as other crimes, at the national and transnational level. A UN working group on border management and law enforcement in relation to the fight against terrorism also promotes the sharing of data for this purpose. [5]

With regard to the EU arena, it should also be noted that among the legislative priorities for 2017, passed by the Council on 13 December 2016, was 'to better protect the security of EU citizens, in particular through greater surveillance of the external borders (through a system of entry and exit, the introduction of "smart borders" and a European system of information and travel authorization)', as well as by 'reinforcing the rules for the purchase and possession of firearms, fighting against terrorism, its financing and money laundering, and sharing information about third-country nationals'.

Indeed, cross-border information management and the effective functioning of border data processing systems can serve as an early warning mechanism. Both strengthen the collective capacity of States to detect, prevent and combat terrorism by facilitating inter-agency cooperation and the timely exchange of information, thus allowing critical decisions to be made in a responsible manner.

I would like to address in this chapter the specific border data management tools that can be useful to tackle terrorism, given that the first step in security intelligence lies in obtaining information, which will then be subject to analysis and examination to turn the information into useful intelligence. As will be discussed, several border databases were created to control the entry of immigrants into European borders, but the information offered by these systems can be used to tackle the threat of another challenge: jihadist terrorism. However, these are two separate phenomena. It is true that the new wave of jihadist attacks has coincided, in the same time period, with the largest migratory crisis that Europe has faced as a result of humanitarian crises and later the Syrian civil war and other conflicts. Nevertheless, they are not the same issue. Jihadist terrorism and immigration have very little in common, however an attempt has been made to link them or to justify certain policies against immigration as a mechanism to combat jihadist terrorism arguing, with weak reasoning, that restricting immigration is a way of preventing the entry of potential terrorists into Europe. [6]

2. *The Importance of the Sharing of Data on Cross-Border Movements within the Schengen Area*

Within the EU, responsibility for designing and applying a domestic legal system for national security rests primarily within the Member States' competences (Article 72

[5] https://www.un.org/counterterrorism/ctitf/es/border-management-and-law-enforcement-relating-counter-terrorism.

[6] Andreu Olesti Rallo, 'La crisis migratoria y la reinstauración de los controles de las fronteras interiores en el espacio Schengen' (2006) 68 *Revista Española de Derecho Internacional* 243–247.

of the Treaty on the Functioning of the European Union (TFEU)). Nonetheless, the Union advocated for the harmonization of domestic legal systems in order to achieve greater effectiveness in the fight against terrorism (Article 29 of the EU Treaty), [7] as well as for cooperation in police and judicial criminal matters, regulated in Title V TFEU, in which Article 83 explicitly refers to terrorism as a serious crime.

The EU's strategy against terrorism has been substantiated mainly through the Common Foreign and Security Policy (CFSP), the former second pillar which continues to be governed by the rules of intergovernmental cooperation. [8] The strategy also relies on the EU's internal policy and the European Area of Freedom, Security and Justice, in which border control, asylum and immigration policies are also laid out. It is a framework where the role of the Parliament and the Commission is clearly established. [9] Regardless, since the entry into force of the Treaty of Lisbon, all of these issues were "communitarized", and the third pillar was rendered unnecessary (Articles 66 and 67 TFEU).

Although the EU's terrorist policy is set out on the basis of the basic principles of harmonization of legislation, cooperation and mutual recognition of judicial decisions, the question of security remains a matter of domestic competence, insofar as it allocates to each state the responsibility to ensure national security. In fact, Article 73 TFEU indicates that, together with the adoption within the EU framework of cooperation in security matters, 'it shall be open to Member States to organize between themselves and under their responsibility such forms of cooperation and coordination as they deem appropriate between the competent departments of their administrations responsible for safeguarding national security'.

Nevertheless, in the fight against terrorism, the need for cooperation between security services and intelligence agencies has become a recurrent issue in the EU, [10]

---

[7] A development of this cooperation can be found, among others, in Article 4 of the Common Position of the Council 2001/931/CFSP of 27 December 2001 on the application of specific measures to combat terrorism; and the Council Decision 2002/996/JHA of 28 November 2002, which establishes a mechanism to evaluate legal systems and their implementation at the national level in the fight against terrorism. See also Council Decision 2003/48/JHA of 19 December 2002 on the implementation of specific measures for police and judicial cooperation to combat terrorism in accordance with Article 4 of Common Position 2001/931/CFSP; and the Council Framework Decision 2002/584 / JHA of 13 June 2002 on the European Arrest Warrant and the surrender procedures between Member States.

[8] This cooperation is reinforced by Article 222 of the TFEU, which stipulates a solidarity clause. This requires the joint action of all EU countries where one Member State is the object of a terrorist attack. However, it is clarified, in the Declaration related to this in Article 222, that none of its provisions 'is intended to affect the right of another Member State to choose the most appropriate means to fulfill its obligation of solidarity with respect to that Member State'. It should also be mentioned in this regard the EU Integrated Response to the Crisis (DIRPC) adopted in 2013.

[9] In fact, these measures were divided between Title IV of the Treaty of the European Community and the former third pillar of police and judicial cooperation in criminal matters.

[10] The need to intensively coordinate data protection due to globalization has become absolutely evident in many other areas. The call to a cooperative exercise in data matters is crucial today, as indicated by Artemi Rallo. See Artemi Rallo Lombarte, 'Cooperación y coordinación entre autoridades de protección de datos', in Artemio Rallo and Rosario García (Eds.), *Hacia un nuevo Derecho europeo de protección de datos* (Tirant lo Blanch 2015) 740.

given that the prevention of new terrorist attacks can be strengthened, among other things, through the establishment of information exchange programmes regarding criminals, borders, financial transactions, displacements, etc. Proactive measures, such as the work that the intelligence services and the security forces do to anticipate and contain future attacks, must have as their starting point the study of the "new" terrorists' behavioural patterns. [11] Cooperation between security and defence agencies is therefore vital. The former are traditionally more focused on homeland security, while the latter are generally preoccupied with external security. This usual separation between internal security and external security is impossible in the combat against terrorism; cooperation among all bodies is crucial.

Council Framework Decision 2006/960/JHA was passed with the aim of promoting this exchange of information in the Schengen area. [12] This established a simplified system of exchange of information and intelligence among the security services of the EU Member States through Europol [13] and Eurojust. This is known as the Schengen Information System (SIS). By making use of this information, Member States' security services could be alerted and warned, among other things, about the entry of terrorist suspects or other criminals, or be informed about the risk of attacks, etc. This information served to prevent a considerable number of terrorist attacks, although the sharing of information did not necessarily guarantee its reliability. It must be noted however that whenever a terrorist attack has occurred the shadow of a lack of cooperation or exchange of information has always loomed in the background of the public debate. [14]

Another instrument that has served to facilitate cooperation on data traffic between the authorities of the Member States and countries associated with the Schengen area is Frontex, the European agency for the management of operational cooperation at the EU's external borders. It was founded in 2004 [15] to facilitate the

---

[11] Gustavo Díaz Matey, 'El papel de la inteligencia en la lucha contra el terrorismo yihadista salafista' (2016) 116 *Revista CIDOB d'Afers Internacionals* 209.

[12] The Schengen Agreement, which establishes the removal of common borders between the countries that make up the Schengen area and creates common controls at their external borders, does not include all EU countries. There are non-EU countries which are in the Schengen area (Iceland, Liechtenstein, Norway and Switzerland) and there are also EU Member States which are not in the Schengen area (French overseas territories, Ireland and United Kingdom).

[13] Article 88 TFEU (formerly Article 30 TEU) states: 'Europol's mission shall be to support and strengthen action by the Member States' police authorities and other law enforcement services and their mutual cooperation in preventing and combating serious crime affecting two or more Member States, terrorism and forms of crime which affect a common interest covered by a Union policy'. It is indicated that among the activities that can be assigned by means of regulation is the collection, storage, treatment, analysis and exchange of information that is shared by Member State authorities or by third countries or bodies.

[14] Among other examples, it was indicated that, in the London attacks of June 2017, the suspects had been in the intelligence services' databases or had been investigated for terrorist connections. A prior flow of information between different services would have facilitated prevention. Díaz Matey (n.11) 221. These same coordination failures between intelligence services came to light after 9/11.

[15] Frontex was set up by EC Council Regulation 2007/2004 establishing a European Agency for the Management of Operational Cooperation at the External Borders.

control of external borders between Member States and third countries and to help to harmonize those border controls. Frontex facilitates cooperation between the border authorities of each EU state, serving as a tool for the exchange of technical knowledge and experience. Although Frontex was born effectively as a mechanism to control migratory flows, it could serve to tackle several security threats such as human trafficking and international terrorism. Among its various activities, which are specifically geared towards controlling migratory flows, the agency carries out risk analysis activities and its findings are shared with Member States and the Commission. Frontex develops and uses information systems which allow for rapid exchange of information between border authorities, acting as a coordinator to build channels between those border authorities.

This information can certainly be relevant in tackling jihadist terrorism. In fact, this topic was one of those analysed at the Frontex Africa meeting which took place in Las Palmas in Gran Canaria on 23 May 2017. It was an event which brought together Frontex and 28 African countries, intelligence directors and border crossing experts. The idea to organize these meetings between Frontex and the African countries came about in 2010 due to the intensity of migratory flows from the African continent to Europe, but also due to the increase in jihadist terrorism in Nigeria, Niger, Mali and Burkina Faso, the rise of Salafist jihadist terrorism in the Maghreb, the attacks perpetrated in Tunisia and the North African origin of the perpetrators of certain terrorist attacks that happened in Europe.

With the primary intention of convergence and information sharing, the Prüm Treaty was agreed in 2005 among several EU countries.[16] The Treaty established a legal framework for strong cooperation between the Member States in the fight against terrorism, cross-border crime and illegal immigration. The contents of the Treaty were subsequently incorporated into the 2008 Council Decision of the same objective and extended to all the States of the area.[17] This was equivalent to extending the provisions of the Schengen framework, hence Prüm is also known as Schengen III.[18] Specifically, it provides for the sharing, between the Contracting Parties, of DNA profiles, fingerprint data, registration records of vehicles and other per-

---

[16] The Prüm Treaty, on the stepping up of cross-border cooperation, particularly in combating terrorism, cross-border crime and illegal migration, was concluded on 27 May 2005, and entered into force on 1 November 2016. It was signed by Belgium, Germany, Spain, France, Luxembourg, the Netherlands and Austria. Over time, more countries have been incorporated.

[17] Council Decision 2008/616/JAI of 23 June 2008 on the implementation of Decision 2008/615/JHA on the stepping up of cross-border cooperation, particularly in combating terrorism and cross-border crime.

[18] As indicated by Gregorio Cámara, Prüm's intention was to increase the rate of progress in the sharing of data and information to cover the objectives described in the fight against terrorism, cross-border crime and illegal immigration. But it did this while working alongside the Community framework and generating a new level of cooperation in these matters among the signatory States. Gregorio Cámara Villar, 'La garantía de los derechos fundamentales afectados por la Convención de Prüm' (2007) 7 *ReDCE* 99.

sonal data. The treaty allows the authorities of other signatory States immediate access to the information contained therein, using reference indexes and contact points. Although the Treaty is of an international nature, in any case, it establishes its compatibility with European standards by providing, in Article 47, that the provisions of the Treaty will only be applicable insofar as they are compatible with EU law. It also establishes that if, in the future, the EU adopts rules that may affect the scope of application of the Treaty, the provisions of the Treaty will no longer be applied. The usefulness of this framework has been demonstrated. Indeed, the provisions in Prüm were a tool which proved useful to French investigators in the aftermath of the Paris terrorist attacks in November 2015.

Regarding the disproportionate relationship that seems to be evident between terrorism and immigration, it should be remembered that one of the very criticisms which was made in relation to the Prüm Treaty was the connection between illegal immigration, terrorism and organized crime; [19] a worrying point but one which, nevertheless, continues to be a recurrent perception.

Controls on the entry and exit of potential terrorists or criminals have been executed at a gradual pace in new tools such as, for example, one that entered into force in 2014: the Visa Information System (VIS). It applies to applicants for short-term Schengen visas. The VIS is connected to all Schengen State consulates in charge of issuing visas and to all crossing points at the external borders. In these border crossings, the VIS allows the border guard to verify that the holder of a biometric visa is indeed the same person who requested it. Police authorities and Europol have access to the system for the detection and investigation of terrorist offences and other serious crimes. In October 2011, the VIS began operating in all Schengen State consulates responsible for the issuance of visas in North Africa, and the system later expanded worldwide.

In any case, we must also recognize that, despite these provisions and the steps towards cooperation, national intelligence services traditionally tend to work on a domestic basis and are wary of the total sharing of all information. However, given the circumstances, it has been necessary to overcome government reluctance to share data in this field. This trend has been changing over time and received a strong boost due in the aftermath of various terrorist attacks suffered by Europe beginning in 2015, [20] right at the point where it seemed that the attacks in Madrid (2004) and London (2005) were a nightmare of the past decade. [21] The warnings from police

---

[19] Ibid, 116.

[20] Julian E. Barnes and Stephen Fidler, 'Brussels Attacks Give New Impetus for more Intelligence Sharing in Europe', *The Wall Street Journal* https://www.wsj.com/articles/brussels-attacks-give-new-impetus-for-more-intelligence-sharing-in-europe-1460952001 accessed 18 April 2016.

[21] The "waved" response to the terrorist phenomenon is characteristic of the EU, consisting of a reinforced reaction only after every occasion in which the terrorist phenomenon becomes more active. R. Coolsaet, 'EU Counterterrorism Strategy: Value Added or Chimera?' (2010) 86 *International Affairs* (Chatam House, The Royal Institute of International Affairs) 857–873; see particularly 869.

forces and analysts of the risk of jihadist terrorism spreading to the European continent became reality in a dramatic manner. [22] Indeed, after the attacks of March 2016, the concept of a "Security Union" was launched as a way to change the system of cooperation for safeguarding the internal national security of each State and move it towards the idea of protecting the security of the Union as a whole. [23]

This need to combat terrorism led to political and regulatory reaction in the EU framework, and in domestic spheres, introducing measures and tools which will be analysed below.

In the Schengen area in particular, a Regulation was adopted in 2016 establishing what is known as the Schengen Borders Code, [24] which constitutes a Code of EU standards for people crossing borders. This is again an example of a law which, although doubtless useful for the prevention of any threat to national domestic security, [25] has as its main objective the control of immigration.

The original Regulation has been amended by another Regulation on the European Border Code, passed in March 2017, [26] which updated the Code in the light of new EU and Member State concerns relating to security and adequate control of immigration. Once again, the concepts of security and immigration were bound together. In summary, it should be noted that the reform obliged Member States to:

a) Carry out systematic controls, by verifying in the relevant databases all persons, including those who enjoy the right to free movement in accordance with EU law (that is, EU citizens and their family members who are not EU citizens) when crossing the external borders. This is a new implementation of the system, since previously the Member States were obliged to systematically verify only third-country nationals who did not have the right to free movement under the relevant EU provisions.

b) Cross-check the identities of people crossing the EU external border against those in databases of police interest (for example, the SIS or the Interpol databases of lost or stolen travel documents). The obligation shall apply to the entry and exit of all external borders of the Schengen area by either land, air or sea.

---

[22] 'La amenaza del terrorismo yihadista' (2016) 1 *Cuadernos del centro memorial de las víctimas del terrorismo* 27–46.

[23] European Commission, 'Communication from the Commission to the European Parliament, the European Council and the Council – delivering on the European Agenda on Security to fight against terrorism and pave the way towards an effective and genuine Security Union', COM (2016) 230 final, 20 April 2016, 2 and 9.

[24] EU Regulation 2016/399 of the European Parliament and of the Council of 9 March 2016 on a Union Code on the rules governing the movement of persons across borders (Schengen Borders Code).

[25] Recital 6 states that 'border control should help to combat illegal immigration and trafficking in human beings and to prevent any threat to the Member States' internal security, public policy, public health and international relations'. In Recital 7, these controls also include the analysis of risks to internal security and the threats that may affect the security of the external borders. Idem in Recital 22.

[26] EU Regulation 2017/458 of the European Parliament and of the Council of 15 March 2017 amending EU Regulation 2016/399 as regards the reinforcement of checks against relevant databases at external borders. Entered into force on 7 April 2017.

In any case, it is necessary to emphasize that many of the measures adopted to secure external borders, despite allegedly being instruments for safeguarding national security, do not have this as their main objective. In a large number of legal or political instruments, the main purpose of such methods of border control is to control immigration, but their potential utility for combatting terrorism is rarely mentioned.

In the same vein of encouraging the sharing of border crossing data, the European Commission proposed the creation of an Entry and Exit System (EES) [27] for capturing data on the entry of third-country nationals into the Schengen area, regardless of whether they have a visa requirement. On 20 November 2017, the EU Council eventually passed the Regulation for the establishment of this System of Entry and Exit, [28] as well as the Regulation amending the Schengen Borders Code in relation to the EES. [29]

The former will allow the establishment of a database of the travel history of third-country nationals, including those suspected of having committed crimes, those who have been convicted of such crimes and those who may be victims of these crimes. The register will be accessible to Member State authorities, more so when access is for police purposes and for the prevention, detection and investigation of terrorism or other serious crimes (point 22). Thus, it will complement and complete the information found in SIS. The Council and the European Parliament must now sign the adopted Regulation. The signed text will be published in the Official Journal of the European Union and will come into force 20 days later.

Despite the fact that SIS can be presented as a tool for contributing to the fight against terrorism, its self-evident primary intention is to control or manage the external borders of the Schengen area to control migratory flows. The same objective is pursued by the new Regulation amending the Schengen Borders Code. In fact, with regard to national entry facilitation programmes, [30] which were already considered in the Schengen Borders Code, it states that border guards must evaluate whether to grant or deny entry to those individuals who present 'a threat to the internal security of any of the Member States' (Article 1(5)). It also establishes that, in certain cases, third-country nationals must provide biometric data for the purpose of border inspections. If a third-country national refuses to provide biometric data for the creation of their individual file or for border checks, a decision to refuse entry must be made.

[27] European Commission, 'Stronger and Smarter Borders in the EU', 6 April 2016.

[28] Regulation of the European Parliament and of the Council establishing an EES to register entry and exit data and refusal of entry data of third country nationals crossing the external borders of the Member States of the EU and determining the conditions for access to the EES for law enforcement purposes and amending EC Regulation 767/2008 and EU Regulation 1077/2011.

[29] Regulation of the European Parliament and of the Council amending EU Regulation 2016/399 in relation to the EES.

[30] Each Member State may establish a voluntary programme ('national facilitation program') in order to allow nationals of a third country, or nationals of a specific third country, who do not enjoy the right of free movement under the law of the Union, to benefit from the facilities referred to in paragraph 2 when crossing the external border of a Member State.

Currently, the RTP or Registered Traveler Program is also under consideration. This would allow rapid entry into the EU for frequent pre-approved travellers from third countries and would be connected to the VIS. Some individual countries already have their own RTP signed with third countries outside the EU (Netherlands, Germany and Finland). [31]

Finally, it should be noted that on 9 June 2017 the EU Council also agreed on a general steering regarding the European Travel Information and Authorization System (ETIAS) proposal. The general steering is the position of the Council for negotiations with the European Parliament, a measure which will clearly be aimed more at curbing illegal immigration than safeguarding security, as ETIAS will allow prior checks and, if necessary, deny travel authorization to visa-free third-country nationals travelling to the Schengen area. [32] The legal procedures to approve ETIAS started in 2016, and the system is expected to be in place by 2021. It is an example of another mechanism that can help to maintain national security, but which is obviously more focused on controlling immigration.

3. *The New Directives on the Processing of Data and the Safeguarding of National Security*

As previously said, the bombings in Paris 2015 and in Brussels 2016 pushed Member States and their institutions to reconsider their security policies and to propose new initiatives to strengthen the fight against terrorism, in particular by reinforcing systematic border checks, arms control procedures and passenger registration. The same attacks accelerated the adoption of Directive 2016/680, of 27 April, on data processing by the authorities for the prevention and prosecution of crime, [33] as well as Regulation 2016/679 on data protection. [34] Likewise, in December of that same year,

---

[31] Fernando Ruíz Domínguez, 'Control de fronteras y tráfico de pasajeros aéreos: ¿seguridad vs libertad?' (2016) 71 *Documento Opinión*, Ieee.es, 1–18.

[32] The system will be applied to visa-free third-country nationals, as well as to those who are exempt from the visa requirement for airport transit. Prior to travelling, individuals will have to obtain an authorization to travel by means of an online application.

[33] EU Directive 2016/680 of the European Parliament and of the Council of 27 April 2016 on the protection of natural persons with regard to the processing of personal data by competent authorities for the purposes of the prevention, investigation, detection or prosecution of criminal offences or the execution of criminal penalties, and on the free movement of such data, and repealing Council Framework Decision 2008/977/JHA. Entered into force in 5 May 2016, and the Member States are required to implement it by 6 May 2018 (at that transposition deadline all Member States, except for Denmark and Spain, have communicated national transposition measures).

[34] EU Regulation 2016/679 of the European Parliament and of the Council of 27 April 2016 on the protection of natural persons with regard to the processing of personal data and on the free movement of such data, and repealing Directive 95/46/EC (General Data Protection Regulation). Entered into force 24 May 2016 and applied by the States by 25 May 2018.

the European Commission presented a draft Directive on combatting terrorism[35] (replacing Framework Decision 2001/475/JHA on the same subject) which was approved on 15 March 2017.[36] The new Directive is primarily concerned with the criminal justice response of the Member States to terrorist offences. It also serves as a reference point for information sharing between national authorities and highlights the importance of electronic evidence by emphasizing the cross-border character of jihadist terrorism and the need for a global and coordinated response to it.

The new Directive 2016/680 on data processing in the prevention and prosecution of crime, mentioned above, which has been fully applicable across the EU since May 2018, opens a new, stricter regime in the area of data sharing between Member States. The Directive applies both to the cross-border processing of personal data and to the processing of personal data by the police and judicial authorities at a purely national level. It should be borne in mind that the previous 2008 Framework Decision, which was replaced by the Directive, only covered cross-border data sharing. The new Directive, indeed, emphasizes the growing need to share information for the prevention of and fight against transnational crime and terrorism. However, it does have its limitations: the Regulation underlines the obligation to guarantee compliance with the basic principles that regulate the protection of personal data (Article 7). Indeed, it establishes minimum standards that must be respected in the processing of data within each Member State; specific rights are entrenched and there are certain limits to the flow of data.

4. *The Passenger Registry (Personal Name Record or PNR)*

Among the information exchange measures for cross-border travel, a much-debated issue was a proposal, which had stalled since 2013, to establish an Air Passenger Registry that could be shared among the EU Member States, known as the Personal Name Record (PNR).

The European Parliament repeatedly expressed concerns over the potentially damaging impact on travellers' privacy.[37] Despite this, and also in response to the attacks in Paris in November 2015, the Council of Ministers of Home Affairs on 4 December of the same year gave the green light for the approval of the Registry, which became the subject of the Directive regulating the use of the PNR for the prevention, investigation

---

[35] COM(2015) 625 final, 2015/0281 (COD) Brussels, 2 December 2015.

[36] EU Directive 2017/541 of the European Parliament and of the Council on the fight against terrorism.

[37] Thus, in April 2013, the European Parliament rejected a proposal to create and use, at the EU level, a PNR Registry due to its doubts about the necessity of the Registry and its concerns about the privacy and data of European citizens.

and prosecution of terrorism and other serious crimes, approved on 21 April 2016.[38] The Directive was required to be implemented by the States within two years of its publication.[39] It would be applicable to flights originating or terminating outside the EU, but Member States could also extend it to cover domestic flights ("intra-EU"). This would require, from the date of implementation, flight service providers to supply state authorities with certain passenger data obtained at the time of booking the flight (for example: name, address, itinerary, whether lone or accompanied passenger, mode of payment, bank cards, telephone numbers, luggage information, travel dates, whether the passenger is a frequent flyer, etc.)[40].

The PNR differs from API (Advanced Passenger Information) which involves the data requested and used by certain countries globally to identify terrorists and "known" criminals through the use of alerts. The PNR registry, however, allows for the risk evaluation of people yet unknown to the authorities. Certain "risk indicators" can be set: for example, whether the reservation has been made online or by a travel agency, whether the ticket has been paid for in cash or by credit card and whether the passenger route shows evidence of a pattern usually used by terrorists. The purpose is to track certain suspicious passengers and, if necessary, prevent threats from materializing by anticipating the commission of certain crimes.

In order to safeguard the fundamental rights relating to the protection of personal

---

[38] EU Directive 2016/681 regulating the use of Passenger Name Record (PNR) data in the EU for the prevention, detection, investigation and prosecution of terrorist offences and serious crime.

[39] At that transposition all Member States, except for Denmark and Spain, have communicated national transposition measures.

[40] The data that will be registered are the following:

1. Name and surname. This is primary registry data, although this will be automatically 'masked' after six months.
2. Travel date. This is essential for the tracking of possible terrorists.
3. Booking date or date of issuance of the ticket.
4. Locator. The booking is identified by this alphanumeric number.
5. Traveller's information – phone number, email.
6. Destination and origin.
7. Other trips. Data regarding the traveller's flights or previous trips.
8. Contact address. This information is not "masked" at six months as with the identity data.
9. Payment method, and whether the ticket was paid for in cash or with a card. With the former, it is possible to track the payment card.
10. Flight seat.
11. Whether travelling alone or in a group. An organized and scheduled trip for a large group of people allows one to discount suspected perpetrators of a planned attack.
12. Facts about the ticket. Rate, round trip, date of purchase.
13. Intermediaries. Travel agency or means of ticket acquisition.
14. Whether the traveller used his ticket or not.
15. Luggage.
16. Bookings, and whether any modification was made to the flight booking.
17. Shared code.
18. General data.
19. Changes in the 18 measures cited.

data, privacy and non-discrimination, the Directive includes a number of limitations on the transfer, processing and storage of PNR data: first, the Directive prohibits the collection and use of sensitive information. Additionally, PNR data can only be stored for a period of five years and must be depersonalized after six months so that the individual to whom it corresponds is no longer immediately identifiable. Passengers also have the right to be informed in a clear manner about the collection of these data and the rights available to them. The Directive requires the establishment of data security mechanisms, responsibility for which is to be allocated to a passenger information unit and a data protection officer. Provisions on data transfer state that the transfer of PNR data to third countries can only occur in very specific circumstances and should be decided on a case-by-case basis, and transfer should only be to 'prevent, detect, investigate and process the crimes of terrorism or serious crimes'. Finally, the Directive states that PNR data cannot be the sole basis for making decisions with adverse legal consequences or consequences of serious impact for the individual concerned. The issue at stake is how to implement this Directive whilst also according the utmost respect to individual privacy.

5. *When Data Crosses the External Border: Data Sharing with Non-EU Third Countries*

5.1. *The Failed PNR Agreement with Canada and the Court of Justice's Requirements Regarding the Transfer of Passenger Data*

The evolution of data and progressive globalization have imposed a need to strengthen the instruments for cooperation between national data authorities covering the original European framework.[41] A flight data transfer agreement was signed in 2006 with the US, which involved sharing information on 34 distinct data types of passengers travelling from Europe with a stopover or final destination in a US airport; the agreement allowed the storage of such data for over five years. The details of the agreement attracted criticism, leading to a review in 2012 which resulted in a reduction of shared data types to 19.[42] A passenger data sharing agreement with Australia has also been in place since 2012.

Canada and the EU negotiated a similar agreement in 2010 on the processing and sharing of passenger name registration data (referred to henceforth as the Agreement). After signing the Agreement in 2014, the European Parliament requested an

---

[41] Artemi Rallo Lombarte (n. 10) 747.

[42] Council Decision 2012/472/EU of 26 April 2012 on the conclusion of the Agreement between the United States of America and the European Union on the use and transfer of passenger name records to the United States Department of Homeland and Security.

opinion from the Court of Justice of the European Union (CJEU) to determine whether it was in accordance with EU law. The response of the CJEU was laid out in its judgment of 26 July 2017, where it declared that this system of data sharing required an 'interference in the fundamental right to respect for private life' and 'the protection of personal data'. The Court acknowledged that such interference with rights may be justified 'for the purpose of public interest', but qualified this with the criticism that the provisions of the Agreement 'are not limited to what is strictly necessary and do not establish clear and precise rules'. In particular, there were not sufficient guarantees regarding "sensitive" data, that is, those revealing information about 'racial or ethnic origin, political opinions, religious or philosophical convictions, membership of organizations or individual health or sexuality'.

Furthermore, the judges were of the opinion that, with regard to data storage by the Canadian authorities, such storage was not justified once the individual had left the country.

The judgment stated that the Agreement should also review the 'clarity and precision' of the data to be shared, and ensure that the 'models and criteria' used are 'specific, reliable and non-discriminatory' and that the data used by Canada are limited to the prevention of terrorism and serious international crimes. The Court also requested that Canada should only be able to communicate this information to a third country that is not a member of the EU if the latter country has an established agreement with the EU. It stated that Canada ought also to establish "passenger rights" in case authorities flout these regulations. Given the above, the judges of the CJEU found that 'the Agreement cannot be concluded in its current form'.

5.2. *Data Sharing with the US: the EU-US Umbrella Agreement and the Privacy Shield*[43]

In relation to data sharing with third countries, it should be remembered that the CJEU once again played an important role in the safeguarding of personal data, as shown in its decision in the *Digital Ireland* case (2014).[44] This involved the negotiation and conclusion of the so-called 'Umbrella Agreement' in 2016,[45] which reinforced the protection of the personal data of Europeans regarding the sharing of such data with the US for the purpose of investigating and fighting crime, including ter-

[43] In this regard, see Fernando López Aguilar, 'La protección de datos personales en la más reciente jurisprudencia del TJUE: Los derechos de la CDFUE como parámetro de validez del Derecho Europeo, y su impacto en la relación transatlántica UE-EEUU' (2017) 39 *Teoría y Realidad Constitucional* 557.

[44] CJEU Case *c-293/12 Digital Rights Ireland*, 8 April 2014.

[45] EU Council Decision 2016/2220 of 2 December 2016 on the conclusion, on behalf of the European Union, of the Agreement between the United States of America and the European Union on the protection of personal information relating to the prevention, investigation, detection, and prosecution of criminal offences. Entered into force 1 February 2017.

rorism.[46] Guarantees were made over the establishment of clear limitations to the use of this data, such as a prohibition on data transfer to third countries without express consent, limits on the retention period of such data, right of access and rectification, a right to communication where data security has been breached and jurisdictional guarantee mechanisms for rights violations.

Furthermore, due to the CJEU decision in the *Schrems case* (2015)[47] the agreement governing commercial data sharing between the US and the EU, known as the 'Safe Harbor Agreement', was declared illegal. This led to the negotiation of new terms which were finalized in the 'EU-US Privacy Shield' of February 2016.

With the new Agreements, the EU, among other things, is protecting itself from massive data flows between other global powers, such as the US, particularly in case of espionage by the US intelligence services (the National Security Agency or NSA). As a matter of principle, and in keeping with the jurisprudence of the CJEU, the EU primarily wishes to avoid the data of its citizens being subject to privacy violations without legitimate justification. The fight against jihadist terrorism is one reason which could justify inter-State data sharing due to the utility of such intelligence, including traveller information, in the pursuit and prevention of new attacks. But such data sharing must occur with a specific objective in mind and only when necessary. Any such action must therefore ensure the protection of legally established guarantees and should be proportionate.

It is clear the American and European visions are different in this balance between privacy and security, particularly with regard to data sharing in the framework of combatting jihadist terrorism. US policy has opted to prioritize national security in a

---

[46] Its objective is to provide additional guarantees to other data transfer agreements already in existence.

[47] CJEU Case C-362/14 *Maximillian Schrems v. Data Protection Commissioner.* After the revelations of Snowden, the Austrian citizen denounced several companies such as Facebook, Microsoft, Skype, Apple or Yahoo for the content of these revelations, which claimed that the companies had been sharing the data of their users with the National Security Agency of the United States (NSA). The CJEU analyzed whether the Safe Harbor Agreement was in accordance with EU regulations. In its judgment, the High Court considered the following:

The laws of the US;

1. 'Regulations that allow public authorities to access the content of electronic communications in a generalized manner injures the essential content of the fundamental right to respect for privacy'.

2. 'Regulations that do not provide for any possibility for the defendant to exercise legal actions to access the personal data that concerns him or to obtain rectification or deletion does not respect the essential content of the fundamental right to effective judicial protection'.

He also explained the following:

3. 'The protection of the fundamental right to respect for private life at the level of the Union requires that exceptions to the protection of personal data and the limitations of such protection do not exceed what is strictly necessary' and that on the contrary the American laws 'authorize in a generalized way the conservation of all the personal data of all the persons whose data have been transferred from the Union to the United States, without establishing any differentiation, limitation or exception according to the objective pursued and without foreseeing any objective criteria that allow circumscribing the access of public authorities to the data and its subsequent use for specific purposes'.

way that is incompatible with the view set out by the CJEU. The reinforcement of this attitude to national security, driven by President Trump, may jeopardize the effectiveness of the Agreements previously mentioned.

6. *Closing Remarks*

Jihadist terrorism is leaving a legacy of pain not only in Europe, but in other parts of the world. The logical response of state governments, including European ones, is the persecution of the perpetrators of such attacks and fundamentally the adoption of measures for the promotion and defence of national security. The suggested responses to terrorism are varied in nature, and many are considered excessive. In the vast majority of cases, they entail a clear restriction of fundamental rights, with an undesirable imbalance between security and freedom. [48] The scale of collection, storage and cross-border sharing of personal data between Member States in criminal and terrorist matters is enormous. The increased access to European databases as well as to commercial data for law enforcement purposes is challenging the balance between privacy and security. Among this variety of measures adopted in defence of national security against terrorism, the restrictions regarding entry requirements at borders and airport control and other points of entry have become especially invasive, and sometimes even discriminatory for individuals travelling from certain areas of the world. [49]

As has been recognized in this chapter, the sharing of data on the transit of individuals across borders is a tool of immense utility in the fight against terrorism. The importance of data sharing with regard to border crossings and shorelines was emphasized by the EU Council in June 2017. [50]

It is self-evident that the combination of two different phenomena, the migration crisis and terrorism, is challenging one of the most precious symbols of the European integration: the free movement in the Schengen area. This merging of the concepts of immigration and terrorism has often been condoned, and tightening of immigration legislation has been justified in the name of anti-terrorism in Europe, where it has been supported to prevent the entry of possible jihadist terrorists. This has become excessive and is akin to saying, for example, 'control borders because the terror-

[48] See, also, Louise Doswald-Beck, *Human Rights in Times of Conflict and Terrorism* (Oxford University Press 2011). Also said by David Cole, 'Enemy Aliens' (2002) 54 *Stanford Law Review* 955. Yuval Shany, 'Human Rights and Humanitarian Law as Competing Legal Paradigms for Fighting Terrorism', in Orna Ben Naftaly (ed.), *International Humanitarian Law and International Human Rights Law: Pas de Deux* (Oxford University Press 2011) 13–33.

[49] Maggie Ibrahim Ibrahim, 'The Securitization of Migration: A Racial Discourse' (2005) 43 *International Migration* 163.

[50] *Council Conclusions on EU External Action on Counter-terrorism* (19 June 2017) (Ref. 10384/17).

ists are coming'. Western countries are faced with global phenomena that demand supranational and coordinated responses, but the two concepts of immigration and terrorism cannot be approached in the same manner. Perhaps, in this, we are beginning to adopt a different vision. Thus, in the Spanish National Strategy Plan presented in 2013, risks and threats to national security were listed and discussed, with terrorism and migratory flows included, on a par with each other, in the same list. In this area there has been a step forward, as in the new National Strategy Plan of December 2017,[51] terrorism is considered a risk to national security, while migratory flows are considered 'challenges which are non-threatening, but may cause vulnerability, provoke situations of instability or lead to the emergence of new threats' (page 12). Indeed, it seems difficult to view migratory flows as threats, rather they can be seen to pose a smaller challenge and it is difficult even to say that novel threats may originate from such flows.

It should also be remembered that there are principles governing these counter-terrorist policies and, in particular, those that regulate border data processing. Thus, the General Assembly of the United Nations has highlighted in more than 60 resolutions related to international terrorism the fundamental importance of guaranteeing respect for human rights in the fight against terrorism. Specifically, in the Resolution approved by the General Assembly of 18 December 2007, on the protection of human rights and fundamental freedoms in the fight against terrorism, the States were called upon 'to ensure that all border control operations, as well as the mechanisms prior to entry, follow clear guidelines and practices and fully respect their obligations under international law', expecially 'refugee law and standards of human rights, regarding those who request international protection'.

Supranational treaties also demand respect for fundamental rights as at the time of crossing frontiers, and the approved rules on data processing impose mandatory guidelines regarding data protection. The CJEU has highlighted these obligations, as discussed previously in this chapter.[52]

Finally, the principle of *favor libertatis* must not be forgotten; the interpretation that offers the greatest guarantees of rights must always be chosen. In accordance with CJEU case-law, any exception to the fundamental principle of the free movement of persons must be interpreted strictly. Therefore, it should be understood that any limitation to entry in the Schengen area, often based on the danger arising from an individual's data, must be applied only if the data reveal the existence of a real, evident and sufficiently serious threat[53] affecting a fundamental interest of the society or its individuals.

---

[51] Spanish National Strategy 2017, 1 December 2017.

[52] It is convenient to remember again what is indicated in the case C-362/14 *Maximillian Schrems v. Data Protection Commissioner*, or in *Digital Rights Ireland c-293/12.*

[53] In this regard, in January 2017, the Commission, together with the Member States and the European External Action Service, began the creation of a matrix which combines risk assessment and detailed elements of vulnerability in order to fulfil settled priorities and to coordinate external strategies.

The question lingering in the background remains the same: how can we achieve a reasonable balance between security and freedom? The issue is that with each new terrorist attack, a greater need to guarantee security is engendered and citizens become more willing to sacrifice a greater share of their own liberty along with the freedom of others.

Cybersecurity and Data Protection in European Union Policies and Rules: The NIS Directive and the GDPR Synergy*

Miriam Viggiano

SUMMARY: 1. Introduction. – 2. Data Protection and Cybersecurity. – 3. Security of Network and Information Systems in EU Policies. – 4. Security of Personal Data Processing. – 5. Conclusion.

1. *Introduction*

In the information society, where technology has completely changed our lives, the news of recent terrorist attacks and the constant threat to stability and peace forces us to consider the issue in relation to the reliability and security of all (national and cross-border) network and information systems and services. They are essential to our society, and affect us all individually and collectively, in commercial, professional, business, economic trends and practices, in an ever more globalised world.

At the 2019 Cyber Defence Pledge Conference, the NATO Secretary General pointed out with concern that 'Cyber-attacks are becoming more frequent, more complex and more destructive. From low-level attempts to technologically sophisticated attacks. They come from states, and non-state actors. From close to home and from very far away', adding that 'Cyber-attacks can be as damaging as conventional attacks', because of the fact that a 'single attack can inflict billions of dollars' worth of damage to our economies, bring global companies to a standstill, paralyse our critical infrastructure, undermine our democracies and have a crippling impact on military capabilities'. [1]

Against this background, it is very important to remember that in 2010, in the US National Security Strategy, under the Barack Obama government, the objective of 'Strengthening Partnership' and implementing the necessary programmes was to be based on the active participation of all the competent institutional bodies (public and private) at national and supranational level, and 'the development of norms for

---

* All views expressed in this chapter are personal and do not represent the views of the Authority where the Author is currently employed.

[1] NATO, Secretary General Jens Stoltenberg, keynote speech at the Cyber Defence Pledge Conference, London on NATO's adaptation to cyber threats, 23 May 2019, https://www.nato.int/cps/en/natohq/opinions_166039.htm.

acceptable conduct in cyberspace; laws concerning cybercrime, data preservation, protection, and privacy' were highly recommended.[2]

Consequently cybersecurity and privacy and data protection issues are all involved in the protection of fundamental rights. The objective of this chapter is to analyse the related key policies outside US, at the European Union (EU) level with reference to EU official documents and legal acts.

2. *Data Protection and Cybersecurity*

Data protection and cybersecurity[3] legal problems may be studied from different points of view. The dominant one is how security (and cybersecurity) policies – that involve the collection, recording, organisation, structuring, storage, use, alignment or combination of personal data[4] – affect or are likely to affect the individual's freedoms including the right to privacy.[5]

---

[2] National Security Strategy, Barack Obama government, May 2010, http://nssarchive.us/NSSR/2010.pdf, 28, where it is indicated that 'Neither government nor the private sector nor individual citizens can meet this challenge alone – we will expand the ways we work together. […] We will work with all the key players – including all levels of government and the private sector, nationally and internationally – to investigate cyber intrusion and to ensure an organized and unified response to future cyber incidents. Just as we do for natural disasters, we have to have plans and resources in place beforehand'. See also National Security Strategy, Barack Obama government, February 2015, http://nssarchive.us/wp-content/uploads/2015/02/2015.pdf; National Security Strategy, Donald Trump government, December 2017, http://nssarchive.us/national-security-strategy-2017/. See also: N.A. Sales, 'Regulating Cyber-Security' (2013) 107 *Nw. U. L. Rev.* 1503; D. Thaw, 'The Efficacy of Cybersecurity Regulation', 30 *Ga. St. U. L. Rev.* 287, 2014; S.J. Shackelford and A.N. Craig, 'Beyond the New Digital Divide: Analyzing the Evolving Role of National Governments in Internet Governance and Enhancing Cybersecurity' (2014) 50 *Stan. J. Int'l L.* 119; S.J. Shackelford, A.A. Proia, Brenton Martell and A.N. Craig, 'Toward a Global Cybersecurity Standard of Care: Exploring the Implications of the 2014 NIST Cybersecurity Framework on Shaping Reasonable National and International Cybersecurity Practices' (2015) 50 *Tex. Int'l L. J.* 305; N.G. Susskind, 'Cybersecurity Compliance and Risk Management Strategies: What Directors, Officers, and Managers Need to Know' (2015) 11 *N.Y.U. J.L. & Bus.* 573; S.Y. Peng, 'Private Cybersecurity Standards: Cyberspace Governance, Multistakeholderism, and the (Ir)Relevance of the TBT Regime' (2018) 51 *Cornell Int'l L.J.* 445; W. Pierotti, 'Cyber Babel: Finding the Lingua Franca in Cybersecurity Regulation' (2018) 87 *Fordham L. Rev.* 405.

[3] For an understanding of 'cybersecurity' see: European Union Agency for Network and Information Security (ENISA), Definition of Cybersecurity: Gaps and Overlaps in Standardisation, December 2015, https://www.enisa.europa.eu/publications/definition-of-cybersecurity.

[4] According to article 4, para. 1, point 1, GDPR, 'personal data' is 'any information relating to an identified or identifiable natural person ('data subject')' and 'an identifiable natural person is one who can be identified, directly or indirectly, in particular by reference to an identifier such as a name, an identification number, location data, an online identifier or to one or more factors specific to the physical, physiological, genetic, mental, economic, cultural or social identity of that natural person'.

[5] There is not enough space in this chapter to examine this issue further. However, for many of the related problems and bibliographical references see: Rosario Serra Cristóbal, 'Processing Personal Data on EU Cross-border Movements to Fight Terrorism', pp. 45–62 in this book.

Another problem, less subject to analysis by legal literature and which will be addressed further, is the complementarity and efficiency of both policies, in the sense that security (and cybersecurity) regulation is – on the contrary – a significant part of privacy and data protection safeguards.

The synergies of cybersecurity and privacy policies are necessary: nowadays, in our modern information society, it is not possible to consider individual privacy without implementing serious security implementation of appropriate technical and organisational measures to ensure cybersecurity of information systems. [6]

In this area, in fact, we must take into account the significant growth of cyber threats in recent years, which have also involved personal data. The European Commission reported that: there were more than '4,000 ransomware attacks per day in 2016'; '80% of European companies experienced at least one cybersecurity incident last year'; '[s]ecurity incidents across all industries rose by 38% – the biggest increase in the past 12 years'; in some Member States '50% of all crimes committed are cybercrimes'; more than '150 countries' and more than '230,000 systems across sectors and countries were affected by Wannycry attack in May 2017 with a substantial impact on essential services connected to the internet, including hospitals and ambulance services'. [7]

As the European Commission has noted, cyber threats come from different actors 'they are often criminal, motivated by profit, but they can also be political and strategic', and for this reason the 'criminal threat is intensified by the blurring of the border between cybercrime and "traditional" crime', considering that 'criminals use the internet both as a way to scale up their activities, and also as a source to find new methods and tools to commit crime'. [8]

3. *Security of Network and Information Systems in EU Policies*

Against this background, in July 2016, the European Parliament and the Council of the European Union adopted the Directive (EU) 2016/1148 'concerning measures

---

[6] In this context, reference is also made to ERCIM (European Research Consortium in Informatics and Mathematics), White paper on Cyber-security and Privacy Research. Version v0.91, Oct. 2014, https://www.ercim.eu/images/stories/pub/white-paper-STM.pdf.

[7] European Commission, Digital Single Market. Building Strong Cybersecurity in Europe, factsheet, December 2018, 1, https://ec.europa.eu/digital-single-market/en/news/resilience-deterrence-and-defence-building-strong-cybersecurity-europe (link 'Full factsheet'). See also European Commission, Joint Communication to the European Parliament and the Council, Resilience, Deterrence and Defence: Building Strong Cybersecurity for the EU, JOIN/2017/0450 final, https://eur-lex.europa.eu/legal-content/EN/ALL/?uri=JOIN:2017:450:FIN.

[8] European Commission, Joint Communication to the European Parliament and the Council, Resilience, Deterrence and Defence: Building Strong Cybersecurity for the EU, 2.

for a high common level of security of network and information systems across the Union', to be transposed by Member States not later than 9 May 2018[9] (hereinafter referred to as 'NIS Directive').

It should be stressed that, as noted in recital 2 of the Directive, 'The magnitude, frequency and impact of security incidents are increasing, and represent a major threat to the functioning of network and information systems'[10] and 'Those systems

[9] For the most recent documents on European policy in this field see in particular: European Commission, Communication from the Commission to the European Parliament, 20.3.2019 COM(2019) 145 final, 'Eighteenth Progress Report Towards an Effective and Genuine Security Union', https://ec.europa.eu/home-affairs/sites/homeaffairs/files/what-we-do/policies/european-agenda-security/20190320_com-2019-145-security-union-update-18_en.pdf. See also European Commission, Joint Communication to the European Parliament and the Council, Resilience, Deterrence and Defence: Building Strong Cybersecurity for the EU, JOIN/2017/0450 final. For cybersecurity EU policies and strategies see also: Regulation (EU) 2019/881 of the European Parliament and of the Council of 17 April 2019 on ENISA (the European Union Agency for Cybersecurity) and on information and communications technology cybersecurity certification and repealing Regulation (EU) No 526/2013 (Cybersecurity Act), https://eur-lex.europa.eu/legal-content/EN/TXT/?uri=CELEX%3A32019R0881; Communication from the Commission to the European Parliament, the European Council and the Council, Eighteenth Progress Report towards an Effective and Genuine Security Union, 20.3.2019 COM(2019) 145 final, https://ec.europa.eu/home-affairs/sites/homeaffairs/files/what-we-do/policies/european-agenda-security/20190320_com-2019-145-security-union-update-18_en.pdf; Joint Communication to the European Parliament and the Council, Resilience, Deterrence and Defence: Building Strong Cybersecurity for the EU, JOIN/2017/0450 final, https://eur-lex.europa.eu/legal-content/EN/ALL/?uri=JOIN:2017:450:FIN; European Commission, Proposal for a Regulation of the European Parliament and of the Council Establishing the European Cybersecurity Industrial, Technology and Research Competence Centre and the Network of National Coordination Centres, 12.9.2018 COM(2018), https://ec.europa.eu/commission/sites/beta-political/files/soteu2018-cybersecurity-centres-regulation-630_en.pdf; Communication from the Commission to the European Parliament and the Council: Making the Most of NIS – towards the Effective Implementation of Directive (EU) 2016/1148 Concerning Measures for a High Common Level of Security of Network and Information Systems across the Union, COM(2017) 476 final 2, 4.10.2017, https://eur-lex.europa.eu/legal-content/EN/TXT/?uri=celex:52017DC0476; Commission Recommendation (EU) 2017/1584 of 13 September 2017 on coordinated response to large-scale cybersecurity incidents and crises, in OJ L 239, 19.9.2017, pp. 36–58; https://eur-lex.europa.eu/legal-content/EN/TXT/?uri=celex:32017H1584; Commission staff working document – Assessment of the EU 2013 Cybersecurity Strategy, SWD(2017) 295 final, 13.9.2017, http://ec.europa.eu/transparency/regdoc/rep/other/SWD-2017-295-F1-EN-0-0.PDF; Directive 2013/40/EU of the European Parliament and of the Council of 12 August 2013 on attacks against information systems and replacing Council Framework Decision 2005/222/JHA (OJ L 218, 14.8.2013, pp. 8–14); Council Directive 2008/114/EC of 8 December 2008 on the identification and designation of European critical infrastructures and the assessment of the need to improve their protection (OJ L 345, 23.12.2008, p. 75); Joint Communication to the European Parliament, the Council, the European Economic and Social Committee and the Committee of the Regions: Cybersecurity Strategy of the European Union: An Open, Safe and Secure Cyberspace, JOIN(2013) 1 final, 7.2.2013, https://eur-lex.europa.eu/legal-content/EN/TXT/?uri=celex:52013JC0001.

[10] A specific definition of 'network and information system' is set out in article 4, para. 1, point 1(a–c), NIS Directive which refers also to point (a) of article 2 of the Directive 2002/21/EC. In this sense, it includes any 'electronic communications network' (transmission systems, switching or routing equipment and other resources which permit the conveyance of signals by wire, by radio, by optical or by other electromagnetic means, including satellite networks, fixed and mobile terrestrial networks, electricity cable systems); any 'device or group of interconnected or related devices, one or more of which,

may also become a target for deliberate harmful actions intended to damage or interrupt the operation of the systems'. Furthermore, in many cases, the incidents referred to also involve a violation of privacy and "personal data breach". [11]

Consequently, the aim of European strategies is to encourage Member States to 'have minimum capabilities and a strategy ensuring a high level of security of network and information systems in their territory', because until the approval of the Directive there were 'very different levels of preparedness' and 'fragmented approaches across the Union'. [12]

Among the instruments designed to obtain the result sought by the European legislator, the Directive provides that all Member States must 'adopt a national strategy on the security of network and information systems' [13] and 'designate national competent authorities, single points of contact and [computer security incident response teams networks] CSIRTs with tasks related to the security of network and information systems'. [14] This is important 'in order to contribute to the development of trust and confidence between Member States and to promote swift and effective operational cooperation'. [15] It has further established 'security and notification requirements for operators of essential services and for digital service providers' as well as the necessity to create 'a Cooperation Group in order to support and facilitate strategic cooperation and the exchange of information among Member States and to develop trust and confidence amongst them'. [16]

A high level of security in network and information systems is achieved and maintained, above all, for specific key and sensitive sectors, such as energy (electricity, oil,

---

pursuant to a program, perform automatic processing of digital data'; any 'digital data stored, processed, retrieved or transmitted' by the above elements 'for the purposes of their operation, use, protection and maintenance'.

[11] See recital 63; as well as article 33, Regulation (EU) 2016/679 of the European Parliament and of the Council of 27 April 2016 on the protection of natural persons with regard to the processing of personal data and on the free movement of such data, and repealing Directive 95/46/EC (General Data Protection Regulation), OJ L 119/1, 4.5.2016 (see below section 4).

[12] Recitals 4–5, NIS Directive.

[13] The '[s]ecurity of network and information systems' is 'the ability of network and information systems to resist, at a given level of confidence, any action that compromises the availability, authenticity, integrity or confidentiality of stored or transmitted or processed data or the related services offered by, or accessible via, those network and information systems' (article 4, para. 1, point 2, NIS Directive).

[14] Article 1, para. 2, points a–e. European Union Agency for Network and Information Security (ENISA), ENISA CSIRT maturity assessment model, final version, 30 April 2019, https://www.enisa.europa.eu/publications/study-on-csirt-maturity.

[15] Article 1, para. 2, point c.

[16] Ibid. See also: Commission Implementing Decision (EU) 2017/179 of 1 February 2017 laying down procedural arrangements necessary for the functioning of the Cooperation Group pursuant to Article 11(5) of the Directive (EU) 2016/1148 of the European Parliament and of the Council concerning measures for a high common level of security of network and information systems across the Union (OJ L 28, 2.2.2017, pp. 73–77; https://eur-lex.europa.eu/legal-content/EN/TXT/?uri=celex:32017D0179).

gas);[17] transport (air, rail, water and road transport); banking; financial market infrastructures; health care sector (including hospitals and private clinics); drinking water supply and distribution; digital infrastructure (internet exchange points–IXPs,[18] Domain Name System–DNS service provider,[19] Top Level Domain–TLD name registries[20]).[21] It will necessarily also cover digital services, such as online marketplaces and search engines, as well as cloud computing services.[22]

In this context, it can be noted that the issues are different: not only do objectives and priorities have to be identified, but also the specific governance framework, which includes 'roles and responsibilities of the government bodies and the other relevant actors', the 'cooperation between the public and private sectors'; 'a risk assessment plan to identify risks';[23] 'a list of the various actors involved in the implementation of the national strategy on the security of network and information systems'.[24]

Operators of essential services and digital service providers have to adopt appropriate measures 'to manage the risks' and 'to prevent and minimise the impact of incidents affecting the security of the network and information systems used for the provision of such essential services'.[25]

For this reason, 'operators of essential services' and 'digital service providers' have to notify the competent authority or the Computer Security Incident Response Teams Networks ('CSIRT')'[26] – respectively – of incidents that have a significant

---

[17] Joseph R. Dancy and Victoria A. Dancy, Terrorism and Oil & Gas Pipeline Infrastructure: Vulnerability and Potential Liability for Cybersecurity Attacks, 2 ONE J 579, 2017: European Union Agency for Network and Information Security (ENISA), Report on Cyber Security Information Sharing in the Energy Sector, November 2016, https://www.enisa.europa.eu/publications/information-sharing-in-the-energy-sector.

[18] An 'internet exchange point' (IXP) is 'a network facility which enables the interconnection of more than two independent autonomous systems, primarily for the purpose of facilitating the exchange of internet traffic' (article 4, para. 1, point 13, NIS Directive).

[19] A 'DNS service provider' is 'an entity which provides DNS services on the internet', i.e.: 'a hierarchical distributed naming system in a network which refers queries for domain names' (article 4, para. 1, points 14–15, NIS Directive).

[20] A 'top-level domain name registry' (TLD) is 'an entity which administers and operates the registration of internet domain names under a specific top-level domain' (article 4, para. 1, point 16, of NIS Directive).

[21] See sectors referred to in Annex II, NIS Directive.

[22] See services referred to in Annex III, NIS Directive.

[23] According to article 4, para. 1, point 9, NIS Directive, a 'risk' is 'any reasonably identifiable circumstance or event having a potential adverse effect on the security of network and information systems'.

[24] Article 7, NIS Directive.

[25] Ibid. See also: European Union Agency for Network and Information Security (ENISA), Good Practices on Interdependencies between OES and DSPs, November 2018, https://www.enisa.europa.eu/publications/good-practices-on-interdependencies-between-oes-and-dsps.

[26] Articles 14 and 16, Directive (EU) 2016/1148. Penalties are provided in case of infringements of national provisions adopted pursuant to the Directive (article 21). See also: Commission Implementing

impact on the continuity of the essential services they provide or that have a substantial impact on the provision of a sensitive service described above that they offer within the Union 'without undue delay'.[27]

An incident is defined as 'any event having an actual adverse effect on the security of network and information systems',[28] such as hacking, theft of data or any other episode linked to the interruption of the continuity of the services. The rationale of their notification to the competent entity is to monitor and assess the impact and effectiveness of the arrangements laid down by the Directive, advising – where necessary – operators of essential services and digital service providers in order to adopt the appropriate technical and organisational measures, helping to foster not only "a culture of risk management" but also the useful best practices to be shared with all operators and providers.[29]

Furthermore, it should be recalled that the 'Cybersecurity Act' was approved in 2019 [30] 'to achieve a high level of cybersecurity, cyber resilience and trust within the

---

Regulation (EU) 2018/151 of 30 January 2018 laying down rules for application of Directive (EU) 2016/1148 of the European Parliament and of the Council as regards further specification of the elements to be taken into account by digital service providers for managing the risks posed to the security of network and information systems and of the parameters for determining whether an incident has a substantial impact (OJ L 26, 31.1.2018, pp. 48–51, in https://eur-lex.europa.eu/legal-content/EN/TXT/?uri=celex:32018R0151).

[27] In the field of '[s]ecurity requirements applicable to trust service providers' see also article 19 of Regulation (EU) 910/2014 of the European Parliament and of the Council of 23 July 2014 on electronic identification and trust services for electronic transactions in the internal market and repealing Directive 1999/93/EC, which established that 'service providers shall take appropriate technical and organisational measures to manage the risks posed to the security of the trust services they provide' and provides the notification requirement to the supervisory body 'of any breach of security or loss of integrity that has a significant impact on the trust service provided or on the personal data maintained therein' ('if a breach of security or loss of integrity concerns two or more Member States, the notified supervisory body shall inform the supervisory bodies in other Member States concerned and ENISA'). Other rules, related to the "security and integrity of networks and services", are provided by article 13a of the Framework Directive 2009/140/EC came into force in 2011.

To better understand the phenomena of security incidents and notification requirements, see also the following European Union Agency for Network and Information Security (ENISA) reports, inter alia: Annual Report Telecom Security Incidents 2018, May 2019, https://www.enisa.europa.eu/publications/annual-report-telecom-security-incidents-2018; Annual Report Trust Services Security Incidents 2017, October 2018, https://www.enisa.europa.eu/publications/annual-report-trust-services-security-incidents-2017; Threat Landscape Report 2017, 15 Top Cyber-Threats and Trends, final version, January 2018, https://www.enisa.europa.eu/publications/enisa-threat-landscape-report-2017; Annual Incident Analysis Report for the Trust Service Providers Analysis of Article 19a annual incident Reports under eIDAS – 2016, October 2017, https://www.enisa.europa.eu/publications/annual-incident-analysis-report-for-the-trust-service-providers; Annual Incident Reports 2016, June 2017, https://www.enisa.europa.eu/publications/annual-incident-reports-2016.

[28] Article 4, para. 1, point 7, Directive (EU) 2016/1148.

[29] For international information security standard see also ISO/IEC 27001, Information Technology – Security Techniques – Information Security Management Systems – Requirements, https://www.iso.org/standard/54534.html; ISO/IEC 27032, Information technology – Security techniques – Guideline for cybersecurity, https://www.iso.org/standard/44375.html.

[30] Regulation (EU) 2019/881 of the European Parliament and of the Council of 17 April 2019 on

Union',[31] giving a new mandate to the European Union Agency for Network and Information Security (ENISA), which has thus become the new 'European Union Agency for Cybersecurity'. In particular, it provides that ENISA has the objective of being 'a centre of expertise on cybersecurity', assisting 'the Union institutions, bodies, offices and agencies, as well as Member States, in developing and implementing Union policies related to cybersecurity', supporting 'capacity-building and preparedness across the Union', promoting cooperation 'among Member States, Union institutions, bodies, offices and agencies, and relevant private and public stakeholders on matters related to cybersecurity', contributing 'to increasing cybersecurity capabilities at Union level in order to support the actions of Member States in preventing and responding to cyber threats, in particular in the event of cross-border incidents'; promoting 'the use of European cybersecurity certification, with a view to avoiding the fragmentation of the internal market', promoting 'a high level of cybersecurity awareness, including cyber-hygiene and cyber-literacy among citizens, organisations and businesses'.[32]

4. *Security of Personal Data Processing*

In 2016, the year in which the NIS Directive was approved, the European Parliament and the Council also adopted the Regulation (EU) 2016/679 on the protection of natural persons with regard to the processing of personal data and on the free movement of such data (General Data Protection Regulation, hereinafter referred to as 'GDPR'),[33] which became fully applicable as from 25 May 2018.

With the GDPR the EU has adopted a new risk-based approach for the protection of personal data and data bases, which has given considerable attention to the 'accountability' of the 'data controller',[34] who has to be responsible for, and able to, demonstrate compliance with the GDPR (article 5, para. 2). In this sense, he or she is obliged to 'implement appropriate technical and organisational measures' and data protection policies, taking into account not only 'the nature, scope, context and purposes of processing', but also 'the risks of varying likelihood and severity for the rights and freedoms of natural persons' (article 24, GDPR).

ENISA (the European Union Agency for Cybersecurity) and on information and communications technology cybersecurity certification and repealing Regulation (EU) No 526/2013.

[31] Article 1.

[32] Article 4, paras. 1–7.

[33] Footnote 11.

[34] The 'controller' is 'the natural or legal person, public authority, agency or other body which, alone or jointly with others, determines the purposes and means of the processing of personal data; where the purposes and means of such processing are determined by Union or Member State law, the controller or the specific criteria for its nomination may be provided for by Union or Member State law' (article 4, para. 1, point 7, GDPR).

As for the security of the processing[35] the controller has 'to ensure a level of security appropriate to the risk' through the integration of the necessary safeguards into the processing, such as the pseudonymisation[36] and the encryption of personal data; to have the ability to 'ensure the ongoing confidentiality, integrity, availability and resilience of processing systems and services' and to 'restore the availability and access to personal data in a timely manner in the event of a physical or technical incident'; to provide a 'process for regularly testing, assessing and evaluating the effectiveness of technical and organisational measures for ensuring the security of the processing'.[37] As for the NIS Directive, in order to evaluate the necessary level of security it is important to understand the risks, in this case, of the personal data processing, arising 'in particular from accidental or unlawful destruction, loss, alteration, unauthorised disclosure of, or access to personal data transmitted, stored or otherwise processed'.[38]

For this purpose, the controller has to adopt specific personal data protection safeguards to protect data – also with appropriate security measures – 'by design',[39]

---

[35] A personal data 'processing' is 'any operation or set of operations which is performed on personal data or on sets of personal data, whether or not by automated means, such as collection, recording, organisation, structuring, storage, adaptation or alteration, retrieval, consultation, use, disclosure by transmission, dissemination or otherwise making available, alignment or combination, restriction, erasure or destruction' (article 4, para. 1, point 2, GDPR).

[36] The 'pseudonymisation' is 'the processing of personal data in such a manner that the personal data can no longer be attributed to a specific data subject without the use of additional information, provided that such additional information is kept separately and is subject to technical and organisational measures to ensure that the personal data are not attributed to an identified or identifiable natural person' (article 4, para. 1, point 5, GDPR). On this issue see: European Union Agency for Network and Information Security (ENISA), Recommendations on Shaping Technology According to GDPR Provisions. An Overview on Data Pseudonymisation, November 2018, https://www.enisa.europa.eu/publications/recommendations-on-shaping-technology-according-to-gdpr-provisions.

[37] Article 32, para. 1, GDPR. On this issue: European Union Agency for Network and Information Security (ENISA), *Handbook on Security of Personal Data Processing*, December 2017, https://www.enisa.europa.eu/publications/handbook-on-security-of-personal-data-processing.

[38] Article 32, para. 2, GDPR. See also article 5, para. 1, point f, where it is indicated that personal data shall be 'processed in a manner that ensures appropriate security of the personal data, including protection against unauthorised or unlawful processing and against accidental loss, destruction or damage, using appropriate technical or organisational measures' ('integrity and confidentiality' principle).

[39] Article 25, para. 1, GDPR. 'Privacy by design' is not a new concept. It may be viewed as a development of 'Privacy-Enhancing Technologies' (PETs), coined in 1995 by the Ontario Privacy Commissioner (IPC) and the Dutch Data Protection Authority. In particular, PET 'refers to coherent systems of information and communication technologies that strengthen the protection of privacy in information systems by preventing the unnecessary or unlawful collection, use and disclosure of personal data, or by offering tools to enhance an individual's control over his/her data. PETs are the technological embodiment of the universal privacy principles contained in fair information practices' (A. Cavoukian, Information & Privacy Commissioner Ontario, Canada, Whole Body Imaging in Airport Scanners: Building in Privacy by Design, March 2009, https://www.ipc.on.ca/wp-content/uploads/Resources/wholebodyimaging.pdf, p. 1). In this framework 'Privacy by Design' is a term coined in the 1990s by Ann Cavoukian, Ontario's Information and Privacy Commissioner 'to address the ever-growing and systemic effects of Information and Communication Technologies, and of large-scale networked data systems', in the sense that it 'anticipates and prevents privacy invasive events before they happen', taking into account it 'is embedded into the de-

that is 'as early as the design phase of a system or application',[40] and, considering 'the amount of personal data collected, the extent of their processing, the period of their storage and their accessibility', 'by default', ensuring – in this sense – that 'only personal data which are necessary for each specific purpose of the processing are processed'.[41] In addition, the respect of the 'data minimisation' principle[42] is also binding, considering it 'can reduce the risks to the data subjects concerned and help controllers and processors to meet their data-protection obligations'[43] referred to in security measures too.

Similar to the NIS Directive, which makes it necessary to set up a 'risk assessment plan' to identify the risks, among the instruments provided by the GDPR for the management of the risk of personal data processing, it should be recalled that it is necessary to carry out a 'risk assessment plan of the impact of the envisaged processing operations on the protection of personal data' (prior to the processing) when there is a 'high risk' to 'the rights and freedoms of natural persons'.[44] In such cases, for example, automated processing which entails 'a systematic and extensive evaluation of personal aspects relating to natural persons', such as profiling, and decisions 'that produce legal effects concerning the natural person or similarly significantly affect the natural person'; processing on a large scale of 'special categories of personal data'[45] or personal data 'relat-

---

sign and architecture of IT systems and business practices', ensuring, in this way, 'that personal data are automatically protected in any given IT system or business practice' (A. Cavoukian, Information & Privacy Commissioner Ontario, Canada, Privacy by Design: The 7 Foundational Principles, 20 August 2009, https://www.ipc.on.ca/wp-content/uploads/Resources/7foundationalprinciples.pdf). On this issue: European Data Protection Supervisor (EDPS), Opinion 5/2018, Preliminary Opinion on Privacy by Design, 31 May 2018, https://edps.europa.eu/data-protection/our-work/publications/opinions/privacy-design_en; European Union Agency for Network and Information Security (ENISA), Privacy and Data Protection by Design – from Policy to Engineering, December 2014, https://www.enisa.europa.eu/publications/privacy-and-data-protection-by-design.

[40] ERCIM–European Research Consortium in Informatics and Mathematics, White paper on Cyber-security and privacy research. Version v0.91, Oct. 2014, https://www.ercim.eu/images/stories/pub/white-paper-STM.pdf, p. 37.

[41] Article 25, para. 2, GDPR. On this issue European Union Agency for Network and Information Security (ENISA), Recommendations on Shaping Technology According to GDPR Provisions, Exploring the Notion of Data Protection by Default, December 2018, https://www.enisa.europa.eu/publications/recommendations-on-shaping-technology-according-to-gdpr-provisions-part-2.

[42] This is the principle relating to processing of personal data on the basis of which personal data shall be 'adequate, relevant and limited to what is necessary in relation to the purposes for which they are processed' (article 5, para. 1, point c, GDPR).

[43] Recital 28, GDPR.

[44] Article 35, para. 1, GDPR. See also: Article 29 Data Protection Working Party, Guidelines on Data Protection Impact Assessment (DPIA) and determining whether processing is 'likely to result in a high risk' for the purposes of Regulation 2016/679, adopted on 4 April 2017, as last revised and adopted on 4 October 2017, https://ec.europa.eu/newsroom/article29/item-detail.cfm?item_id=611236.

[45] I.e. 'personal data revealing racial or ethnic origin, political opinions, religious or philosophical beliefs, or trade union membership, [...] genetic data, biometric [...], data concerning health or data concerning a natural person's sex life or sexual orientation' (article 9, GDPR).

ing to criminal convictions and offences';[46] processing concerning 'systematic monitoring of a publicly accessible area on a large scale' (e.g. video surveillance) are included.[47] The 'data protection impact assessment' (DPIA), in fact, contains – inter alia – 'an assessment of the risks to the rights and freedoms of data subjects' and 'the measures envisaged to address the risks, including safeguards, security measures and mechanisms to ensure the protection of personal data' applied by the data controller.[48]

In some cases, furthermore, after the DPIA, the data controller has to consult the supervisory authority ('prior consultation') whether 'the processing would result in a high risk in the absence of measures taken by the controller to mitigate the risk'.[49]

Finally, another instrument concerning the personal data security measures is the "notification" – as in Directive (UE) 2016/1148 – of a personal 'data breach' to the national data protection supervisory authority, within 72 hours, when there is 'a breach of security leading to the accidental or unlawful destruction, loss, alteration, unauthorised disclosure of, or access to, personal data transmitted, stored or otherwise processed'[50] (except 'the personal data breach is unlikely to result in a risk to the rights and freedoms of natural persons').[51] Moreover, the data controller has to communicate the personal data breach to the data subject where the personal data breach 'is likely to result in a high risk to the rights and freedoms of natural persons'.[52]

Heavy administrative fines are provided in the case of GDPR infringements and national supervisory authorities have to apply them, ensuring that the imposition in each individual case is effective, proportionate and dissuasive, by following the specific criteria laid down by the GDPR.[53] It is important to remember that the controller who contravened the data protection by design and by default rules (article 25) and the 'data minimisation' principle (article 5); DPIA and prior consultation of the supervisory authority requirements (articles 35–36), or data security and data breach dispositions (articles 32-34), are also subject to a fine of – depending on the infringed article – up to 10 000 000/20 000 000 EUR or, in the case of an undertaking, up to 2/4 per cent 'of the total worldwide annual turnover of the preceding financial year, whichever is higher'.[54]

---

[46] Article 9, GDPR.

[47] See article 35, para. 3, points a–c, GDPR.

[48] Article 35, para. 7, points c and d, GDPR.

[49] Article 36, GDPR. See also: Article 29 Data Protection Working Party, Guidelines on Data Protection Impact Assessment (DPIA) and determining whether processing is 'likely to result in a high risk' for the purposes of Regulation 2016/679, p. 18.

[50] Article 4, para. 1, point 12, GDPR.

[51] Article 33, GDPR. See also: Article 29 Data Protection Working Party, Guidelines on Personal Data Breach Notification under Regulation 2016/679, adopted on 3 October 2017, as last revised and adopted on 6 February 2018, https://ec.europa.eu/newsroom/article29/item-detail.cfm?item_id=612052; European Data Protection Supervisor (EDPS), Guidelines on Personal Data Breach Notification for the European Union Institutions and Bodies, 21 November 2018, https://edps.europa.eu/sites/edp/files/publication/18-12-14_edps_guidelines_data_breach_en.pdf.

[52] Article 34, GDPR.

[53] Article 83, para. 1, GDPR.

[54] Article 83, para. 4-5, GDPR. See also: Article 29 Data Protection Working Party, Guidelines on

For the sake of completeness, it should be stated that, simultaneously to the GDPR, the EU has also adopted Directive (EU) 2016/680 on the processing of personal data 'or the purposes of the prevention, investigation, detection or prosecution of criminal offences or the execution of criminal penalties, and on the free movement of such data'[55] which constitute the "data protection package" 2016. Moreover at the supranational level, processing of personal data of the Union bodies and institutions is covered by Regulation (EU) 2018/1725.[56] This Directive and Regulation provide similar data protection safeguards to the above mentioned.[57]

In the light of the foregoing, a partial overlapping of interests and legal instruments concerning "security of network and information systems" and "personal data protection" guarantees can be deduced – which are set out, respectively, by the NIS Directive[58] and the GDPR (as well as the "comprehensive data protection framework" which includes Directive (EU) 2016/680, Regulation (EU) 2018/1725 and Directive 2002/58/EC) – concerning accountability, responsibility, roles, risk assessment plans and incident notifications. Differences remain in sectors, subjects, risks and competent supervisor entities. In particular, the NIS Directive covers the specific sectors and services referred to in its annexes II[59]–III[60] and the risk to which it refers is limited to potential adverse effects on the security of network and information systems. On the contrary, the GDPR (and the other EU data protection legislation) is not limited to the mentioned sectors and the concept of risk covers not only security risk, but also the risk

the application and setting of administrative fines for the purposes of the Regulation 2016/679, adopted on 3 October 2017, https://ec.europa.eu/newsroom/article29/item-detail.cfm?item_id=611237.

[55] Directive (EU) 2016/680 of the European Parliament and of the Council of 27 April 2016, OJ L 119/89, 4.5.2016.

[56] Regulation (EU) 2018/1725 of the European Parliament and of the Council of 23 October 2018 on the protection of natural persons with regard to the processing of personal data by the Union institutions, bodies, offices and agencies and on the free movement of such data, and repealing Regulation (EC) No 45/2001 and Decision No 1247/2002/EC (OJ, L 295/39, 21.11.2018). The data protection legal framework is completed also by the 'Directive on privacy and electronic communications' (Directive 2002/58/EC of the European Parliament and of the Council of 12 July 2002 concerning the processing of personal data and the protection of privacy in the electronic communications sector, amended by Directive 2009/136/EC), which includes specific rules about 'Security of processing' and 'data breach' (article 4). See also the 'Proposal for a Regulation of the European Parliament and of the Council concerning the respect for private life and the protection of personal data in electronic communications and repealing Directive 2002/58/EC (Regulation on Privacy and Electronic Communications)', currently discussed in the European Parliament and Council (https://eur-lex.europa.eu/legal-content/EN/TXT/?uri=CELEX%3A52017PC0010).

[57] See Directive (EU) 2016/680: article 26 for 'accountability'; article 27 for 'data protection by design and by default', article 27 and article 28 for 'data protection impact assessment' and 'prior consultation'; articles 29–32 for 'Security of processing' and 'data breach'; article 57 for 'penalties'.

See also Regulation (EU) 2018/1725: article 19 for 'accountability'; article 20 for 'data protection by design and by default', articles 39 and 40 for 'data protection impact assessment' and 'prior consultation'; articles 33–35 for 'security of processing' and 'data breach'; article 66 for 'penalties'.

[58] But see also Regulation (EU) 910/2014 (article 19); Directive 2009/140/EC (article 13a).

[59] Energy (electricity, oil, gas); transport (air, rail, water and road transport); banking; financial market infrastructures; health care (including hospitals and private clinics); drinking water supply and distribution; digital infrastructure (IXPS, DNS service providers, TLD name registries).

[60] Online marketplace, search engine and cloud computing service.

to the rights and the freedoms of natural persons. With regard to security incidents, furthermore, in case personal data are involved (data breach), a double notification is still required, for the different competence profiles, to the competent authority or the CSIRT identified by Member States and to the data protection supervisory authority.

5. *Conclusion*

It is necessary to build a society where citizens can use new technologies but are also aware of the risks that these may entail: cybersecurity 'is critical to both our prosperity and our security', as 'our daily lives and economies become increasingly dependent on digital technologies' so 'we become more and more exposed'.[61] It has long been recognised that security incidents 'are diversifying both in terms of who is responsible and what they seek to achieve. Malicious cyber activities not only threaten our economies and the drive to the Digital Single Market, but also the very functioning of our democracies, our freedoms and our values'.[62]

It is also currently well known that one of the problems we have to face is the development of next-generation digital technologies. The growing availability of the Internet of Things (IoT) devices,[63] artificial intelligence,[64] blockchain,[65] quantum

---

[61] European Commission, Joint Communication to the European Parliament and the Council, Resilience, Deterrence and Defence: Building Strong Cybersecurity for the EU, JOIN/2017/0450 final, p. 2.

[62] Ibid. This is also clear in the above-mentioned Cyberspace National Security Strategy of United States of America, December 2017, http://nssarchive.us/national-security-strategy-2017/, where it is underlined 'Malicious state and non-state actors use cyberattacks for extortion, information warfare, disinformation, and more. Such attacks have the capability to harm large numbers of people and institutions with comparatively minimal investment and a troubling degree of deniability. These attacks can undermine faith and confidence in democratic institutions and the global economic system. Many countries now view cyber capabilities as tools for projecting influence, and some use cyber tools to protect and extend their autocratic regimes. Cyberattacks have become a key feature of modern conflict' (p. 31).

[63] European Union Agency for Network and Information Security (ENISA), Baseline Security Recommendations for IoT in the context of Critical Information Infrastructures, November 2017, https://www.enisa.europa.eu/publications/baseline-security-recommendations-for-iot; European Union Agency for Network and Information Security (ENISA), IoT Security Standards Gap Analysis Mapping of Existing Standards Against Requirements on Security and Privacy in the Area of IoT, December 2018, https://www.enisa.europa.eu/publications/iot-security-standards-gap-analysis. See also: Charlotte A. Tschider, 'Regulating the Internet of Things: Discrimination, Privacy, and Cybersecurity in the Artificial Intelligence Age' (2018) 96 *Denv. L. Rev.* 87; Peter Swire and Jesse Woo, 'Privacy and Cybersecurity Lessons at the Intersection of the Internet of Things and Police Body-Worn Cameras' (2018) 96 *N.C. L. Rev.* 1475; Y. Shen and P.-A. Vervier, 'IoT Security and Privacy Labels', in M. Naldi, G.F. Italiano, K. Rannenberg, M. Medina and A. Bourka (eds), *Privacy Technologies and Policy, 7th Annual Privacy Forum*, APF 2019, Rome, Italy, June 13–14, Proceedings (Springer 2019), 136.

[64] A. Deeks, N. Lubell and D. Murray, 'Machine Learning, Artificial Intelligence, and the Use of Force by States' (2019) *Journal of National Security Law and Policy*, Vol. 10, Issue 1, 1–26. See also Maria Orefice, 'Artificial Intelligence and the Right to Privacy in the Times of Terrorism', pp. 79–94 in this book.

[65] T.I. Kiviat, 'Beyond Bitcoin: Issues in Regulating Blockchain Tranactions', (2015) *Duke Law*

computing,[66] 5G (i.e. the fifth-generation cellular network technology)[67] and big data analytics[68] will increase the risks if cybersecurity is not prioritised in their design,[69] Europe expects '[t]ens of billions of "Internet of Things" devices [...] to be connected to the Internet by 2020',[70] and identifies that a 'failure to protect the devices which will control our power grids, cars and transport networks, factories, finances, hospitals and homes could have devastating consequences and cause huge damage to consumer trust in emerging technologies'.[71]

Furthermore, what it is essential to understand is that there is certainly a continuous process with an uncompensated acceleration greater than what we can expect.

We should also correct one misunderstanding, which has often arisen: we cannot consider security and privacy – and, particularly, cybersecurity and data protection safeguards – as a medium or long-term objective, but as a "physiological condition" of the functioning of the networks and information systems as well as data bases, without which we face a "defective product", which, as such, must not be used because it could have dangerous effects.

Journal, Vol. 65, Issue 3, 569–608; A.N. Longman, *The Future of Blockchain: As Technology Spreads, It May Warrant More Privacy Protection for Information Stored with Blockchain*, North Carolina Banking Institute, Vol. 23, 111–138.

[66] Jeong Woon Choi, 'Quantum Computation and Its Influence on Cybersecurity' (2018) *Charleston L. Rev.*, Vol. 12, 393.

[67] M.R. Bradley and V. Rotty, 'Vincent, Fixing the Glitch: The Smart Rollout of 5G Small Cell Wireless Networks Balancing the Private and Public Interests' (2019) *South Dakota Law Review*, Vol. 63, Issue 3, 483–509.

[68] European Union Agency for Network and Information Security (ENISA), Privacy by Design in Big Data. An Overview of Privacy Enhancing Technologies in the Era of Big Data Analytics, December 2015, https://www.enisa.europa.eu/publications/big-data-protection. See also: S. Hoffman, 'Big Data Analytics: What Can Go Wrong?' (2018) *Indiana Health Law Review*, Vol. 15, Issue 2, 227–246; K.A. Houser and D. Sanders, 'The Use of Big Data Analytics by the IRS: Efficient Solutions or the End of Privacy as We Know It', (Summer 2017) *Vanderbilt Journal of Entertainment & Technology Law*, Vol. 19, Issue 4, 817–872; T.J. Kraft, 'Big Data Analytics, Rising Crime, and Fourth Amendment Protections', (Spring 2017) *University of Illinois Journal of Law, Technology & Policy*, Vol. 2017, Issue 1, 249–274; D. Sorkin, J. Lai and M. Cuevas-Trisan, 'Legal Problems in Data Management: Ethics of Big Data Analytics and the Importance of Disclosure', (Spring 2015) *John Marshall Journal of Information Technology and Privacy Law*, Vol. 31, Issue 4, [xi]–656; O. Tene and J. Polonetsky, 'Big Data for All: Privacy and User Control in the Age of Analytics' (2013) *Northwestern Journal of Technology and Intellectual Property*, Vol. 11, Issue 5, [xxvii]–274.

[69] European Commission, Joint Communication to the European Parliament and the Council, Resilience, Deterrence and Defence: Building Strong Cybersecurity for the EU, p. 2.

[70] Ibid. See also Cybersecurity Act, recital (2) where it is indicated that 'Digitisation and connectivity are becoming core features in an ever growing number of products and services and with the advent of the internet of Things (IoT) an extremely high number of connected digital devices are expected to be deployed across the Union during the next decade. While an increasing number of devices is connected to the internet, security and resilience are not sufficiently built in by design, leading to insufficient cybersecurity'.

[71] European Commission, Joint Communication to the European Parliament and the Council, Resilience, Deterrence and Defence: Building Strong Cybersecurity for the EU, p. 2.

Cyber threats and attacks will be not an exemption or a limited phenomenon of a restricted number of cases anymore, but "the rule". So, the specific components of this "physiological condition" must be – inter alia – "digital resilience", the ability to make a "dynamic adaptation" and, as recently stated, "cyber-hygiene".

In fact, cybersecurity means not only the ability to predict and prevent cyber threats, but also to manage and withstand them, mitigating the negative effects and consequences, assuring the continuity of services.[72]

Moreover, acknowledging that technology changes rapidly, in June 2017, it was recognised by the European Council, as well as by the Global Strategy on Foreign and Security Policy for the European Union, that our 'future security depends on transforming our ability to protect the EU against cyber threats: both civilian infrastructure and military capacity rely on secure digital systems'.[73]

In this sense, the issue is not only related to technology, but also to human behaviour, which 'is equally important' in terms of cyber-hygiene; 'namely, simple, routine measures that, where implemented and carried out regularly by citizens, organisations and businesses, minimise their exposure to risks from cyber threats, should be strongly promoted'.[74]

Cybersecurity and data protection are inseparable, essential to the essential to the objectives discussed above and to the coherence of the renewed EU strategies. The NIS Directive and GDPR (as well as the "comprehensive data protection framework"[75]) represent a positive starting point and are both good steps forward, but they need to be fully implemented, enforced and monitored. However, they are not comprehensive, especially if one considers that, for example, the NIS Directive is limited to certain sectors and excludes others.[76] It is essential to develop synergy between the competent and supervisory authorities concerning the NIS Directive and GDPR.

To this end, Europe will have to work on these issues, and pay more attention to

---

[72] As European Commission has noted: 'Cybersecurity incidents are unpredictable, often occur and evolve within very short periods of time and therefore affected entities and those with responsibilities as regards responding to and mitigating the effects of the incident must coordinate their response quickly. Furthermore, cybersecurity incidents are often not contained with any specific geographical area and may occur simultaneously or spread instantly across many countries' (Commission Recommendation (EU) 2017/1584 of 13 September 2017 on coordinated response to large-scale cybersecurity incidents and crises, OJ L 239, 19.9.2017, pp. 36–58, https://eur-lex.europa.eu/legal-content/EN/TXT/?uri=celex:32017H1584, point 4).

[73] European Commission, Joint Communication to the European Parliament and the Council, Resilience, Deterrence and Defence: Building Strong Cybersecurity for the EU, JOIN/2017/0450 final, p. 2.

[74] Recital 8, Cybersecurity Act. See also: European Union Agency for Network and Information Security (ENISA), Review of Cyber Hygiene Practices, December 2016, https://www.enisa.europa.eu/publications/cyber-hygiene.

[75] See also Directive (EU) 2016/680, Regulation (EU) 2018/1725 and Directive 2002/58/EC (above referred to in section 4).

[76] For example agrifood or defence sector.

education and training, which are the other challenges of the future. This is because, – in the words of the NATO Secretary General, 'cyber goes beyond technology' and '[t]he people behind the technology are just as important. We need to build a strong and diverse workforce of future cyber defenders [...]. Because we have always been able to change when the world is changing'.[77]

[77] NATO, Secretary General Jens Stoltenberg, keynote speech at the Cyber Defence Pledge Conference, London on NATO's adaptation to cyber threats, 23 May 2019, https://www.nato.int/cps/en/natohq/opinions_166039.htm.

Artificial Intelligence and the Right to Privacy in Times of Terrorism

Maria Orefice

SUMMARY: 1. Introduction. – 2. Privacy in the Age of Artificial Intelligence. – 3. The Advent of New Technologies and the Reasonable Expectation of Privacy for Big Data. – 4. The General Data Protection Regulation 2016/679/EU between Limits and Openness to Challenges of AI.

1. *Introduction*

Terrorism in ordinary times raises several questions related to the compression of fundamental rights: a massive control of people's private lives, an overexposure to potential discrimination based on ethnicity or religion and a departure from the constitutional principle of the presumption of innocence.

With the advent and rise of technological innovation, the Internet of Things (IoT) and artificial intelligence (AI) systems, developed by governments and private individuals, the risk is that machine-to-machine decisions are taken by automatic choices, determined without a test of legitimization of the principles of precaution and proportionality, without determining the degree of probability that the risk will mature into actual concrete damage and without comparing a future and uncertain security benefit to the damage to existing and indelible freedoms.

The policymaker has moved towards the criminalization of the alleged danger of crimes or attempts to commit offences. In fact, in 2019, a person was arrested in Wales for the first time thanks to facial recognition technology and the US police agencies are now using analysis software more often to identify potential criminals, even if they are uncertain of the reliability of the data.

Every day our lives become more and more connected to the Internet, which means that the Internet of Things will soon be the Internet of Data, easy to control and to hack. AI is already present in our daily lives in areas such as self-driving vehicles, robotic surgery, chatbot and voice recognition.

With the use of AI, these data are processed dynamically, not simply saved in databases, but processed, correlated and translated for purposes other than those that had led to their acquisition. When these data are personal, AI raises questions concerning the protection of privacy and the rectitude of the behaviour of businesses towards consumers.[1]

---

[1] Roberta Angelini, 'Intelligenza Artificiale e governance. Alcune riflessioni di sistema', in Franco

When the fear of terrorism prevails in ordinary life to the point that liberties are sacrificed *hic et nunc* in favour of the uncertain security of tomorrow, it should be held firm that freedom and democracy are the only assets worthy of being defended in times of terrorism.[2]

We should ask: is it proportionate (in the balance between the threat of terrorism and the enjoyment of fundamental freedoms) to use the data of all (suspected and unsuspected), collected, extracted or bought through continuous monitoring, sometimes even without our knowledge, for one apparent purpose of public security or even worse for a hidden purpose, such as that of orienting our electoral choices as demonstrated by the Cambridge Analytica scandal?[3]

Starting from an international regulatory context that saw the emergence of the laws of fear,[4] which will not be the object of our analysis for reasons of space, we will analyse the evolution of the concept of privacy over time, in relation to the massive collection of data (big data) and in consideration of the challenges that AI poses today. Then we will try to analyse the supranational legislator's response to the growing need to protect the freedoms which, precisely because they are constantly threatened, need stronger protection.

On the contrary, new technologies and AI could not only positively influence the relationship between the central state and citizens and create opportunities for simplification of public services (filling out questionnaires and forms, surveying the needs of the population, limiting information asymmetries, etc.), but above all to provide citizens with tools for controlling and disposing of their personal data, extending the spaces of protection of the personal sphere, in order to enable an AI *ethics by design*.

The European legislator seems to have taken some steps in this direction, with Regulation 2016/679, fully applicable from 25 May 2018, which generally includes some provisions for those who processes personal data of European citizens, including those outside the European territory. By way of example, but in no way exhaustive, one of the most interesting news articles is cited: when data processing has more than one purpose, the link between the original and the additional purpose must be taken into account, and where the latter is different, the specific consent of the party concerned will be necessary, this obviously does not mean that companies will not

Pizzetti (ed.), *Intelligenza Artificiale, protezione dei dati personali e regolazione* (Torino, Giappichelli 2018) 297.

[2] David E. Adelman, 'Harmonizing Methods of Scientific Inference with the Precautionary Principle: Opportunities and Constraints' [2004] 34, *Environmental Law Reporter* 10133.

[3] Zeynep Tufekci, 'Facebook's Surveillance Machine' [2018] *New York Times* https://www.nytimes.com/2018/03/19/opinion/facebook-cambridge-analytica.html accessed 19 March 2018; Jennifer Cobbe, 'Reining in Big Data's Robber Barons' [2018] http://www.nybooks.com/daily/2018/04/12/reining-in-big-datas-robber-barons/ accessed 10 April 2018.

[4] Giovanna De Minico, 'La risposta europea al terrorismo del tempo ordinario: il lawmaker e il giudice' (2017) X(2) *Osservatoriosullefonti.it* 3; Cass R. Sunstein, *Laws of Fear: Beyond the Precautionary Principle* (Cambridge, Cambridge University Press 2005).

adopt unfair business practices, given that the AI provides tools that amplify the possibilities of abuse, but that companies will be able to take the challenge of *privacy compliant* to compete in the market and strengthen consumer trust.

The European legislator is moving in the direction of securing the fundamental values on which democratic societies are based, with the aim of making effective the protection of the fundamental right to the protection of personal data recognized to by European citizens by the Nice Charter and, at the same time, to promote the free circulation of data, as recognized by Recital 7 of the Regulation.

This regulation must be read looking at the technological development already underway, looking for potential dangers and defining the legal problems that may lead to the development of our society, possibly dissolving the nodes on the rethinking of the legal categories that technological evolution invokes and will increasingly demand in the future.

2. *Privacy in the Age of Artificial Intelligence*

To effectively protect privacy in the era of AI, of the IoT, of the massive data production and of the anti-terrorist hyper-control, it is necessary to understand the current issues that its protection poses.

We will now examine how privacy has evolved over time and how its definition is evolving. The notion of privacy[5] cannot be called unifying.[6] It has taken on different values in the past, due to historical and social contexts. In recent times, regardless of where it has been discussed, it has increasingly tended to be conceived as an antiquated concept and even, in the worst case, harmful, anti-progressive, excessively expensive and hostile to economic, social and political well-being.

---

[5] Antonio Baldassarre, *Privacy e Costituzione. L'esperienza statunitense* (Roma, Bulzoni 1974) 64; Antonio Baldassarre, *Diritto della persona e valori costituzionali* (Torino, Giappichelli 1997); Cesare Massimo Bianca, 'Tutela della privacy. Note introduttive' (1999), *Nuove leggi civili commentate* 2-3; Francesco Bilotta, 'L'emersione del diritto alla privacy', in Agostino Clemente (eds), *Privacy* (Padova, Cedam 1999) 54; Giuseppe Busia, 'Riservatezza (diritto alla)' (2000) *Digesto delle discipline pubblicistiche* 476; Giovanni Buttarelli, *Banche dati e tutela della riservatezza* (Milano, Giuffrè 1997); Antonio Cataudella, 'Riservatezza (diritto alla)' (1991) *Enciclopedia giuridica*, 1; Ettore Giannantonio, Mario G. Losano and Vincenzo Zeno-Zencovich (eds), *La tutela dei dati personali. Commentario alla legge n. 675/96* (Padova, Cedam 1999); Roberto Pardolesi (eds), *Diritto alla riservatezza e circolazione dei dati personali* (Milano, Giuffrè 2003); Stefano Rodotà, 'Persona, riservatezza, identità. Prime note sistematiche sulla protezione dei dati personali' (1997) 4 *Rivista critica del diritto privato* 583; Stefano Rodotà, 'Privacy e costruzione della sfera privata. Ipotesi e prospettive' (1991) XXII *Politica del diritto* 525; Stefano Rodotà, *Tecnologie e diritti* (Bologna, Il Mulino 1995) 106; Stefano Rodotà, 'Controllo e riservatezza a garanzia della privacy ma senza i "lacci" della Burocrazia' (1997) *Guida al Diritto* 10.

[6] Sergio Niger, *Le nuove dimensioni della privacy: dal diritto alla riservatezza alla protezione dei dati personali* (Padova, Cedam 2006) XI 1-254.

The consequences of a 'bad definition'[7] of privacy, however, are foreseeable and manifest when privacy and its values, presumably obsolete, must be balanced against the imperatives of defence of national security, economic efficiency and protection of entrepreneurship; in these cases, most of the time the protection of privacy comes out on the losing side.

In fact, the list of its counterweights is long and constantly growing. Recent innovations introduced by social media, mobile platforms, cloud computing, data mining and predictive analytics threaten to tip the balance in favour of the value to be balanced against confidentiality, deploying privacy in permanent opposition to progress, knowledge and security.

Privacy in Greece was intended as 'deprivation' or refusal to accept or pursue public offices. The attention paid to the care of a private space, in the opposite sense of the public dimension, excluded the political commitment that was considered the most important aspect of human life to the point that: 'a man who lived only a private life and who, like the slave, [...] could not enter the public sphere or that, like the barbarian, [...] chose not to establish such dominion, he was not fully human'.[8]

In this sense, 'a life spent outside the common world acquired an almost antisocial connotation',[9] so much so that it was believed that in an ideal society there was no need for a private sphere in which to seek refuge because this need was considered a pretext to escape from ethical and social obligations.[10]

With the passing of time and with the evolution of societies the concept of privacy has been reversed, delimiting, in clear opposition to the past, an essential sphere for the full expression of human faculties, an instrument of protection of human dignity to the extent that it allows the individual not to be discriminated against, to act autonomously, to freely develop one's own personality and to participate autonomously in the political and social life of the country.

The result is the demarcation of an inalienable and inviolable place of intimacy in which everyone must be able to leave his or her mask in tranquillity and security, free to potter around in one's slippers,[11] without the fear of being seen or spied on.

With the information society this *ius solitudinis*[12] has undergone profound changes, becoming almost an oxymoric claim to participation, knowledge, control over all the information that can name a person. Privacy today, in other words, would take on a further significance that would be directed by the identical and intimate need for freedom. The needs of defence and national security, highlighted by the recent

---

[7] Raymond Shih Ray Ku, 'Privacy is the problem' (2009–2010) 19 *Widener Law Journal* 873.

[8] Hannah Arendt, *Vita activa: la condizione umana* (Alessandro Dal Lago tr., Milano, Bompiani 2001) 19.

[9] Francesca Fabris, 'Il diritto alla privacy tra presente, passato e futuro' (2009) 1 in *Tigor – A.I* 95.

[10] Niger, *Le nuove dimensioni della privacy: dal diritto alla riservatezza alla protezione dei dati personali*, 3.

[11] Ibid, 4.

[12] Right to be let alone.

incidents of terrorism, on the one hand and the new market strategies, on the other, have transformed the company into a daily surveillance network that invests the generality of the affiliates. [13]

In the first case, as monitoring is no longer limited to exceptional periods, it exposes the universality of people and, not only dangerous ones, to a previously unimaginable visibility; [14] in the second, the mercantilist logic of the personalized product increases the risk that the consumer may be discriminated against on account of his or her opinions, religious beliefs, health conditions and intentionally addressed to certain contents or goods.

In the light of what has been expressed so far, the protection of privacy today should try to answer this question: 'Can we consider the subject whose past and present are recorded in detail and who is totally at the mercy of other subjects, public or private, even strangers, from whom he must resign himself to being expropriated of his data to be free and adequately protected?'

The techniques for interfering in the lives of individuals have developed a slow and continuous erosion of the prerogatives of the person, no longer 'integrated' physically and psychically. The risk is to turn a person into a mere object that can be manipulated, nullifying every fragment of dignity.

There is an unprecedented expansion of the field of interference of public power in privacy, which corresponds to the strict reduction of guarantees: the intrusive subject is the public power, whose intrusion is far more intense than the private one, then be subjected to limits. [15]

Then confidentiality, stretching its meaning, should cover these spaces, transforming itself into 'protection of existential choices against public control and social stigmatization' [16] or 'as the demand for social instruments that protect us from the risk of being simplified, objectified and judged out of context'. [17] It would no longer be the old passive claim to be let alone, but an active claim aimed at controlling one's own data, which can well translate into the request not to be seen by third parties and thus meet with the solitary matrix of privacy, but through new protection tools that allow everyone to control their data on the Internet.

This 'new' question of privacy would preserve a need for protection of one's own interior – matured over time and dictated by social change – from prying eyes and external invasions, though no longer connected to the character of the materiality of the space within which the individual moves.

---

[13] De Minico, *Costituzione. Emergenza e terrorismo* (Napoli, Jovene 2016).

[14] Ibid.

[15] Sandro Staiano, 'Diritto alla riservatezza e potere pubblico' (2017) 17 *Federalismi.it* 4.

[16] Rodotà, *Privacy, libertà, dignità. Discorso conclusivo della Conferenza internazionale sulla protezione dei dati*, 26th International Conference on Privacy and Personal Data Protection, Poland, Wroclaw, 14–16 September 2004, http://www.garanteprivacy.it/web/guest/home/docweb/-/docweb-display/export/10492932.

[17] Ibid.

In this technological panorama, the protection of privacy is necessary because it becomes even more necessary as the risk increases that the invasion may result in conditioning or discrimination, which would prevent the individual from exercising his liberties.

Given that modern technologies are so sophisticated that they can penetrate the everyday life of each individual, the demand for privacy increases the protection spaces and the instruments of control, parallel to the invasion of those technologies.

Consequently, in the concept of privacy, a reversal of the route with respect to its Greek origins is affirmed: its protection would no longer represent deprivation from a social life but a condition of inclusion in the society of participation, [18] in the sense that only protection from the conditioning that may derive from the use-abuse of new technologies will make the participation of the individual free to society. Since it was considered a quality typical of the subject attentive to its 'particular' it has become the essential tool for the exact opposite: the conscious and autonomous participation in public life.

Not only that, privacy is also a brake that becomes even stronger as the interference techniques become more refined. It serves to block the invasions of its private field from public interference from both private and public entities [19]. The right to privacy assumes the appearance of a 'conceptual container', [20] within which all modes of protection of personal freedom guaranteed to the individual by the State converge. The privacy would have in *re ipsa* an elasticity directly proportionate to the forms of intrusion, so today it would acquire a much wider scope and would require, therefore, a variable protection, certainly stronger than in the past.

Having assumed this definitional flexibility, a close link exists between privacy and dignity, to the extent that dignity assumes the form of freedom of self-determination; this relationship stands as a fundamental factor of contrast against forms of mass control and requires the addressing and stemming of the growing and convulsive phenomenon of data mining.

The ultimate aim is to protect the dynamic and emerging subjectivity of individuals from the abuse of commercial and governmental actors, who are interested in making individuals and communities fixed and predictable.

Thus described, privacy would be far from antiquated: in the form of freedom from surveillance, public or private, it becomes fundamental to the affirmation of conscious citizenship, an indispensable structural feature of democratic political systems. [21] A similar construction is also fundamental to the capacity for innovation, so

---

[18] Ibid.

[19] William M. Beaney, 'The constitutional right to privacy in the Supreme Court' (1962) *Supreme Court Review* 212-251.

[20] Alessandro Mantelero, *Il costo della privacy tra valore della persona ragione d'impresa* (Milan, Giuffré 2007) 1.

[21] James Campbell and others, 'Privacy Regulation and Market Structure' (2015) 24(1) *Journal of Economics & Management Strategy* 47–73.

that even the perception of privacy as 'anti-innovation' would be a non sequitur.

The innovation that manifests itself in commercial and social contexts, in fact, is the result of the free interaction of particular commercial and social values. A commercial culture that sees privacy as a threat to its knowledge production practices encourages forms of unfair competition. But a society that values innovation respects privacy and gaming processes and encourages experimentation from which innovation, as we shall see below, is derived. In short, it is privacy raids that damage individuals, progress and innovation. An understanding of social phenomena that gives the right relevance to effective privacy protection requires a structural approach to legislation.

The legislative strategies aimed at achieving these objectives should make the data control systems transparent and accountable. Moreover, they should respect the private (not necessarily physical) space of each subject because it is a dynamic subjectivity on which liberal democracy and innovation rely on, since it is in interstitial spaces – within information processing frameworks – that they prosper and, therefore, European or supranational privacy legislation should focus precisely on maintaining these spaces. [22]

3. *The Advent of New Technologies and the Reasonable Expectation of Privacy for Big Data*

The protection of the personal sphere, understood as freedom not to be interfered with in the choices made in the private sphere, [23] a precondition of the freedom of self-determination, was recognized only in 1965 to the individual, as part of the conjugal relationship, limited to the family.

This notion has gradually been extended, but only with the emergence of new technologies and the first forms of AI, privacy has been pushed further to extend to the whole community [24] to the point that today it would result in everyone's right to maintain control of personal data, [25] or data collected from electronic devices that are used daily, which, if combined, are able to reveal the most intimate details of an individual's existence.

It cannot be denied that technological innovation has made the sense of protection of the sphere of a person who escapes the arbitrary exercise of power expand along with the predictive algorithms.

[22] Cohen, ibid.

[23] Griswold v. Connecticut [1965] U.S. 381(479).

[24] Maria Francesca De Tullio, 'La privacy e i big data verso una dimensione costituzionale collettiva' (2016) 4 *Polica del Diritto* 642.

[25] Cohen, ibid.

American jurisprudence, in its many rulings, [26] has shown that privacy covers everything the owner assumes to be private, even if physically released from his or her material availability.

It should be added that this protection, as is repeatedly reiterated by the Supreme Court, must be assured to the suspect, even during a flagrant arrest. This clarification serves to highlight how much stronger is the protection of the subject against whom no investigation has yet been initiated, but, on the other hand, is monitored daily by the app managers of his smartphone for profit motives or by governments for security reasons.

From what has been argued it is clear that the expectation of privacy covers and extends to information that comes out of the material sphere within which the subject can exercise a lordship over things.

Likewise, the fact that in using the smartphone the subject accepts that the information entered in it is saved on servers located in an area outside the smartphone cannot mean that the subject wanted to give up his or her privacy.

The daily use of electronic devices does not annul the expectation of protection of those who use them but puts at risk the protection of privacy and threatens liberty constantly, so only an increase in the scope of privacy and the tools to protect it will be able to provide adequate protection of the liberty of individuals and the community in general.

Those who use smartphone applications for social networking or e-commerce services give their personal data to Over The Top operators ('OTT') 'allowing' access to their geolocation information, camera data, gallery data, search history, contacts, personal agenda, etc., these data are transferred and stored in the servers on duty.

We ask ourselves: if data is no longer in the strict availability of its owner because it is part of a public or private database, i.e. maintained and managed, even temporarily by the subject offering the specific service required, do we say that the owner of that data intends to give up his or her privacy and then when he or she consents to be monitored, they completely loses control of the information that identifies it?

On this point it may be of interest to mention the Supreme Court of the United States case Whalen v. Roe [27]. In fact, the Court ruled on the constitutional legitimacy of a New York State law that had set up a centralized computerized archive containing the names and addresses of all the people who had been prescribed narcotics. This computer system, however, although created to avoid data loss, made the identities of patients easily divulged, causing concern to the data owners, who feared that their information could be revealed, with the risk that drug addicts would be branded as such, and therefore discriminated against, in violation of their fundamental rights, in particular the privacy rights.

---

[26] Griswold v. Connecticut [1965] U.S. 381 (479); Whalen v. Roe [1977] U.S. 429 (589); Katz v. United States [1967], U.S. 389 (347); Olmated v. United States [1928] U.S. 227 (439); State v. Earls [2013] NJ 214 (564).

[27] Whalen v. Roe [1977] US 429 (589).

In this case, the Court considered that the collection of information affects 'two privacy interests':

1. an 'individual interest in avoiding disclosure of personal matters'. In assessing the non-disclosure interest, the Court found that in the specific case the security measures employed by the law in question to protect the identities of the recipients of the requirements were sufficient to ensure that personal data would be protected by the public domain. The Court also found that the legal guarantees adequately protected the interest not to disclose personal information.

2. an 'interest in independence in making certain kinds of important decisions'. In this regard, the Court stated that the decision in question was whether the necessary medicine would be acquired and used, i.e. how much conditioning would be derived by the patient who was supposed to take it, in other words would he or her have renounced the medicine if it hadn't been filed?

Moreover, Judge Stevens, prophetically, in that ruling left open the possibility that some databases in the future might not be 'constitutionally acceptable' if they were not adequately protected against misuse.

He points out here that the Court, while rejecting the appellant's claim, acknowledged that the right to privacy includes, on the one hand, the interest in checking one's personal data, on the other, the interest in making free decisions (informational privacy and privacy of autonomy). The former refers to the control over one's own data and the second to the possible interference of third parties in the personal choices of an individual who makes use of services.

Now, in the light of this case study and of the excellent US jurisprudence, it is necessary to distinguish between the physical dimension and the proprietary dimension in the daily use of our data. The former would include the profiles of the unauthorized invasion of spaces in which a person holds a reasonable expectation of confidentiality; the later would include issues related to the unauthorized commercial exploitation of data. It follows that the privacy as described so far, declined in a modern key and not in its eremitical version, will also cover data that have come out of the material availability of the subject to which they belong and will demand to know purposes, places, times, methods of treatment and security techniques.

So, if we want to apply the reasoning of the Court to the object of our investigation, we will verify: 1) the presumed maintenance of data in the private sphere by its owner; 2) the interest not to disclose the data; and 3) the interest in making independent and autonomous decisions about the transfer of data.

These three verifications are resolved in the following question: When the subject grants the OTT access to his or her personal data, in order to take advantage of a service and the OTT apparently continues to 'maintain the material control' of the data it produces (which will be stored on his cellular phone) can the subject 'reasonably' expect that the public or private custodian carefully conserves his or her data and that the custodian does not use it for his own purposes, or when he or she hands over his smartphone does he or she definitively and consciously renounce the control of his or her data?

In order to answer this question, users should know the conditions of the service, i.e. which uses will be intended for their data, in which type of cataloguing they will be submitted, in which places they will be stored and what security measures will be taken to protect the data, but above all users should be able to continue using the service by denying access to the service provider or should be able to choose differentiated protection levels. This did not happen with Cambridge Analytica. [28]

Many people today provide their personal data on the web and social networks, without relaxing their privacy expectations because they do not know the terms of the service, the purposes for which the data are collected or otherwise are willing to negotiate them in order to have an efficient e-mail service or to benefit from messenger or WhatsApp and communicate with close and distant relatives and friends.

Users often accept the general conditions of the contract only to eliminate temporary consent screens (cookies) that block the page on which they are browsing. These general conditions are often too vague or too technical for the average user of the Internet, where the relationship between the cost of the service and the profitability of the data, extrapolated from the uses – considering the economic position of the supplier and the consumer – is clearly disproportionate.

The apparently free acceptance of users, without which they would be forced to give up the service, allows companies to exploit for any purpose personal information, e-mails, religious and political beliefs, highly personal photographs and videos, in which the facial recognition algorithms and the determination of the surrounding environment can be used to outline behaviours and habits, age, sex, friends, the type of places frequented and the types of products purchased.

The data can reveal if a person is likely to have a heart attack and can therefore determine the price of the insurance premium, forcing that person to pay the higher rate or may predict that a particular person will fail to repay a mortgage loan, causing the bank to deny them financing, or that another person intends to commit a crime by having him arrested in advance. The prediction would degrade self-determination and may prove to be incorrect if the data, on the basis of which it is made, are not correct, with serious consequences for the fundamental freedom of individuals.

The new technological landscape imposes new rules to protect self-determination against data determinism. [29] If a person visits pro-jihadist sites he or she will not nec-

---

[28] Zeynep Tufekci, 'Facebook's Surveillance Machine' [2018] *New York Times* https://www.nytimes.com/2018/03/19/opinion/facebook-cambridge-analytica.html accessed 19 March 2018; Jennifer Cobbe, 'Reining in Big Data's Robber Barons' [2018] http://www.nybooks.com/daily/2018/04/12/reining-in-big-datas-robber-barons/ accessed 10 April 2018.

[29] Viktor Mayer-Schönberger and Kenneth N. Cukier, *Big Data. Una rivoluzione che trasformerà il modo di vivere e già minaccia la nostra libertà* (Milano, Garzanti 2013) 30.

essarily commit a crime, but if the intelligent algorithm[30] foresees that he may do so, the Authorities could intervene with a preventive arrest or limit this person's freedom.

In the proposed case there would be a risk of subverting the content of the offensive principle, [31] or the notion of 'potential harm' in the definition of exposure to danger would be broadened, undermining its constitutional roots. If it is true that the principle of legality, in the formal sense, provides that in the abstract any fact can become a crime, since it is sufficient that a law be published that considers it so, it is equally true that the hierarchy of sources privileges the constitutional provisions.

Then, the free action of individuals would risk being threatened by a sort of 'data dictatorship', [32] which may seem far-fetched today, but could well be adapted to the authoritarian drift of a democratic state. The data may or may not be correct, but they may be disclosed to those that the owner of the data did not want them to know and that they were not and are not required to know. If this model has a positive aspect, on the one hand, to combat tax evasion, for example, on the other hand, it has a negative aspect for the client of insurance companies, which can impose a higher premium, replacing urinalysis, which is certainly more expensive than an assessment of the habits, interests, hobbies and diseases of the insured would be.

To hide the data, in extrema ratio, the individual could renounce the freedom to choose the contents to be accessed and the sites to visit on the Net, self-limiting his freedom of expression for fear of being spied on. In such a scenario, the 'interest in independence in making certain kinds of important decisions and therefore the privacy of autonomy would be undermined at its root.

The prediction would replace self-determination and, therefore, the 'black box' of the individual, which today gathers all his or her data, would become the new beating heart of the individual's privacy, which is based on the principles of modern constitutionalism, so to defend it would mean to defend the dignity of the individual, rereading the fundamental maps of national and European rights in an evolutionary key.

In fact, the respect for the dignity of the human person cannot be derogated even from the legislator.

---

[30] Giovanna De Minico, 'L'algoritmo giuridico è intelligente ma deve tenr conto delle differenze' [2020] *Il sole 24 ore* accessed 22 june 2020, 29.

[31] Giovanni Fiandaca and Enzo Musco, *Diritto penale Parte generale* (Bologna, Zanichelli 2014) 213–220; Giovanni Fiandaca and Enzo Musco, *Diritto penale Parte speciale* (Bologna, Zanichelli 2012) 1, 505–509; Ferrando Mantovani, *Diritto penale Parte generale* (Padova, Cedam 2013) 209–215; Domenico Pulitanò, *Diritto penale* (Torino, Giappichelli 2013) 208–220.

[32] Mayer-Schönberger and Cukier, 237.

4. *The General Data Protection Regulation 2016/679/EU between Limits and Openness to the Challenges of AI*

On 4 May 2016, after a troubled four-year legislative process, the text of the EU Data Protection Regulation 2016/679/EU[33] was published in the Official Journal of the European Union. After 20 days it officially entered into force and became definitively applicable directly in all member countries starting from 25 May 2018.
The new Regulation certainly made a noteworthy contribution to the discipline of new phenomena[34] that have taken root in the network, as can be seen from the legal nomenclature used: the extension of the list of definitions concerning the protection of personal data of Article 2 of the previous law 95/46/EC, today Article 4 of the EU Regulation.

More fitting descriptions are added to the technological context, such as profiling, genetic data, biometric data, the right to portability and so on.[35]

The definition of 'consent of the interested party' has also changed, which Article 6 sets as the cornerstone of the lawfulness of processing personal data. According to this provision, the treatment must be rooted in a suitable legal basis and in a series of foundations that, in principle, coincide with those provided for by the old Privacy Code, that is, in addition to consent, the fulfilment of contractual obligations, vital interests of the data subject or third parties, the legal obligations to which the data controller is subject and the public interest or the exercise of public authority and the legitimate prevailing interest of the data controller or third parties to whom the data are communicated.

With reference to the definition of sensitive data in the digital society, in the Regulation EU/2016/679 the term 'Big Data' is never used, nor is it highlighted that an aggregation of personal data can reveal "more than sensitive" information on users. Just think of the geolocation data that can reveal if a person attends places of worship, and consequently his or her religious beliefs. This gap is symptomatic of a deficient regulatory apparatus. A failure to recognize a phenomenon that only takes into account the profiling, which is hinted at in the new Regulation, cannot give any legal protection to the persons to whom the Big Data belongs.

Therefore, those rapid information requests that ask for personal data as payment

---

[33] Regulation (EU) 2016/679 of the European Parliament and of the Council of 27 April 2016 on the protection of natural persons with regard to the processing of personal data and on the free movement of such data, and repealing Directive 95/46/EC (General Data Protection Regulation).

[34] Gaetano Arnò, *La tutela della privacy nella rete Internet* (Torino, Giappichelli 2002); Peter Carey, *E-privacy and Online Data Protection* (London, Butterworths 2002); Lawrence Lessing, *Code and Other Laws of Cyberspace* (New York, Basic Books 1999); Andrea Lisi, *La privacy in Internet* (Napoli, Esselibri Simone 2003).

[35] Ioana Gheorghe-Badescu, 'Le nouveau règlement général sur la protection des données, Quoi de neuf?' (2016) *Revue de l'Union européenne* 466.

for the service they offer for generic and non-homogeneous purposes, but which do not shed light on the fact that aggregation of data exposes the "more than sensitive" data of the person, would seem in sharp contrast to the regulatory provisions and must therefore be rewritten. Moreover, with reference to the further requirement of explicitness that is required for the processing of sensitive data, which is a more robust requirement than the other type of consent, generally, this 'explicit' or manifest consent is granted in writing or electronically and is accompanied by a handwritten or digital signature, although under certain conditions it can be inferred based on the active behaviour of the interested party. In this way, albeit within certain limits, spaces are opened for forms of consensus derived from concluding behaviours, expressed through positive actions on the part of the interested party, not by simply identifying or otherwise harbingers of discretion. 'Explicit consent' is also needed for consent to decisions based on automated processing such as profiling.

Profiling, intended as 'any form of automated processing of personal data consisting in the use of such personal data to evaluate certain personal aspects related to a natural person' and 'in particular to analyze or predict aspects concerning professional performance, economic situation, health, personal preferences, interests, reliability, behaviour, location or movement of that physical person', would require explicit consent, but a legal artifice would loosen its effectiveness. According to the definition given by the Regulation, the analysis of the data in their archives with information technology (IT) tools, the processing of which is subjected to the prior assessment of a person – possibly before the use of the data themselves, for example in order to adapt and verify the data themselves – does not constitute profiling. Therefore, no strengthened consent would be needed to carry out such an analysis.

Among the exceptions to the granting of consent, another is added: Recital 43 and Article 9 specify that public entities should not, as a rule, seek consent for the processing of personal data. The Regulation explicitly clarifies that the legitimate interest of the holder does not constitute a suitable legal basis for the treatments conducted by the public authorities in the performance of their respective tasks.

Further limitations are contained in Article 23, which states that the law of the Union or of the Member State to which the data controller or data processor is subject may limit, by legislative measures, the scope of the obligations and rights referred to in Articles 12–22 and 34, on transparency, information and access to personal data, rectification and cancellation, opposition and automated decision-making concerning individuals, if this limitation respects the essence of fundamental rights and freedoms and is a necessary and proportionate measure in a democratic society to safeguard a range of values, amongst them national security, public security the prevention, investigation, detection and prosecution of offences or the execution of criminal sanctions, including the safeguarding against and prevention of threats to public safety.

The exceptions contained in Article 23 that derogate, for example, from the right to portability for the reasons already listed risk being too vague to incorporate discretionary meanings also among Member States. On the contrary, uniform and well-defined derogations cancel the spaces within which abuse can be hidden.

Effective protection would require that the consumer be granted adequate safeguard, considering the peculiarities of the Network[36] and the rapid development of AI systems, but its consistency is soft in the new Regulation.[37]

A consensus that becomes a 'transfer of data' and therefore the transfer of confidential information, the most intimate of users, cannot be said to be valid or compatible with the provisions of the EU Regulation, which however fails to keep up with the technologies, because it omits the regulation of cases now consolidated on the Internet.

Big Data: the information that is collected and combined every day becomes, in the information society, hypersensitive data that affect the explication of users' freedoms to the point that they themselves constitute the core of those unavoidable fundamental freedoms, but the European Regulation does not mention this.

Notwithstanding this, although the terms 'Big Data' and 'Artificial Intelligence' do not appear in the text of the Regulation, a series of principles are defined that could be the bridge to the future development of sustainable AI algorithms and 'ethics by design'.

Even if there is not yet a shared definition of AI, the core of these systems lies in the ability of the algorithms to learn from the data with which they are fed and create new data analysing the reality in which they operate to make decisions about the behaviour to be taken.

The opportunities that smart machines can offer to humanity are unimaginable, even if simultaneously the impact they can have on human rights is worrying, as widely described in the Recommendation adopted by the Parliamentary Assembly of the Council of Europe on 28 April 2017 'Technological Convergence, Artificial Intelligence and Human Rights'.

The Regulation lays down a number of principles that can be adapted to the context of AI. First, the transparency of the algorithms that are used in the processing of personal data in which data are involved, and also the 'privacy by design' requirement, which is an insurmountable hinge for machine programming and algorithm design; secondly, the accountability of the data controller for the effects that the machines he or her developed or controlled can have on the rights of the data subjects. This responsibility also translates into the obligation to assess the risks that the proceedings involve for the freedoms and rights of persons (Data protection impact assessment 'DPIA', following the Regulation) and to adopt technical and organization-

---

[36] Viktor Mayer-Schönberger and Yann Padova, 'Regime Change? Enabling Big Data through Europe's New Data Protection Regulation' (2016) XVII *The Columbia Science & Technology Law Review* 315-335.

[37] Olivia Tambou, 'Protection des données personnelles: les difficultés de la mise en oeuvre du droit européen au déréférencement' (2016) *Revue de référence en droit européen*, 249.

al measures adequate to the risks involved in the processing, as well as security measures.

However, it is not always the case that the exact methods to be used by the algorithm and the effects thereof are knowable in advance, particularly as AI is powered by machine learning and deep learning systems that aim to allow the machines to learn by adopting behaviours that the programmers themselves had not foreseen.

The report of the Commission nationale de l'informatique et des libertés (CNIL) 'Comment permettre à l'homme de garder la main?' [38] reviews the possible effects of the use of AI on the rights and freedoms of individuals and proposes a public platform to gather together the algorithms used by everyone rather than to evaluate the content of them to verify their effects.

The precautionary principle should also be extended to the field of AI to develop a prior assessment of the impact of AI algorithms on the basis of available practices, in order to link the new AI products to this type of assessment.

These systems will need to be developed in ways that provide for the control and predictability of behaviours. This is covered by Article 22 of the Regulation which recognizes an AI under human control, which allows human intervention to interrupt treatments or deactivate the machines.

These principles are translated into the need to insert ethical principles into the language of algorithms[39] that will help the machines decide when it is appropriate to apply the precautionary principle. Therefore, privacy by design should be the starting point for regulation and enforcement based on the protection of non-negotiable rights and prevailing on market logic, such as life, self-determination, for this the owner and the whole chain involved in the treatments respect the principle of loyalty defined by the CNIL.

The European Supervisory Authorities, the European Committee for the Protection of Personal Data and the European Commission have been assigned the role of being authors of a European Data Protection Governance, [40] which will have to take into account the work of European institutions with the aim of adapting European legislation to cover the practical applications of growing technological innovation under development and to adequately protect the right to personal data protection by strengthening consumer confidence and promoting free movement of data.

---

[38] 'Comment permettre à l'homme de garder la main? Les enjeux éthiques des algorithmes et de l'intelligence artificielle', https://www.cnil.fr/sites/default/files/atoms/files/cnil_rapport_garder_la_main_web.pdf accessed December 2017; The Norwegian Data Protection Authority, Artificial Intelligence and Privacy Report, January 2018.

[39] Giuseppe D'Acquisto and Maurizio Naldi, *Big Data e Privacy by Design* (Torino, Giappichelli 2017) 186.

[40] Franco Pizzetti, 'La protezione dei dati personali e la sfida dell'intelligenza artificiale', in Franco Pizzetti (ed.), *Intelligenza Artificiale, protezione dei dati personali e regolazione* (Torino, Giappichelli 2018) 186.

Fighting Terrorism Online: Censorship, Platforms and Freedom of Expression across the Atlantic

Giovanni De Gregorio

SUMMARY: 1. Censorship, Terrorism and Online Platforms. – 2. Freedom of Expression across the Atlantic. – 3. Tackling Online Terrorist Content in Europe. – 4. Tackling Online Terrorist Content in the US. – 5. Online Terrorism and Private Enforcement of Fundamental Rights. – 6. Conclusions.

1. *Censorship, Terrorism and Online Platforms*

Censorship is not a new phenomenon. History shows that freedom of expression has been subject to restrictions to control the dissemination of information and ideas.[1] In particular, terrorism is one of the predominant examples demonstrating how public actors justify limitations to the flow of information across society to avoid the spread of propaganda and violent values.

The relationship between censorship and terrorism is of particular concern when the debate is framed in the digital environment.[2] Unlike in the past where the channels of communication were usually centralised and controlled by the public authority and the creation and distribution of information was governed by traditional media outlets, the decentralised nature of the Internet has allowed each user to freely share thoughts with a global community just through the use of an Internet connection. The case of live streaming of terrorism shootings during Christchurch attacks in New Zealand is emblematic.[3]

Although the evolution of the digital environment has fostered freedom of expression, the evident drawbacks cannot be neglected. Primarily because of the difficulties

[1] For a brief introduction to the evolution of censorship see Jurgen Wilke, 'Censorship and Freedom of the Press' (European History Online, 8 May 2013) http://ieg-ego.eu/en/threads/european-media/censorship-and-freedom-of-the-press accessed 19 November 2018.

[2] Jeffrey Kaplan, 'History and Terrorism' (2011) 98(1) *Journal of American History* 101; Gerard Chaliand and Arnaud Blin (eds), *The History of Terrorism. From Antiquity to ISIS* (University of California Press, 2016).

[3] Eleanor Ainge Roy, '"No Right to Livestream Murder": Ardern Leads Push Against Online Terror Content' *The Guardian* (24 April 2019) https://www.theguardian.com/world/2019/apr/24/christchurch-call-ardern-leads-push-against-online-terror-content accessed 30 April 2019.

in monitoring the vast amount of content uploaded by users, the Internet has become a channel in which to pursue illicit aims such as terrorism.[4] Thanks to the possibilities offered by modern social media, cyberspace has become an area of attention in terms of hate, radicalisation and terrorism.[5] Indeed, the Internet has amplified the opportunities for terrorist organisations to exploit the Web to pursue purposes such as propaganda or recruitment. Before the advent of the digital environment, terrorist recruiters had to rely on human contacts, for example, at religious premises since, unlike the Internet, mainstream media such as TV and newspapers could not be considered available instruments for terrorist organisations in western countries. Today, however, the Internet enables terrorist groups to connect and share their values across the globe not only with individuals but also with other terrorist organisations.[6]

One of the similarities between terrorism and the Internet is their cross-border nature involving different jurisdictions and, therefore, national and supranational laws. Nevertheless, whilst it is not particularly difficult to define the online dimension as being a digital space which differs from the atomic world, the same consideration does not apply when defining acts of terrorism.[7] Although national and international instruments have been adopted since 2001, there is still no agreed definition of it.[8] For example, in some jurisdictions, an order to eliminate a comment on a terrorist video could be considered proportionate. Whereas, in other states, the same situation could be covered by the right to free speech. Terrorist content are forms of expression. Therefore, the primary question is how the detection and taking down of alleged terrorist content online comply with the rule of law and respect the freedom of expression of users.

---

[4] Europol, 'European Union Terrorism Situation and Trend Report 2018' (2018) https://www.europol.europa.eu/activities-services/main-reports/european-union-terrorism-situation-and-trend-report-2018-tesat-2018 accessed 11 June 2019.

[5] Alexander Tsesis, 'Terrorist Speech on Social Media' (2017) 70(2) *Vanderbilt Law Review* 651; Ariel V. Lieberman, 'Terrorism, the Internet, and Propaganda: A Deadly Combination' (2017) 95(9) *Journal of National Security Law & Policy* 95; Anne Alya and Others, 'Terrorist Online Propaganda and Radicalization' (2017) 40(1) *Studies in Conflict & Terrorism* 1; Thane Rosenbaum, 'The Internet as Marketplace of Madness – and a Terrorist's Best Friend' (2017) 86 *Fordham Law Review* 591; Giovanna De Minico, 'Internet and Fundamental Rights in Time of Terrorism' (2015) *Rivista AIC* https://www.rivistaaic.it/images/rivista/pdf/4_2014_De%20Minico.pdf accessed 10 September 2018.

[6] Anne Stenersen, 'The Internet: A Virtual Training Camp?' (2008) 20 *Terrorism & Political Violence* 215; Lee Jarvis and Others (eds), *Terrorism Online: Politics, Law and Technology* (Routledge, 2015).

[7] This is a well-known issue in the debate on law and terrorism. See, in particular, Stella Margariti, *Defining International Terrorism: between State Sovereignty and Cosmopolitanism* (Springer, 2017); Gus Martin, *Understanding Terrorism: Challenges, Perspectives, and Issues* (Sage, 2017); Alex P. Schmid, 'The Definition of Terrorism', in Alex P. Schmid (ed.), *The Routledge Handbook of Terrorism Research* (Routledge, 2011), 39; Boaz Ganor, 'Defining Terrorism: Is One Man's Terrorist Another Man's Freedom Fighter?' (2002) 3(4) *Police Practice and Research* 287.

[8] Although, recently, international Treaties, UN Security Council resolutions and other international and regional instruments addressing terrorism-related issues have been adopted, there is still no an internationally agreed definition of terrorism. As a result, these notions are addressed in accordance with state laws and policies, leading to considerable discrepancies between different domestic frameworks.

However, the flow of terrorist content online is a critical challenge for constitutional states even from a transnational perspective. The Internet constitutes another layer of complexity for constitutional states. Without dealing with the issues relating to the so-called 'dark web', it is necessary to mention the role of online platforms in favouring the sharing of messages, contacts or content which convey terrorist values. [9] The private nature of online platforms raises issues about the extent to which constitutional states can interfere with their freedom to run their businesses. In particular, the relevance of this observation can be understood by considering that both the EU and US exempt online intermediaries from liability for hosting third-party content.

Public and private censorship limiting expressions or the uploading of online content interferes with freedom of expression. This consideration leads to wonder how constitutional states can ensure that public authorities adopt legal rules ensuring legal certainty and respect of the rule of law. In other words, the primary challenge consists of understanding how constitutional legal orders can address terrorist threats online because of their cross-border character and the involvement of online platforms in the dissemination of such content. [10]

However, the well-known narrative regarding the Internet as promoting illicit activities should not lead one to consider the digital environment as the primary source through which terrorism is spread across society. The cyberspace has only amplified a complex situation. [11] Therefore, when dealing with the boundaries of freedom of expression online regarding alleged terrorist content, it is necessary to bear in mind that fighting online terrorism is only one of the steps in countering the problem. This observation does not mean that the Internet is not playing an important role for terrorist organisations since this channel provides a free instrument of global communication not only for propaganda purposes but also to get illegal goods such as weapons or to obtain financing. [12] Nevertheless, when address-

---

[9] Raphael Cohen-Almagor, 'The Role of Internet Intermediaries in Tackling Terrorism Online' (2017) 86 *Fordham Law Review* 425.

[10] For example, finding objective criteria to identify online content conveying terrorist messages is not easy,nor is drawing a line between hate speech, violence, violent extremism, radicalisation and terrorism. See Anne Aly and Others (eds), *Extremism Online, New Perspectives on Terrorism and the Internet* (Routledge, 2018); David Lowe, 'Prevent Strategies: The Problems Associated in Defining Extremism: The Case of the United Kingdom' (2017) 40(12) *Studies in Conflict & Terrorism* 917; Francesca Galli, *The Law on Terrorism: The UK, France and Italy Compared* (Bruylant, 2015); Alex P. Schmid, 'Violent and Non-Violent Extremism: Two Sides of the Same Coin' (International Center for Counterterrorism (ICCT) Research Paper, May 2014) https://www.icct.nl/download/file/ICCT-Schmid-Violent-Non-Violent-Extremism-May-2014.pdf accessed 30 May 2018.

[11] See Paul Gill and Others, 'Terrorist Use of the Internet by the Numbers' (2017) 16(1) *Criminology & Public Policy* 99; Ines von Behr and Others, 'Radicalisation in the Digital Era: The Use of the Internet in 15 Cases of Terrorism and Extremism' (Rand Corporation, 2013) https://www.rand.org/content/dam/rand/pubs/research_reports/RR400/RR453/RAND_RR453.pdf accessed 30 May 2018.

[12] Michael Jacobson, 'Terrorist Financing and the Internet' (2010) 33(4) *Studies in Conflict & Terrorism* 353.

ing content concerning terrorist activities, the attention should not be only focused on the Internet as the source of the problem. Adopting this last approach could hinder the freedoms and rights of the users, without solving the terrorist threat which is an atomic issue by nature. Fighting terrorism online with a generally preventive approach could reduce the opportunities to rely on the Internet not only for illicit purposes but, especially, for lawful ones.

At this point, it is also necessary to clarify that these questions only matter for democratic states whose legal system is based on the rule of law. However, as far as authoritarian regimes are concerned, the extension of public powers is less problematic because of the lack of strict constitutional limits. In other words, authoritarian regimes could be in a better position to tackle terrorism than constitutional states. This conclusion highlights the core of the problem. Constitutional states fight an unequal battle against terrorism since they address an enemy which is not bound by the respect of any rule and, as a consequence, enjoys a competitive advantage against public authorities which are, instead, subject to procedures compliant with the rule of law and obliged to respect fundamental rights.

Against this background, this chapter aims to provide the legal framework for countering terrorist content online by looking at how public actors, at the national and supranational level, and online intermediaries can tackle this threat and pursue public interest objectives such as security while protecting fundamental rights. In other words, it is necessary to strike a fair balance between three primary interests: ensuring the right to freedom of expression, as a cornerstone of a democratic society; tackling online terrorism to guarantee public interests such as security; protecting the freedom to conduct business of online platforms.

Within this complex constitutional exercise, this chapter analyses the EU and US legal strategies to tackle terrorist content shared through online platforms. The first part of the chapter frames the debate across the Atlantic by examining how freedom of expression enjoys a different degree of protection in the EU and the US from a constitutional law standpoint. Then, the second part addresses the attempts of the EU and the US to address online terrorism from a comparative perspective. The last part of this chapter focuses on the issue of private enforcement of fundamental rights with a specific focus on the introduction of new rights to increase the degree of transparency and accountability of online platforms when moderating online content, especially that which is of a terrorist nature.

2. *Freedom of Expression across the Atlantic*

In this scenario of doubt and terror, it is necessary to provide a general overview of how freedom of expression is protected in the EU and US constitutional legal order. Whilst the right to free speech in the US enjoys broad protection as the scope of the

First Amendment shows,[13] the protection of freedom of expression is subject to a more cautious approach in Europe.[14]

The European Convention on Human Rights ('Convention' or 'ECHR'),[15] the Charter of Fundamental Rights of the European Union ('Charter' or 'CFREU')[16] and national constitutions recognise freedom of expression as a fundamental right in Europe. Such a multilevel framework of protection is the result of a historical path towards democracy and pluralism on which the French Declaration of the Rights of Man and of the Citizen can be considered the first milestone.[17]

More specifically, Article 10(1) ECHR recognises that each individual has the right to free speech from two perspectives: the freedom to impart information and receive it 'without any public interference and regardless of frontiers'.[18] Although, at first glance, this statement can be considered an absolute recognition of freedom of expression in the European framework, however, according to Article 10(2) of the Convention, the exercise of this fundamental right can be limited 'since it carries with it duties and responsibility'.

Taking the opposite approach to the US freedom of speech enshrined in the First Amendment, Article 10(2) ECHR prescribes that freedom of expression can be restricted only by law and when it is necessary in a democratic society for specific reasons which represent hard-core public interests prevailing over the rights of individuals.[19] Moreover, the prohibition of abuse of rights is another restriction to the

---

[13] Richard Albert, 'The Unamendable Core of the United States Constitution', in Richard Albert (ed.), *Comparative Perspective on the Fundamental Freedom of Expression* (Wolters Kluwer, 2015), 13; Ronald Jr. Krotoszynski, *The First Amendment in Cross-Cultural Perspective* (New York University Press, 2006); Eric Berendt, *Freedom of Speech* (Oxford University Press, 2005).

[14] Oreste Pollicino and Marco Bassini, 'Free Speech, Defamation and the Limits to Freedom of Expression in the EU: A Comparative Analysis', in Andrej Savin and Jan Trzaskowski (eds), *Research Handbook on EU Internet Law* (Edward Elgar, 2014); Vincenzo Zeno-Zencovich, *Freedom of Expression. A Critical and Comparative Analysis* (Routledge, 2008).

[15] The Convention for the Protection of Human Rights and Fundamental Freedoms (1950).

[16] Charter of Fundamental Rights of the European Union [2012] OJ C 326/391.

[17] The Declaration of the Rights of Man and of the Citizen (1789). According to Art. 11: 'The free communication of thoughts and of opinions is one of the most precious rights of man: any citizen thus may speak, write, print freely, except to respond to the abuse of this liberty, in the cases determined by the law'.

[18] ECHR (n 15), according to Art. 10(1): 'Everyone has the right to freedom of expression. This right shall include freedom to hold opinions and to receive and impart information and ideas without interference by public authority and regardless of frontiers'. See *Handyside v United Kingdom* [1976] 1 EHRR 737; *Jersild v Denmark* [1994] 19 EHRR 1.

[19] Ibid, according to Art. 10(2): 'The exercise of these freedoms, since it carries with it duties and responsibilities, may be subject to such formalities, conditions, restrictions or penalties as are prescribed by law and are necessary in a democratic society, in the interests of national security, territorial integrity or public safety, for the prevention of disorder or crime, for the protection of health or morals, for the protection of the reputation or rights of others, for preventing the disclosure of information received in confidence, or for maintaining the authority and impartiality of the judiciary'. It is worth observing that

right to free speech. Indeed, Article 17 ECHR provides a general upper limit for the exercise of fundamental rights enshrined in the Convention according to which the exercise of a right should not preclude or limit the exercise of other rights 'to a greater extent than is provided for in the Convention'.[20]

This paradigm of protection can also be found in the EU framework of fundamental rights. Although Article 11 of the Charter does not seem to include any restriction to freedom of expression,[21] this lack does not mean that freedom of expression enjoys broader protection in the EU constitutional order. Any fundamental right enshrined in the Charter shall be read together with Articles 52(1) and 54 CFREU.[22] The former establishes the principle of legality for the restriction of freedom of expression, clarifying that measures placing legal limitations on fundamental rights shall respect the 'essence of those rights and freedoms'. Moreover, limitations need to comply with the principle of necessity, pursue objectives of general interest recognised by the Union or protect the rights and freedoms of others.[23]

In addition, Article 54 prohibits the abuse of rights consisting of the 'destruction of any of the rights and freedoms recognised in this Charter or at their limitation to a greater extent than is provided for herein'. According to such non-exhaustive considerations, it is possible to understand that the right to free speech in Europe does not enjoy absolute protection, but, as is the case for all the other fundamental rights, needs to be balanced *ex post* by European Courts or *ex ante* by lawmakers.

---

the Strasbourg Court has applied these exceptions narrowly, also in the field of terrorist content requiring restrictions that are necessary and proportionate. It should only refer to forms of expression that manifestly incite, glorify or justify violence, hatred or other forms of intolerance relating to terrorist activities, going beyond a mere declaration of sympathy. Moreover, 'terrorist content' needs to be contextualised in the specific case, taking into account different factors such as the authors and their public influence. See, in particular, *Stomakhin v Russia* [2018]; *Roj TV A/S v Denmark* [2018]; *Belek and Velioğlu v Turkey* [2015]; *Bidart v France* [2015]; *Perinçek v Switzerland* [2015]; *M'Bala M'Bala v France* [2014]; *Hizb Ut-Tahrir and Others v Germany* [2012].

[20] Ibid, according to Art. 17: 'Nothing in this Convention may be interpreted as implying for any State, group or person any right to engage in any activity or perform any act aimed at the destruction of any of the rights and freedoms set forth herein or at their limitation to a greater extent than is provided for in the Convention'.

[21] CFREU (n 16), according to Art. 11(1): 'Everyone has the right to freedom of expression. This right shall include freedom to hold opinions and to receive and impart information and ideas without interference by public authority and regardless of frontiers'.

[22] Ibid, according to Art. 52(1): 'Any limitation on the exercise of the rights and freedoms recognised by this Charter must be provided for by law and respect the essence of those rights and freedoms. Subject to the principle of proportionality, limitations may be made only if they are necessary and genuinely meet objectives of general interest recognised by the Union or the need to protect the rights and freedoms of others'.

[23] Cases C-402/05 P and C-415/05 P [2008] *Kadi and Al Barakaat International Foundation v Council and Commission of the European Communities*; Case C-539/10 P [2012] *Al-Aqsa v Council and Pays-Bas/Al-Aqsa*; Case C-293/12 and C-594/12 [2014] *Digital Rights Ireland Ltd v Minister for Communications, Marine and Natural Resources, Minister for Justice, Equality and Law Reform, The Commissioner of the Garda Síochána, Ireland and the Attorney General, and Kärntner Landesregierung, Michael Seitlinger, Christof Tschohl and Others.*

Unlike the EU framework, as already expressed, in the US constitutional legal order, freedom of expression is considered a quasi-absolute right. In particular, in order to understand when a violation of the right to freedom of speech occurs, the US Supreme Court applies a strict scrutiny test according to which any such law should be 'narrowly tailored to serve a compelling state interest'.[24] This test aims to assess whether the 'state action' was narrowly tailored and serves a compelling state interest.[25] The right to free speech can be limited only in exceptional cases according to the case law of the US Supreme Court over time.[26] However, there are concerns in relation to exceptionalism.[27] Indeed, an approach which is based on exceptional cases could lead to undermining speech due to the increase in the role of public actors in ensuring national security, especially the powers of law enforcement bodies. Similar considerations could be extended to the role of the courts in interpreting such expression.

In the next sections, these non-exhaustive considerations on freedom of expression across the Atlantic provide a constitutional insight as to why the EU and US have followed a different path in the fight against online terrorism.

3. *Tackling Online Terrorist Content in Europe*

Recently, terrorist attacks in the EU have triggered a new wave of debates concerning the fight against terrorism, especially, in the online environment. The need to enhance action in the digital environment has been supported, *inter alia*, by the European Council which called for industry to 'develop new technology and tools to improve the automatic detection and removal of content that incites to terrorist acts. This should be complemented by the relevant legislative measures at EU level, if necessary'.[28]

---

[24] Eugene Volokh, 'Freedom of Speech, Permissible Tailoring and Transcending Strict Scrutiny' (1997) 144 *University of Pennsylvania Law Review* 2417.

[25] *Holder v Humanitarian Law Project*, 561 U.S. 1 [2010], 130 S.Ct. 2705. In this case, the Court analysed whether the government interest was compelling, and the national security and foreign affairs satisfy this high bar. See, also, Daphne Barak-Erez and David Scharia, 'Freedom of Speech, Support for Terrorism, and the Challenge of Global Constitutional Law' (2011) 2 *Harvard National Security Journal* 1.

[26] The First Amendment does not preclude the criminalisation of speech whose aim is to incite to hate or lead to imminent harm. In *Brandenburg v Ohio*, [1969] 395 U.S. 444, 447, the Supreme Court stated: 'The constitutional guarantees of free speech and free press do not permit a State to forbid or proscribe advocacy of the use of force or of law violation except where such advocacy is directed to inciting or producing imminent lawless action and is likely to incite or produce such action'. See Tsesis (n 5); Elisabeth Zoller, 'The United States Supreme Court and the Freedom of Expression' (2009) 84(3) *Indiana Law Journal* 885.

[27] Alan K. Chen, 'Free Speech and the Confluence of National Security and Internet Exceptionalism' (2017) 86 *Fordham Law Review* 397.

[28] European Council Meeting Conclusions (June 2017) http://www.consilium.europa.eu/media/23985/22-23-euco-final-conclusions.pdf accessed 20 May 2018. Similarly, the European Parliament

Within this framework, before addressing the measures adopted in the EU for this purpose, it is worth focusing on legal regime of online intermediaries for the content they moderate. Apart from terrorist websites and illegal activities through the dark web, as already stressed, terrorist content is usually spread through the digital channels offered by online platforms. Therefore, platforms such as social media perform the role of gatekeepers governing the flow of terrorist information online. [29]

The primary starting point is the liability regime established by Directive 2000/31/EC (hereinafter, 'e-Commerce Directive'). [30] More specifically, the e-Commerce Directive establishes an exemption for hosting providers (e.g. social media) from the general obligation to monitor online content published by users. [31] This exemption is justified by the need to prevent online intermediaries from being overburdened by an *ex ante* online checking activity which would *de facto* preclude them from running their business. [32]

Nevertheless, this exemption is not absolute. The obligation to remove specific online content applies if platforms become aware of the presence of illicit content hosted in their online space. [33] In this case, the exemption from liability does not apply and the provider is obliged to take action to remove the content. In other words, the e-Commerce Directive provides for a liability regime similar to that of content providers in the event that the former becomes aware of the illegal nature of the content published by users through their services. [34] In this case, the service provider cannot rely on the above-mentioned exemption and, therefore, will be forced to intervene by removing the content if it is not to be held liable.

Combining the ban on general monitoring with the system of liability for third-

---

urged platforms 'to strengthen measures to tackle illegal and harmful content', while asking the Commission to issue proposals to address these issues. See Resolution of 15 June 2017 on online platforms and the digital single market (2016/2276(INI)).

[29] Emily B. Laidlaw, 'A Framework for Identifying Internet Information Gatekeepers, in International Review of Law' (2012) 24(3) *International Review of Law, Computers & Technology* 263.

[30] Directive 2000/31/EC of the European Parliament and of the Council of 8 June 2000 on certain legal aspects of information society services, in particular electronic commerce, in the Internal Market (Directive on e-Commerce) OJ L 178/1. See in particular, Andrej Savin, *European Internet Law* (Edward Elgar, 2013); Rosa J. Barcelo and Kamiel Koelman, 'Intermediary Liability in the e-Commerce Directive: So Far so Good, but It's not Enough' (2000) 4 *Computer Law & Security Report* 231.

[31] Ibid, Art 15. See, in particular, Case C-70/10 [2011] *Scarlet Extended SA v Société belge des auteurs, compositeurs et éditeurs SCRL (SABAM)* ECR I-11959; Case C-360/10 [2012] *Belgische Vereniging van Auteurs, Componisten en Uitgevers CVBA (SABAM) v Netlog NV*.

[32] Ibid. Recital 42 of the Directive clarified that the *ratio* of such exemption of liability aims not to overwhelm platforms that perform activities which are 'purely technical, automatic and passive'.

[33] Ibid, Art. 14.

[34] Joint Cases C-236/08, C-237/08, C-238/09 [2010] *Google France SARL and Google Inc. v Louis Vuitton Malletier SA, Google France SARL v Viaticum SA and Luteciel SARL and Google France SARL v Centre national de recherche en relations humaines (CNRRH) SARL and Others* ECR I-02417; Case C-324/09 [2011] *L'Oréal SA and Others v eBay International AG and Others* ECR I-06011.

party illicit behaviours, public actors would hardly rely on hosting providers to limit the spread of illicit conduct online. As a result, on the one hand, online intermediaries cannot be obliged to monitor online content and, on the other hand, they are shielded by a system based on their passive role or lack of control. This system recognises the fundamental role of online platforms in moderating online content. [35] Nevertheless, Articles 12(3) and 14(3) do not exclude the possibility of a court or administrative authority requiring an online intermediary to terminate or prevent an infringement. Moreover, the latter specifies also that Member States can establish procedures 'governing the removal or disabling of access to information'. Within this framework, it is necessary to recall two Recitals of the e-Commerce Directive which clarify the limits of the general ban on monitoring. [36] Indeed, this ban applies only to general monitoring obligations without involving those aimed at addressing specific cases. Furthermore, Member States can require online intermediaries to apply duties of care, which can reasonably be expected from them and which are specified by national law, in order to detect and prevent certain types of illegal activities.

Within this framework, the e-Commerce Directive does not define the meaning of 'illegal content'. The lawful or unlawful nature of content is determined by specific legislation at the EU level as well as by national law. In the past, the EU has adopted legislative measures to define which content should be considered unlawful. These policies include the Directive 2011/92/EU to combat the sexual abuse and sexual exploitation of children and child pornography, [37] Directive (EU) 2017/541 ('Terrorism Directive'), [38] Directive (EU) 2019/790 ('Copyright Directive') [39] and Directive (EU) 2018/1808 on the amendments to Audiovisual Media Services Directive ('AVMS Directive'). [40]

---

[35] Furthermore, even subject to the implementation of Member States, Art. 15(2) requires online platforms to inform 'the competent public authorities of alleged illegal activities undertaken or information provided by recipients of their service or obligations to communicate to the competent authorities, at their request, information enabling the identification of recipients of their service with whom they have storage agreements'.

[36] e-Commerce Directive (n 30), Recitals 47–48.

[37] Directive 2011/92/EU of the European Parliament and of the Council of 13 December 2011 on combating the sexual abuse and sexual exploitation of children and child pornography, and replacing Council Framework Decision 2004/68/JHA [2011] OJ L 26/1.

[38] Directive (EU) 2017/541 of the European Parliament and of the Council of 15 March 2017 on combating terrorism and replacing Council Framework Decision 2002/475/JHA and amending Council Decision 2005/671/JHA [2017] OJ L 88/6.

[39] Directive (EU) 2019/790 of the European Parliament and of the Council of 17 April 2019 on copyright and related rights in the Digital Single Market and amending Directives 96/9/EC and 2001/29/EC [2019] OJ L 130/92.

[40] Directive (EU) 2018/1808 of the European Parliament and of the Council of 14 November 2018 amending Directive 2010/13/EU on the coordination of certain provisions laid down by law, regulation or administrative action in Member States concerning the provision of audiovisual media services (Audiovisual Media Services Directive) in view of changing market realities [2018] OJ L 303/69.

With regard to online terrorism, the Commission proposed a Regulation to tackle terrorist content online ('Regulation on Terrorist Content') in September 2018,[41] then voted on by the European Parliament in April 2019 (first reading).[42] The Regulation on Terrorist Content aims to establish a clear and harmonised legal framework to tackle the misuse of hosting services for the dissemination of terrorist content online to guarantee the smooth functioning of the internal market.[43]

According to Recital 1, this goal would be achieved by reinforcing legal certainty for hosting service providers, reinforcing users' trust in the online environment and by strengthening safeguards to the freedom of expression, the freedom to receive and impart information and ideas in an open and democratic society and the freedom and pluralism of the media.[44] Even more importantly, the Regulation on Terrorist Content is oriented to the full respect of the fundamental rights protected in the Union's legal order and, especially, in the Charter.[45]

These aims are also achieved through the territorial scope of application including hosting service providers offering services in the Union, irrespective of their place of establishment.[46] The broad scope of application could encourage platforms to apply the EU Standard of Protection on a global scale to avoid setting different procedures of content moderation. However, despite the broad territorial scope of application, the Regulation on Terrorist Content only applies to hosting providers offering their services to the public. As clarified, neither cloud providers nor electronic communi-

[41] Proposal for a Regulation of the European Parliament and of the Council on preventing the dissemination of terrorist content online, COM(2018) 640 final. See Joris van Hoboken, 'The Proposed EU Terrorism Content Regulation: Analysis and Recommendations with Respect to Freedom of Expression Implications' (2019) Transatlantic Working Group on Content Moderation Online and Freedom of Expression https://www.ivir.nl/publicaties/download/TERREG_FoE-ANALYSIS.pdf accessed 12 May 2019; Aleksandra Kuczerawy, 'The Proposed Regulation on Preventing the Dissemination of Terrorist Content Online: Safeguards and Risks for Freedom of Expression' (2018) CITIP https://cdt.org/files/2018/12/Regulation-on-preventing-the-dissemination-of-terrorist-content-online-v3.pdf accessed 10 April 2019; Martin Scheinin, 'The EU Regulation on Terrorist Content: An Emperor without Clothes', verfassungblog.de (31 January 2019) https://verfassungsblog.de/the-eu-regulation-on-terrorist-content-an-emperor-without-clothes/ accessed 14 April 2019; Joan Barata, 'New EU Proposal on the Prevention of Terrorist Content Online' (2018) *CIS Stanford Law* https://cyberlaw.stanford.edu/files/publication/files/2018.10.11.Comment.Terrorism.pdf.

[42] European Parliament legislative resolution of 17 April 2019 on the proposal for a regulation of the European Parliament and of the Council on preventing the dissemination of terrorist content online (COM(2018)0640 – C8-0405/2018 – 2018/0331(COD)).

[43] The Regulation on Terrorist Content needs to be contextualised in the framework of the Recommendation on measures to effectively tackle illegal content adopted by the Commission in March 2018. This document is the non-binding implementation of the political guidelines defined by the Communication on tackling illegal content online launched in September 2017. In particular, the Commission provided a set of operational measures to be taken by public and private actors regarding the detection and removal of illegal content, especially in the field of terrorist content.

[44] Ibid, Recital 1.

[45] Ibid, Recitals 6–7.

[46] Ibid, Art. 1(2).

cations services as defined in Directive (EU) 2018/1972 are included in the definition of hosting providers.[47] Moreover, it excludes content which is disseminated for educational, artistic, journalistic or research purposes, or for awareness raising purposes against terrorist activity, and content which represents an expression of polemic or controversial views in the course of public debate.[48] This choice reflects the interest of the Union to focus on hosting providers whose activity of dissemination of online content can affect society. From another perspective, the Regulation on terrorist content tries to strike a fair balance between different interests exempting content shared for research and journalistic purposes.

Concerning the definition of terrorist content, unlike the original text proposed by the Commission, the Regulation on Terrorist Content does not distinguish between 'terrorist offences' as established by the Terrorism Directive and 'terrorist content'. Indeed, it defines the latter by referring to the legal basis established by the former like 'inciting the commission of one of the offences listed in points (a) to (i) of Article 3(1) of Directive (EU) 2017/541', and 'where such conduct, directly or indirectly, such as by the glorification of terrorist acts, advocates the commission of terrorist offences, thereby causing a danger that one or more such offences may be committed intentionally'.[49] It is worth observing that the definitions of the Terrorist Directive were conceived in the field of criminal law. Whereas, in this case, these rules could also apply to non-criminal measures such as removal orders which are also applied by online platforms implementing a private standard of safeguards.

The Regulation on Terrorist Content clarifies that hosting services shall act in a diligent, proportionate and non-discriminatory manner, and with due regard to the fundamental rights of the users and take into account the fundamental importance of the freedom of expression and information in an open and democratic society.[50] In any case, unlike the Copyright Directive,[51] the Regulation on Terrorist Content does not prejudice the application of the safe harbour regime established by the e-Commerce Directive. Hosting providers are only required to inform the competent authorities and expeditiously remove the content of which they became aware.

Besides, the Regulation on Terrorist Content provides that national competent authorities can issue removal orders and lay down requirements for hosting service providers to remove content as soon as possible and, in any case, within one hour of the receipt of a removal order.[52] This obligation could be particularly burdensome

---

[47] Ibid, Art. 2(1)(1).

[48] Ibid, Art. 1(2)(a).

[49] Ibid, Art. 2(1)(5).

[50] Ibid, Art. 3(1).

[51] Copyright Directive (n 39), Art. 17.

[52] Regulation on Terrorist Content (n 42), Art. 4(2). Removal orders shall provide: '(a) identification of the competent authority via an electronic signature issuing the removal order and authentication

for small and medium-sized online platforms for various reasons. It would be sufficient to focus on the resources to implement an effective system of removal or the need to hire human resources on a 24/7 basis. As a result, this rule would increase the competitive advantage of consolidated platforms with potential effects on competition. Furthermore, it cannot be excluded that, in order to comply with the one-hour term, some platforms would rely on automated processing of content which could lead to errors or inaccuracy affecting fundamental rights, especially freedom of expression. Recital 38 refers to this situation suggesting that the competent authority should take into account whether the hosting service provider is a start-up or a small and medium-sized business. This decision should be determined on a case-by-case basis. In any case, Member States should avoid penalties encouraging the removal of content which is not terrorist content.

Where hosting providers cannot comply with the removal order because of reasons *force majeure* or of *de facto* impossibility not attributable to the hosting service provider, including for technical or operational reasons, or the removal order contains manifest errors or does not contain sufficient information to execute the order, the hosting provider shall inform, without undue delay, the competent authority, explaining the reasons. [53] These provisions aim to define a fair balance between the need to tackle terrorist content and the freedom to conduct business in the internal market.

Moreover, the Regulation on Terrorist Content not only establishes reacting measures but also specific provisions to mitigate the risks of exposure to terrorist content. [54] More specifically, hosting providers can adopt specific measures to protect their services against the public dissemination of terrorist content. It is interesting to observe how, even in this case, the principle of proportionality plays a crucial role by requiring hosting providers to 'take into consideration' 'the risk and level of exposure to terrorist content, the fundamental rights of the users, and the fundamental importance of the right to freedom of expression and the freedom to receive and impart information and ideas in an open and democratic society'. [55]

Nevertheless, the implementation of these measures should not prejudice the application of the measures established by the amendments to the AVMS Directive and the regime of the e-Commerce Directive. It is worth observing that some examples of

of the removal order by the competent authority; (b) a detailed statement of reasons explaining why the content is considered terrorist content and a specific reference to the categories of terrorist content listed in Article 2(5); (c) an exact Uniform Resource Locator (URL) and, where necessary, additional information enabling the identification of the content referred; (f) easily understandable information about redress available to the hosting service provider and to the content provider, including redress with the competent authority as well as recourse to a court as well as deadlines for appeal; (g) where necessary and proportionate, the decision not to disclose information about the removal of terrorist content or the disabling of access to it referred to in Article 11'.

[53] Ibid, Art. 4(7–8).

[54] Ibid, Art. 6(1).

[55] Ibid.

the duties applicable to hosting providers can be found in the appropriate measures introduce by the amendments to the AVMS Directive addressed in this section. The Regulation on Terrorist Content establishes that video-sharing platform providers, as hosting providers, 'shall take appropriate measures to tackle the dissemination of terrorist content in accordance with Article 28b, paragraph 1(c) and paragraph 3 of Directive (EU) 2018/1808'.[56]

If hosting providers have received a substantial number of removal orders, competent authorities can ask these providers to set necessary, proportionate and effective additional specific measures which, in any case, should not lead to the obligation of general monitoring or the use of automated tools.[57]

Among the safeguards proposed, the Regulation on Terrorist Content increases the degree of transparency by requiring hosting providers and competent authorities to disclose information about their activities concerning terrorist content.[58] Even more importantly, hosting providers are required to provide human oversight and verification to ensure 'the right to freedom of expression and freedom to receive and impart information and ideas in an open and democratic society'.[59] Furthermore, in order to ensure the right to remedy, against the decision of the hosting provider, content providers whose content has been removed or access to it disabled can complain requesting reinstatement of the content. In this case, the hosting provider is obliged to provide 'comprehensive and concise' information on the removal or disabling of access to terrorist content and the possibility of contesting the decision,[60] except when the competent authority decides, based on objective evidence and considering the proportionality and necessity of such a decision, not to disclose information for reasons of public interest such as security.[61] Despite the importance of this new users' right, it is not clear how hosting providers will implement these new provisions, especially those concerning the motivation and reinstatement of content. The 'Regulation on Terrorist Content only requires hosting providers to promptly examine every complaint they receive and provide information about the outcome of moderation within two weeks of receipt. The motivation should be provided only when hosting providers refuse to reinstate the content at stake.

---

[56] Ibid, Art. 3(2b).

[57] Ibid, Art. 6(4). The request shall take into account, in particular, the technical feasibility of the measures, the size and economic capacity of the hosting service provider and the effect of such measures on the fundamental rights of the users and the fundamental importance of the freedom of expression and the freedom to receive and impart information and ideas in an open and democratic society. The hosting provider can request to revoke the decision, and, in this case, the competent authority shall provide a reasoned decision within a reasonable period of time after receiving the request by the hosting service provider.

[58] Ibid, Arts. 8–8(a).

[59] Ibid, Art. 9.

[60] Ibid, Art. 10-11.

[61] Ibid, Art. 11(3).

Another relevant piece of legislation in the EU concerns the field of audiovisual services addressing video-sharing platforms. The amendments to the AVMS Directive aim, *inter alia*, to protect minors and citizens from hate speech in the digital environment. Within this framework, video-sharing platforms' liability continues to be covered by Articles 14 and 15 of the e-Commerce Directive.[62] In other words, audiovisual hosting providers should be protected from liability related to the content stored in their online spaces, as established by Article 14.

According to Article 28-*ter*, Member States require video-sharing platforms to adopt appropriate measures to protect minors from audiovisual content which may impair their physical, mental or moral development. The AVMS Directive also aims to protect the general public from audiovisual content containing hate speech, child pornography, racism and, especially, public provocation to commit a terrorist offence as set out in Article 5 of Terrorism Directive.

The meaning of 'appropriate measure' is specified.[63] For example, video-sharing platforms should consider the nature of the content, the possible harm it may cause, the characteristics of the category of person to be protected, the rights and legitimate interests of the subjects involved, including also those of video-sharing platforms and users, and the public interest. The AVMS Directive provides a list of appropriate measures.[64] The role of Member States is to establish mechanisms to assess the degree of appropriateness of these measures through their national regulatory authorities, together with mechanisms to ensure there is a facility to complain and redress related to the application of appropriate measures.

Nevertheless, the EU approach has not been the only preventive measure in the

---

[62] Directive (EU) 2018/1808 (n 40), Art. 28-*ter*(1).

[63] Ibid, Art. 28-*ter*(3).

[64] Ibid. However, it is not clear if the list is exhaustive. In particular, these criteria consist of: '(a) including and applying in the terms and conditions of the video-sharing platform services the requirements referred to in paragraph 1; (b) including and applying in the terms and conditions of the video-sharing platform services the requirements set out in Article 9(1) for audiovisual commercial communications that are not marketed, sold or arranged by the video-sharing platform providers; (c) having a functionality for users who upload user-generated videos to declare whether such videos contain audiovisual commercial communications as far as they know or can be reasonably expected to know; (d) establishing and operating transparent and user-friendly mechanisms for users of a video-sharing platform to report or flag to the video-sharing platform provider concerned the content referred to in paragraph 1 provided on its platform; (e) establishing and operating systems through which video-sharing platform providers explain to users of video-sharing platforms what effect has been given to the reporting and flagging referred to in point (d); (f) establishing and operating age verification systems for users of video-sharing platforms with respect to content which may impair the physical, mental or moral development of minors; (g) establishing and operating easy-to-use systems allowing users of video-sharing platforms to rate the content referred to in paragraph 1; (h) providing for parental control systems that are under the control of the end-user with respect to content which may impair the physical, mental or moral development of minors; (i) establishing and operating transparent, easy-to-use and effective procedures for the handling and resolution of users' complaints to the video-sharing platform provider in relation to the implementation of the measures referred to in points (d) to (h); (j) providing for effective media literacy measures and tools and raising users' awareness of those measures and tools.

European context. Whereas the Commission has followed a multi-stakeholder approach in the lack of any EU binding measure, some Member States have proposed bills and enacted legislation to tackle online terrorism.

In 2016, France attempted to criminalise the mere consultation of online content promoting terrorism.[65] According to the amendment to the criminal code, the act of habitually accessing online public communication services that exhibit messages, images or representations that directly encourage the commission of terrorist acts, or defend these acts, when this service has the purpose of showing images or representations of these acts that consist of voluntary harm to life, is punishable by two years imprisonment and a fine of €30,000. Nevertheless, this rule does not apply when access is in good faith in the course of normal professional activity aimed to inform the public, conducting scientific research or for use as evidence in court. In February 2017, the French Constitutional Council declared this provision unconstitutional arguing that it introduces a disproportionate interference with the right to freedom of communication.[66] A governmental bill was adopted immediately after this decision. The amended provision required that the conduct of the user is accompanied by the intent to adhere to the ideology expressed by these services.[67] Even with this amendment, the Constitutional Council again invalidated the bill in December 2017,[68] considering the new condition to be insufficient to avoid a disproportionate interference with the right to free speech. In July 2019, the French Parliament adopted a new law to tackle the spread of hate speech (first reading).[69] The law requires social media platforms to remove hateful content within 24 hours of the users' notice. Failure to comply with this rule could lead to fines of up to 4 per cent of the social media's global revenue.

However, this French attempt is not unique in the Union. In June 2017, a new German law, known as NetzDG,[70] was adopted obliging online platforms with more than two million users in Germany to take action to handle illegal content hosted by them within 24 hours of being notified of it.[71] The NetzDG applies to all content

---

[65] Loi no. 2016-731 Art. 18 [2017], Art. 421-2-5-2.

[66] Decision no. 2016-611 QPC [2017].

[67] Loi no. 2017-258 Art. 24 [2017], Art. 421-2-5-2.

[68] Decision no. 2017-682 QPC [2017].

[69] Proposition de Loi visant à lutter contre les contenus haineux sur internet (2019).

[70] Gesetz zur Verbesserung der Rechtsdurchsetzung in sozialen Netzwerken – NetzDG BGBl. I S. 3352 [2017].

[71] Thomas Wischemeyer, 'What is Illegal Offline is Also Illegal Online – The German Network Enforcement Act 2017', in Bilyana Petkova and Tuomas Ojanen (eds), *Fundamental Rights Protection Online: The Future Regulation of Intermediaries* (Elgar, 2019); Holger Lutz and Sebastian Schwiddessen, 'The New German Hate Speech Law – Introduction and Frequently Asked Questions: Summary and FAQ on Scope and Requirements of Germany's Intensively Debated New Law to Combat Hate Speech and Fake News' (2017) 18(4) *Computer Law Review International* 103; Aleksandra Kuczerawy, 'Phantom Safeguards? Analysis of the German Law on Hate Speech NetzDG' (Ku Leven Blog, November 2017) https://www.law.kuleuven.be/citip/blog/phantom-safeguards-analysis-of-the-german-law-on-hate-speech-netzdg/ accessed 24 May 2018.

which is considered illicit according to this law.[72] Furthermore, regarding the subjective scope of application, the law applies broadly to all profit-making platforms allowing users to share or publish online content. However, the law exempts service providers with less than two million users in Germany; or providing editorial content; or intended for individual communication or the dissemination of specific content. With regard to content the nature of which is not evidently illicit, the NetzDG gives companies seven days extra time to decide whether to eliminate the online content at issue. Such extra time can be extended in specific cases provided by law. Platforms can also delegate the decision-making regarding the lawfulness of processed content to a self-regulation institution.[73] At the end of the process, the platform shall immediately notify the notice provider and the user of any decision together with its reasoning.

Moreover, providers that receive more than 100 complaints per year are obliged to publish two German-language annual reports explaining, *inter alia*, the mechanisms to detect the presence of unlawful content, the criteria to assess the signalled content, how the provider handles the complaints and the number of complaints received. Furthermore, platforms covered by the scope of NetzDG shall make monthly reviews of their processes for handling notices rectifying inadequacies. Failure to comply with these rules would trigger the application of fines up to five million euros according to Section 4.

In 2019, the UK adopted the Counter-Terrorism and Border Security Act 2019 introducing new criminal provisions amending the Terrorism Act adopted in 2000.[74] Among the amendments introduced, the law criminalises 'the publication of an item of clothing, or any other article, in such a way or in such circumstances as to arouse reasonable suspicion that the person is a member or supporter of a proscribed organisation'.[75] Another provision punishes the act of watching or accessing information online that is likely to be useful to a person committing or preparing acts of terrorism.[76]

Within this framework, the European approach shows an increasing amount of attention to the spread of terrorist content online and the role of online platforms as channels to foster the dissemination of this content. The next section examines the US framework underlining the reasons for a different approach to online terrorist content.

---

[72] The NetzDG refers to the German criminal code and, in particular, to paras 86, 86a, 89a, 91, 100a, 111, 126, 129–129b, 130, 131, 140, 166, 184b together with paras 184d, 185-–187, 241, 269.

[73] Network Enforcement Act (n 70). According to Section 3(2)(3): '[...] the 7-day time limit may be exceeded if: a) the decision regarding the unlawfulness of the content is dependent on the falsity of a factual allegation or is clearly dependent on other factual circumstances; in such cases, the social network can give the user an opportunity to respond to the complaint before the decision is rendered; b) the social network refers the decision regarding unlawfulness to a recognised self-regulation institution pursuant to subsections (6) to (8) within 7 days of receiving the complaint and agrees to accept the decision of that institution'.

[74] Counter-Terrorism and Border Security Act [2019].

[75] Ibid, Section 2.

[76] Ibid, Section 3.

4. *Tackling Online Terrorist Content in the US*

Although the EU approach to tackling the spread of terrorist content online has evolved over the last few decades, the US framework has not followed the same path.

Like the e-Commerce Directive, the US Communications Decency Act ('CDA') provides an exemption of liability for content hosted by social media. [77] The CDA is based on the dichotomy between content and service provider where the latter 'shall be treated as the publisher or speaker of any information provided by another information content provider'. [78] In other words, online platforms are considered just as channels of communication without any responsibility for third-party conduct. Besides, according to the Good Samaritan rule, providers are not liable when they limit access to 'objectionable' material. In other words, this provision allows online intermediaries to freely restrict access to content such as pornography or offensive speech.

Two years after the CDA was adopted, the Digital Millennium Copyright Act (DMCA) of 1998 afforded immunity to intermediaries of intellectual property infringement enabled by their networks. [79] This US legislation plays a crucial role since it provides another important instrument in the framework of online intermediaries' liability: the so-called 'notice-and-takedown' system. The DMCA has established that online intermediaries are not responsible where they have no actual knowledge that the material is infringing; do not receive a financial benefit from infringing activity; upon notification of alleged infringement, expeditiously remove content or block access to it. These two measures constitute the general framework of online intermediaries' liability in the US.

However, other than these rules, the US has not adopted specific measures to address the issue relating to the spread of illicit content through online platforms. At the EU level, as already seen, the European institutions have shown an interest in this phenomenon and started a dialogue with online platforms. Whereas, in the US, the government has focused more on direct monitoring of social media speech to detect terrorist behaviour or threats to national security. This is the consequence of a political choice resulting from the 9/11 terrorist attack the effect of which in terms of legal measures has led, *inter alia*, to the adoption of the US Patriot Act. [80]

Notwithstanding, in the US, terrorism has captured the political attention since 2001, the protection of free speech, as recognised by the First Amendment of the US

---

[77] Communications Decency Act, 47 U.S.C. § 230.

[78] Ibid, Section 230(f)(3): 'any person or entity that is responsible, in whole or in part, for the creation or development of information provided through the Internet or any other interactive computer service'.

[79] Digital Millennium Copyright Act, 17 U.S.C. § 512.

[80] *United States v Mehanna* [2013] 735 F.3d 32, 44 (1st Cir.). This recent and well-known US case involved Tarek Mehanna who was charged and convicted of various offences among which was the conspiracy to provide material support to terrorists through social media.

Constitution, has led to a more defensive approach regarding the activity of private actors, especially in the digital environment. Whereas, in the EU, the limits to free speech enshrined in national constitutions as well as in the Charter and in the Convention could explain why the Union and its Member States address online content in a different way. Indeed, the US Constitution, in particular, the First Amendment, limits the power of government to interfere with a platform's free speech even in those cases where they contribute to spreading obnoxious and offensive expressions. [81]

Moreover, the strict scrutiny applied by the Supreme Court limits any restriction to freedom of expression. Two landmark decisions of the US Supreme Court provide examples of how freedom of expression enjoys broad protection online. In 1997, *Reno v American Civil Liberties Union* was the first major US Supreme Court case addressing the regulation of the digital environment. [82] More specifically, the case originated from the US attempt to limit access to online content prohibited for minors. The Supreme Court considered specific parts of the CDA as unconstitutional since the provisions were excessively vague and indeterminate, thus, violating the First Amendment. The decision was essentially based on the US liberal approach to free speech expressed by the metaphor 'free marketplace of ideas'. [83] Within this framework, the Internet was considered as an instrument to expand freedom of speech. [84]

More recently, the Supreme Court has dealt with a case involving the prohibition of sex offenders from accessing social media websites. [85] This ban originated from a law enacted by the North Carolina General Assembly in 2008. [86] The US Supreme Court was called to answer whether, under the First Amendment precedents, such a law is permissible, 'both on its face and as applied to the petitioner – who was con-

---

[81] *Scales v United States* [1961] 367 U.S. 203, 229.

[82] *Reno v American Civil Liberties Union* [1997] 521 U.S. 844. See also *Ashcroft v American Civil Liberties Union* [2002] 535 U.S. 564; *Ashcroft v Free Speech Coalition* [2002] 535 U.S. 234.

[83] Daniel E. Ho and Frederick Schauer, 'Testing the Marketplace of Ideas' (2015) 90 *New York University Law Review* 1161; Eugene Volokh, 'In Defense of the Market Place of Ideas / Search for Truth as a Theory of Free Speech Protection' (2011) 97(3) *Virginia Law Review* 591; G. Brazeal, 'How Much Does a Belief Cost? Revisiting the Marketplace of Ideas' (2011) 21(1) *Southern California Interdisciplinary Law Journal* 2; Matthew Gentzkow and Jesse M. Shapiro, 'Competition and Truth in the Market for News' (2008) 22(2) *Journal of Economic Perspectives* 133; Joseph Blocher, 'Institutions in the Marketplace of Ideas' (2008) 57(4) *Duke Law Journal* 820; Paul H. Brietzke, 'How and Why the Marketplace of Ideas Fails' (1997) 31(3) *Valparaiso University Law Review* 951; Alvin I. Goldman and James C. Cox, *Speech, Truth, and the Free Market for Ideas* (Cambridge University Press, 1996); Ronald Coase, 'Markets for Goods and Market for Ideas' (1974) 64(2) *American Economic Review* 384.

[84] 521 U.S. 844 (n 82), according to the Supreme Court: 'The dramatic expansion of this new marketplace of ideas contradicts the factual basis of this contention. The record demonstrates that the growth of the Internet has been and continues to be phenomenal. As a matter of constitutional tradition, in the absence of evidence to the contrary, we presume that governmental regulation of the content of speech is more likely to interfere with the free exchange of ideas than to encourage it. The interest in encouraging freedom of expression in a democratic society outweighs any theoretical but unproven benefit of censorship'.

[85] *Packingham v North Carolina* [2017] 582 U.S. 15 1194.

[86] N.C.G.S. §14–202.5.

victed based on a Facebook "post" in which he celebrated the dismissal of a traffic ticket'. According to the Court, social media are considered to be a 'protected space' under the First Amendment for lawful speech. As observed by Justice Kennedy, differently from the past, today it is not difficult to define the spaces for the exchange of public views: 'It is cyberspace – the "vast democratic forums of the Internet" [...] and social media in particular'.[87] The restriction in question violates the First Amendment since North Carolina could protect children through less restrictive means, such as prohibiting conduct that often presages a sexual crime, like contacting a minor or using a website to gather information about a minor.

As a result, the high level of protection of online free speech together with the (consequent) exemption of liability of online platforms, could lead to considering that these actors are not subject to a specific rule concerning terrorist content. However, this consideration does not mean that online platforms are allowed to support terrorist activities.[88] Despite the exemption of liability established by the CDA, in several cases online platforms have been sued for terrorist matters such as deaths in terrorist attacks. More specifically, the plaintiffs have complained that social media provided material support for terrorist attacks.[89]

Hence, within this framework, the fight against online terrorism is based on each platform's policy. Indeed, unlike in the EU framework where a multi-stakeholder approach has led public actors and platforms to cooperate to tackle illicit content, in the US social media companies have autonomously developed their own policy to address the spread of such content. In particular, Facebook, YouTube, Twitter and Microsoft have created the Global Internet Forum to Counter Terrorism as a consequence of the social complaints relating to the role of online platforms in tackling illicit activities online. The aim of this forum is to develop standards regarding transparent report mechanisms and the use of detection automated techniques.[90]

Beyond these voluntary measures, it is necessary to mention that, in 2015, the US Congress proposed a bill aimed at obliging Internet companies to report to the government when obtaining 'actual knowledge' of any 'facts and circumstances' related to 'terrorist activity'. In other words, the provision tried to enhance the cooperation between online platforms and the government, similarly to the rule enshrined in Article 15(2) of the e-Commerce Directive. The primary problem was related to definitions. Section 603 of the Intelligence Authorization Act for Fiscal Year 2016 (S. 1705)

---

[87] 582 U.S. 15 1194 (n 85).

[88] 395 U.S. 444, 447 (n 26).

[89] See, in particular, *Fields v Twitter* [2016] 217 F. Supp. 3d 1116, 1118 (N.D. Cal.), affirmed by the US Court of Appeals for the 9th Circuit in 2018.

[90] The US government has also worked with social media and technology companies to increase transparency and react against terrorist activities on their platforms. In 2017, the inter-agency Global Engagement Center (GEC) was established to counter foreign state and non-state propaganda and disinformation efforts aimed at undermining US national security interests. The GEC was codified into law in the National Defense Authorization Act (NDAA).

did not define the meaning of 'terrorist activity', which raises significant First and Fourth Amendment concerns. The only point of reference regarding the term 'terrorist activity' can be found in 18 U.S.C. § 842(p), which prohibits a person from distributing information relating to explosives if the person has knowledge that the recipient intends to use the information to commit a violent crime. Section 603 did not clarify the content of the report since both companies and users were uncertain as to what exactly triggers the mandatory reporting requirement. The primary concern was that the broad definition could lead to encouraging self-censorship to avoid the reporting obligation. As a result, it cannot be ruled out that, in order to comply with this obligation, even lawful activity such as research or journalism dealing with terrorism would be subject to monitoring or removed.

More recently, although it is in a different field, the SESTA-FOSTA package,[91] although addressing not terrorism content, could impact on platforms' liability system by inserting an exception to Section 230 of the CDA. Irrespective of the scope of the law, which does not deal with terrorist content online, it is possible to consider this approach as a step towards a potentially new approach even in the US framework.

5. *Online Terrorism and Private Enforcement of Fundamental Rights*

At this point, it is worth focusing on the role of online platforms as private actors involved in the enforcement of the rules against terrorist content. The vast amount of content moderated on a global scale leads these actors to set the standard of protection of fundamental rights online.[92] Online platforms are private actors and, as a result, they aim to maximise profit rather than pursue public interests. More specifically, putting in place content monitoring technologies or complying with other general obligations concerning the monitoring of content requires resources which would harm profits.[93] Therefore, the risk to be held liable or sanctioned encourages online platforms to manage content at their own convenience (i.e. collateral censorship).[94] In other words,

---

[91] Allow States and Victims to Fight Online Sex Trafficking Act [2017] H R 1865.

[92] Giovanni De Gregorio, 'From Constitutional Freedoms to the Powers of the Platforms: Protecting Fundamental Rights Online in the Algorithmic Society' (2019) 11(2) *European Journal of Legal Studies* 65; Luca Belli and Niccolo Zingales (eds), *Platform Regulations: How Platforms are Regulated and How They Regulate Us* (FGV Direito, 2017); Natali Helberger and Others, 'Governing Online Platforms: From Contested to Cooperative Responsibility' (2018) 34(1) *The Information Society* 1; Kate Klonick, 'The New Governors: The People, Rules, and Processes Governing Online Speech' (2018) 131 *Harvard Law Review* 1598; Orla Lynskey, 'Regulating Platform Power' (2017) *LSE Legal Studies Working Paper 1* http://eprints.lse.ac.uk/73404/1/WPS2017-01Lynskey.pdf accessed 1 September 2018.

[93] Steven Beale, 'Online Terrorist Speech, Direct Government Regulation, and the Communications Decency Act' (2017) 16(1) *Duke Law & Technology Review* 333.

[94] Jack Balkin, 'Old-School/New-School Speech Regulation' (2014) 127 *Harvard Law Review* 2296.

regulatory solutions imposing monitoring and removal obligations on online intermediaries and providing fines for failure to comply with such rules can increase the degree of private censorship because online platforms would be encouraged to remove content to avoid liability, especially that of which the illicit nature is not evident.

In this way, this scenario contributes to increasing the power of online platforms to moderate online expressions, including, terrorist content. Even the decision to remove or maintain terrorist content is left to the decisions of private actors which, without any legal provision regarding their decision-making, perform functions traditionally belonging to public authority. For example, when moderating content, online platforms exercise a role similar to that of the judiciary which is the only authority, together with the lawmaker, entitled to balance fundamental rights and decide on the lawfulness of online content. For example, the scope of the notion of 'terrorism' and the predominance of the public interest is interpreted by online platforms which, as private actors, are not obliged either to pursue the public interest or to protect fundamental rights. If, even public authorities, especially the judiciary, could encounter difficulty in deciding whether online content constitutes an act of terrorism, the primary concern is how online platforms can balance those fundamental rights at stake without any public safeguard.

Furthermore, online platforms base their decisions on their Terms of Services (ToS) which, similarly to the law, can be considered as the legal basis according to which platforms exercise their powers. By defining the criteria according to which decisions are enforced, as well as the procedural and technical tools underpinning their ToS, online platforms contribute to determining the rules on which content are moderated, exercising a sort of quasi-legislative power. Although this autonomy is limited in some areas, for example data protection, the global application of their services and the lack of any legal rules regulating online content moderation leave a significant amount of political discretion in the hands of platforms when drafting their ToS or other internal guidelines concerning content moderation.

Against this background, the use of automated processes to perform online content moderation activities raises further concerns about the protection of fundamental rights. On the one hand, algorithms can be considered as technical instruments facilitating a platform's functionalities, such as the organisation of online content. On the other hand, such technologies can constitute technical self-executing rules, obviating even the need for a human executive or judicial function. The biggest concern is the low level of decision-making transparency, which strongly affects users' fundamental rights.[95]

---

[95] Algorithms raise serious concerns in terms of transparency due to the unpredictable automated results which limit the diffusion of online content whose unlawfulness is detected by machines. See Frank Pasquale, *The Black Box Society. The Secret Algorithms that Control Money and Information* (Harvard University Press, 2015); Matteo Turilli and Luciano Floridi, 'The Ethics of Information Transparency' (2009) 11(2) *Ethics and Information Technology* 105; Tal Zarsky, 'Transparent Predictions' (2013) 4 *University of Illinois Law Review* 1507.

It is not serendipitous that the EU Commission has intervened to protect fundamental rights by striking a fair balance between the different interests at stake.[96] In particular, by taking as its reference the Regulation on Terrorist Content, the EU approach does not focus on monitoring and filtering obligations but on the transparency of the content moderation process and remedies against platforms' decisions as two ex-post solutions that can mitigate the risk of collateral censorship. Indeed, proposing specific rules regarding the process according to which platforms decide how to remove a specific content could constitute a fair balance between the different interests at stake. These transparency obligations, consisting, for example, of the reason for a specific decision of removal, would allow users to rely on clear rules regarding the removal of their content and could contribute to increasing the cooperation with the public authorities in dealing with terrorist content online. This obligation would not involve online content *per se* but only the possibility for users to understand and react to the removal or blocking of their online content by private actors. In particular, human intervention would introduce a procedural safeguard to understand the reasons for decisions on online content.

6. *Conclusions*

The increasing availability of terrorist content and its dissemination through online platforms leads one to wonder how constitutional states should deal with this situation. As should be clear by now, the detection and removal of illegal content online are two of the primary challenges when countering online terrorism.

The EU and US strategies against online terrorism have highlighted the paradoxical situation in which constitutional states find themselves when addressing illicit online content, especially terrorist content. The biggest challenge concerns not only terrorist content online but the role of online platforms in disseminating and moderating these expressions. On the one hand, public actors have indirectly entrusted private actors to police content in the digital environment by implementing a system of exemption of liability for third-party content.[97] On the other hand, even the opposite choice based on a pervasive public control over online content would have entailed risks of censorship and overregulation of private activities. In other words, the need for public actors to take into consideration, on the one hand, the protection of the freedom to conduct an online platform business and the freedom of expression of users and, on the other hand, the need to tackle the spread of illicit content explains why the enforcement of policies to fight online terrorist content is complex.

---

[96] Aleksandra Kuczerawy, 'The Power of Positive Thinking: Intermediary Liability and the Effective Enjoyment of the Right to Freedom of Expression?' (2017) 8(3) *Journal of Intellectual Property, Information Technology and Electronic Commerce Law* 226.

[97] Joel R. Reidenberg, 'States and Internet Enforcement' (2004) 1 *University of Ottawa Law & Techonology Journal* 213.

Despite this common challenge, the EU and US have adopted two different approaches concerning the fight against online terrorism. Whilst, the US has maintained a liberal approach by extending the scope of the First Amendment to the online environment, the EU has firmly demonstrated its intent to regulate online platforms as also shown by the plan to adopt the so-called Digital Services Act in 2020. In order to understand the reasons for these two different approaches, the paradigm of freedom of speech across the Atlantic can provide a non-exhuastive clue. Indeed, in the US framework, the broad protection afforded online platforms through the right to free speech restricts the attempts to regulate platforms' activities. On the contrary, the constitutional protection of freedom of expression in the EU has encouraged the adoption of new safeguards to protect other interests such as security and transparency in platforms' decision-making processes.

The above-mentioned general framework has highlighted the primary issues regarding the role of constitutional states and platforms in tackling terrorist content. Nevertheless, fighting online terrorism is only a part of the strategy to counter this threat and online terrorism should not be subject to measures which are stricter than those which apply to the offline world. In this scenario, one of the core questions is whether public security or other public interests should justify pervasive public surveillance measures and the monitoring of citizens to address the threat of terrorism even in the digital environment. In this case, it should be recalled that unlike terrorist organisations, which are not bound by any rule, constitutional states have to take into consideration their role in ensuring the protection of fundamental rights. In this context, it should be borne in mind that this asymmetry should not influence the balancing of public interests and fundamental rights. Such balancing is crucial, especially when the expansion of public interest could be used as an argument to justify a reduction in the level of protection of fundamental rights and lead to a dangerous turmoil for democracy.

Freedom of Speech and Social Networks in the Age of Terrorism: A Comparative Analysis

Fulvia Abbondante

SUMMARY: 1. Hate Speech: An Uncertain Definition. – 2. Freedom of Speech in the Age of Terrorism: the USA Case. – 3. Hate Speech on Social Networks in the USA. – 4. European Models of Offline and Online Freedom of Speech. – 5. Hate Speech on the Internet in Europe between Private and Collateral Censorship. – 6. European Union Proposal on the Prevention of Terrorist Content Online. New Regulation, Old Issues. – 7. Conclusion.

1. *Hate Speech: An Uncertain Definition*

The concern that the contemporary jurist feels in investigating the thorny question of limits to the freedom of expression is born, not only from the usual difficulty of imagining a relatively stable point of balance between the protection of this fundamental right and other values, but also from the inadequacy of the traditional conceptual categories he has been confronted with until today when the relationship freedom/limits is transferred into the intangible dimension of the Internet Network. The critical factors appear even more evident when addressing the theme of hate speech, because of the intrinsic difficulty of finding a consistent and satisfactory definition of this phenomenon even in the offline world. As a matter of fact, it is arduous to obtain a homogenous juridical description of this kind of expression. It is, in general, hard to distinguish hate discourse from a simple criticism (which, in some cases, uses strong words without any intention of incitement to hate), because the content of speech is conditioned by the context, the intention of the speaker and the impact on the public. [1] Moreover it is complex to define the term "hate" in a clear manner since it is an emotion that everyone expresses in a different way. However, according to numerous international and supranational documents hate speech might be classified as all forms of expression addressed to a collectivity of people because they belong to a discriminated group in a way that promotes, incites or justifies hatred. [2] Two positions on the constitutional compatibility of the regulation of hate speech confront each

[1] Andrew Sellars, 'Defining Hate Speech' (2016) 20 Berkman Klein Center Research Publication https://ssrn.com/abstract=2882244 accessed 10 December 2016.

[2] Thomas Davidson and others, 'Automated Hate Speech Detection and the Problem of Offensive Language' (Proceedings of the Eleventh International AAAI Conference on Web and Social Media 11 March 2017) https://www.aaai.org/ocs/index.php/ICWSM/ICWSM17/paper/view/15665/14843.

other. On the one hand, some scholars underline the importance of freedom of expression for personal self-determination and for deliberative development of public opinion so that any restriction of this right has to be limited only in particular cases.[3] On the other hand, there are those who emphasize the role of hate speech in intimidating vulnerable groups and attacking their sense of dignity with the result that the free speech of minority communities is limited and the principle of equality is compressed.[4] Recently other kinds of hate speech have emerged such as propaganda and an apology for terrorism. In this scenario the values at stake are freedom of speech and national security. Many countries have adopted national legislation which has restricted fundamental freedoms to protect public order. With the development of the Internet and the opportunity for each user to spread their thoughts easily and globally, the question of hate speech has raised new and unprecedented issues. The method of communication is not a secondary aspect – as it clearly emerges – since the Internet has turned the diffusion of thought from quantitatively limited and circumscribed (in time and space) into a capillary, global and permanent phenomenon. This chapter analyses the problems related to the regulation of hate speech and terrorist speech both offline and online by comparing the different approaches and solutions in the USA, European countries and the European Union.

2. *Freedom of Speech in the Age of Terrorism: the USA Case*

As mentioned above western democracies have reacted to hate speech by taking two different approaches in offline reality. The first, adopted in the USA, is to guarantee the marketplace of ideas in a broad manner according to a formula used by Judge Holmes.[5] It is important to underline that the claim of a marketplace of ideas is the result of a long and oscillating jurisprudence of the Supreme Court of the USA. For instance, during the McCarthy era the reference to a 'clear and present danger' was used to compress the freedom of speech altogether.[6] In short, from the decision *Bran-*

[3] Lee C. Bollinger, *The Tolerant Society: Freedom of Speech and Extremist Speech in America* (Oxford University Press 1986); Robert C. Post, 'Legitimacy and Hate Speech' (2017) (32) *Constitutional Commentary* 651.

[4] Mary Ellen Gale, 'Reimagining the First Amendment: Racist Speech and Equal Liberty' (1991) *St. John's Law Review* (65) 119; Robert Delgado, 'Words that Wound: A Tort Action for Racial Insults, Epithets and Name Calling', in Mari Matsuda and others (eds), *Words that Wound: Critical Racial, Assaultive Speech and the First Amendment* (Westview Press 1993); Alexander Tsesis, 'Dignity and Hate Speech: Regulation of Hate Speech in a Democracy' (2009) *Wake Forest Law Review* (44) 17–23; Jeremy Waldron, *The Harm in Hate Speech* (Harvard University Press 2012).

[5] *Abrahms v. United States* (Holmes, dissenting opinion) (1919) 250 U.S. 616; *Gitlow v. New York* (1925) 268 U.S.652.

[6] *Schenck v. United States* (1919), 249 U.S. 47, 52; *Frohwerk v. United States* (1919) 249 U.S. 204; *Debs v. United States* (1919)249 U.S. 211.

deburg vs. *Ohio*, speech is unprotected only when it is able to determine concrete action, as is the case with violent speech, true threats, fighting words, i.e. those manifestations of thought characterized by strong violence and danger, as well as all those forms of expression that are translated on a factual level. Also the racist propaganda speech, both the purely verbal and the one that makes use of symbols recalling the National Socialist ideology or the cross burning, must be considered protected when the use of such emblems is obviously aimed at instigating violence and hatred, though they do not create a danger of immediate execution. The First Amendment, therefore, is considered a super constitutional value and every limitation is subject to strict scrutiny. After 9/11 and the increasing number of terrorist attacks, the Congress of the USA has approved many laws which impose a strong limitation on fundamental rights. For the purposes of this work, a relevant precedent is the judgment of *Holder vs. Humanitarian Law Project* of 2010,[7] in which the Supreme Court has assessed, for the first time, compatibility with First Amendment of Section 2339 A and Section 2239 B, introduced to counter international terrorism through the Antiterrorism and Effective Death Penalty Act ('AEDPA'), modified on several occasions over the past decade.[8] The first provision more generally punishes anyone who 'provides material support or resources or conceals or disguises the nature, location, source or ownership of material support or resources, knowing or intending that they are to be used in preparation for, or in carrying out, a violation [...]' to terrorists. The Statute defines 'material support' as 'any property, tangible or intangible, or service, including currency or monetary instruments or financial securities, financial services, lodging, training, expert advice or assistance, safe houses, false documentation or identification, communications equipment, facilities, weapons, lethal substances, explosives, personnel (one or more individuals who may be or include oneself), and transportation, except medicine or religious materials'. For the purposes of the commission of the crime, the term 'training' is understood as imparting or teaching specific skills while the formula 'expert advice or assistance' means providing advice or assistance through the use of technique, science or other specialized knowledge. The second provision, instead, introduced after the September 11 attacks, punishes those 'who consciously provide material support or resources to a foreign terrorist organization, or attempts or conspires to do so'. The identification of subversive organisms is determined by the Executive power that periodically draws up a list of organizations that can threaten the security of the USA. In the above mentioned – and highly criticized – Supreme Court sentence, the expression material support, is meant as 'training and expert assistance', despite being an activity of pure thought – as it imparts specific skills or knowledge – differently from other forms of communication which have a general content; it can be a material support to organizations included in the government list and give rise to a hypothesis of coordinated speech prohibited by federal law. The validity of the

---

[7] *Holder v. Humanitarian Law Project* (2010) 561 U.S. 1.

[8] The Antiterrorism and Effective Death Penalty Act of 1996, Pub. L. No. 104-132, 110 Stat. 1214.

AEDPA is justified taking for granted that national and international security are interests worthy of protection and some forms of material support can also be realized with the use of peaceful speech and with the assumption – hypothetical as well as indirect – that the activities, realized through a manifestation of thought, can provide the implementation of terrorist structures. In such cases according to the supreme judges it is not necessary to follow the 'present and clear danger' formula and to consider the intention to commit an imminent illegal action but the mere awareness of certain types of activities is sufficient – including those carried out by the Humanitarian Law Project – in coordination with foreign terrorist organizations included in the list. The vagueness of the argument is evident as the Supreme Court does not clarify the criteria by which independent speech could be distinguished from coordinated speech. The Constitutional Court, reinterpreting the content of the federal law, introduces a double limitation to freedom of expression: the first based on the content of the message, the second on the identity of the recipients of such a message.[9] In a wider perspective, however, this second point opens the door to a further and dangerous extension of the limits to free speech that, by its very nature, is expressed in a relational dimension. The conceptual core of a marketplace of ideas implies interaction between subjects, who are bearers of different ways of conceiving reality; it is just the exchange of the different visions of the world that guarantees self-government and the search for truth. In a society characterized, thanks to the Internet, by the circulation of ideas through the connection of billions of people, in every place on the globe, it seems difficult to imagine a communication that does not take into account at least profiles of international relations.[10] Moreover, the extensive scope that the higher judges applied to material support through the use of speech could harm other constitutionally guaranteed rights, such as the right of research or the right of information, since they are also realized through collaboration, obviously for legitimate purposes, with organizations deemed illegal by the Federal Government. Consequently, it would not be just to condemn terrorist thought in and of itself (since a precise classification of the criminal case does not exist) but rather every manifestation of thought that includes forms of "contact" (legal or illegal) between the agent and subversive organizations, identified by the Secretary of State. During McCarthyism, one of the most obscure periods in overseas democracies, the Court was careful to trace the boundary lines between unprotected thought, precisely equipped with a subversive potential, that could endanger national security, and thought, characterized by strong elements of criticism, that was nevertheless worthy of protection.[11]

---

[9] Daphne Barak, Erez and David Scharia, 'Freedom of Speech, Support for Terrorism, and the Challenge of Global Constitutional Law' (2011) (2) *Harvard National Security Journal* 1; David Cole, 'The First Amendment's Borders: The Place of Holder v. Humanitarian Law Project in First Amendment Doctrine' (2011) (6) *Harvard Law and Policy Review*, 147.

[10] Timothy Zick, 'Falsely Shouting Fire in a Global Theater: Emerging Complexities of Transborder Expression' (2012) (65) 1 *Vanderbilt Law Review* 126.

[11] David Cole, 'The New McCarthyism: Repeating History in the War in Terrorism' (2003) (38) *Harvard Civil Rights-Civil Liberties Law Review* 1.

3. *Hate Speech on Social Networks in the USA*

It is important to be clear about how the problem of balancing freedom of speech in relation to terroristic hate speech is being debated in the USA when we consider the Web. In the USA, the Web is seen as a neutral element of the diffusion of thought and, because of its characteristic, it is considered to deserve protection as it allows for the exchange of ideas, the enrichment of public debate and therefore the emergence, within the competition between ideas, of truth. The role played by members in Internet in the diffusion of incitement to racial, ethnic, religious hatred and terrorism does not affect the application of the First Amendment, which, of course, is about relationship between the freedom of the individual and authority and not that of private companies such as Internet Service Providers (ISPs) who have the task of spreading thought.

It is also clear that the original discipline viewed with disfavour a regulation which limited the medium through which the expressions are transmitted. Section 230 (1) lett. a) of the Communication Decency Act, in fact, expressly excludes the liability of the providers.

As a consequence, the lack of any hard regulation has instead generated forms of self-regulation totally managed by the social networks through the notice and take down mechanism. [12] Over time, however, the swirling expansion of the hate pyramid has induced the most influencial platforms to introduce control through the use of algorithms based on recognition indexes, or groups of experts who verify the alerts coming from other users and remove content considered offensive. Consequently, the social media has been more interested in inserting in its terms and conditions specific rules aimed at preventing the dissemination of repugnant messages. One might also notice the existence of two different models of autonomous regulation within the most widespread platforms.

The first model, adopted by YouTube, provides general contractual rules between the user and the social medium: the lack of responsibility on the part of ISPs for the contents conveyed by users is reiterated. Community guidelines present a generic reference to company policy which does not support content promoting or allowing violence against people or groups of people regardless of their background. The second model provides a more precise regulation and it has had the most widespread affect on the social networks from a global point of view.

Twitter – which originally was characterized by a very tolerant attitude – has recently amended the terms of access for users, including a specific section dedicated to illicit conduct. The latter is understood as any activity aimed at defaming or directly attacking or threatening other people on the basis of race, ethnicity, national origins,

---

[12] Jennifer M. Urban, Joe Karaganis and Brianna L. Schofield (2017), *Notice and Takedown in Everyday Practice*, UC Berkeley Public Law Research Paper No. 2755628 https://ssrn.com/abstract=2755628 accessed 22 March 2017.

sexual orientation, gender identity, religious affiliation, age, disability or illness. The section also specifies that an account will be denied to those whose primary goal is to incite hatred against any of the categories indicated above.

Facebook, on the other hand, has separated the contractual terms from the Statement of Rights and Responsibilities. In the latter document hate speech is identified as any expressive form that contains attacks addressed to people because of race, ethnicity, national origins, sexual orientation, gender identity, belonging to a religious group, age, disability or illness.

Terrorist propaganda, which has proliferated in an uncontrolled manner thanks to automatic dissemination mechanisms, follows the contractual rules of the platforms provided for seditious speech; in fact, ad hoc federal and state laws that explicitly impose forms of involvement of the ISPs in the fight against fundamentalist subversion do not yet exist.

Congress too tries to limit free expression on the Internet. In 2015, Senators Dianne Feinstein (Democrat) and Richard Burr (Republican) proposed *Combat Terrorist Use of Social Media Act* that would introduce a reporting obligation for social media to federal officials if they know of online terrorist activities. The bill, approved by the Homeland Security Commission Governmental Affairs, however, was not discussed due to the electoral deadline. Resubmitted with similar content in 2016 by another Republican senator, it was rejected by the same Commission as 'any government involvement in the use of social media runs the significant risk of impacting the right of individuals having nothing whatsoever to do with terrorism'. The Government's resistance to introducing these forms of legislation is due, in particular, to the strong deployment of civil rights defence organizations which, until today, have been able to block all proposals on the matter. Moreover, part of the scholars had already criticized the 2015 bill for its substantial unenforceability, since the duty to notify the competent authorities arose only when the intermediary has current knowledge of the terrorist activity. It is clearly impossible without a preventive monitoring action able to reveal to platforms the existence of a subversive conduct in progress. [13]

It emerges that in the USA the control of freedom of speech within the rules of the platforms in an inhomogeneous manner with the effect that the breadth of definition of hateful conduct remains at the discretion of each provider.

4. *European Models of Offline and Online Freedom of Speech*

A completely different case is Europe, where the punitive measures against incitement to hatred, based on ethnic and racial grounds, have been incorporated into legal systems as a part of militant democracy.

[13] Susan Klein and Crystal Flinn, 'Social Media Compliance Programs and the War Against Terrorism' (2017) (8) *Harvard National Security Journal* 53.

However, the gradation of these measures has different shades. Only Germany has introduced an express limitation on racist speech in the criminal code in the name of human dignity. Examples of countries that have adopted a special legislation on hate speech beyond the criminal code include Belgium (Law of 30 July 1981 on the Punishment of Certain Acts Inspired by Racism and Xenophobia), France (Section 24 in the Press Law of 1881), Ireland (The Prohibition of Incitement to Hatred Act 1989), the UK (Section 18(1) of the Public Order Act of 1986); Italy (L. n. 654 of 1975, modified first in 1993, and then in 2006). Although these laws establish the punishment of pure thoughts, the judges have limited the application of sanctions only when there is a danger of imminent illegal action.

As far as online discipline is concerned, Germany was the first European country to introduce a law which asks the platform to remove manifestly illegal content (under criteria set out in German law) within 24 hours and a longer timeframe for the other illicit content but does not establish a new liability regime and does not transform speech that was previously legal into illegal. The primary aim is set up a new compliance regime under which the complaints management is to become more transparent and presumably more effective. [14]

The Act establishes three different types of obligations the providers must fulfil.

To guarantee transparency the law imposes an obligation on each provider to publish a report in the middle of every year in which each of the following must be indicated: a) the efforts made by the provider to prevent the spread of offensive content on its platform; b) the criteria and procedures used to cancel or remove content; c) the number of complaints made and the reasons for them; d) information on the organization of the unit responsible for analysis of the reports; e) the number of complaints received and transmitted to a group of third party experts in case of differing decisions; f) the time taken (within 24 hours/48 hours/1 week) between reporting and blocking or removing illegal content; g) the measures used to communicate to both complainant and user the outcome of the assessment. [15]

The second category of obligations consists of publication on each provider's website of a complaint scheme that is easily identifiable, always easily accessible and, obviously, in German.

In any case, it is compulsory to communicate to the person who spread the hate content (identified according to hypothesis of criminal offenses contemplated by the German penal code) the reasons for its removal. Finally, the social networks must appoint an appropriate body to evaluate the complaint or an entitled person to exam-

---

[14] Sandra Schmitz-Berndt and Christian M. Berndt, 'The German Act on Improving Law Enforcement on Social Networks: A Blunt Sword?', https://ssrn.com/abstract=3306964 accessed 14 December 2018).

[15] Marco Bassini and Giulio Enea Vigevani, 'Primi appunti su fake news e dintorni', http://www.medialaws.eu/wp-content/uploads/2017/10/Bassini-Vigevani.pdf (2017), 19; Victor Claussen 'Fighting Hate Speech and Fake News. The Network Enforcement Act (NetzDG) in Germany in the Context of European Legislation' (2018) *N. Rivista dir. dei media* 14–15.

ine the complaint. The infringement of these obligations carries fines from a minimum of €500,000 up to a maximum of €1,000,000 for the platform itself.

The German law recognizes the potential liability of intermediaries that omit to control not only content inciting hate crimes but also every form of illicit thought. [16] The text raises numerous doubts about the use of very general terms such as 'manifestly illegal content' and a very short period in which to remove or block the content. The delicate, evaluative task is left to a private company, through a unespecifed proxy, in contrast to the soft law rules (which are analysed below) not because of an entrepreneurial option but as a result of the legislator's choice. [17]

5. *Hate Speech on the Internet in Europe between Private and Collateral Censorship*

The Web is considered with much suspicion and concern in Europe. European Court of Human Right ('ECHR') has committed itself to underlining and pointing up the capability of the Web of harming fundamental rights – through the use of word and images – rather than being a potential means of expression of freedom of speech. [18]

This substantial unease about the negative characteristics of the Internet clearly appears when analyzing the emergency legislation that has flourished since the succession of terrorist attacks in many European countries, which was gradually followed by the tightening of repressive and preventive measures and the addition of new criminal hypotheses (such as incitement to terrorism and glorification of terrorism – which implies an exacerbation of the sanctions if crime is carried out through the Internet: this view identifies the potential diffusivity of the medium).

In fact, after the deadly attacks on Charlie Hebdo, France has introduced – based on the state of emergency proclaimed by President Hollande – an obligation for service providers to remove or block all the sites that praise and glorify terrorism according to a black list drawn up by the ad hoc body set up by the Minister of the Interior. The law does not seem to impose this obligation of removal on the social networks thus rendering it ineffective, in practical terms, at achieving the intended purpose. [19]

Italy has also introduced a very similar system providing for the drafting of a list of websites used by terrorist associations, subject to periodic updating by the police and postal police forces. [20] After selecting the collected data it is possible to oblige

[16] Sandra Schmitz-Berndt and Christian M. Berndt (n. 14).

[17] Marco Bassini and Giulio Enea Vigevani (n. 15).

[18] Oreste Pollicino, 'La prospettiva costituzionale sulla libertà di espressione nell'era di Internet' (2018) (1) *Rivista dir. dei media* 34.

[19] Décret n. 2015-125 du 5 février 2015 http://www.legifrance.gouv.fr.

[20] L. 17 aprile 2015, n. 43 G.U. Serie Generale n. 91 20 aprile 2015.

'connectivity providers' to inhibit access to sites included in the list when the judges request it. However, it is imposed that, where there are hard evidence to believe that specific crimes are carried out for terrorist purposes with the help of the Internet, information management providers can be ordered to remove all illicit material accessible to the public, guaranteeing, if technically possible, the use of content unrelated to illegal conduct. Although with some precautions, due to the presence of a reserve of jurisdiction sanctioned by Article 21 of the Constitution, regarding the preparation of the list of dangerous or suspicious sites, the intervention of the judge required by the law has a purely notarial value, since the legislator does not clarify whether it is possible to expand or reduce the list on the basis of the assessment about the actual danger of the suspect and, in any case, no reasonable time limit to carry out this verification is given. Some scholars note that in the Italian case the legislation only respects the role of guarantee of the judge formally as the final decision is in the hands of the Government.[21]

In addition to some mandatory measures introduced by individual States, in 2016 the European Commission signed a Code of Conduct on countering illegal hate speech[22] involving the most important social networks operating on the Internet. Such platforms have committed themselves to removing hate content – referring both to encouragement of racial hatred or incitement to terrorism – within 24 hours of receiving a report by users of illegal content, according to the terms of contract and community guidelines, and to setting up mechanisms to remove or block the illegal content.

This is a soft regulation and therefore not binding on private parties, falling within forms of cooperation between public and private companies – in other words voluntary delegate enforcement – that have already been tested for other forms of offences, such as the infringement of copyright.[23]

However, as many scholars have noted the Code poses many risks to the right to freedom of expression. As specified above, platforms can remove posts and content initially according to the company terms of service[24] and only when necessary in accordance with the national law, transposing the Framework Decision 2008/913/JHA.[25]

---

[21] Giovanna De Minico, *Costituzione. Emergenza e terrorismo* (Jovene 2016).

[22] Commission, 'Code of Conduct on Countering Illegal Hate Speech Online' (2016) http://ec.europa.eu/justice/fundamentalrights/files/hate_speech_code_of_conduct_en.pdf accessed 9 March 2017.

[23] Giancarlo F. Frosio, 'The Death of "No Monitoring Obligations": A Story of Untameable Monsters' (2017) (8:3) *Journal of Intellectual Property, Information Technology and e-Commerce Law, JIPITEC,* https://www.jipitec.eu/issues/jipitec-8-3-2017/4621/#N1030D.

[24] Teresa Quintel and Carsten Ullrich, 'Self-Regulation of Fundamental Rights? The EU Code of Conduct on Hate Speech, Related Initiatives and Beyond', in Bilyana Petkova and Tuomas Ojanen (eds), *Fundamental Rights Protection Online: The Future Regulation of Intermediaries* (Edward Elgar 2019).

[25] Council Framework Decision 2008/913/JHA of 28 November 2008 'on combating certain forms and expressions of racism and xenophobia by means of criminal law', https://eur-lex.europa.eu/legal-content/en/ALL/?uri=CELEX%3A32008F0913.

The second relevant point is the lack of transparency about the mechanisms that manage the take down procedures which generally are carried out by algorithmic or artificial intelligence. Moreover, there is no mention in the Code of the users' right to appeal the decisions on removing or blocking through counter notice or before a Court. [26]

Subsequently, in September 2017, the European Commission [27] adopted a Communication to harmonize and give effect to the fight against illegal content. The key points of this new soft law document are: 1) the forecast of proactive measures by online platforms through the use of algorithms filtering the content stored in them; 2) the Communication clarifies that Article 14 of the e-Commerce Directive (which prevents States from introducing a general obligation to monitor content) would apply to service providers that merely host information of a third party without control over the content. However, when proactive measures are adopted platforms become aware of illegal content so that also mere hosting providers are liable; 3) in particular hypotheses the timeframe of deletion is shorter than the 24 hours provided in the Code (i.e. when a trusted flagger notifies the platform of hateful content because of expertise on this subject); 4) in order to prevent illicit content from being disseminated the Commission suggests the use of database hashes or automatic stay down procedures; 5) the Communication encourages platforms to give out information about the amount of content removed or blocked, the measures adopted and the time needed to remove the content and invites platforms to introduce a counter notice mechanism. As can be observed the documents of September 2017 try to clarify the loophole of the Code of Conduct. The European Union's increased attention to the protection of the right to freedom of expression is to be appreciated but the non-binding nature of the Act gives platforms wide discretion in deciding which rules are enforceable.

These two soft law precedents are completed by the Recommendation on measures to effectively tackle illegal content online published in March 2018. [28] This document represents a further tool to clarify ambiguous and contradictory parts of the Code of Conduct and Communication. [29]

First of all, it improves transparency for the platforms whenever they have submitted notices and followed the counter notice procedure. In brief, users are able to report any illicit content via a user-friendly mechanism so that service providers can explain the reasons why content should be blocked or removed. Secondly, platforms

[26] Giancarlo Frosio, 'From Horizontal to Vertical: An Intermediary Liability Earthquake in Europe' (2017) (2) *Oxford Journal of Intellectual Property Law and Practice* 565.

[27] Commission, Communication from the Commission to the European Parliament, the Council, the European Economic and Social Committee and the Committee of the Regions, 'Tackling Illegal Content Online: Towards an Enhanced Responsibility of Online Platforms', COM. (2017) 555 final.

[28] Commission, 'Commission Recommendation of 1.3.2018 on Measures to Effectively Tackle Illegal Content Online', COM. (2018) 1177 final, Brussels, 1 March 2018.

[29] Teresa Quintel and Carsten Ullrich (n. 24).

should inform content providers of any removal or blocking allowing them to contest the decision whenever there is no clarity about the illegality of the content. Moreover, the introduction of proactive measures to prevent the disseminating of illegal content is also required. When platforms choose the use of these instruments, they should give particular attention to data protection regulation and draw up appropriate safeguards, human controls and review procedures.

Regardless of the fact that these Acts are not binding, the introduction of proactive measures poses other issues relating to freedom of expression. First of all the existence of these provisions seems to reduce the exception liability of Article 14 of e-Commerce Directive. [30] Although there are no explicit sanctions for the conduct of intermediaries, the fear of a more intense discipline or of a probable liability leads to the suppression of legal content determining a collateral censorship effect thanks to lack of transparency in the removal or blocking procedures, which, in the end, leaves the balancing of the values at stake to private companies that they will be encouraged to pursue economic interests or to refuse to pay fines without any regard for the effective protection of fundamental rights.[31] Algorithm technologies are thought to satisfy business interests so that the adaptation of those tools to legal parameters does not ensure the accuracy of their actions [32] and they are prone to errors (false positive detecting legal material or false negative failing to remove illegal material). [33] Nor is the use of 'human in the loop principle' sufficient to assure the diligence and efficiency with which the illegal content will be removed. In fact, it is not clear who are human experts, what kind of expertise they have and if they are adequately trained. Furthermore the choice to recruit staff is dependent on the financial capacity of each platform. Moreover providers are not enticed to create sophisticated communication channels with any kind of guarantee of economic return. [34]

Finally the preference to apply unilateral rules arranged exclusively by social networks (different from one another and depending on the diverse company policies of providers) creates a jeopardy effect in the taken solutions that are not in accordance

---

[30] European Parliament and Council, Directive 2000/31/EC of 8 June 2000 on 'certain legal aspects of information society services, in particular electronic commerce, in the Internal Market'.

[31] Jack M. Balkin, 'Free Speech and Hostile Environments' (1999) (99:1) *Columbia Law Review*, 2295; Jack M. Balkin, 'Old School New School Speech Regulation' (2014) *Faculty Scholarship Series*, 4877 https://digitalcommons.law.yale.edu/fss_papers/4877; Jack M. Balkin, 'Free Speech in Algorithm Society Big Data, Private Governance, and New School Speech Regulation' (2018) *Faculty Scholarship Series*, 5160 https://digitalcommons.law.yale.edu/fss_papers/5160.

[32] Molly K. Land and Jay D. Aronson, 'The Promise and Peril of Human Rights Technology', in M. Land and J. Aronson (eds), *New Technologies for Human Rights Law and Practice* (Cambridge University Press 2018).

[33] Eugene Coche, 'Framework Online', https://papers.ssrn.com/sol3/papers.cfm?abstract_id=3280904, 3 December 2018; Miriam Buiten, Alexandre de Streel and Martin Peitz 'Rethinking Liability Rules for Online Hosting Platforms', https://ssrn.com/abstract=3350693 on March 11, 2019; Christina Angelopoulos and Stijn Smet, 'Notice-and-Fair-Balance: How to Reach a Compromise between Fundamental Rights in European Intermediary Liability' (2016) 8:2) *Journal of Media Law*, 266.

[34] Miriam Buiten, Alexandre de Streel and Martin Peitz (n. 33) 8.

with international human rights standards representing a clear exception to the rule of law.[35]

6. *European Union Proposal on the Prevention of Terrorist Content Online. New Regulation, Old Issues*

The proposal for a new Regulation on prevention of terrorist content online[36] is the first attempt to establish obligations that go beyond the voluntarist approach followed by the European Union until now but critical points and contradictions are present in this draft, too.

However, when compared with the soft law precedents the first change in the new Act is its subject. The proposal concerns only terrorist content.

It is easy to observe that its definition is different from that contained in Directive 2017/541 on combating terrorism[37] which establishes 'the public provocation to commit a terrorist offence' is considered as 'the distribution, or otherwise making available by any means, whether online or offline, of a message to the public, with the intent to incite the commission of (terrorist offences)', and in particular 'where such conduct, directly or indirectly, such as by the glorification of terrorist acts, advocates the commission of terrorist offences, thereby causing a danger that one or more such offences may be committed'. Such public provocation 'is punishable as a criminal offence when committed intentionally'.

The new draft, in contrast, introduces the possibility of removing content that 'incit[es] or advocat[es], including by glorifying, the commission of terrorist offences, thereby causing a danger that such acts be committed'. Albeit the two clauses look similar the reference to the term "incitement" identifies a much broader and vaguer notion compared with 'the advocacy of the commission of terrorist offences' included in the Directive mentioned above. In this way the proposal should leave more discretionary power to Member States that would have the opportunity to clamp down on extreme but legal expressions such as journalistic work on terrorism.[38]

---

[35] Eugene Coche (n. 33) 6.

[36] Council of the European Union, 'Proposal for a Regulation on Preventing the Dissemination of Terrorist Content Online General Approach', 14978/18, Interinstitutional 3 December 2018, https://www.parlament.gv.at/PAKT/EU/XXVI/EU/04/57/EU_45743/imfname_10862334.pdf.

[37] European Parliament and Council, Directive 2017/541 of 15 March 2017 'on combating terrorism and replacing Council Framework Decision 2002/475/JHA and amending Council Decision 2005/671/JHA, OJ L 88, 31.3.2017', https://eur-lex.europa.eu/legal-content/EN/TXT/?uri=celex%3A32017L0541.

[38] Joan Barata, 'New EU Proposal on the Prevention of Terrorist Content Online, An Important Mutation of the E-Commerce Intermediaries' Regime' (October 2018) http://cyberlaw.stanford.edu/files/publication/files/2018.10.11.Comment.Terrorism.pdf.

Another highly uncertain point is whether the new proposal amends Directive 2017/541 with the consequence that the terrorist content on the Internet is not punishable and only subject to removal or blocking. [39]

According to Recital 10 there is no distinction between active or passive hosts so a broad range of services are covered. Moreover there is no provision excluding small service providers.

In line with the Communication and Recommendation approach the proposal incorporates an obligation named 'duties of care'. Article 3 establishes a general obligation for hosting services to 'take appropriate, reasonable and proportionate actions ..., against the dissemination of terrorist content and to protect users from terrorist content'. When doing so, these actors shall act in a 'diligent, proportionate and non-discriminatory manner, and with due regard to the fundamental rights of the users and take into account the fundamental importance of the freedom of expression and information in an open and democratic society'. Differently from the past in this mandatory rules on infringement prevention is introduced not to remove terrorist content notified by Member States and users but to prevent its spread. So that States shall establish penalties if hosts fail to include these rules in their terms and conditions. As some scholars have noted the platforms – in the absence of clear criteria on how to achieve duties of care – are also forced to block legal content. [40]

Apart from this general obligation, Article 4 specifies that competent authorities will have the power to order hosting service providers to remove or disable access to content. The timeframe to carry out these measures is truncated to a single hour, a very short time that will put the platforms under pressure. A one-hour deadline is completely impracticable for small providers, who do not have the capacity to employ staff to be available for potential removal orders 24 hours a day. [41] According to the proposal the removal order has to indicate information about feasible redress to the hosting service provider and the content service provider. Instead, according to the Recommendation the challenge against removal order before the Court is permitted, without specify what Court is. As some scholars noted the vagueness of these clauses about redress and appeal does not qualify as an effective remedy. The lack of clarity about how much time is needed to revise the appeal and, in the case of a successful answer, what the procedure is to put the removal content back on the Web makes the remedy irrelevant. [42] Only in a few cases is it possible to exclude every form of liability. Whenever there are multiple failures in removal orders the competent authorities will apply a financial penalty of 4% of the global business of the hosting provider.

---

[39] Ibid, 6.

[40] Ibid, 7.

[41] Aleksandra Kuczerawy, 'The Proposed Regulation on Preventing the Dissemination of Terrorist Content Online: Safeguards and Risks for Freedom of Expression', for Center for Democracy and Technology, https://ssrn.com/abstract=3296864 accessed December 5, 2018.

[42] Ibid, 9–10.

Article 5 is the most problematic because it lays down the power of competent authorities or the relevant Union Body to send a referral to hosting service providers which have expeditiously given a voluntary assessment of the content and its compliance with the terms of service. After the assessment the hosting service provider informs the relevant authorities about its decision and timing. This mechanism introduces an apparently voluntary measure but instead it represents a delegation of responsibility for the enforcement [43] that would be adopted by Member States incompatible with Article 52.1 of the European Union Charter as it is not provided by law, but rather by the private rules established by hosting service providers.

Article 10 of the proposed Regulation states that hosting service providers should establish effective and accessible complaint mechanisms as a safeguard that content has been removed (or access to it disabled) as a result of a referral or of a proactive measure. The complaint mechanisms would allow content providers to submit a complaint against the action of the hosting service provider to require reinstatement of the content. Furthermore, the Article establishes that hosting service providers should promptly analyse every complaint they receive. They should also reinstate any content the removal of which (or disabling of access to) was unjustified, without undue delay. This prevision that introduces such a form of redress is important but not sufficient. As mentioned above, assessment of content will be conducted according to terms and conditions which, in many cases, consider the removal acceptable. Moreover, hosting service providers have no interest in publishing again content that they have previously removed, even if the decision was based on a mistake. Only when it attracts negative media attention do the platforms reupload the content. [44]

Finally and in continuity with the Communication and Recommendation, Article 6 contains a group of proactive measures, including automated means, regarding their content monitoring with the aim of 'preventing the re-upload[ing] of content' and 'detecting, identifying and expeditiously removing or disabling access to terrorist content'. This approach is not new and is a European trend. The recent approval of the Audio Visual Media Service [45] and Copyright Directive proposal incorporate the same solution. No penalties are applied and it may look closer to a desideratum than an actual legal obligation.

In Article 6 paragraph 2 it is also established that the competent authorities can request the hosting service provider, which has received an order that has become final, to submit a report within three months on the specific proactive measures taken. Moreover the competent authorities may require the platform to install an automated machine where the arranged voluntary actions are deemed weak. These clauses create many risks. The first is that the use of technical measures is expensive and they can on-

---

[43] S. Stalla-Bourdillon, 'Chilling ISPs ... When Private Regulators Act without Adequate Public Framework' (2010) (26) *Computer Law & Security Review*, 290.

[44] Aleksandra Kuczerawy (n. 41) 2.

[45] European Parliament and of the Council, Directive (EU) 2018/1808 of 14 November 2018.

ly be borne by the big companies impacting on proper competition between giants and small entrepreneurs.[46] The second danger is that with the introduction of proactive measures the role of the platforms will change rapidly. Although the required technical tools are directed to find particular groups of content effectively they have to examine the entire platform and then recognize any content that should be deleted. Combining these two measures it appears evident an infringement according to Article 15 of the e-Commerce Directive that prevents the State from imposing general monitoring obligations as interpreted by CJEU. In *Sabam v. Netlog*[47] the European judges ruled that requiring a filtering mechanism that would oblige hosting providers to actively monitor almost all the data relating to each of its service users in order to prevent any future infringements would constitute imposing general monitoring, which is prohibited by the above mentioned Directive. Even if we wanted to consider this obligation not general but addressed to specific contents (although it is difficult, in practice, to make a distinction between a general monitoring obligation and a specific monitoring obligation),[48] it is evident a progressive delegation to enforcement of law[49] exclusively on the platforms through a regulation which allows private censorship[50] and the death of 'no monitoring obligations.'[51] Finally the proposal aims not only to prevent the uploading of identified terroristic content through comparison with the existing database but also to detect new terroristic content that has not yet been identified. The use of artificial intelligence is not able to stop misidentification of content thus potentially presenting an elevated danger to freedom of speech.

7. *Conclusion*

As Jack M. Balkin noted 'the twentieth century model is a dyadic model: the state is on one side, speakers and publishers are on the other', so 'During the early age of the

---

[46] Miriam Buiten, Alexandre de Streel and Martin Peitz (n. 33) 42.

[47] European Court of Justice, *Sabam v. Netlog* Case C-360/10 http://curia.europa.eu/juris/liste.jsf?num=C-360/10&language=EN.

[48] Etienne Montero and Quentin Van Enis, 'Enabling Freedom of Expression in Light of Filtering Measures Imposed on Internet Intermediaries: Squaring the Circle?' (2011) (27) *Computer Law & Security Review*, 21.

[49] Aleksandra Kuczeraw, 'Safeguards for Freedom of Expression in the Era of Online Gatekeeping', (2017) (3) *Auteurs & Media*, 292–303; Joan Barata, 'New EU Proposal on the Prevention of Terrorist Content Online' (2018) *CIS Stanford Law* https://cyberlaw.stanford.edu/files/publication/files/2018.10.11.Comment.Terrorism.pdf.

[50] Laura De Nardis, 'The Privatization of Free Expression' in Pranesh Prakash and others (eds), *Global Censorship. Shifting Modes, Persisting Paradigm* https://law.yale.edu/system/files/area/center/isp/documents/a2k_global-censorship_2.pdf (Information Society Project, Yale Law School; Access to Knowledge for Development Centre 2015).

[51] Giancarlo F. Frosio, 'Reforming Intermediary Liability in the Platform Economy: A European Digital Single Market Strategy' (2017) (118:7) *Northwestern University Law Review*, 19.

Internet, people imagined that territorial governments would lose much of their power to control speech'.[52] It's not completely true: what has changed is just the method of control. Platforms become special purpose sovereigns who govern populations of end-users without any guarantee of procedural benefits.[53] This position is confirmed by observing the European Union regulation on hate speech and terrorist speech on the Web. In the past soft law regulation has prevailed whereas currently the self- coregulation model is the preferred one. Specifically censorship of illegal content is entrusted to the Internet service providers by governments which delegate the power[54] to decide which types of content are legal, with the possibility that content which is not illicit will be deleted. The pressure of public power on the social media has a chilling effect on freedom of speech or in an indirect way the silencing of dissent.

The soft laws, the German law and the new regulation proposal – but in general all law of fears – are a kinds of rules which act for the purpose of prevention and independently of the concrete possibility to commit a more serious offence by the authors with a strong and unjustified limitation of fundamental rights.[55] The uncoordinated and rapid change of national and supranational rules creates, moreover, a great uncertainty about the application of appropriate norms with a large number of misunderstandings and mistakes that oblige media platforms to overblock the content uploaded online. Add to this the fact that the decision to remove or block content is generally – as suggested also in the latest European documents – entrusted to algorithms or a group of experts without consistent procedural benefits. The war against terror on the Internet is now totally in the hands of providers but this has negative implication for the freedom of expression, the rule of law and due process.

---

[52] Michel Meyerson, '"Speaker" Within the New Media' (1995) (71) *Notre Dame L. Rev.* 79, 118; Jack M. Balkin, 'Free Speech is a Triangle' (2018) (118:7) *Columbia Law Review*; Symposium: A First Amendment for All. Free Expression in an Age of Inequality (2011) (118: 7) *Columbia Law Review*.

[53] Ibid, 2015.

[54] Luca Belli and Cristina Sappa, 'The Intermediary Conudrum: Cyber-Regulators, Cyber-Police or Both?' (2017) (8) *Journal of Intellectual Property, Information Technology and Electronic Commerce Law, JIPITEC*, 183.

[55] Giovanna De Minico, 'Internet and Fundamental Rights in Time of Terrorism' (2016) (4) https://www.rivistaaic.it/images/rivista/pdf/4_2014_De%20Minico.pdf 1.

Freedom of Expression behind the Incitement to Terrorism in a Globalised World by the Internet

Germán M. Teruel Lozano

SUMMARY: 1. Introduction. – 2. The Difficulty of Harmonising an Offence of Incitement to Terrorism in the Supranational Sphere. European Legislation as a Paradigm. – 3. In Search of a Common Standard with Respect to Incitement to Terrorism as a Limit to the Freedom of Expression: The Jurisprudence of the ECHR as It Contrasts with the Doctrine of the US Supreme Court. – 4. The Internet and the Challenges for the Fight Against Terrorism. – 5. In Conclusion: A Lege Ferenda Proposal for an Offence of Incitement to Terrorism Compatible with the Highest Standards of Protection for the Freedom of Expression.

1. *Introduction*

Terrorism has become one of the greatest threats to Western society in the twenty-first century. Our democracies must confront terrorist attacks which aim to terrorise the population and destabilise, if not destroy, our model of coexistence. Terrorism seeks not only to cause harm, but to accompany it with a forceful message. It has been said that terrorism is a "theatre";[1] a tragic representation with an immense communicative force. There is not the slightest doubt that terrorist activities have found, in the Internet, a new space in which to be developed and fomented; something which, as will be examined, presents new challenges.

It is precisely in the struggle against these terrorist acts which horrify our societies that these latter must simultaneously affirm their commitment to democratic ideals. The necessity of confronting an evil of such size, with such great risks, is subject to significant tension between our values and fundamental principles, especially those upon which rights-based criminal law has been built.[2] With respect to this, 'criminal law of the enemy' finds its paradigm in the terrorist: no longer citizens, terrorists have permanently abandoned society and now attack it.[3] To neutralise these ene-

---

[1] Jan-Peter Loof, 'Restricting free speech in times of terror: an ECHR perspective', Afshin Ellian and Gelijn Molier (ed.), *Freedom of speech under attack* (Eleven 2015), 185.

[2] Cfr. Luigi Ferrajoli, *Diritto e ragione. Teoria del garantismo penale* (Ed. Laterza 2004), and *Il paradigma garantista* (Editoriale Scientifica 2014).

[3] Cfr. Günther Jakobs, 'Kriminalisierung im Vorfeld einer Rechtsgutverletzung' (1985) 97 *Zeitschrift für die gesamte Strafrechtswissenschaft* 75 or Id., 'Bürgerstrafrecht und Feindstrafrecht' (2004) 21

mies, one is justified in weakening constitutional safeguards and diminishing proportionality of criminal response. [4] Thus new crimes surface: provocation and incitement to terrorism, but also glorification and justification, proselytism and recruitment, grooming and travel for terrorist purposes or aiding such purposes, and even a simple Web search for terrorist content could be classed as a crime. [5]

This chapter will focus on studying crimes of incitement to terrorism from a European perspective, including indirect forms such as apologia or glorification, and the specific features of punishment available for these behaviours when conducted via the Internet. In particular, the classification offered under Directive 2017/541 of the European Parliament and Council, dated 15 March, will be taken as a reference, relative to the fight against terrorism. Similarly, insofar as these crimes encroach on freedom of expression, a more adequate standard of protection will be sought in light of the jurisprudence of the European Court of Human Rights, contrasting it in turn with that of the US Supreme Court. All of the above will enable the realisation of a proposal for a rights-based redefinition of these crimes, one which responds to the needs derived from the dissemination of these types of messages via the Internet. This will be an attempt to seek an efficacious response to terrorist barbarity without abandoning the principles of our civilisation, upon which the rights-based constitutional State is founded.

2. *The Difficulty of Harmonising an Offence of Incitement to Terrorism in the Supranational Sphere. European Legislation as a Paradigm*

The necessity of prevention in the face of terrorism has led, among other things, to the attempt to punish the incitement or even glorification of terrorism, as previously mentioned. In the wake of 9/11, nations became aware of the nature of a new danger: international terrorism. In contrast to other forms of "classic" terrorism with a national outlook, a terrorism that transcended national barriers had appeared with clarity, threatening the entire World and taking on the reality of globalisation. Moreover, this was a terrorism with a profile associated with religious fundamentalism. [6] All of this required a coordinated response between countries – unilateral responses were not enough; a necessity amplified, as will be seen, when the terrorist phenomenon spread through the Internet.

Ritsumeikan Law Review 93. More specifically on terrorism, cfr. Id., 'Terroristen als Personen im Recht?' (2005) 117 (n. 4) *Zeitschrift für die gesamte Strafrechtswissenschaft* 839. See also Gunther Jakobs and Manuel Cancio Meliá, *Derecho penal del enemigo* (Aranzadi 2006).

[4] In a critical sense, cfr. Francisco Muñoz Conde, 'El nuevo Derecho penal autoritario', *El derecho ante la globalización y el terrorismo* (Tirant lo Blanch 2004); and Jesús-María Silva Sánchez, *La expansión del Derecho Penal. Aspectos de la política criminal en las sociedades postindustriales* (Civitas, 2001).

[5] Cfr. Conseil Constitutionnel, 2017-682 QPC 15/12/.2017.

[6] Cfr. Loof (n. 1), 202.

However, this coordinated action between nations also faces hurdles. On the one hand, the very definition of what is meant by terrorist acts is disputed. Furthermore, as far as this chapter is concerned, when the intent is to criminalise acts of incitement or apologia which presuppose the *prima facie* exercise of a fundamental freedom, countries maintain varying standards with respect to the recognition and limits of such freedoms.

Such is the situation that in the international sphere it has not yet been possible to reach an agreement which enforces an offence for the incitement of terrorism, although this has been possible in other spheres.[7] In 2001, in reaction to the 9/11 attacks, the Security Council issued a resolution in which it was recognised for the first time that 'inciting terrorist acts [is] also contrary to the purposes and principles of the United Nations'.[8] It was to be some years later, again following a terrorist attack – this time in London – and in a unique political context,[9] that for the first time the Security Council agreed to urge all Member States 'to adopt such measures as may be necessary and appropriate' in order to 'prohibit by law incitement to commit a terrorist act or acts'.[10] It was not clarified whether Member States were to prohibit direct incitement only, or indirect incitement as well – in fact, the reference to 'the justification or glorification (*apologie*)' remained relegated to the preamble. Nor was it ascertained whether the proscription was required to carry criminal sanction. The binding nature of the aforementioned resolution might even be thrown into question, as it may simply constitute an appeal to States rather than an international legal obligation.[11] Similarly, the same resolution recognises 'the importance that, in an increasingly globalised world, States act cooperatively to prevent terrorists from exploiting sophisticated technology, communications and resources to incite support for criminal acts'. And it simultaneously affirms the commitment to respecting freedom of expression.

In the European context, it has been possible to go beyond this, despite notable differences from the outset between Member States, the majority of which did not previously specifically penalise incitement to or glorification of terrorism, although

---

[7] Cfr. the 'International Convention on the Elimination of All Forms of Racial Discrimination' (art. 4) or the 'Additional protocol to the convention on Cybercrime, concerning the criminalisation of acts of a racist and xenophobic nature committed through computer systems' (28/01/2003).

[8] United Nations. Security Council R 1373 (2001).

[9] Daphne Barak-Erez and David Scharia, 'Freedom of speech, support for terrorism, and the challenge of global constitutional law' (2011) 2 *Harvard National Secutiry Journal* 1, 20, states: 'Three elements that facilitated the adoption of this landmark resolution': 'The first element is the political circumstances of the time: the Council was meeting with the eleven of heads of states, only two months after the bombing attacks in London and one year after the Beslan attack [...]. The general feeling was that the Security Council was expected to take a significant initiative. Second, the adoption of the Council of Europe Convention on the Prevention of Terrorism, on May 15, 2005, three months before the resolution was adopted [...]. The third element was the United Kingdom's understanding of anti-terrorism'.

[10] Resolution 1624 (2005) United Nations. Security Council. Vid. Barak-Erez and Scharia (n. 9).

[11] Cfr. Göran Rollnert Liern, 'Incitación al terrorismo y libertad de expresión: el marco internacional de una relación problemática' (2014) 91 *Revista de Derecho Político* 231, 235.

such acts could be sanctioned on a case-by-case basis with the application of general offences. [12] In 2005, the States which were Parties to the Council of Europe Convention 196 on the prevention of terrorism (16/05/2005) undertook, under Article 5 of the same, to criminalise acts of public provocation to commit terrorist crimes. A qualification was added that these acts were not considered 'terrorist crimes'. [13] As stated in the explanatory report, it was preferable to put in place a general phrase (public provocation) in lieu of specific phrases, rendering the direct or indirect nature of the incitement irrelevant for the application of the law. [14] The dissemination or any other form of publicising provocative messages is penalised, but two cautionary notes are added: 'first, there has to be a specific intent to incite the commission of a terrorist offence, which is supplemented with the requirements in paragraph 2 (see below) that provocation be committed unlawfully and intentionally'. [15] Secondly, 'the result of such an act must be to cause a danger that such an offence might be committed', [16] but without the act necessarily leading to the enactment of the terrorist act. [17] 'When considering whether such danger is caused, the nature of the author and of the addressee of the message, as well as the context in which the offence is committed shall be taken into account'. [18] With respect to the public nature of the dissemination, the latter implies that the message must have been "easily" accessible to the public, which excludes private communication. [19] Among the examples laid out in the Report are Internet posts or the creation and collation of hyperlinks to facilitate their viewing, as well as the printing of posts, speeches in places accessible to others, and the use of communications media. [20] It is doubtful, in my view, to con-

[12] Cfr. Council of Europe, *"Apologie du terrorisme" and "incitement to terrorism"*, 2004.

[13] Cfr. Explanatory report to the Council of Europe Convention on the prevention of terrorism, 16/05/2005, § 77.

[14] Cfr. Explanatory report to the Council of Europe Convention on the prevention of terrorism, 16/05/2005, § 96. It also explains: 'Direct provocation does not raise any particular problems in so far as it is already a criminal offence, in one form or another, in most legal systems. The aim of making indirect provocation a criminal offence is to remedy the existing lacunae in international law or action by adding provisions in this area' (§97). 'The provisions allow Parties a certain amount of discretion with respect to the definition of the offence and its implementation. For instance, presenting a terrorist offence as necessary and justified may constitute the offence of indirect incitement' (§ 98).

[15] Explanatory report to the Council of Europe Convention on the prevention of terrorism, 16/05/2005, § 99.

[16] Explanatory report to the Council of Europe Convention on the prevention of terrorism, 16/05/2005, § 100.

[17] Council of Europe Convention on the prevention of terrorism, art. 8.

[18] Explanatory report to the Council of Europe Convention on the prevention of terrorism, 16/05/2005, § 100.

[19] Cfr. Explanatory report to the Council of Europe Convention on the prevention of terrorism, 16/05/2005, § 102–103.

[20] Cfr. Explanatory report to the Council of Europe Convention on the prevention of terrorism, 16/05/2005, § 104.

sider 'public' the use of technological media such as the Internet in spreading messages via email or exchanging material in a chat or forum. However, according to the explanatory report, this certainly ought to be considered public dissemination.[21] In any case, the Convention also expressly incorporates an obligation to respect human rights and especially freedom of expression when judging and trying these crimes (Art. 12).

The European Union has furthermore committed to responding in a collective manner to terrorism. The first initiative was the Council Framework Decision 2002/475/JHA of 13 June 2002 on combating terrorism, even though this only addressed the penalty for recruitment (Art. 4). In 2008[22] it was amended to, among other things, criminalising provocation to commit a terrorist crime (Art. 3.2.a) as in 'offences linked to terrorist activities' (that is to say, external to terrorist crimes in the proper sense). This regulation has been replaced by the Directive (EU) 2017/541 of the European Parliament and Council of 15 March 2017. The description of terrorist provocation encompassed by this new legislation did not change the basic elements of the definition of the crime as offered under the Framework Decision, and was maintained in the Commission's proposal for a Directive.[23] Specifically: (1) The *public distribution or dissemination* in any form of *provocative messages* in a direct or indirect manner will be penalised as advocated by the commission for *terrorist crimes* (defined in the same European legislation).[24] (2) *Presenting a risk* that such crimes may be committed. A risk that, as indicated in the Preamble, must be assessed according to the circumstances of the case.[25] Thus, this offence is a crime of endangerment, rather than injury, and the Directive seems to exclude the conception of such a crime as an abstract endangerment. In fact, if we examine the literal wording of the European legislation, it may be understood that the offence should pose a specific risk of damage (specific endangerment), or at least a "potential" danger (hypothetical endangerment). (3) An *intention*, which must cover all aspects of the crime and thus necessitates an intention to incite.[26]

[21] Cfr. Explanatory report to the Council of Europe Convention on the prevention of terrorism, 16/05/2005, § 104.

[22] Council Framework Decision 2008/919/JHA of 28 November 2008.

[23] COM(2015) 625 final.

[24] A danger could be defined as a probable relationship between a fact and a harmful event. In this sense, the offence of terrorism will be the 'harmful event' that we want to prevent but which is likely to occur as a consequence of the action (public spread of the messages which directly or indirectly incite the commission of these acts).

[25] The Directive (EU) 2017/541 of the European Parliament and Council of 15 March 2017 sets: 'In each concrete case, when considering whether such a danger is caused, the specific circumstances of the case should be taken into account, such as the author and the addressee of the message, as well as the context in which the act is committed. The significance and the credible nature of the danger should be also considered when applying the provision on public provocation in accordance with national law' (10).

[26] Cfr. Directive (UE) 2017/541 of the European Parliament and of the Council of 15 March 2017, § 17.

Among the more innovative aspects of this wording, what is striking is that, for the first time, glorification is explicitly included in the description of behaviour as a form of indirect incitement;[27] and that the dissemination of these types of messages via the Internet is specifically acknowledged.[28] Article 21 has even been adjusted with measures to eliminate and block Internet content which contains incitement to terrorist acts. Moreover, European lawmakers have demonstrated their respect for fundamental rights and accordingly provisioned a specific article (Art. 23). This has not mitigated the doubts that continue to be raised regarding this legislation which distinctly advocates legal intervention and, furthermore, continues to lack a clear definition of the behaviour it prohibits and the degree of danger which justifies criminal sanction,[29] as previously mentioned. This latter point, as will be seen, is the key to a description of the crime which can fulfil the requirements that stem from the need to adequately protect the freedom of expression. The fact that there is currently no set standard between countries at the time of writing may mean that one Member State, holding itself to a higher standard for the protection of freedom of expression, can question a legal judgement handed down in another country for a crime if, for example, it is based on a general capacity to be harmful (hypothetical or potential danger) and not on the existence of a concrete or specific danger.

[27] This mention was introduced in the first reading by the Council and the Parliament. The Directive explains: 'The offence of public provocation to commit a terrorist offence act comprises, inter alia, the glorification and justification of terrorism or the dissemination of messages or images online and offline, including those related to the victims of terrorism as a way to gather support for terrorist causes or to seriously intimidate the population' (§ 10). And the European Commission's Proposal (COM(2015) 625 final) establishes: 'Under this provision are considered as punishable acts, for example, the glorification of suicide bombers, encouragement to join violent jihad, direct invitations to kill non-believers, justification of terrorism or the dissemination of messages or images of brutal assassinations as a way to gain publicity for the terrorists cause or prove their power, where such behaviour actually creates the risk that terrorist acts will be committed and provided that the messages are disseminated with the purpo"se of furthering terrorist activities (not necessarily those of a specific terrorist organisation). Such messages and images may also include those denigrating victims of terrorism, including their families. The provisions were also meant to ensure that dissemination of messages through the Internet encouraging the commission of terrorist offences or providing for terrorist expertise was made punishable.'

[28] Cfr. Information Note. General Secretariat of the Council, 21.02.2017 (doc. 6338/17).

[29] In a critical sense, cfr. Opinion of the European and Social Committee on the 'Proposal for a directive of the European Parliament and of the Council on combating terrorism and replacing Council Framework Decision 2002/475/JHA on combating terrorism' 2016/C 177/09: 'The Committee considers that it is dangerous for any democracy to legislate against anticipated crimes (criminalising offences or crimes which have not yet been committed)' (§ 15) and 'As freedom of the press and freedom of speech are guaranteed, it is unclear when informing the public of a terrorist attack ceases to be information and becomes provocation' (§ 3.2.2.4).

3. *In Search of a Common Standard with Respect to Incitement to Terrorism as a Limit to the Freedom of Expression: The Jurisprudence of the ECHR as It Contrasts with the Doctrine of the US Supreme Court*

One of the current difficulties in reaching a consensus at the international and European level regarding the crime of incitement to and glorification of terrorism is precisely the differing standards of protection of the freedom of expression. In the European domain, the system of reference is the European Convention as defined by the European Court of Human Rights ('ECHR'). While it is true that the ECHR must be considered the *"lowest" common denominator* (starting from a high standard) that all Member States must undertake to respect, this does not prevent countries from adopting higher standards for the recognition and protection of a right. For that reason, although this chapter focuses primarily on Europe, it is useful to examine the contrast with the approach of the US Supreme Court. Significant differences exist between the European and US perspectives in the approach to limiting freedom of expression in the face of speech that incites violence, and more specifically terrorism, which justifies a comparative study of the two. As will be seen, whilst in Europe one observes an inclination in favour of justifying this type of limitation, in the USA an indirect route has been adopted so as to avoid clashing with the US First Amendment. [30]

The differences between the two systems are evident from the constitutional recognition of freedom of expression itself. [31] Thus, on the one hand, the current European Convention which declares in Article 10 that 'everyone has the right to freedom of expression', immediately cautions that exercising the same entails 'duties and responsibilities' and 'may be subject to such formalities, conditions, restrictions or penalties as are prescribed by law and are necessary in a democratic society' for the protection of other values (national security, territorial integrity, the protection of the reputation or rights of others ...). Under Article 17 of the Convention, there may even be exclusions *ratione materiae* from being protected under the Convention when the exercising of any fundamental rights seeks 'to engage in any activity or perform any act aimed at the destruction of any of the rights and freedoms set forth herein or at their limitation to a greater extent than is provided for in the Convention'. On the other hand, in contrast to the European approach, the US Constitution's First Amendment radically declares that 'Congress shall make no law [...] abridging the freedom of speech, or of the press ...'. Nonetheless, it is true that the broad constitutional recognition has not impeded the limitation of this freedom in the USA, under a severe scrutiny from the Supreme Court.

---

[30] Cfr. Barak-Erez and Scharia (n. 9), pp. 14 ss.

[31] Cfr. Stefan Sottiaux, 'The "Clear and Present Danger" Test in the Case Law of the European Court of Human Rights' (2003) 63 *ZaöRV* 654 ss.

Further, with regard to incitement to and glorification of terrorism, the European Court of Human Rights has had to deal with a variety of cases, setting out a jurisprudence which presents few clear-cut cases. With this in mind, on the one hand we should highlight a first group of sentences related to convictions for incitement to terrorist violence in Turkey, [32] and, on the other, a second group for convictions derived from glorification of terrorism, where the most relevant sentence was in the Leroy v. France case, [33] after which there has been a series of decisions also related to Turkey among the incitement to and glorification of terrorism. [34] Some conclusions can be drawn from the examination of this jurisprudence.

The first conclusion is that there is an interference of freedom of expression when penalising an incitement to or glorification of terrorism. In these situations, we would be facing a conflict that should be resolved according to the triple test designed by the Court of Strasbourg (legal provision, legitimate purpose and necessity in a democratic society). In this sense, this type of provocative speech will not be excluded *ratione materiae* from the scope of the Convention by virtue of Article 17. [35]

Secondly, it is not possible to criticise in every case the punishment of apologias as being inconsistent with the freedom of expression, even if such discourses do not contain a direct incitement to violence. [36] As we will discuss, the tenor of such expressions will be only one of the aspects to consider within the context in which the speech takes place. Notwithstanding, the European Court has emphasised the difficulty of punishing terrorist glorification. [37]

Thirdly, the degree of control commanded by the European Court or, in other words, the degree of discretion granted to the Member States, is modulated by various factors. Thus, for example, when it comes to political discourse or matters of general interest, there is a tighter degree of control, whilst if national security is at

---

[32] Cfr. ECtHR Zana v. Turkey apl. n. 69/1996/688/880 (25.11.1997); Incal v. Turkey apl. n. 22678/93 (9.06.1998); Sürek v. Turkey (n. 1) apl. n. 26682/95; Gerger v. Turkey apl. n. 24919/94; Sürek y Özdemir v. Turkey apl. n. 23927/94; Ceylan v. Turkey apl. n. 23556/94; Arslan v. Turkey apl. n. 23462/94; and Sürek v. Turkey (n. 3) apl. n. 24735/94 (8.07.1999).

[33] ECtHR Leroy v. France apl. 36109/03 (2.10.2008). Previously, ECtHR Hogefeld v. Germany apl. n. 35402/97 (20.01.2000). More recently, ECtHR Stomakhin v. Russia apl. 52273/07 (9.05.2018).

[34] Cfr. ECtHR Taşdemir v. Turkey apl. n. 38841/07 (23.02.2010); and ECtHR Savgin v. Turkey apl. n. 13304/03 (2.02.2010); Gül and others v. Turkey apl. n. 4870/02 (8.06.2010); Kiliç and Eren v. Turkey apl. n. 43807/07 (29.02.2012); and Yavuz y Yaylali v. Turkey apl. n. 12606/11 (17.12.2013).

[35] Other cases in which the ECtHR has applied art. 17 ECHR, ECtHR, Kasymakhunov and Saybatalov v. Russia apl. n. 26377/06 (14.03.2013), and Hizb Ut-Tahrir and others v. Germany apl. n. 31098/08 (12.06.2012). See also ECtHR Norwood v. United Kingdom apl. n. 23131/03 (16.11.2004).

[36] Cfr. ECtHR Leroy v. France apl. 36109/03 (2.10.2008), § 37; or Yavuz y Yaylali v. Turkey apl. n. 12606/11 (17.12.2013) § 51.

[37] ECtHR Leroy v. France apl. 36109/03 (2.10.2008), § 37: 'En particulier, et comme le montrent les travaux du Conseil de l'Europe en la matière (paragraphes 20 et 21 ci-dessus), la principale difficulté réside dans la possibilité de punir l'apologie du terrorisme sans entraver les libertés fondamentales telle que la liberté d'expression.'

stake in cases of incitement to violence in conflict-ridden contexts, the Court will allow a larger degree of discretion.[38] With respect to the fight against terrorism in particular, the Strasbourg Court has specified that a 'fair balance' must be found between respect for fundamental rights and freedom of expression and the legitimate right of a democratic society to protect itself against terrorist acts.[39]

Fourth, in the application of the Strasbourg test to convictions for crimes of incitement or glorification of terrorism, no problems have arisen in relation to legal coverage, despite the frequent criticism of the lack of clarity in these criminal offences.

Fifth, national security and even territorial integrity have been conceded by the European Court as legitimate reasons to justify the punishment of acts of incitement to terrorist violence when they occur in a context of conflict. The defence of order and the prevention of crime have also been acknowledged as legitimate justifications.[40]

Sixth, in judging whether the restrictions are 'necessary in a democratic society', the European Court holistically reviews the facts of the case, including both the content of the discourse and the context in which it occurred.[41] The problem is that the Court of Strasbourg has not provided a clear blueprint in relation to the degree of danger that justifies a sanction of this kind.[42] If we analyse cases in which the Court has adjudicated that there was a violation of the Convention we will see that in the majority of them, following a review of the content and context of the relevant speech, the Court concludes that there was no actual incitement to violence.[43] Additionally, when evaluating the need for the interference, the Court takes other factors

---

[38] Cfr. ECtHR Ceylan v. Turkey apl. n. 23556/94 (8.07.1999) § 34; and ECtHR Stomakhin v. Russia apl. 52273/07 (9.05.2018) § 86, 92.

[39] Cfr. ECtHR Zana v. Turkey apl. n. 69/1996/688/880 (25.11.1997) § 55; Ceylan v. Turkey apl. n. 23556/94 (8.07.1999), § 28; and Leroy v. France apl. 36109/03 (2.10.2008), § 37.

[40] Cfr. ECtHR Leroy v. France apl. 36109/03 (2.10.2008), § 40.

[41] The ECtHR Ceylan v. Turkey apl. n. 23556/94 (8.07.1999), § 32.III, sets: 'the Court must look at the interference in the light of the case as a whole, including the content of the impugned statements and the context in which they were made. In particular, it must determine whether the interference in issue was 'proportionate to the legitimate aims pursued' and whether the reasons adduced by the national authorities to justify it are "relevant and sufficient". In doing so, the Court has to satisfy itself that the national authorities applied standards which were in conformity with the principles embodied in Article 10 and, moreover, that they based themselves on an acceptable assessment of the relevant facts.'. Previously, cfr. ECtHR Zana v. Turkey apl. n. 69/1996/688/880 (25.11.1997), § 51.iii.

[42] In this sense, Giovanni Bonello, 'Freedom of expression and incitement to violence', in Josep Casadevall et al. (eds), *Freedom of expression: essays in honour of Nicolas Bratza, president of the European Court of Human Rights* (Wolf Legal Plublishers 2012), 351, has concluded: 'fails to distinguish sufficiently between dangerous and non-dangerous "incitement"'. Cfr. Loof (n. 1), in toto, and Rollnert Liern (n. 11), 239 y ss.

[43] Cfr. ECtHR Incal v. Turkey apl. n. 22678/93 (9.06.1998), § 50: 'Although the reference to "neighbourhood committees" appears unclear, those appeals cannot, however, if read in context, be taken as incitement to the use of violence, hostility or hatred between citizens'. Also, cfr. ECtHR Arslan v. Turkey apl. n. 23462/94 (8.07.1999), § 48; Gerger v. Turkey apl. n. 24919/94 (8.07.1999), § 50; Sürek and Özdemir v. Turkey apl. n. 23927/94 (8.07.1999), § 61; Savgin v. Turkey apl. n. 13304/03 (2.02.2010), § 45, and Dmitriyevsky v. Rusia apl. n. 42168/06 (3.10.2017), § 107.

into account, for example, if it is a political discourse, or the general interest,[44] and the type of penalty (its severity,[45] or whether it had been a preventive restriction[46]). Conversely, when the European Court perceives that, given its content and context, a speech can be perceived as a form of incitement to violence, albeit indirect, then it is generous in giving a large degree of discretion to countries, as previously stated, and consequently, the Court usually considers the measures that have been adopted as necessary.[47] If it were possible to view a pattern in this, the Court of Strasbourg at best assesses the ability or capacity to incite, but does not judge the specific causality between the speech and its probable outcome; that is to say, the greater or lesser probability and imminence of verifying the damage – the actual level of danger that arises.[48] This has been a controversial topic in the Court, where certain judges have claimed that in order to justify the need for restriction of such freedoms, it is necessary to evaluate whether there exists a sufficiently real and compelling danger,[49] and even that, in certain decisions – whilst it is true these are rather isolated – the Court itself appears to have set out the criteria for 'clear and present danger', concluding that the sanctions imposed ought to be deemed 'unnecessary' despite the violent

---

[44] Cfr. ECtHR Incal v. Turkey apl. n. 22678/93 (9.06.1998), § 54; Gerger v. Turkey apl. n. 24919/94 (8.07.1999), § 48; Arslan v. Turkey apl. n. 23462/94 (8.07.1999), § 46; Sürek and Özdemir v. Turkey apl. n. 23927/94 (8.07.1999), § 60; and Dmitriyevsky v. Rusia apl. n. 42168/06 (3.10.2017), § 95.

[45] Cfr. ECtHR Arslan v. Turkey apl. n. 23462/94 (8.07.1999), § 49; Gerger v. Turkey apl. n. 24919/94 (8.07.1999), § 51; Sürek and Özdemir v. Turkey apl. n. 23927/94 (8.07.1999), § 62.

[46] Cfr. ECtHR Incal v. Turkey apl. n. 22678/93 (9.06.1998), § 56 and Çetin and others v. Turkey apl. n. 40153/98 (13.02.2003), §§ 57 ss.

[47] Cfr. ECtHR Zana v. Turkey apl. n. 69/1996/688/880 (25.11.1997), §§ 59-62; and Sürek v. Turkey (n. 1 and n. 3) (8.07.1999). In the ECtHR Dmitriyevsky v. Rusia apl. n. 42168/06 (3.10.2017), § 99 the Court concludes: 'Another factor is whether the statements, fairly construed and seen in their immediate or wider context, *can be seen* as a direct or indirect call to violence or as a justification of violence, hatred or intolerance. The Court has held, in particular, that where such remarks incite violence against an individual, a public official or a sector of the population, the State enjoys a wider margin of appreciation when examining the need for an interference with freedom of expression'.

[48] Cfr. ECtHR Zana v. Turkey apl. n. 69/1996/688/880 (25.11.1997), § 60: 'had to be regarded *as likely to* exacerbate an already explosive situation in that region'. In this sense, ECtHR Sürek v. Turkey (n. 1) apl. n. 26682/95 (8.07.1999), § 62 was polemic because it concluded that the message had 'a clear intention to stigmatise the other side to the conflict by use of labels' and presupposed 'an appeal to bloody revenge by stirring up base emotions and hardening already embedded prejudices which have manifested themselves in deadly violence'; and the ECtHR Sürek v. Turkey (n. 3) apl. n. 24735/94 (8.07.1999), § 40: 'In such a context the content of the article *must be seen as capable of inciting* to further violence in the region'. Cfr. Rollnert Liern (n. 11), 25.

[49] In this sense, see the votes of Judge Palm and Judges Tulkens, Casadevall and Greve, and also Judge Bonello who claimed to incorporate the 'clear and present danger test' in the ECtHR Sürek v. Turkey (n. 1) apl. n. 26682/95 (8.07.1999). In a similar sense, see the votes in the ECtHR Gerger v. Turkey apl. n. 24919/94 (8.07.1999); Sürek and Özdemir v. Turkey apl. n. 23927/94 (8.07.1999); Ceylan v. Turkey apl. n. 23556/94 (8.07.1999); Arslan v. Turkey apl. n. 23462/94 (8.07.1999); and Sürek v. Turkey (n. 3) apl. n. 24735/94 (8.07.1999). And votes of Judges Sajó, Zagrebelsky and Tsotsoria to the ECtHR Féret v. Belgium apl. n. 15615/07 (16.07.2009). See also the critics of Judge Keller to the ECtHR Stomakhin v. Russia apl. 52273/07 (9.05.2018).

'tone' literally contained in the verbalisations being penalised.[50]

In cases where there was no direct provocation, merely language which glorified terrorism or made an apologia for its perpetrators, the evaluation of the context becomes even more important. Thus, the Court has granted Member States a large degree of discretion and, consequently, justifies conviction for these crimes even when there was no explicit incitement to violence.[51] As such, it has accepted that certain forms of identification with a terrorist group, in particular, the glorification of its acts or members, the denigration of its victims or the encouragement of financing such a group, may be criminally sanctioned without an indictment of the danger that arises in actuality.[52] As Jan-Peter Loof concludes, in light of this jurisprudence, 'the link between the publication and the potential consequences, however, does not need to be a strong or direct one, nor does the author have to show a clear intent to incite'.[53]

The US attitude, on the contrary, is very different. In its approach to provocative speech,[54] the US Supreme Court refers to the test of 'clear and present danger', alt-

---

[50] Cfr. ECtHR Gül and others v. Turkey apl. n. 4870/02 (8.06.2010), §§ 40-42, in which the Court concludes that: 'by shouting these slogans, the applicants did not advocate violence, injury or harm to any person. Furthermore, neither in the domestic court decisions nor in the observations of the Government is there any indication that there was a *clear and imminent danger* which required an interference such as the lengthy criminal prosecution faced by the applicants.'. Cfr. ECtHR Kiliç and Eren v. Turkey apl. n. 43807/07 (29.02.2012), §§ 28–29.

[51] Cfr. ECtHR Leroy v. France apl. 36109/03 (2.10.2008). Also see ECtHR Tasdemir v. Turkey apl. n. 38841/07 (23.02.2010); Kiliç and Eren v. Turkey apl. n. 43807/07 (29.02.2012), §§ 28–29; and Yavuz and Yaylali v. Turkey apl. n. 12606/11 (17.12.2013).

[52] Cfr. ECtHR Yavuz and Yaylali v. Turkey apl. n. 12606/11 (17.12.2013), § 51: 'La Cour relève que la propagande est souvent conçue comme une diffusion déterminée des informations à sens unique influençant la perception publique des événements, des personnes ou des enjeux. Le fait que les informations sont à sens unique n'est pas per se une raison pour limiter la liberté d'expression. Une restriction peut être prévue notamment pour empêcher l'endoctrinement terroriste des personnes et/ou des groupes susceptibles d'être influencés dont le but est de les faire agir et penser d'une manière voulue. Ainsi, la Cour accepte que certaines formes d'identification avec une organisation terroriste et surtout la glorification de cette dernière peuvent être considérées comme un soutient du terrorisme et incitation à la violence et la haine. De même, la Cour admet que la dissémination de messages d'éloge de l'auteur d'un attentat, le dénigrement des victimes, l'appel à financer des organisations terroristes ou d'autres comportements similaires peuvent constituer des actes d'incitation à la violence terroriste (voir paragraphes 24 et 26 ci-dessus). Dans ces circonstances, l'article 10 n'interdit pas en tant que telle toute restriction. Cependant, une telle restriction sera soumise à un examen le plus scrupuleux de la Cour (voir, mutatis mutandis, Association Ekin, précité, § 56)'.

[53] Loof (n. 1), p. 215.

[54] In other speeches the Supreme Court has designed other tests such us fighting words. Cfr. Chaplinsky v. New Hampshire, 315 U.S. 568 (1942), where the Court decided not to protect speeches which *inflict injury* and others which *tend to incite an immediate breach of peace*. This criteria has been changed later by the Supreme Court (Cohen v. California, 403 U.S. (1971), 15, and Lewis v. New Orleans, 415 U.S. (1974), 130. See also, Gregory v. Chicago, 394 U.S. (1969), 111; Garner v. Lousiana, 368 U.S. (1961), 368; and Terminello v. Chicago, 337 U.S. (1949), 1. And the Supreme Court has also concluded that it is possible to limit freedom of expression when there are *true threats*: when 'the speaker means to communicate a serious expression of an intent to commit an act of unlawful violence to a particular individual or group of individuals, see, *e. g.*, ibid. The speaker need not actually intend to carry out the

hough this has been refined over the course of time in an intriguing jurisprudence.[55] This test sprang from the pen of Judge O. W. Holmes in the Schenck v. United States sentencing,[56] and was gradually imposed on the 'bad tendency' test which originated from the English *common law*.[57] This was a jurisprudence that, in addition, was initially influenced by the risk to security that certain extremist speeches could represent during wartime – it took place during the First World War – which led to the Supreme Court's liberality in placing restrictions on the freedom of expression. Notwithstanding this, the particularly famous votes of Judges O. W. Holmes and L. Brandeis[58] continued to permeate throughout US judicial culture. Thus, in the case of Dennis v. United States,[59] the Court attempted to reach, as Sottiaux notes,[60] 'an equilibrium between freedom of expression and national security' during the Cold War, and applied the test of 'clear and present danger' although still with a degree of flexibility, taking into account two fundamental factors: the gravity of evil to be averted, and the probability that it could be verified.[61] A grave evil could justify

threat. Rather, a prohibition on true threats protects individuals from the fear of violence and the disruption that fear engenders, as well as from the possibility that the threatened violence will occur. *R. A. V., supra*, at 388. Intimidation in the constitutionally proscribable sense of the word is a type of true threat, where a speaker directs a threat to a person or group of persons with the intent of placing the victim in fear of bodily harm or death' (Virginia v. Black et al., 538 U.S. (2003), 343). See also, Watts. v. United States, 394 U.S. (1969), 750. Cfr. Frederik M. Lawrence, 'Violence-conducive speech: punishable verbal assault or protected political speech', in Michael Kretzmer and Peter Kershman Hazan (ed.), *Freedom of speech and incitement against democracy* (Kluwer Law International 2000), pp. 24 ss.; and Teresa Rodríguez Montañés, *Libertad de expresión, discurso extremo y delito* (Tirant lo Blanch 2011), 145 ss.

55 Cfr. Sottiaux (n. 31); Kretzmer and Kershman Hazan (ed.), *Freedom of speech and incitement against democracy* (Kluwer Law International 2000), 3–10; 11–31; 102–118; and Rodríguez Montañés (n. 54), 159 ss.

56 Schenck v. United States, 249 U.S. (1919), 47.

57 Cfr. Debs v. United States, 249 U.S. (1919), 211; Frohwerk v. United States, 249 U.S. (1919), 204; or, moreover, Abrams v. United States, 250 U.S. (1919), 616.

58 In this sense, see the votes of judges Holmes and Brandeis in Abrams v. United States, 250 U.S. (1919), 616: 'we should be eternally vigilant against attempts to check the expression of opinions that we loathe and believe to be fraught with death, unless they so imminently threaten immediate interference with the lawful and pressing purposes of the law that an immediate check is required to save the country.'. See also Gitlow v. People, 268 U.S. (1923), 652, where these judges concluded: 'Every idea is an incitement. [...] The only difference between the expression of an opinion and an incitement in the narrower sense is the speaker's enthusiasm for the result'. And, in Whitney v. California, 247 U.S. (1927), 357, 375, Judges Brandeis and Holmes define the test in this manner: 'no danger flowing from speech can be deemed clear and present unless the incidence of the evil apprehended is so imminent that it may befall before there is opportunity for full discussion'.

59 Dennis v. United States, 341 U.S. (1951), 494, 584. See also Stromberg v. California, 283 U.S. (1931), 359; DeJonge v. Oregon, 299 U.S. (1937), 353; and Herndon v. Lowry, 301 U.S. (1937), 242.

60 Sottiaux (n. 31), 665.

61 Sottiaux (n. 31), 662. Related to the application of the Judge L. Hand's test, as an alternative to the Holmes-Brandeis vision, Sottiaux has concluded that: 'Hand's approach was thus more speaker-centred, focussing less on probable consequences of the expression than Holmes' standard' (Sottiaux (n. 31), 665). See also Kretzmer and Kershman Hazan (n. 55), 11 ss.

criminal sanction of a discourse, even when the risk was not imminent. Subsequently, in Yates v. United States[62] the Court did not apply the test but annulled the conviction because the jury had based it on the distinction between 'advocacy of abstract doctrine' and 'advocacy of action', when, in the view of the Supreme Court, 'the essential distinction is that those to whom the advocacy is addressed must be urged to *do* something, now or in the future, rather than merely to *believe* in something'. Therefore, it was a criterion based more on the content of a message than on its dangerousness. It was in Brandenburg v. Ohio[63] that the Supreme Court, in a decision *per curiam*, expressed the current formulation of the test of 'clear and present danger', defining it as: 'the principle that the constitutional guarantees of free speech and free press do not permit a State to forbid or proscribe advocacy of the use of force or of law violation' except in the case of 'such advocacy is directed to inciting or producing imminent lawless action and is likely to incite or produce such action'. There are thus two factors to take into account when determining whether an intervention is legitimate: (1) The subjective intention to incite; (2) Whether the discourse is capable of imminently producing any illegal action.[64] Thus, this test, which combines subjective factors but also integrates prosecution of effective and imminent dangerousness, forms the nucleus of the proposal made by Judges O. W. Holmes and L. Brandeis.[65]

Furthermore, the US Supreme Court, as mentioned, has shown a 'clear willingness to prohibit speech when it is linked to a terrorist organization in a manner that supports its activity'.[66] Specifically, in the case of Holder v. Humanitarian Law Project, the Supreme Court accepted that advisory activity in international law and humanitarian aid could be sanctioned as a form of collaboration with terrorist organisations under the US Patriot Act, considering that it was not mere political discourse being sanctioned but rather a form of terrorist collaboration and, consequently, the higher interest of defending against terrorism came into play.[67] It thus avoided having to apply the more rigorous test that would have corresponded to understanding that the First Amendment was at stake.

In my view, when we encounter messages which incite terrorism, with the exception of those which can be clearly understood as material collaboration with terrorism, their prosecution should be conducted in consideration of the freedom of expression. This is clear when dealing with incitement to violence, either directly or

[62] Yates v. United States, 354 U.S. (1957), 298.

[63] Brandenburg v. Ohio, 395 U.S. (1969), 444. After, see Hess v. Indiana, 414 U.S. (1973), 105, 109.

[64] Cfr. Sottiaux (n. 31), 664. More in general, Larry Alexander, 'Incitement and freedom of speech', in Kretzmer and Kershman Hazan (eds), *Freedom of speech and incitement against democracy* (Kluwer Law International 2000), 105 ss.

[65] Alexander (n. 64), 105: 'the Court's decision represented a refinement of the Homes and Brandeis "clear and present danger" test'.

[66] Barak-Erez and Scharia (n. 9), 19.

[67] Cfr. Rodríguez Montañés (n. 54), 203 ss.

even indirectly through apologetic discourses or glorifying terrorist activities or their perpetrators. It is also clear when dealing with speeches which are offensive to victims of these attacks, although in these cases the rule of reference would no longer be to the dangerousness of the discourses, but to their abusive or injurious capacity. A supposed limit is that of indoctrination cases. This type of discourse, rather than being treated as a form of material collaboration, I believe should be considered a disguised provocation and, therefore, one should assess to what extent it poses a risk that such acts are committed, in accordance with the applicable rule, to judge the appropriateness of curtailment of the freedom of expression. In this regard, between the more lenient rule of the European Court of Human Rights, based on the dangerous capacity of the provocative nature or content of the message, and the more restrictive rule of the US Supreme Court of 'clear and present danger' in its current formulation, I consider that it would be preferable to opt for the latter, as will be explained below in more detail. Momentarily, I simply wish to highlight, in the words of Judge Bonello, that what is 'unacceptable is not incitement to violence, but the immediate capacity of words to beget actual violence'. [68] This is a notion which the US Supreme Court has managed to weave into its test, but which has not been incorporated in Europe, although this would be desirable. [69]

4. *The Internet and the Challenges for the Fight Against Terrorism*

One of the characteristics of the terrorist phenomenon of the twenty-first century is precisely its cross-boundary, global nature. [70] This is a trait which has made the Internet a fertile ground for conducting terrorist activities (that is, acts of cyberterrorism, the examination of which is beyond the scope of this chapter), and for the dissemination of messages, slogans and incitement to commit terrorist acts. [71] Most notably, it is concerning to see how terrorists can use the Internet to radicalise vulnerable groups of people in our society. At the same time, it is unclear what the best response is to this situation in which the Web nowadays is a source of radicalisa-

---

[68] Bonello (n. 42), 353.

[69] Cfr. Bonello (n. 42), 355, who concluded: 'The "immediate lawless action" doctrine, which never entered the Court's case law by the front door, here peeps indistinctly through a window'.

[70] Cfr. Loof (n. 1), 202, and Yael Ronen, 'Incitement to terrorist acts and international law' (2010) 23 *Leiden Journal of International Law* 645, 659 ss.

[71] In this sense, the European Commission's Proposal for a Directive (COM(2015) 625 final) recognises: 'Terrorist groups have demonstrated advanced skills in the use of the Internet and new communication technologies to disseminate propaganda, interact with potential recruits, share knowledge, plan and coordinate operations. The Internet and social media have notably offered new opportunities for radical and terrorist groups to target vulnerable audiences and thereby facilitate recruitment and/or self-radicalisation'. See also 164 (2005) United Nations Security Council.

tion[72] and it is debated whether repressive measures or censorship is the best method of confronting this problem.[73]

In any case, the debate remains open and, as we have seen, the legislation which punishes provocation and terrorist apologia has begun to specifically account for their extension into the digital sphere. However, from a substantive point of view, I agree with R. Bustos that the same legal principles ought to apply online 'as far as possible',[74] and the limitations to freedom of expression and the definition of punishable conduct must remain unchanged. What differs is the evaluation of the greater or lesser impact that these messages may have when disseminated via these technologies and the specific characteristics that arise in the enforcement of laws when regulating these media. This being the situation, in my view there are two features of Internet communication that constitute a challenge for legal response to acts of terrorist provocation that are conducted using these platforms.[75] On the one hand, a significant feature is the global and decentralised nature of the Web, which lacks borders and an epicentre of control. On the other hand, the Internet is a multifaceted medium: it allows interpersonal communication, whilst simultaneously being a medium of mass communication; it is a multidirectional method of communication, and may also be used for bilateral communication and to transmit any item which can be recorded (data, videos, photos …). In short, the Internet offers a dispersed and spontaneous medium of communication, where anonymity can be maintained and where it is relatively easy to duplicate content.

All of the above, from the perspective of a legal response, suggests, first of all, the need to draft international agreements in order to define prohibited behaviours and to coordinate responses. When a global phenomenon is at stake, it is difficult to be able to respond effectively without international action. However, at the same time, as we have been able to see, because the standards of protection of the freedom of expression are so disparate as is the notion of what may be considered terrorism, it has become a challenge to compose a harmonious response. Second, it is necessary to demarcate acts involving private communication, protected not only by freedom of expression but also by secrecy of communication, from cases of online dissemination

---

[72] Cfr. Rafael Bustos Gisbert, 'Libertad de expresión y control de la Red', in Miguel Revenga Sánchez (ed.), *Terrorismo y Derecho bajo la estela del 11 de septiembre* (Tirant lo Blanch 2014), 166; and Ezekiel Rediker, 'The incitement of terrorismo in the Internet: legal standards, enforcement, and the role of the European Union' (2015) 36 *Mich. J. Int'l L.* 321, 323 ss.

[73] Cfr. Tufyal Choudhury, 'The Terrorism Act 2006: Discouraging terrorism', in Ivan Hare and James Weinstein, *Extreme speech and democracy* (Oxford University Press 2009), 463–487, In this sense, see also Directive (EU) 2017/541 of the European Parliament and of the Council § 31.

[74] Cfr. Bustos Gisbert (n. 72), 164 and 170.

[75] Cfr. Germán Teruel Lozano, 'Perspectivas de los derechos fundamentales en la sociedad digital' (2016) 9 *Fundamentos. Cuadernos monográficos de teoría del estado, derecho público e historia constitucional* 215; Id., 'El Derecho ante el nuevo paradigma tecnológico de Internet', in Joaquín Sarrión Esteve et al. (ed.), *Estudios de investigación europea para jóvenes investigadores. Construyendo ciudadanía. Europa, crisis y oportunidades* (Comares 2015); and Bustos Gisbert (n. 72), 165 ss.

of messages, which, whilst not available to the entire world, must be considered public communication. This is without a doubt relevant to the justification of punishing provocation or incitement. Ultimately, the need to remove illicit content from the Internet and to identify its perpetrators requires international cooperation, as mentioned above, as well as direct collaboration with the service providers. It is difficult for States acting alone to effectively hand out verdicts if they cannot rely on the cooperation of Internet service providers, given that there isn't a centralised system of control. Hence, the European Clean IT initiative to collaborate with the technology industry in the fight against the spread of terrorist messages on the Internet [76] and the Proposal for a Regulation of the European Parliament and of the Council on preventing the dissemination of terrorist content online.[77] In this regard, I would like to emphasise the risks that the adoption of identification measures to end anonymity on the Internet [78] may entail, as well as the risk of private censorship as a consequence of controlling the content published by Internet users.[79]

With this in mind, with respect to crimes of incitement to terrorism on the Internet, I would conclude by reiterating the need to construct a global agreement on the matter, as has been accomplished in other domains,[80] in a manner which maintains a high standard of respect for the freedom of expression, because it is precisely the safeguarding of this freedom which ensures the effectiveness of the measures that are adopted. It is not by further repression that the objectives of the fight against terrorism will be achieved. In fact, we must avoid excessive criminalisation which may result in victimising radicals or marginalising debates by hiding them in the depths of the Web instead of bringing them to the surface so that they may be defeated with better arguments, in cooperation with the communities involved in them. At the same time, we must work to establish agreements on the design, architecture and coding of the Internet, and develop technical methods in collaboration with the digital industry to share and expunge the Internet of illicit messages and identify their authors, without compromising the open and plural nature of cyberspace.

---

[76] Cfr. Rediker (n. 72), 348 ss.

[77] Cfr. COM(2018) 640 final.

[78] Cfr. David Kaye, *Report on encryption, anonymity, and the human rights framework*, 22/05/2015.

[79] Cfr. Germán Teruel Lozano, 'Freedom of speech and new means of censorship in the digital era' [2014] 2 *Percorsi Costituzionali* 560; and Id., 'Libertades comunicativas y censura en el entorno tecnológico global' (2017) 12 *Revista de la Escuela Jacobea de Posgrado* 75.

[80] Cfr. Council of Europe Convention on Cybercrime, 23.11.2011.

5. *In Conclusion: A Lege Ferenda Proposal for an Offence of Incitement to Terrorism Compatible with the Highest Standards of Protection for the Freedom of Expression*

From necessity springs virtue. Thus, it has been possible to discuss throughout this chapter the need to bring about a synchronised response at an international level, and especially at the European level, towards conduct which leads to the provocation or the glorification of terrorism. However, at the same time, the inadequacies of the current international and European legislative framework have been made evident, as well as the desire to build within Europe a higher standard of protection for the freedom of expression than has been defined heretofore by the European Court of Human Rights, following the lead of the test designed by the US Supreme Court in Brandenburg v. Ohio. Although the recent European Directive has made indubitable progress, I consider it apt to set out more conclusively certain points that remain unresolved and may lead to distortions in their implementation by Member States. Hence, now, we modestly try to make a virtue of this need to address terrorist incitement by proposing a re-reading of the criminal classification propounded by the European Directive, ensuring that this adheres to the highest standard of protection of freedom of expression.

As such, when dealing with crimes of incitement or provocation to terrorism, it is necessary to look at the following factors. Firstly, the objective elements of the act, the conduct therein and the form of incitement (direct or indirect, explicit or implicit – depending on which is preferable) and the nature of its public exposure; secondly, the outcome (whether it is defined as a concrete/specific danger outcome, as proposed in this chapter); Thirdly, one is obliged to analyse the danger, understood as the likelihood that, as a consequence of the provocation, rooted in a dangerous outcome, a specific harmful event will take place (which will henceforth be referred to as a 'feared harmful outcome'); Finally, we address the subjective element of the crime (*mens rea*).[81]

In this sense, although there may be suspicions in the punishment of apologias,[82]

---

[81] Cfr. UN Secretary-General's report on the protection of human rights and fundamental freedoms while countering terrorism – 28/08/2008 – (UN Doc. 6/63/337), § 62, which states: 'for States to comply with international protections of freedom of expression, laws should only allow for the criminal prosecution of direct incitement to terrorism, that is, speech that directly encourages the commission of a crime, is intended to result in criminal action and is likely to result in criminal action'. Or the Explanatory report to the Council of Europe Convention on the prevention of terrorism, §§ 99–100.

[82] Cfr. UN Secretary-General's report on the protection of human rights and fundamental freedoms while countering terrorism – 28/08/2008 – (UN Doc. 6/63/337), § 61: 'Incitement must be separated from glorification. If the first may be legally prohibited, the second may not. In the context of the fight against terrorism a troubling trend has been the proscription of the glorification of terrorism, involving statements which may not go so far as to incite or promote the commission of terrorist acts, but nevertheless applaud past acts. While such statements might offend the sensitivities of individual persons and

for my part I understand that any form of provocation must be punishable regardless of whether it has been carried out in a manner which is, to any degree, direct or explicit. As E. Barendt indicates, '[a]ny speech which is understood by its audience as inciting the use of force or law violation might be held a criminal offence, provided the Brandenburg criteria are satisfied'.[83] And as will be seen, the crux of criminal sanction lies in the adequate evaluation of dangerousness, accompanied by a provocative intention, and not in the manner in which the specific discourse is transmitted.[84] Thus, not only must directly provocative expressions be penalised, so too must indirect or covert forms of apologia or glorification of terrorist acts or their perpetrators. In this way, the position of the European Directive can be adopted here, although its typical wording can be improved; in particular, the difference between what is advocated, which is not necessarily a terrorist crime in itself (for example, the apologia of its perpetrators or other criminal acts), and the feared harmful outcome (crimes of terrorism).

Similarly, the requirement standard for public exposure should be adequately outlined, especially taking into account the specificities presented by online dissemination where publicly open communications are intermingled with those which are private but may reach a large audience. Something which may also take place is discourse in a public place but in front of a relatively limited audience. Therefore, it is necessary to detail what is meant specifically by 'public' as a general requisite, taking into account, on the one hand, the channel or location of dissemination (whether it is a private channel or location or whether it is open to an undefined public), and on the other hand, the potential audience which may have received the message.[85] All of this must be regardless of whether the message is disseminated in the analogue or digital world. In this sense, I believe that a suitable definition of the crime must cover

---

society, particularly the victims of terrorist acts, it is important that vague terms of uncertain scope such as 'glorifying' or 'promoting' terrorism not be used when restricting expression. Incitement can be understood as a direct call to engage in terrorism, with the intention that this will promote terrorism, and in a context in which the call is directly causally responsible for increasing the actual likelihood of a terrorist act occurring. In their fight against terrorism and in order to respect the freedom of expression, States should be careful to differentiate the two notions.'

[83] Eric Barendt, 'Incitement to, and glorification of, terrorism', in Ivan Hare and James Weinstein (eds), *Extreme speech and democracy* (Oxford University Press 2009), 455.

[84] Cfr. Ronen (n. 70), 665: 'The other elements of the offence, in particular the probability of harm test and the *mens rea*, can serve as safeguards against such abuse, without rendering the entire project ineffectual'. See also Rediker (n. 72), 346.

[85] Cfr. Directive (EU) 2017/541 of the European Parliament and Council of 15 March 2017, art. 5, and the Explanatory Report to the Council of Europe Convention on the prevention of terrorism, which concludes: 'The term "to the public" makes it clear that private communications fall outside the scope of this provision' (§ 103); 'In order to make a message available to the public, a variety of means and techniques may be used. For instance, printed publications or speeches delivered at places accessible to others, the use of mass media or electronic facilities, in particular the Internet, which provides for the dissemination of messages by e-mail or for possibilities such as the exchange of materials in chat rooms, newsgroups or discussion fora' (§ 104). As Ronen (70), p. 667, says: 'The determination whether a specific speech was 'public' or 'private' should take into account the totality of circumstances, such as the number of members of the public involved, and the openness and accessibility of the place or speech'.

messages which are disseminated through channels or in public spaces that have been made accessible to an indeterminate number of people, but also messages that have been distributed in private channels or spaces if the recipients constitute a large group. In the latter case – if dealing with private communication – one must take into account the actual recipients, rather than the potential recipients as when disseminated via a public medium or space. Then, it will be the judge who assesses the specific circumstances in relation to the risk that is engendered. In this sense, I doubt that the Legislator would foresee aggravating factors in the case that the message is disseminated via a medium which makes it accessible to a large number of people, given that to a considerable extent is already inherent in the definition of basic conduct. What appears relevant in my view, as is done in the European Directive, is that specific laws are put in place in order that judges may order the blocking or filtering of certain online messages, requiring in this case collaboration with service providers.[86]

In any case, as mentioned, the crux of the offence lies in the definition of dangerousness. Consequently, one must define the feared harmful outcome, which can be none other than the enactment of terrorist crimes.[87] According to what has been examined, messages may lead to incitement in various forms, but it is necessary to clarify that it is the risk of incitement to terrorist activities being carried out that is at stake. In short, the public dissemination of such messages *may* persuade others to commit terrorism offences as defined by national laws which follow the European guidelines that have unified the issue. However, the key in this is dangerousness, understood in terms of probability – which would also add the requirement of imminence – that the outcome we wish to prevent (terrorist crimes) occurs. That is why I have emphasised the term 'may' previously, since it is necessary to give it a standard meaning.

At this point, the European Directive and the Europe Convention go hand in hand. In both cases, as we have seen, the legal precepts require a danger being created that terrorist acts are committed, but without clarifying whether it is a specific danger or the potential capacity of the act itself. Be that as it may, this particular danger or capacity should be assessed in response to various circumstances: the nature of the author and the recipients of the message, the context, etc.[88] Something that, as stated, excludes the conception of these crimes as abstract dangers. This would adequately respond to the requirements of the case law of the European Court of Human Rights, which, as has also been discussed, has justified interference with the freedom of expression in the face of incitement to terrorism whenever a provocative capacity

---

[86] See also the Proposal for a Regulation of the European Parliament and of the Council on preventing the dissemination of terrorist content online, 12.09.2018 (COM(2018) 640 final).

[87] Cfr. Ronen (n. 70), 661 ss.

[88] Cfr. Cfr. Explanatory report to the Council of Europe Convention on the prevention of terrorism, 16/05/2005, § 100, and Directive (EU) 2017/541 of the European Parliament and of the Council, § 10.

has been established. But, in light of what has been analysed in this chapter, is this criterion sufficient to satisfy the highest standard of protection as defined by the US Supreme Court in Brandenburg?

In my judgement, it is not. The interpretation of the phrase 'likely to incite or produce unlawful action' is key. In this respect, I consider that such an interpretation, as has been applied by the US Supreme Court, requires that it be verified that the message in question is directly responsible for creating a clear and imminent risk that terrorist acts may occur. It must be proven, taking into account the specific circumstances of the case, that the likelihood of such acts being committed as a consequence of the message has increased. As the UN Secretary-General has pointed out, [89] terrorist provocation can only be punished when 'it is directly causally responsible for increasing the current likelihood of a terrorist act occurring'. Therefore, it will be necessary to prove that the dissemination of the message has been a relevant element for the generation of the risk or dangerous situation (although it has not been the exclusive factor). But, in addition, this has to be 'imminent', with a minimal delay in time. Hence, as the Johannesburg principles declare, it is necessary to prove that 'there is a direct and immediate connection between the verbalisation and the likelihood of such violence'. [90]

Only in this manner can the assessment of dangerousness be given true consistency. In trying these crimes it is necessary to assess complex social phenomena that can be triggered as a result of the dissemination of a message, which is impossible to judge in the medium or long term. So much so that, if the danger is remote, the judges would have to base their judgment more on politico-social assumptions than on a real evaluation of danger, and would end up making a verdict based on how the speech 'sounds' to them, and whether it seems provocative or incendiary to a degree but without a factual basis that proves its actual dangerousness. Likewise, it should be borne in mind that this type of crime promotes criminal intervention based on the danger that other people may carry out certain harmful acts and not on the damage that in itself generates the dissemination of those messages. Can we hold the person who disseminates a message responsible for something which, over time, others may do? In all honesty, I find it very difficult to apportion blame to provocative conduct that generates risks which are spread out over time. That is why, however serious the evil that we wish to avoid, I believe that the concurrence of both requirements (high probability and imminence) cannot be dismissed when penalising this type of provocative behaviour. [91]

This, translated into a specific configuration of crime, requires designating it as a

---

[89] UN Secretary-General's report on the protection of human rights and fundamental freedoms while countering terrorism – 28/08/2008 – (UN Doc. 6/63/337), § 61.

[90] Johannesburg Principles on national security, freedom of expression and access to information (1995), art. 19.

[91] Cfr. Barendt (n. 83), 461.

specific or concrete danger in which, upon application, the judges must assess all the circumstances of the case (the content of the message, means of dissemination, audience, context ...) [92] to prove that as a consequence of the dissemination of the provocative message, a dangerous situation has been created that allows us to observe that it is highly probable and imminent that third parties commit terrorist offences. What is not necessary, logically, is to verify the terrorist acts themselves. The crime is one of risk.

From a subjective perspective (*mens rea*) there must be an intention to incite, even if the message was mere apologia. In other words, in order to punish this type of conduct, it must be proven that the author who spreads the message had the intention of provoking others to commit terrorist crimes. [93] However, what I do not believe that it is necessary to add in these cases is the malice that is characteristic of terrorist offences insofar as they are not recognised as terrorist offences in the strictest sense.

Contrary to the argument of this chapter will be opposed grounds of efficacy, and the excessive restriction of its punitive scope, making criminalisation an unhelpful tool for the preventative fight against terrorism. [94] Faced with such considerations we must be aware that the clear recognition of freedom of expression certainly involves risks but we must have confidence in the maturity of our societies. And it is precisely this confidence which leads us to understand that when the risk is not imminent and the danger is distant, then our response must be "more" and "better" discourse – policies that allow us to fight against speech corrupting our society – rather than repression (and much less criminal punishment). In fact, as noted above, the censorship of this type of discourse may have contraindications and its effectiveness is not proven; it can submerge the spaces of radicalisation of terrorists in the darkness of the Internet and, especially when we refer to cases linked to discourses of religious extremism, it may be the communities themselves that work together to reject extremist discourse. [95] In some cases, it can even generate attraction towards the forbidden and victimise those who are punished for spreading radical messages. In addition, as Enric Barendet has recognised, among other arguments opposing these types of measures, we must remember that 'to extend the scope of the criminal law by proscribing speech encouraging terrorism is dangerous', for the reason that 'it allows the government to prosecute extreme political speech it dislikes, perhaps for very good reason,

[92] Cfr. Directive (EU) 2017/541 of the European Parliament and of the Council § 10.

[93] Cfr. Directive (EU) 2017/541 of the European Parliament and of the Council § 17; the Explanatory Report to the Council of Europe Convention on the prevention of terrorism, 16/05/2005, § 99; the UN Secretary-General's report on the protection of human rights and fundamental freedoms while countering terrorism – 28/08/2008 – (UN Doc. 6/63/337), § 61 and the OSCE/COE Expert workshop and office for democratic institution and human rights.

[94] For example, cfr. Ronen (n. 70), 668.

[95] Cfr. Choudhury (n. 73), 463–487 and, in the same book, Savage y Liht, 'Radical religious speech: The ingredients of a binary world view', 488–507. Also see Rediker (n. 72), 323 ss.; and the Directive (EU) 2017/541 of the European Parliament and of the Council § 31.

while not intervening in other circumstances where it is more sympathetic to the speech', moreover a 'further reason for that is the Terrorist Act offense may well exercise some "chilling effect" on freedom of political speech which the government accepts is not caught by the new law'. [96]

In this manner, in an attempt to redefine the criminal classification proposed by the European Directive in accordance with a high standard of recognition of freedom of expression, I would propose the following formulation that could be used by the Member States when implementing European regulations:

> 'Those who directly or indirectly and regardless of the medium used, intentionally incite publicly or disseminate among a large number of people messages to incite terrorist offences [typified in Articles x], generating [a climate of hostility that represents] a clear and present danger that these offences are committed will be punished with the penalty of [...]'.

Finally, as previously mentioned, in order to guarantee the effectiveness of the fight against terrorism, this crime would have to be accompanied by other measures of police cooperation and, above all, the development of mechanisms to remove illicit content from the Internet. [97] Additionally, we must also create instruments to prevent radicalisation on the Internet and collaborate with the most vulnerable groups and communities in our societies. [98]

---

[96] Barendt (n. 83), 453.

[97] Rediker (n. 72), 348–351.

[98] Cfr. Opinion of the European and Social Committee on the 'Proposal for a directive of the European Parliament and of the Council on combating terrorism and replacing Council Framework Decision 2002/475/JHA on combating terrorism' (2016/C 177/09), § 1.6: 'The Committee considers that tools to prevent radicalisation must be developed as part of a broader programme which factors in the social, economic, cultural, religious and political causes of the spread of this type of threat, and that they must be coordinated with action to combat and punish terrorism. However, radicalisation does not automatically mean predisposition or integration to violence. Prevention policies and programmes must target individuals and groups most predisposed to use violence for the purpose of terrorism. The role of civil society is crucial in dealing with the conditions which Foster radicalisation and the predisposition to use violence'. See also the European Commission Proposal for a Regulation of the European Parliament and of the Council on preventing the dissemination of terrorist content online, 12/09/2018 (COM(2018) 640 final).

Parameters towards a Fundamental Right of Accessing the Internet and Its Restrictions: The Case of Terrorism

Cláudio de Oliveira Santos Colnago

SUMMARY: 1. Introduction. – 2. The Lessig Theory: Law, Norms, Markets and Architecture. – 3. Internet Access as a Human Right: Symbolism and Scope of Protection. – 4. Access Restriction and Terrorism: Concrete Cases and Real Issues. – 5. Conclusion.

1. *Introduction*

This chapter intends to address the following problem: how to determine the proper parameters for limiting a fundamental right to access the Internet? If it is true that Internet access may be considered a human right (due to technology evolution and all the effects that it brings to individuals and society as a whole), it is also feasible to infer that such a right should not be interpreted in an absolute way.

Therefore, it would be natural to allow some sort of limitations or restrictions to this recently developed human right, considering that a basic parameter for interpreting all sorts of human rights is that none of them is absolute. Moreover, every single fundamental position may have to give way to a different one, in order to strike a proper balance in concrete situations. However, these limitations cannot be stablished in an arbitrary way, but must satisfy minimal legal and constitutional requirements or standards in order to be considered admissible from a human rights perspective, duly developed in an argumentative way in each case. In order to verify whether limitations to human rights are considered to be valid, one criterion that has been used by scholars and legal actors is the proportionality technique, which proposes a way to rationally balance different human rights, depending on the facts.

The research will focus on the question regarding which variables may be applied to the restriction of access to the Internet and how these parameters articulate with the growing problem of terrorism in the digital age. Thus, the chapter will address matters from different perspectives, from the lawfulness of restricting access to someone who is serving time for terrorism, to proper strategies that may be combined with access limitation in order to fight such hideous crimes, without criminalizing innocent behaviour.

Since Internet regulation theory may benefit from the theoretical model created by Lawrence Lessig (the four constraints theory, first articulated in 'Code and Other Laws of Cyberspace' and then strengthened in 'Code: Version 2.0', which are: Law,

Norms, Market and Architecture), this author will be our base-theory to be used alongside the proportionality adjudication technique, in order to provide a robust proposition in answer to the main question elected as the research focus.

2. *The Lessig Theory: Law, Norms, Markets and Architecture*

Certainly many aspects may influence human behaviour: from weather conditions to chemical or psychological factors or even cultural and ideological elements, what is certain is that human complexity cannot be reduced in an absolute way to a few invariable factors. Therefore, we may say, even paradoxically, that there is no absolute certainty regarding the human phenomenon, even though this condition should not stop us from searching for an answer, even if it is a transitory one, always subject to possible refutations. This is the great mark of scientific statement: the possibility of being tested in an intersubjective way, as in an attempt to disprove them. [1] It is in this context of seeking more objectivity on human behaviour that we may insert the theme of restraints on individual freedom or "forces" of regulation on the work of Lawrence Lessig.

With no intention of excluding other factors that may influence human behaviour, Lessig identifies four kinds of restraints that may be present in a certain society: Law, Norms, Market and Architecture. Law regulates through the public force – if one doesn't behave according to its mandate, the government may force someone to do so (with due process). Law, in the model conceived by Lessig, refers to the whole set of legal rules stablished by the government. [2] Acting in a different way are Norms, which function as a diffuse force – a community may force someone to act in a certain way based solely on others' expectations regarding an individual and its desire for them to "fit in" (i.e., a smoking habit may be considered something foolish or a natural habit, depending on the group). As pointed out by Greenleaf, norms '... cause us to frown on racist jokes or sexist language, to tell the truth about our age where concessions might be available, and to observe other conventions both because we have been brought up to feel guilty if we act otherwise', in addition to the fear of being rejected by a specific group. And he proceeds by explaining that 'Norms also aid the observance of the sanctions of law by making us guilty about breaking laws even if the likelihood of enforcement is next to nil'. [3]

We may consider that both Law and Norms have in common the fact that they

---

[1] Karl Raimund Popper, *A lógica da pesquisa científica*, Trad. Leonidas Hegenberg and Octanny Silveira da Motta, 16 (São Paulo: Cultrix, 2008) 42, 46.

[2] Ronaldo Lemos, *Direito, tecnologia e cultura* (Rio de Janeiro: Editora FGV, 2005) 21.

[3] Graham Greenleaf, 'An Endnote on Regulating Cyberspace: Architecture vs Law?' (1998) *University of New South Wales Law Journal*, Vol. 21, Number 2 'Electronic Commerce: Legal Issues for the Information Age'. Available at http://papers.ssrn.com/sol3/papers.cfm?abstract_id=2188160.

work with the basic concept of undesired consequences – institutionalized by the government with the Law, and totally disperse when it comes to Norms. The Market constrains an individual's behaviour through price – something that is cheap is prone to be done, and what is expensive has a tendency to have restricted access. As well put by Leonardi, the Market restraints exist due to an elaborate structure of statutes and norms that define what can be bought and sold and how this may be accomplished. [4]

Architecture, in its own way, regulates by simply putting barriers and paths in someone's way – think how we tend to reduce a car's speed in a street full of potholes, or even how we are constrained to exercise ourselves in a building where there are no elevators. As explained by Lessig: 'That I cannot see through walls is a constraint of my ability to snoop', 'That I cannot read your mind is a constraint on my ability to know whether you are telling me the truth', 'That I cannot lift large objects is a constraint on my ability to steal'. And he concludes: 'These features of the world – whether made, or found – restrict and enable in a way that directs or affects behavior. They are features of this world's architecture, and they, in this sense, regulate'. [5]

When transported to the Internet, the architecture constraint is dominant, since everything we do online is dependent on the code by which applications are programmed. The code itself, though, cannot be developed in an arbitrary way, as we pointed out in an earlier work: 'The code, that is usually programmed by ISPs [Internet Service Providers] according to their own ideology and beliefs, should comply with fundamental rights, in a way that these regulate the code – and not the other way around'. [6]

This innovative approach to human behaviour has been widely used as a base theory for legal scholars around the world [7] and may help us understand the different aspects of Internet regulation. On the other hand, we must stress that this model is applicable not only to Internet issues, but to almost every aspect of regulating one's conduct. [8] As described by Lessig: [9]

---

4 Marcel Leonardi, *Tutela e privacidade na Internet* (São Paulo: Saraiva, 2012), 161.

5 Lawrence Lessig, 'The New Chicago School' (1998A) *The Journal of Legal Studies*, Vol. XXVII, June, 663.

6 Cláudio de Oliveira Santos Colnago, The Right to be Forgotten and the Duty to Implement Oblivion: A Challenge to Both "Old" and "New" Media', Paper presented at the IX World Congress of Constitutional Law, Oslo, Norway, 16–20 June 2014. Available at https://www.jus.uio.no/english/research/news-and-events/events/conferences/2014/wccl-cmdc/wccl/papers/ws14/w14-colnago.pdf.

7 Giovanna de Minico, 'Internet e le sue fonti' (2013) *Osservatorio sulle fonti*, Fasc. 2/2013. Available at www.osservatoriosullefonti.it. Vasileios Karagiannopoulos, *China and the Internet: Expanding on Lessig's Regulation Nightmares* (2012) Vol. 9. Available at http://script-ed.org/?p=478.

8 Ronaldo Lemos, *Direito, tecnologia e cultura* (Rio de Janeiro: Editora FGV, 2005), 21.

9 Lawrence Lessig, 'The Law of the Horse: What Cyberlaw Might Teach' (1999) *Harvard Law Review*, Vol. 113, 546.

> The threats to values implicit in the law – threats raised by changes in the architecture of code – are just particular examples of a more general point: that more than law alone enables legal values and law alone cannot guarantee them. If our objective is a world constituted by these values, then it is as much these other regulators – code, but also norms and the market – that must be addressed. Cyberspace makes plain not just how this interaction takes place, but also the urgency of understanding how to affect it.

Even though these different restraints do not regulate human conduct with the same intensity, we may think about a combined analysis of the restraints, or the substitution of one for another, in order to achieve a proper public goal. [10] There is no hierarchy on these restraints, even though it would be proper to consider that some of them tend to be more effective (i.e. architecture) and others tend to be more democratic (i.e. law in current western societies). Lessig's approach also considers two different kinds of regulation – direct and indirect. In the former regulation is directly applicable to the targeted individual, in the latter the restraint focuses on another restraint that, in its turn, will be effective in achieving the actual regulation goal. Just think of the numerous cases of tax withholding by companies concerning their employees' income.

Regarding this subject, Mayer-Schoenberger points out that indirect regulation is much less transparent and, therefore, less prone to accountability, unlike direct regulation. [11] Contemporary regulation, consequently, should consist of a combination of both direct and indirect elements, in a holistic approach. [12] So, the proper form of regulation limiting human liberty should always take into account the option that is more inclined to achieve the goals set by public interest, as long as it is compatible with fundamental constitutional values.

This brief introduction to Lessig's regulation model was necessary as a contextualization tool, since Internet access is a multi-level phenomenon that will depend and be conditioned by the different restraints that may affect one's ability to be part of the Net. The main approach in this chapter is the qualification of Internet access as a human right and the proper restrictions that may be stablished as legal restraints to it. The other restraints on human behaviour, though, play a fundamental role in the justification of a legal obstacle to access the Net and may contribute to deciding whether some restrictions will in fact pass the proportionality test.

---

10 Lawrence Lessig, 'The New Chicago School' (1998A) *The Journal of Legal Studies*, Vol. XXVII, June, 664.

11 Viktor Mayer-Schoenberger, 'Demystifying Lessig' (2008) *Wisconsin Law Review*, Vol. 4, 718.

12 Ian Brown and Christopher T. Marsden, *Regulating Code: Good Governance and Better Regulation in the Information Age* (Cambridge, MA: MIT Press, 2013) 2435.

3. *Internet Access as a Human Right: Symbolism and Scope of Protection*

A chapter that proposes to address the Internet as a human right and its conflict with the need for security against terrorism could not be fully developed without referring to the immensely relevant report presented by the United Nation's Special Rapporteur on the promotion and protection of the right to freedom of opinion and expression, Frank La Rue, on the U.N. General's Assembly of 16 May 2011. In this document, La Rue [13] stated:

> Unlike any other medium, the Internet enables individuals to seek, receive and impart information and ideas of all kinds instantaneously and inexpensively across national borders. By vastly expanding the capacity of individuals to enjoy their right to freedom of opinion and expression, which is an 'enabler' of other human rights, the Internet boosts economic, social and political development, and contributes to the progress of humankind as a whole.

No one would ever discuss the importance of Internet access in the everyday life of the 21st century, since it is present in almost every aspect of society, from public services to elections. The generality of this common sense statement may produce an almost automatic agreement regarding its merit, whilst recognizing that Internet access as a human right does not solve all the issues regarding its restriction. It is relevant to stress, on the other hand, that we also tend to perceive more benefits than downsides in the consideration of a human right to access. The mere vocation of the Internet to be an instrument against absolute government power, as stated by Frosini, [14] could well be considered as a strong argument for considering it a human right. One must remember, though, that if the Internet presents itself as a mechanism that favours putting the government in check, it can also be adapted in order to favour unlimited power and dictatorships. The Internet is a plastic reality and this characteristic must not be forgotten.

As pointed out by De Hert and Kloza, '… before such a new right to freely use the Internet is recognised, one should take into account what is already protected and how'. [15] Emphasizing the point, we may refer to the following excerpt of an earlier work of ours:

---

[13] Frank La Rue, 'Report of the Special Rapporteur on the promotion and protection of the right to freedom of opinion and expression'. United Nations, 2011. Available at http://www2.ohchr.org/english/bodies/hrcouncil/docs/17session/A.HRC.17.27_en.pdf.

[14] Tommaso Edoardo Frosini, 'L'accesso a Internet quale diritto fondamentale', in Pollicino, Bertolini *et al.* (org.), *Internet: regole e tutela dei diritti fondamentali* (Milan: Università Commerciale Luigi Bocconi, 2013) 36–42.

[15] P. De Hert and D. Kloza, 'Internet (Access) as a New Fundamental Right. Inflating the Current Rights Framework?' (2012) *European Journal of Law and Technology*, Vol. 3, No. 3.

> Therefore, we may say that the Internet has played a major role on strengthening the core value that guides the application of human rights: the human dignity. The act of giving individuals a tool for developing their own ideas and sustaining their opinions without previous filters represents a major role on the recognition of persons as human beings, whose dignity is not any different from any other fellow human. [16]

Hence, the acceptance of Internet access as a human right plays a symbolic role, since it may be an initial approach to trigger proper public policies in order to expand its reach and protect individuals from arbitrary measures, taken both by the government and by private entities, which may exclude one's individual freedom to be on the Net. However, considering it as a human right attracts the well stablished dogmatic structures conceived by legal scholars in order to define what is protected and what is not. This includes defining its scope of protection, its essential content, the criteria for stablishing proper limitations and the proportionality test.

Approaching the human right's scope of protection is to identify the facts and situations that are effectively protected by that fundamental position. The delimitation of the right's scope is something usually done at the same time as the definition of the proper limitations to which it is subject. Thus, defining the scope of protection to the human right of accessing the Internet may lead us to consider that there is a basic safeguard against arbitrary and/or unreasonable restrictions on being part of the Net – that may be enacted both against governments and private entities (such as Internet providers, for example). Moreover, such a consideration also fuels the creation of public policies in order to reduce the huge gap known as "digital divide". [17] Since there is not a specific text providing the right of access, for it is derived from other human rights (an "implicit" right), the burden of developing its scope must be undertaken with extreme caution and be directed towards its connection with the rights at stake.

It is certain that the usual broad way that human rights are referred to in international treaties has a clear goal of including, abstractly, all individuals. However, this aspect should not lead to an absolute conception of human rights, since such an idea has never been accepted amongst the international community. Take the 1789 Universal Declaration of Rights of Man and of the Citizen, the fourth article of which article already conceived the possibility of limiting (even if exceptionally) human rights by government action:

---

[16] Cláudio de Oliveira Santos Colnago, 'Freedom of Expression and Internet: Should Judges Apply a Preferred Position Doctrine to Cases Involving the Internet?' Paper presented on the IX World Congress of Constitutional Law, Oslo, Norway, 16–20 June 2014. Available at http://www.jus.uio.no/english/research/news-and-events/events/conferences/2014/wccl-cmdc/wccl/papers/ws8/w8-colnago.pdf.

[17] From a global perspective, by the end of 2018 around 40 percent of the world's population was online. One of the world's challenges is to turn Internet access "universal", accessible to basically anyone. Available at http://www.internetlivestats.com/internet-users/.

> Art. 4th. Liberty consists of doing anything which does not harm others: thus, the exercise of the natural rights of each man has only those borders which assure other members of the society the enjoyment of these same rights. These borders can be determined only by the law.

Hence, the practical application of broad and generic legal references to human rights reserves innumerable difficulties in establishing its scope of protection and its limits, which should be initially oriented by the aforementioned premise – one cannot conceive any human right position as absolute, since it depends on its concrete interweaving with other fundamental human rights. However, human rights should not have limitations imposed that are so burdensome as to drain out their essential content. From the human rights perspective, limitations are natural, but should follow a proper balance to be construed according to concrete parameters. This is the point at which the proportionality technique gains a proper space in the human rights phenomenon.

As stated by Sweet and Mathews, in a comprehensive study[18] regarding the increase in proportionality adjudication as a global technique regarding human rights, 'Over the past half-century, most of the world's most powerful high courts have adopted PA [Proportionality Adjudication] to deal with the most politically salient, and potentially controversial, issues to which they could expect to be exposed.' According to what has already been stressed in an earlier paper of ours, 'The proportionality technique has been applied on every major constitutional culture for years, and has in its favour a standardizing effect on the different constitutional cultures'.[19]

Proportionality adjudication consists of a three to four step verification regarding a restriction of a human right, which is strictly scrutinized regarding its form, goal and effects. The growth in the use of this technique as a tool to solve human rights cases may bring with it a threat to the rights themselves, depending on how the instrument

---

[18] Alec Stone Sweet and Jud Mathews, 'Proportionality Balancing and Global Constitutionalism' (2008) *Faculty Scholarship Serie,* Paper 14 http://digitalcommons.law.yale.edu/fss_papers/14.

[19] Cláudio de Oliveira Santos Colnago (2014), 'The Right to be Forgotten and the Duty to Implement Oblivion: A Challenge to Both "Old" and "New" Media', Paper presented on the IX World Congress of Constitutional Law, Oslo, Norway, 16–20 June, available at https://www.jus.uio.no/english/research/news-and-events/events/conferences/2014/wccl-cmdc/wccl/papers/ws14/w14-colnago.pdf. As noted by Bernhard Schlink, 'Constitutional cultures with a doctrinal tradition will progressively be transformed in the direction of a culture of case law. The often-praised asset of proportionality analysis is its flexibility; from case to case, facts may be assessed differently and rights and interests weighed and balanced differently. The case-specific configuration of facts, interests and rights becomes more important and more significant than the doctrine that surrounds the case. Judges become more interested in finding the proportional solution for the case than in a decision that fits into established doctrine or helps to modify and refine it. On the other hand, the principle of proportionality has a certain structuring quality and potency that introduces a minimal doctrinal element into constitutional cultures with a case-law tradition'. (Bernhard Schlink, 'Proportionality in Constitutional Law: Why Everywhere but Here?' (2012) *Duke Journal of Comparative & International Law,* Vol. 22. Available at http://scholarship.law.duke.edu/cgi/viewcontent.cgi?article=1290&context=djcil).

is applied – its misuse may weaken human rights, instead of strengthening them.[20] This is why the application of the technique must follow the strict and serious argumentative path described, among other, by Sweet and Mathews:[21]

> 'In the paradigmatic situation, PA [Proportionality Adjudication] is triggered once a *prima facie* case has been made to the effect that a right has been infringed by a government measure. In its fully developed form, the analysis involves four steps, each involving a test. First, in the "legitimacy" stage, the judge confirms that the government is constitutionally-authorized to take such a measure. Put differently, if the purpose of the government's measure is not a constitutionally legitimate one, then it violates a higher norm (the right being pleaded). The second phase – "suitability" – is devoted to judicial verification that, with respect to the act in question, the means adopted by the government are rationally related to stated policy objectives. The third step – "necessity"– has more bite. The core of necessity analysis is the deployment of a "least-restrictive means" (LRM) test: the judge ensures that the measure does not curtail the right any more than is necessary for the government to achieve its stated goals. PA is a balancing framework: if the government's measure fails on suitability or necessity, the act is per se disproportionate; it is outweighed by the pleaded right and therefore unconstitutional. The last stage, "balancing in the strict sense," is also known as "proportionality in the narrow sense." If the measure under review passes the first three tests, the judge proceeds to balancing *stricto senso*. In the balancing phase, the judge weighs the benefits of the act – which has already been determined to have been "narrowly tailored," in American parlance – against the costs incurred by infringement of the right, in order to determine which "constitutional value" shall prevail, in light of the respective importance of the values in tension, given the facts'.

The proportionality technique may not be an infallible way of protecting human rights development, but it tends to be a criterion to be used globally in order to accommodate the different perspectives regarding such an intricate matter. Its application, though, should not be the end, but the mere beginning of the argument. This is due to the fact that the steps inherent to the proportionality adjudication are not strict rules, but broad argumentative paths to be filled with meaning by an appropriate reasoning. With these premises in mind we may now stablish a proper approach to the main theme itself – Internet access and suitable restrictions to this right when confronted with terrorism.

---

[20] In Brazil, for example, the misuse of proportionality has led to a situation in which freedom of expression is in practice a weaker right than the protection of privacy (Cláudio de Oliveira Santos Colnago, 'Freedom of Expression and Internet: Should Judges Apply a Preferred Position Doctrine to Cases Involving the Internet?', Paper presented on the IX World Congress of Constitutional Law, Oslo, Norway, 16–20 June 2014. Available at http://www.jus.uio.no/english/research/news-and-events/events/conferences/2014/wccl-cmdc/wccl/papers/ws8/w8-colnago.pdf).

[21] Alec Stone Sweet and Jud Mathews, 'Proportionality Balancing and Global Constitutionalism', (2008) *Faculty Scholarship Series*, Paper 14, available at http://digitalcommons.law.yale.edu/fss_papers/14.

4. *Access Restriction and Terrorism: Concrete Cases and Real Issues*

As explained by Randall Law, 'Terrorism is a strategy that makes use of certain tactics; in other words, terrorism is a means to an end – although often one that eventually overshadows the putative goals toward which its users ostensibly strive'. The same author abandons an unproductive search for a precise and perfect definition of the phenomenon, opting for a broad approach. Therefore, he discusses about terrorism either as '... a communicative act intended to influence the behavior of one or more audiences', that can also be understood '... as a set of tactics; as an act of symbolic and provocative violence; and as a cultural construct'. One of its primary and essential elements consists of the '... ability of violent actors to ensure that news of their acts and intentions reaches their target audiences, sometimes through direct impact', but in a more probable and effective way, '... through rumors, government responses, newspapers, television, entertainment sources, and countless other forms of information dissemination'.[22] That's exactly where terrorism and Internet intersect: the ability to spread data (correct or incorrect) virtually by anyone to anywhere.

In the same way, Lozano recognizes that 'Terrorism seeks not only to cause harm, but to accompany it with a forceful message. It has been said that terrorism is a "spectacle"; a tragic representation with an immense communicative force'. Addressing the matter on its core, Lozano unveils the difficulties of dealing with terrorism online, since '... it is unclear what the best response is to this situation in which the Web nowadays is a source of radicalisation and it is debated whether repressive measures or censorship is the best method of confronting this problem'.[23]

Consequently, if Internet access may be considered a human right, the same applies to human life protection, which is severely threatened in the occurrence of terrorist attacks and intimidations. Thus, it is useful to lay out some parameters and standards that may be applied to consider which would be proper limitations to the fundamental right of accessing the Internet when balanced with security policies, destined to deal with terrorist threats and prevent terrorist attacks. These standards may be better understood if argumentatively construed based on concrete scenarios that take in considerations Lessig's constraints theory, which is why we set out a few questions regarding limitations to accessing the Internet due to security issues in a broad way.

Whatever the solutions may be for combating terrorism on the Internet, there should be balanced policies on the matter of human rights, since the ultimate victory of terrorism would be converting the methods of the Constitutional State into terrorist ones. That's why the limitation of a human right can't affect its basic core, as stated by de Minico, in the sense that '... the legislator has to limit the fundamental

---

[22] Randall D. Law, *Terrorism* (Themes in History) (Polity Kindle Edition 2016).

[23] Germán M. Teruel Lozano, 'The Internet, Incitement to Terrorism and Freedom of Expression in the European Framework', Paper presented on the X World Congress of Constitutional Law, Seoul, South Korea, June 18-22, 2018.

rights to the strict necessary and ensure that to a given compression of a certain right will correspond a probable advantage for a counter-posed value'. If that doesn't happen, '... the regulation would be illegitimate and politically inadequate'. That also discharges any option for a policy of absolute control over individuals, since according to de Minico, 'controlling everyone is like controlling no one'. [24]

So, some issues that may arise from contrasting the human right of access to the basic public policy of security (specifically on assessing terrorist threats) may be divided into two large topics, such as: a) access limitations, and b) ISPs' collaboration, both of them having in mind the necessity of intelligence processing of data. To propose an answer to these questions, we intend to articulate Lessig's constraints theory with the proportionality adjudication technique, in order to construe an answer that can be put to the test according to the different legal, social, economic and architectural contexts that may be presented to anyone trying to strike a balance between freedom and security.

One aspect that should be clear is that there is no space for absolute solutions, in both senses. Neither do humans have total protection against data collection nor can the government simply collect data from anyone for any purpose. This has been well noted by Orefice, who formulates the question: '[I]s it proportionate (in the balance between the threat of terrorism and the enjoyment of fundamental freedoms) to use the data of all (suspected and unsuspected)' which are 'collected, extracted or bought through continuous monitoring, sometimes even without our knowledge, for one apparent purpose of public security ...?' [25] Even though a clear answer would be "no", that still leaves us with the necessity of striking a balance somewhere in the middle between the two absolute solutions preemptively discharged.

4.1. *Internet Access Limitations and Terrorism*

Our first impulse when considering Internet access a human right is to think of it in a "common-sense" way – which looks upon the concept of human rights as something invulnerable and, therefore, an absolute. As stated before, this first impression seems simple, even though it is completely misleading – human rights are not about absolute positions, but about how limitations on them may be legitimately justified by social and public values. Contaminated by that first impression, a natural tendency would be to consider that no one should be prohibited from accessing the Internet, due to its remarkable value to human culture and development in general. Even though the latter is true, it does not mean that use of the Net can't be restricted – it only means that limitation can happen, but not in an arbitrary way.

[24] Giovanna De Minico, 'Internet and Fundamental Rights in Time of Terrorism' (n. 4 2015) *Rivista della associazione italiana dei constituzionalisti* 4.

[25] Maria Orefice, 'Artificial Intelligence and the Right to Privacy in the Times of Terrorism', Paper presented at the X World Congress of Constitutional Law, Seoul, South Korea, 18–22 June 2018.

Consequently, there are two premises we may adopt when dealing with restrictions to Internet access: 1) there is no such a thing as immunity from restrictions, since no human right is an absolute and 2) the restriction cannot be too intense or extreme in order to preserve a minimum of the human right's core. So, limitations to a human right can be placed, but there must be a legitimate procedure for them, under the proportionality perspective, which takes us to the three to four steps referred by Sweet and Mathews: 1) legitimacy, 2) suitability/adequacy, 3) necessity, 4) proportionality in the strict sense.

Therefore, on the clash between Internet access and the value "security", we must consider that the restrictions should pass the test whenever they are actually intended to enhance safety and there are no deviations from this stated objective. Although, if the government starts to impose restrictions on the pretence of making its citizens secure, but it is actually using a specific policy in a discriminatory way, the human right limitation will not pass the proportionality test, due to the lack of legitimacy. Take a hypothetical situation in which the government imposes abstract restrictions that are applied in a discriminatory and arbitrary way, such that they are applied more strictly with certain ethnic groups or foreigners and less strictly with others.

Since the first test is confirmed, it is necessary to analyse the suitability/adequacy of the limitation, which means that the restriction on Internet access is not only rationally related to the security goal, but it also has a potential of actually improving security. In addition, on the necessity test, one must scrutinize if the restriction imposed by the government on accessing the net is not excessively intrusive, or more than necessary for obtaining the goal of security. Said in another way, the necessity step imposes government to always use the least restrictive instrument possible, if it has the same efficacy as the more intrusive one. Finally, on the proportionality on the strict sense, the public policy (restriction on accessing the Internet) must be inspected as a matter of importance and intensity. This means that there must be a proportional relation between how intense the restriction is and how important the human right is, on a scale considering the concrete facts.

Surely, the last step is not as objective as the other three, since it presupposes classifying the restriction according to an intensity scale (for example: (1) non-intrusive, (2) intrusive and (3) very intrusive restriction) and also defining the importance of the human right on a concrete facts basis (i.e. (1) less important, (2) important, (3) very important). In this abstract consideration, the limitation would be valid if there is a direct proportionality between the importance of the right and the intensity of the restriction. So, a restriction that is (3) very intrusive would be justified for a (1) less important or (2) important right, but possibly not for a (3) very important one. In the same way, a (1) non-intrusive limitation would be justified independently on the weight attributed to the human right.

But how can we determine exactly when a restriction is non-intrusive or very intrusive? How do we classify a human right as "less important" or "very important" in the actual scenario? There is no absolute answer or guaranteed pathway to answer these questions, other than that they must be construed argumentatively, interpreting all the relevant aspects. However, the proportionality test can be combined with Lessig's framework for restraints as a way of helping the interpretation of these relevant aspects.

Hence, when dealing with Internet access restrictions due to the value of security, there are two specific restraints on the Lessig framework that should be highlighted: Market and Architecture. The first one is pertinent because the cost of access may determine how easy it is for data to be shared and also on the grounds of the possibility of terrorists gaining control of specific access providers. The second may determine the very shape of technology used by the access providers – one that can facilitate or hinder the collaboration of private actors mentioned in the next topic. Of course, that Law (either hard or soft) plays a crucial role in the matter, since this is the force of regulation that will actually create the context for imposing the others, and Norms may contribute or disturb the acceptance of some restrictions.

Then what kind of access limitations could be pertinent to the enhancing of security? There are some clear and fairly obvious situations, like, for example, forbidding a convicted terrorist to use the Internet while he serves his time. When it comes to extending this prohibition after the fulfilment of the jail time, however, the matter becomes more intricate. If the goal is to avoid the continuity of criminal behaviour, the restriction could be considered legitimate and also adequate, since terrorism has been using the widespread Internet for planning and executing attacks. The limitation could also pass the necessity test, since there wouldn't be a less intrusive way of preventing new terrorist acts by that person, considering the popularity of the Net among terrorist groups. When it comes to the proportionality test in the strict sense, the hypothesis shows an important right – not very important in the case, since there are other forms of communication besides the Internet that would still be available. Conversely, we may consider the restriction to be non-intrusive, precisely because there would be still another instrument that could be used to communicate. Therefore, this could be considered a valid restriction.

But what if the competent government authorities have reason to believe that, instead of preventing the convicted and recently freed terrorist from accessing the Internet, they could better enforce security by monitoring him, in a way that could eventually lead to other malefactors? This takes us to ISPs' collaboration, the subject of the next section.

4.2. *Collaboration with ISPs*

Due to its nature and quick pace of growth, the Internet has posed a real challenge to traditional government regulations, including the ones destined to protect human rights. The sovereignty of the national state and its "hard law" was not as operational as the code of applications. Thus, the current framework actually demands a lot of private collaboration in regulating the digital environment. The importance and intricacy of collaboration with ISPs to enforce human right provisions on the Internet has been well explained by De Gregorio:[26]

> The need for public actors to take into consideration, on the one hand, the protection of the freedom to conduct business of online platforms and free speech of the and, on the other hand, the need to tackle illicit contents have made the policy to tackle terrorist contents hosted by platforms constitute a reason which explains why the fight against terrorist online contents for Constitutional States is so complex.

The theme of collaboration with ISPs in order to restrain terrorism from spreading online is a rich one, in which Lessig's concept of architecture/code prevails as a way of enforcing conduct. However, since the main topic of our discussion deals with the human right of accessing the Internet, we must be alert to the fact that only a specific group of the broader category known as 'Internet Service Providers' (ISPs) is pertinent to our research: the Internet Access Providers (IAPs). The IAPs are the companies that provide services that make it possible for individuals to have access to the Internet.[27]

Consequently, the present topic intends to address how the collaboration of IAPs with authorities can be considered as a limitation to the right to access the Internet. Also, the effectiveness of the cooperation is dependent on what information the IAPs may or may not access. In Brazil, for example, governing law (Federal Statute 12.965, from 23 April 2014) provides in its Article 14 that in the provision of a connection, whether free or at cost, it is prohibited to retain users' records of access to Internet applications. Such a provision has a lot of relevance to the case, since the current architecture (hardware and software) of IAPs' tools tends to allow access to these logs. Architecture, in this case, is being limited by Law – a limitation that may not be very effective.

It should be remembered that companies may have to enforce some human rights and, therefore, may have to comply with some duties and standards before government. When it comes to Internet access versus terrorism, a immediate topic is the collection of data and the sharing of it with the law enforcement authorities. This kind of procedure could be considered a restriction on free access (not as in "free beer", but as in "free speech"), since accessing the Internet presupposes a freedom to search without undue government impositions. Previous general and extensive content filtering by IAPs should not be adopted as a general rule, due to its heavy economic costs. Rights may have costs, but duties tend to cost even more. Conversely, whenever technology simplifies (Architecture) and reduces the cost (Market) of filter-

---

[26] Giovanni de Gregorio, 'Countering Pro-Terrorism Online Contents: Censorship, Platforms and Freedom of Expression in the Transnational Constitucional Order', Paper presented on the X World Congress of Constitutional Law, Seoul, South Korea, 18–22 June 2018.

[27] Marcel Leonardi, *Responsabilidade civil dos provedores de serviços de internet* (Editora Juarez de Oliveira 2005), 22.

ing and processing specific data that could be tagged as "red flags" (for example, exchange of data with words referring to bombing, killing, exploding, terror, etc.), it should be adopted as a policy by IAPs to share this data with the government.

One may question whether the access to the data should only be admissible with a warrant, since it would be a search that would demand probable cause to be valid. In our opinion, this would have been adequate for the reality existed before the Internet. The huge amount of data generated by the most diverse applications would make the security activity almost impossible. Instead of worrying about the sharing of data between private companies and the government, a correct and more updated human rights framework would require the proper judicial orders only for the actual use of the data for more intrusive proceedings, such as physical searches and arrests.

The need to update the meaning of human rights safeguards has already been developed by Lessig,[28] applying what he calls 'translation'[29] to deal with the practical matter of the constitutionality of a 'worm',[30] in the context of the US Constitution. His classic lesson is stated as follows:

> Is the worm, then, constitutional? That depends on your conception of what the Fourth Amendment protects. In one view, the amendment protects against suspicionless governmental invasions, whether those invasions are burdensome or not. In a second view, the amendment protects against invasions that are burdensome, allowing only those for which there is adequate suspicion that guilt will be uncovered. The paradigm case that motivated the framers does not distinguish between these two very different types of protections, because the technology of the time wouldn't distinguish either. You couldn't– technically– have a perfectly burdenless generalized search in 1791. So they didn't–technically–express a view about whether such a search should be constitutionally proscribed. It is instead we who must choose what the amendment is to mean.
>
> (…) It may not be easy to imagine systems that follow an individual wherever he goes, but it is easy to imagine technologies that gather an extraordinary amount of data about everything we do and make those data accessible to those with the proper authorization. The intrusiveness would be slight, and the payoff could be great.

[28] Lawrence Lessig, *Code version 2.0* (New York: Basic Books, 2006) 22–23.

[29]'To know what values are relevant, however, we need a method for putting values into a new context. I begin this part with an account of that method. The values I will describe are part of our tradition, and they need to be interpreted and made real in this context. Thus, I begin this part with one approach that the law has developed for recognizing and respecting these values. This is the interpretive practice I call "translation". A translator practises a fidelity to earlier commitments to value. Latent ambiguities are those instances where fidelity runs out. We have nothing to be faithful to, because the choices we now face are 'choices that our forbears did not' (Lawrence Lessig, *Code version 2.0* (New York: Basic Books, 2006), 156).

[30] 'A "worm" is a bit of computer code that is spat out on the Net and works its way into the systems of vulnerable computers. It is not a "virus" because it doesn't attach itself to other programs and interfere with their operation. It is just a bit of extra code that does what the code writer says. The code could be harmless and simply sit on someone's machine. Or it could be harmful and corrupt files or do other damage that its author commands.' (Lawrence Lessig, *Code version 2.0* (New York: Basic Books, 2006) 20).

Thus, this way of considering data sharing between IAPs and the government, with an update on the individual safeguards (judicial order only needed to use the data for more intrusive proceedings, not applicable for the sharing itself) due to Lessig's translation, should be subject to a proportionality test. Since the goal of collecting the data is to prevent terrorism and enhance security, a human rights value, it should be considered a legitimate goal. On the suitability/adequacy test, there is a natural and obvious conclusion that with more data being subject to scrutiny the possibility of preventing attacks due to intelligence work is enriched. On the necessity aspect, the safeguard proposed (judge's authorization previous to any invasive actions) makes this kind of cooperation the least intrusive option, acquiring the goal in the same way. On the proportionality, in a strict sense, test, the restriction can be considered non-intrusive (since the data can only be actually used with a judicial authorization) and the correlated human right (security), a very important one, considering the current context with the rise of terrorist attacks all over the world.

Therefore, the proper interpretation calls for a limited collaboration between IAPs and government, conditioned by the economic viability (Market) and technological availability (Architecture), when it comes to users' data being shared. Moreover, the sharing isn't authorized for legal use by the government, until there is a demonstration of probable cause. This way, the enormous amount of data doesn't get lost in the haystack that is the Internet today, without discharging the human rights safeguards that are much needed to avoid abuse of power.

5. *Conclusion*

The issue of Internet access as a human right and its intertwining with security against terrorism raises innumerable questions regarding the proper way to secure and protect both human rights values in a balanced way. This involves defining the proper limitations to it and the different aspects of regulation (Law, Norms, Market and Architecture) that may influence the intensity of the limitation. If it is certain that no right is absolute, one must also wonder if the limitation does not affect its essential core. Thus, applying the proportionality test to a specific set of concrete hypotheses in which free access to the Internet may collide with the need for security against terror, we propose answers based on the proportionality adjudication technique, specifically the ones that are more likely to happen, involving direct and indirect limitations and the collaboration of private IAPs. We hope that this may be a first step towards much broader studies regarding the topic, always with one requisite in mind: human rights must be applied in a balanced way, in order to fulfil the majority of them – and not one single position.

National Sovereignty, Security, and Internet Governance: Impact on Constitutional Principles and Challenges for the Human Rights of Internet Users

Andrey A. Shcherbovich

In 2016, the State Duma (Russian Parliament) adopted a package of anti-terrorist amendments to the legislation that was developed by Deputy Irina Yarovaya and member of the Council of the Federation Viktor Ozerov (the so-called *Yarovaya Law*). It is necessary to pay special attention to the impact of the so-called Yarovaya Law on the constitutional rights and freedoms of citizens. These amendments provide the disclosure of personal data to the competent authorities. Third parties (employees of state bodies) become aware of the privacy of citizens, their correspondence and other data, access to which by any third party other than the addressee would be restricted in normal circumstances.

1. *Social and Political Context*

The Internet, being a supranational environment that does not recognize state borders, serves as a guarantee for positive changes in society. The needs of people of the twenty-first century standing before the scientific community the issue of inclusion in the set of basic human rights and the rights of new approaches to their implementation, which develop rights proposed in the Universal Declaration of Human Rights of 1948 and other international instruments.

Russian Internet users' understanding of the traditional legal culture is that the Internet is a space, free from any legal regulation. This freedom should not be understood as anarchy, but the Internet could be an asylum for freedom of expression, as well for the freedom of thought.

The Internet, directly or indirectly, affects the realization of all constitutional rights. It affects the realization of the constitutional freedom of expression and of the right and access to information, but through the right of access information people are realizing other constitutional rights. That is why this sphere is so important in terms of legal regulation.

The Internet has global characteristics not only in the geographical, but also in the social and legal sense of the word, as it affects a wide range of social relations. Due to the specific nature of the Internet, we are in great need of adequate legal regulation of the relevant relationships that are developing online.

2. *The Problem of "Sovereignty" on the Internet*

In recent years the principle of ensuring the security of the Russian Federation in creating information systems, their operation and protection of information are increasingly coming to the fore in the development of legislation in the field of governance of information and the Internet. This principle becomes dominant in the development of new laws in this area. Russian officials refer to the "digital" or "information" sovereignty of Russia, but largely this can be attributed to the complex geopolitical position of the country.

Over the last few years the Russian legislator has developed a number of initiatives aimed at the regulation of the Internet. Among them there were provisions to block resources containing extremist information, or aimed at violation of the law on conducting political rallies. Other provisions 'localized' personal data of Russian citizens (obling the use of databases located only in the Russian Federation). Anti-terrorist amendments provided for disclosure of user-generated content to the law-enforcement agencies at their request. Other initiatives by the Russian Ministry of Communications aimed at import substitution in the field of information technologies. All these initiatives are evidence of the general policy of the digital (information) sovereignty of Russia. [1]

At the end of April 2014, Maxim Kavzhdaradze, member of the Council of Federation, the upper house of the Russian Parliament, proposed the creation of a purely domestic Internet inaccessible from abroad, with the exception for the Customs Union. This internal segment of the Internet is to be named after a cartoon movie character named Cheburashka. The author of the proposal later clarified that his proposal would be applied exclusively to scientific information.

The explanatory memorandum to the draft Federal Law 'On the invalidation of the Federal Law on the organization of public and municipal services', noted that the implementation of the Law leads to the transformation of Russia into an electronic virtual cross-border society in which the core functions of the state executive power

[1] See: A.A. Saveliev, *Itemized Commentary to the Federal Law of July 27, 2006 No 149-FZ 'On Information, Information Technologies and Information Protection'* (Zakon, 2015). ConsultantPlus Legal Reference System.

in reality are carried out by intermediaries. These intermediaries are transnational corporations that own the financial system, and the Internet itself, where this interaction will be carried out. The attributes of the state will be preserved, but the real power will inevitably belong to the owners of the system that sells the information services, i.e. banks and supranational corporations.

The authors of the invalidation bill stated that Federal Law No 210-FZ is incompatible with the fundamental principle of the Constitution, which proclaims the Russian Federation to be a sovereign state. Its implementation will lead to the danger of dismantling the sovereignty of Russia and the whole nation state. These concerns are quite typical of the Russian legislator in this area. [2]

The head of the State Duma Security and Anti-Corruption Committee Irina Yarovaya, stated that the Internet is destroying the notion of boundaries, the concept of sovereignty. Modern communications make it possible to invade the sovereign domestic interests and violate the principles of national security. According to Irina Yarovaya, the additional powers of the FSS (Russian security service) will allow special services to carry out their tasks more efficiently.

There is a trend towards "sovereignization" in the state regulation of the Internet in Russia. Without understanding the essence of the Internet as a global network, Russian legislators are trying to extend the concept of sovereignty to relations on the Internet. Here we need to consider these initiatives in terms of the principle of constitutionalism, as well as the foundations of the functioning of the Internet.

China has achieved a high level of digital sovereignty by prohibiting or restricting access to the Chinese market by foreign Internet companies (Facebook, Google, Twitter) and developing the Chinese social media platforms such as RenRen and Sina Weibo. Most of the data belonging to Chinese citizens and institutions are stored on servers in China. On 1 September 2015, a similar law entered into force in Russia. [3]

The Chinese project named Golden Shield that blocks and filters content harmful to the ruling Communist Party has been very successful, as the government decided to control the Internet at an early stage of its development. Liu Wei, Minister of the Information Office Internet China at the second Sino-Korea Roundtable, said: 'Just as the seventeenth century showed the expansion of national sovereignty over parts of the maritime space and the twentieth on the airspace, national sovereignty is currently expanding in cyberspace [...] no cyberspace can exist without sovereignty'. [4]

Chinese users wishing to access blocked sites can use proxies, which provide ac-

---

[2] Explanatory note to the draft Federal Law *'On the invalidation of the Federal Law of July 27, 2010 No 210-FZ "On the organization of the provision of state and municipal services"'*. ConsultantPlus Legal Reference System.

[3] Federal Law No. 242-FZ of July 21, 2014 '*On Amendments to Certain Legislative Acts of the Russian Federation Regarding the Clarification of the Procedure for Handling Personal Data in Information and Telecommunication Networks'* (Amended on December 31, 2014). ConsultantPlus Legal Reference System.

[4] J. Kurbalija, *An Introduction to Internet Governance* (DiploFoundation, 2014).

cess to third-party servers to avoid censorship, but most users will not attempt to bypass censorship because of the presence of internal spies.

It seems that the concept of sovereignty over the Internet is impossible. Because of unclear jurisdiction, it is difficult to distinguish national segments of the Internet. Experts could allocate only language segments. Indeed, even if the website is registered on the national top-level domain of the particular country (like *.ru* for Cyrillic *.рф* for Russia), it could be owned by not only its citizens and legal entities, but also by foreign citizens and legal entities.

From the point of view of global security policies, development of the Internet really amplifies the relationship and even interdependence between states. However, one should regard this as a positive factor.

The current Constitution of the Russian Federation establishes the sovereignty of the Russian Federation. Its fourth article proclaims sovereignty as one of the foundations of the constitutional system and sets out the legal and territorial guarantees of the state sovereignty of Russia: 'The sovereignty of the Russian Federation extends throughout its territory. The Russian Constitution and federal laws have supremacy throughout the Russian Federation. The state ensures the integrity and inviolability of its territory'. [5]

By a definition made by the Supreme Court of the Russian Federation, Russian sovereignty implies the supremacy, independence and autonomy of state power, the fullness of legislative, executive and judicial power of the state on its territory and independence in international relations. It is an essential quality characteristic of the Russian Federation as a state, being one of the most essential features of its constitutional-law status. [6]

In general, we can say the sovereignty concept in constitutional and international law has been not only preserved but strengthened. However, this approach based on the recognition of the absolute sovereignty of states has various shortcomings, the number and value of which increases with time. The world order based on its interpretation of the concept of sovereignty has faced criticism which has strengthened over time. The concept of the absolute sovereignty of the state as a phenomenon began to be criticized because it is, on the one hand, unrealizable, and, on the other, inappropriate, and even dangerous. Indeed, the unlimited governmental power of any state is impossible in any country, even in absolute monarchies.

Unlimited power of the state is impossible and unacceptable in a constitutional state, because this understanding contradicts the principle of constitutional government, which presupposes the existence of a system of limitation of state power in or-

---

[5] *Constitution of the Russian Federation.* Adopted by popular vote on December 12, 1993. Taking into account the amendments introduced by the *Laws on Amendments* to the Constitution of the Russian Federation. ConsultantPlus Legal Reference System.

[6] See: Decision of the Supreme Court of the Russian Federation of September 12, 2012 on case No AKPI12-1128. ConsultantPlus Legal Reference System.

der to prevent arbitrariness in relationships with the people and citizens.[7]

Information technologies can affect the sovereignty of states. It is possible to say even that the national state is losing its sovereign powers in the context of the globalization of information. National states had transferred part of their sovereignty to supranational bodies even prior to the emergence and development of the global Internet. In addition, different social and political groups, institutions, horizontal and vertical networks were destroying the usual bulkhead between foreign and domestic politics.

Being aware of the existence of gaps in the legislation regulating the Internet, Russian legislators offer different initiatives to regulate relations on the Internet, particularly restricting the rights of Internet users.

The vast majority of bills and proposals concern the introduction of new restrictions on the dissemination of information and the facilitation of the surveillance of citizens. Below some examples of these legislative initiatives are given. There is an analysis of a number of regulations adopted by the Russian Federation in the sphere of regulation of the Internet. These examples illustrate the approaches of the Russian legislator to regulating the Internet.

3. *Internet Sovereignty Bill*

On February 12, 2019, the State Duma, the lower house of the Russian Federal Parliament, adopted in the first reading the draft bill on Internet "sovereignty" in Russia. Three hundred and thirty-four deputies voted in favour and 47 against the document. At the same time, representatives of the private sector, civil society and the Accounting Chamber (Russian parliamentary controlling authority) expressed criticism regarding this bill, because its implementation may require billions of dollars from the national budget.

The explanatory note to the bill [8] states that the draft Federal Law, which is officially called 'On Amendments to Certain Legislative Acts of the Russian Federation', was prepared to take into account the aggressive nature of the US National Cybersecurity Strategy, adopted in September 2018. [9]

Under these conditions, the note argues, protective measures are necessary to ensure the long-term and stable operation of the Internet in Russia and to increase the

---

[7] See: I.A. Alebastrova, *Constitutionalism as the Legal Basis for Social Solidarity. Monograph* (Prospekt, 2016).

[8] The explanatory note to the draft Federal Law '*On Amendments to Certain Legislative Acts of the Russian Federation'*, adopted in the first reading on February 12, 2019 (State Duma of the Russian Federation). http://sozd.duma.gov.ru/bill/608767-7 accessed March 11, 2019.

[9] *US National Cyber Strategy* (The White House, September 2018). https://www.whitehouse.gov/wp-content/uploads/2018/09/National-Cyber-Strategy.pdf accessed March 11, 2019.

reliability of the Russian Internet resources. The bill determines mandatory rules for traffic routing and organizes control over the compliance with those rules. It creates an opportunity to minimize the transfer abroad of data exchanged between Russian users.

The bill also identifies cross-border connection lines and traffic exchange points. Their owners and operators will be obliged to provide the opportunity for centralized traffic management in case of emergency. In other words, the bill creates a special emergency infrastructure to guarantee the performance of Russian digital resources on occasions when it is not possible to connect to foreign route servers.

Control over the implementation of the provisions established by the new law will be entrusted to the Federal Service for Supervision in the Sphere of Communications, Information Technologies and Mass Communications (Roskomnadzor). [10]

There is a need to be ready if the country will be disconnected from the global Internet – said the President of Russia, Vladimir Putin, meeting with representatives of Russian agencies and the press. At the same time, according to the Russian leader, the new cyberdefence is supposed to be utilized only as a reaction to threats coming from foreign states. The President called the Internet an 'invention of intelligence services' which 'listen, see and read what you say', reinforcing that with no Internet they will not be able to do so.

In this sense, the President continued the isolation of Russia from the global network which will impose 'tremendous harm to itself' not only economically, but also politically, but such a scenario is 'theoretically possible'.

Adoption and implementation of the law on "Internet sovereignty" may create uncertainty for Russian digital businesses and the extension would require significant budget expenditure including the expansion of the powers of Roskomnadzor. These observations are clarified in the response to the bill, issued by the Expert Council under the Government of Russian Federation. [11]

Notably, the experts pointed out that the requirement for telecom operators to 'transfer the complete scheme of their network and traffic routing to Roskomnadzor' is technically impracticable. They explained that this is not possible, as the network is constantly expanding and updating.

In addition, the experts stressed that the bill's authors refer to the potential threat to the Russian segment of the Internet, but do not specify what that threat is. The government also considered that the amendments would expand the powers of Roskomnadzor, entrusting it with functions to eliminate all threats to the integrity and security of the Internet, which the law now assigns to the ministerial level or the Government of Russia. The transfer and consolidation of the functions of regulation,

---

[10] Federal Service for Supervision in the Sphere of Communications, Information Technologies and Mass Communications (Roskomnadzor). https://rkn.gov.ru/ accessed March 11, 2019.

[11] *With sovereignty in tomorrow. Experts at the government estimated the cost of autonomous Internet* (*Kommersant*, No 238 of December 25, 2018). https://www.kommersant.ru/doc/3842329 accessed March 11, 2019.

supervision and direct management of the communications industry to Roskomnadzor 'carries unacceptable risks' the experts say.

In November 2017, President Putin demanded that the experts engage in the development of autonomous Internet control systems, which would remove the "domination" of the United States from the Russian segment of the network.

Importantly, the Ministry of Communications and Mass Media together with the Ministry of Foreign Affairs was tasked with developing an agreed position with the association of Brazil, Russia, India, and China ('BRICS') on the creation of a BRICS domain name route server system, which would "duplicate" the existing domain name system, [12] would be independent of the control of international organizations and would protect the number of Russian users from "targeted impacts".

4. *Law*

It is necessary to designate creation of number of registries of domain names, indexes of pages of sites on the Internet containing information, prohibited for dissemination in the Russian Federation. This law introduced so-called blacklists. [13] These initially included websites that contain information relating to the three categories: propaganda for pedophilia, drug addiction and suicide.

The Russian Association of Electronic Communications ('RAEC') highlights the possible negative consequences of the application of this law. Among them is the blocking of bona fide resources located on the same IP-address as resources holding illegal content. [14]

In other words, this law could possibly give rise to outrageous decisions being made by the blacklist operators. Moreover, those blacklists would be introduced on the basis of the decree of the government (not the Federal Law), [15] even though according to the Russian Constitution rights and freedoms may only be restricted by the court and according to the Federal Law. In this case, this principle is violated. It should be also mentioned that technologically blacklists disturb the operability of the Internet. Thus,

---

[12] *Domain Name System (Wikipedia).* https://en.wikipedia.org/wiki/Domain_Name_System accessed March 11, 2019.

[13] Federal Law No. 139-FZ of July 28, 2012 (as amended on October 14, 2014) *'On Amendments to the Federal Law "On Protection of Children from Information Harmful to Their Health and Development! and Certain Legislative Acts of the Russian Federation'*. ConsultantPlus Legal Reference System.

[14] See: RAEC position on the initiative of the Safer Internet League (*RAEC*, February 1, 2013) http://raec.ru/live/position/5898/ accessed March 11, 2019.

[15] See: Resolution of the Government of the Russian Federation No. 1101 of October 26, 2012 (Edited on October 12, 2015) *'On the unified automated information system Unified register of domain names, indexes of pages of sites in the information and telecommunication network 'Internet' and network addresses, allowing to identify sites in the information and telecommunication network 'Internet' containing information, the dissemination of which is prohibited in the Russian Federation'*. ConsultantPlus Legal Reference System.

even before the introduction of blacklists there was the incidence of the court decision on a single Livejournal blog, as a result of which access to the whole LiveJournal blog platform was partially blocked in Russia. [16]

There is a problem with bringing the legislation of the Russian Federation in line with international law standards and principles. However, because of the specific features of the Internet, there is a complete void of organic principles applicable to it in international law. The Russian legal system traditionally does not recognize international soft law rules, only international treaties. However, outside the European Union or the United States, even the "soft law" rules in this field are in the stage of formation and development.

Under international law, states are legally bound to respect, protect and fulfil the rights of their citizens. Governments have the primary responsibility for the implementation of human rights within their jurisdictions. The duty to protect requires governments to protect citizens from violations of human rights committed by other actors, including business and nongovernmental organizations. States are also required to take appropriate measures to investigate, punish and redress the violations of human rights that occur within their territory or jurisdiction.

Other participants in public relations, including on the Internet, also bear responsibility within the framework of the international regime in the field of human rights. The Universal Declaration of Human Rights calls on 'every person and every organ of society' to promote and respect human rights. Despite the fact that these charges do not equate to legal obligations, even if they are not recognized as such in accordance with national legislation, they are certainly an integral part of the existing social rules that should be respected by all the stakeholders.

The 'Charter of Human Rights and Principles for the Internet' is the result of many years work by the 'Internet Rights and Principles Dynamic Coalition', an open international community within the framework of the Internet Governance Forum (IGF). The Charter not only lists the basic responsibilities of states, but also contains recommendations. Governments' responsibilities are to ensure the observance of human rights by private companies, and the recommendations for other entities is how they should behave in order that their actions do not violate human rights on the Internet. As of today, the Charter still only exists in draft form.

5. *The Law of Extrajudicial Blocking of Websites*

In particular, experts are challenging Federal Law No. 398-FZ of December 28, 2013 'On Amendments to the Federal Law on Information, Information Technolo-

---

[16] See: A. Golitsyna, V. Kholmogorova and M. Galkin, *LJ is partially inaccessible* (*Vedomosti*, June 26, 2009), www.vedomosti.ru/newspaper/articles/2009/06/26/zhzh-chastichno-nedostupen accessed March 11, 2019.

gies and Information Protection'. The law allows Roskomnadzor (executive authority under the auspices of the Ministry of Telecommunications) to immediately block out websites that circulate calls for riots and other extremist information without court decisions [17] only under the instruction of the Prosecutor General's Office of the Russian Federation.

This initiative came from the interdepartmental commission on combating extremism. It is supposed to tighten the law as a result of two measures. The first one was to allow a request to block resources to be granted not only by the Prosecutor General's Office, but also by the regional supervisory agencies, as Russia is a federal state.

The second one was to consider as a sufficient basis for making such a request the presence on the site of not only calls for "unlawful" actions, but also of any "xenophobic" information.

'Lugovoi Law' (named after its author, Deputy of the State Duma Andrey Lugovoi) came into force on February 1, 2014. According to Alexander Zharov, the head of Roskomnadzor, in mid-March 2015, during the operation of this law about 6500 websites, located at 3300 unique IP addresses, were blocked.

Among the first resources to be blocked without a court decision were opposition media resources. Human rights activists believe that the law is an instrument of Internet censorship in Russia. The Human Rights Council under the President of the Russian Federation stated that this law seriously restricts the constitutional rights and freedoms of citizens. [18]

Experts on the 'Sanitation of the Law' project note that the so-called 'Lugovoi Law' contradicts Russian and international legislation, contains inaccurate language that allows broad interpretation, introduces additional tools for state regulation of the Internet, is a tool with which to put pressure on the network media and opposition resources and restricts the right to freedom of speech and freedom of assembly. The law should be completely abolished, and the previously introduced principle of extra-judicial Internet blocking and "blacklists" should be revised. [19]

6. *Localization of Personal Data of Russian Citizens*

There is a convention of the Council of Europe on Protection of Individuals with regard to Automatic Processing of Personal Data. [20] Russian legislation on personal

---

[17] Federal Law No. 398-FZ of December 28, 2013 *'On Amendments to the Federal Law 'On Information', Information Technologies and Information Protection'*. ConsultantPlus Legal Reference System.

[18] *An even larger offensive law on freedom on the Internet is being prepared* (*Human Rights in Russia,* March 31, 2015), www.hro.org/node/21789 accessed March 11, 2019.

[19] *The law on extrajudicial blocking of Internet sites. Conclusion of the public council* (Sanitation of the Law project, 2014). http://sanatsia.com/reestr-zakonov/579/ accessed March 11, 2019.

[20] Convention for the Protection of Individuals with Regard to Automatic Processing of Personal Data (Strasbourg, January 28, 1981). ConsultantPlus Legal Reference System.

data does not comply with this convention. The main legal problem in this area is the localization of personal data of Russian citizens.

Localization of personal data of Russians, introduced by amendments to the Federal Law 'On Personal Data' (Law No. 242-FZ),[21] is inconsistent with the nature of the Internet as a universal network aimed at international data transfer. There are many concerns about the realization of the constitutional rights and freedoms of citizens contained within this law. In fact, the adoption of this law was an unprecedented measure that could affect the existence of the entire Internet in Russia.

Since September 1, 2015 Internet services dealing with the personal data of Russian citizens were able to processing such data using servers located exclusively in Russia. The document includes online stores, social networking, ticket reservation services, hotels and other services. It refers to Russian companies that store data abroad and to foreign organizations that deal with clients from Russia.

The law has caused quite a strong reaction in the online community and among Internet industry experts. The authors of the document are accused of producing a law that cannot be realized in practice, it does not ensure the security of Russian citizens, but complicates their lives and hampers the development of the Internet in Russia.

The reasoning for the adoption of the law formulated by its authors are as follows. Many people are registered in the social networks, buy goods and receive services through the Internet. A significant portion of these services could be placed abroad, mainly in the United States and Europe. As a result, credit card information, passport details and correspondence, including e-mail, could be accumulated by intelligence services of the states concerned.

As stated by one of the developers of the law, First Deputy Chairman of the State Duma Committee on Information Policy, Information Technology and Communications, Vadim Dengin, the majority of Russians are strictly against the storage of their personal data abroad and wish to store their personal data inside Russia. In other case, personal data may fall into the hands of fraudsters as a result of a hacker attack on foreign intelligence services.[22]

The law regulates the duties of the personal data operators to ensure the recording, systematization, accumulation, storage, clarification (updating, changing), retrieval of personal data of Russian Federation citizens on servers located in the territory of the Russian Federation, and the disclosure of the location of these servers.

Based on an enforceable court decision, Roskomnadzor, being the authorized body for the protection of the rights of personal data subjects, is entitled to limit ac-

---

[21] Federal Law No. 242-FZ of July 21, 2014 '*On Amendments to Certain Legislative Acts of the Russian Federation Regarding Specification of the Procedure for the Processing of Personal Data in Information and Telecommunication Networks*' (as amended on December 31, 2014). ConsultantPlus Legal Reference System.

[22] A. Filimonov, '"*We must share!" or protection of personal data of Russians from the foreign special services*' (*Garant.ru,* August 14, 2014). www.garant.ru/article/559071/ accessed March 11, 2019.

cess to information processed in violation of the personal data legislation of Russian Federation. The law defines the procedure for limiting access to that information. For this purpose, Roskomnadzor created the automated information system 'Register of violators of the law on personal data'.

Here we are talking about the balance between security and freedom on the Internet. These localization amendments to the law on personal data actually ban cross-border transfer of personal data. However, Council of Europe Convention for the Protection of Individuals with Regard to Automatic Processing of Personal Data, and the law on personal data generally allow cross-border transfer of personal data.

The list of endangered resources provided by the law doesn't mention specific attributes of the Internet, like foreign domain names, Domain Name System ('DNS') addresses, static IPs, also participating in the transmission of personal data. Application of the law on personal data to databases containing this information actually paralyzes the entire Russian segment of the Internet, because basic mechanisms of regulation of the global network are situated outside Russia. These large-scale restrictions are almost impossible under current conditions, but those provisions create the legal basis for this.

The current law on personal data limits the citizen's right to cross-border transfer of personal data, in cases where the citizen has given personal consent to the transfer. These restrictions are in conflict with Articles 23 and 29 of the Constitution of the Russian Federation.[23] The issues surrounding personal data have become the object of political speculation because the authors of the law did not take into account the supranational nature of the Internet. The law covers social networks, airline and hotel bookings and other services of foreign origin.

Russian companies also store their data on servers abroad. It is much cheaper and more convenient than opening servers in Russia simply to comply with the law. Moreover, Russian citizens and companies are opening servers abroad to facilitate access to these resources from other countries.

This law complicates the functioning of the Internet in Russia. Many companies will not rent a server in Russia just to comply with the law because of its redundancy. The law creates additional obstacles for transboundary transfer of personal data.

7. *Yarovaya Anti-terrorist Laws*

On June 24, 2016, the State Duma adopted a package of anti-terrorism provisions, developed by the deputy Irina Yarovaya and member of the Council of Federation Viktor Ozerov. After the first reading, some of the most resonant rules of the bill

---

[23] A. Ivanov, *Keeping of personal data abroad from the point of view of Russian law* (Zakon, 2015. No 1). ConsultantPlus Legal Reference System.

were relaxed or deleted. However, some of the provisions, criticized by ICT industry representatives,[24] remained in the document.

These amendments, better known as the 'Yarovaya Law', included provisions obliging telecom operators and Internet companies to store text messages, user conversations, as well as 'the image, sound, video and other communications' for up to six months. Since the introduction of these norms, telecom operators have been required to provide access to all personal data requested to law enforcement agencies without a court order.

The Yarovaya Law tightens the terms of various "extremist" articles of the Criminal Code, including Article 282 (for 'inciting hatred or hostility, and humiliation of human dignity'), through which it is regularly indicted for Internet users. The amendments also equate public calls to terrorist activity or justification of terrorism on the Internet to the same actions in the media (Article 205.2 of the Criminal Code).

According to the amendments, network operators must keep the information on the facts of reception, transmission, delivery and (or) processing of voice and text messages, including their contents, as well as images, sounds or other communications of users. On special request, operators must provide the above-mentioned information to the law enforcement agencies conducting operational and investigative activities, or the security services of the Russian Federation. They should submit information disclosing the users of communication services and other information necessary to carry out tasks on these bodies, as prescribed in the federal laws.[25]

In addition, it is necessary to pay special attention to the impact on the constitutional rights and freedoms of citizens of the so-called Yarovaya Law. The law is implemented in two stages. First stage comprises the statistical details of each user's traffic, but the second stage comprises decrypted transmitted data (messages, texts, images, sounds, etc.). Third parties (employees of state bodies) become aware of the personal data of citizens, their correspondence and other information, access to which by any third party other than the addressee should be prohibited or at least restricted in normal circumstances.

However, before drawing any conclusion about the impact of the Yarovaya Law on the constitutional rights of citizens, it is necessary to recall the aims of its adoption. These legislative amendments have been made in order to protect the security of the state and citizens from the terrorist threat, which, according to clause 3 of Article 55 of the Constitution of Russia, provide legal grounds for restrictions of some rights in accordance with the federal law.

---

[24] '*edia: the government softened the "Yarovaya Law", recognizing constructive criticism' (znak.com,* January 22, 2018). https://www.znak.com/2018-01-22/smi_pravitelstvo_smyagchilo_zakon_yarovoy_priznav_kritiku_konstruktivnoy accessed March 11, 2019.

[25] Draft Federal Law No. 1039149-6 *'On Amending Certain Legislative Acts of the Russian Federation Regarding the Establishment of Additional Measures to Counter Terrorism and Ensure Public Security'.* Submitted to the State Duma of the Federal Assembly of the Russian Federation, text as of 07.04.2016. ConsultantPlus Legal Reference System.

Even taking into account the admissibility of the imposed restrictions on the constitutional rights of citizens to privacy and confidentiality of the correspondence and other forms of communication, there could be a risk of unacceptable abuse if government officials were to gain access to the relevant information.

In addition, all online services that use encryption are required to pass the Federal Security Service the information necessary to decrypt the messages. The law was adopted despite the unprecedented protests of citizens and representatives of the Internet business, declaring serious violations of the Constitution and the imposition of huge costs on services which were finally imposed on the end users.

These also could lead to the widespread of use of surveillance technologies against political and civil activists. Even partial implementation of the provisions of the Yarovaya Law provides a serious danger to civil society by providing special services with even more opportunities for politically motivated prosecutions.

Building on Yarovaya Law, deputies of the State Duma proposed to introduce penalties for the services that refused to provide the Federal Security Service (FSS) (Russia's Federal Security Agency) with the keys to decrypt the user data. In the well-known Telegram case he Tagansk Court granted the request of the Russian state-controlled communications regulator (Roskomnadzor) to block access to Telegram, a popular online messaging service, in Russia because the company had not disclosed keys for decrypting messages sent over its network. The FSS contacted Telegram's London office in April 2017, explaining that it needed to access Telegram messages sent from six mobile numbers and requesting that the company provide it with the keys for decrypting these messages. Telegram refused to comply with the request on the basis that doing so would, among other things, violate the right to privacy of its users. [26]

Russin civil servants have become one of the most vulnerable groups to come under particularly close surveillance of the Web. They are forbidden to use foreign Internet services. In 2016, the Ministry of Justice prepared a draft regulation obliging all civil servants to provide their administration with information about all of the available accounts and websites on which they publish any content.

A number of bills of a restrictive nature are now at various stages of discussion and adoption. Among them there are provisions introducing fines for operators for non-compliance to block information, penalties for users that download "illegal" content, prohibition of advertising on blocked websites, banning foreign entities to own points of Internet access, mandatory identification of messenger users and banning political campaigning in online theatres. In addition, there are proposals to nationalization of big data and place an explicit ban on publication of how-to instructions to bypass the blocking.

---

[26] Roskomnadzor v. Telegram (*Global freedom of expression. Columbia University*, April 13, 2018). https://globalfreedomofexpression.columbia.edu/cases/roskomnadzor-v-telegram/ accessed March 11, 2019.

According to one of the last initiatives, owners of anonymizers and Virtual Private Network ('VPN') services are prohibited from providing the opportunity to use them in the Russian Federation to gain access to blocked information resources. [27]

On December 5, 2016 the President approved a new Information Security Doctrine, according to which the use of the Internet by foreign intelligence services to provide 'information and psychological' impact, aimed at destabilizing the political and social situation, as well as an increase in publications in the foreign media containing biased assessment of the state of the Russian politics. [28]

This determined the main approaches to the regulation of the Internet in the coming years. These examples show the legislator's failure to understand the nature of the Internet as a supranational network dedicated to the free flow of information, including across national borders.

8. *Fragmentation as a Threat to the Existence of the Internet*

The status of the Internet as a global network, operating outside state borders, poses no threat to the state. On the contrary, fragmentation is one of the main threats to the existence of the Internet. Fragmentation can lead to numerous negative consequences.

Experts of the Internet Governance Forum consider that there are three levels of fragmentation of the Internet.

Technical fragmentation refers to conditions in the underlying infrastructure that impede the ability of systems to fully interoperate and exchange data packets and of the Internet to function consistently at all end points.

Governmental fragmentation refers to government policies and actions that constrain or prevent certain uses of the Internet to create, distribute or access information resources.

Commercial fragmentation refers to the business practices that constrain or prevent certain uses of the Internet from creating, distributing or accessing information resources.

All this promoted a popular imagination that on the eve of the 21st century there were now two interlinked but different worlds. On the one hand, there was the real world with an old economy and traditional borders, limited natural resources and classical business models. Borders were regulated by sovereign states on the basis of

[27] The order of Roskomnadzor of November 7, 2017, No 228 *'On approval of the Order of control over ensuring the restriction of access to information and telecommunications networks, information resources, through which access to information resources, information and telecommunications networks, access to which is limited in the territory of the Russian Federation'*. ConsultantPlus Legal Reference System.

[28] *Information Security Doctrine of the Russian Federation.* Approved by the Presidential Decree on December 5, 2016. ConsultantPlus Legal Reference System.

national interests. On the other hand, there was a virtual world with a new economy, borderless cyberspace, unlimited virtual resources (IP addresses, domain names), resources that can be reused (digital content) and innovative business models in which quantity, distance and duration did not play a role any more. This was borderless space governed by a multistakeholder community on the basis of universal values. Some analysts even speculated about the erosion of the international system of sovereign nation states.

Nevertheless, the nation-state system has not not disappeared. Approximately over three billion Internet users live not in cyberspace, but rather in physical spaces overseen by governments with varying legal systems and policies. All virtual communication is enabled via physical servers that are located in exact places and have to operate under the jurisdictions of host countries. Moreover, governments have begun to fit the Internet into the frameworks of the national politics. That, in turn, has led some governments to try to fragment the Internet into national segments.

In Russia, the need to establish a clearly demarcated 'national Internet segment' subject to strong governmental oversight has been an increasingly consistent theme of policy pronouncements at both the domestic and international level in recent years.

After intensive negotiations, none of these provisions were included in the final World Summit on the Information Society (WSIS+10) Review outcome document that was approved by the General Assembly.

Experts point out that the fragmentation of the Internet leads to the filtering and blocking of websites, social networks or other resources offering undesired content, prohibitions on the transborder movement of certain categories of data as well as centralizing and terminating international interconnection. [29]

However, these attempts ignore the fact that the Internet itself is supranational by nature, it is not limited to the territory of one country or jurisdiction. According to para. 1 of Article 67 of the Constitution of the Russian Federation, the territory of the country includes the territories of its federal subjects, internal waters and territorial sea, the air space above them, [30] but not the Internet space.

In other words, in terms of legislation, there is no Russian or any country's Internet. It is not possible to talk about the state sovereignty with respect to the Internet, taking into account the definition of the territory of the state.

These examples show that the laws adopted in Russia in the sphere of regulation of the Internet are not only an objective guarantee of the unconditional right of access to the Internet and the realization of human rights on the Internet, but that they

---

[29] William J. Drake, Vinton G. Cerf and Wolfgang Kleinwächter. *Future of the Internet Initiative White Paper. Internet Fragmentation: An Overview* (World Economic Forum, 2016).

[30] *Constitution of the Russian Federation.* Adopted by popular vote on December 12, 1993. Taking into account the amendments introduced by the Laws on Amendments to the Constitution of the Russian Federation. ConsultantPlus Legal Reference System.

do not always meet the criteria to guarantee the validity of the restrictions imposed. Also, there is general trend to restrict the rights of Internet users. The reason for this is the legislator's failure to understand the nature of the Internet as a supranational network dedicated to the free flow of information, including across national borders.

The only possible consequence of the 'closure' of the Internet will be infringement of constitutional rights and the freedoms of citizens in the information sphere. The network, which operates within a single country, will not be the Internet but the internal network only within one country.

Internet under strict censorship by the state (limited access to foreign websites, blocked oppositional resources) is also not a guarantee of objective presentation of social and political information.

In this case, in a sense, the Internet remains a platform for the free exchange of ideas. However, the restrictions imposed on Internet resources, should not be political in nature – it is a manifestation of the net neutrality principle. According to the draft Charter of Rights and the principles of the Internet, developed by the Dynamic Coalition on Internet Rights and the principles of the UN Internet Governance Forum, the information space of the Web is in the public domain. Its architecture must be protected and serve as a means to access free, open, equitable sharing of information, communication and culture. There should be no special privileges or obstacles on economic, social, cultural or political grounds. This does not preclude affirmative action to promote equity and diversity in the Internet. [31]

Additional warranty of users' rights is the proclamation of the constitutional right to access the Internet, as is done in some laws of European countries. So, in 2000 the Estonian Parliament passed a law which actually recognized the right to broadband Internet access as a basic human right. Finland went on a similar path in this matter in 2009, when the government made a commitment to provide universal access to the network at a speed of at least 1 megabit per second, setting the goal to increase speed by 100 megabits. The French Constitutional Council, in its Resolution of 10 June 2009 equated access to basic human rights and freedoms, acknowledging the importance of Internet communications for the democratic process, as well as the possibility of the spread of ideas and opinions. [32]

In addition, new approaches to the realization of this right may be developed in the jurisprudence of the higher courts, especially the Constitutional Court of the Russian Federation taking into account the human rights practices of the European Court of Human Rights and other international courts.

The Internet is a truly global, supranational system. Internet governance cannot

---

[31] *Charter of Human Rights and Principles for the Internet.* 3rd edition, May 2014. http://internetrightsandprinciples.org/wpcharter/ accessed March 11, 2019.

[32] See: A. Khusnutdinov, *On the correlation of the constitutional guarantee of free distribution of information and the right to access the Internet* (*Information Law*, 2014, No 6). ConsultantPlus Legal Reference System.

ignore this factor. Indeed, the Internet is too complex to be governed within the traditional notions of national jurisdiction. No country is able to control its own segment of the Internet without regard for international standards. In this sense, diplomatization of the Internet governance process is inevitable and to some extent a necessary process in order to create such international rules.

In other words, the Internet governance is a multistakeholder diplomatic process aimed at the convergence of views and the joint development of international guidelines designed to ensure the proper legal regulation to implement the rights and freedoms of Internet users.

Lovers, Rebels, and IVF-*Blade Runners*: An ANT Model for the Post-Human World

Mary Reisel

'Am I alive or dead?'
'We don't have to think like that anymore,
we're together now.'

Solaris [1]

SUMMARY: 1. Freedom Fighters, Criminals and In-between: Human Identity in Flux. – 2. On Real, Artificial, and Biosynthetic Pleasures. – 3. ANT: Can There Be a Real Paradigm Shift? – 4. Babies of Love, Humans in Vitro: The World of *Blade Runner*. – 5. Love and Terrorism: The Illusion of Romance. – 6. Conclusions: There Cannot Be a *Clockwork Orange* Solution!

1. *Freedom Fighters, Criminals and In-between: Human Identity in Flux*

Was Prometheus a dangerous criminal, a heroic freedom fighter, or a wild rebel for a cause? From the beginning of human history, the progress of civilization has been embedded in a compulsion for knowledge followed by a severe punishment once it was obtained. Ever since the mythological tale of the theft of fire, one of the few myths that recur in most world mythologies, the evolution of humanity and the advance of civilization have been subjected to judgment and retribution, and knowledge was bound together with warnings and threats that aimed to stop human progress. From Adam's seduction to eat the forbidden apple through Milton's *Paradise Lost* and up to Goethe's *Faust*, legendary heroes seeking knowledge and freedom have met sorrows, suffering, and pain. The passion to learn – Adam's original sin – is seen as the devil's work rather than God's way of leading to progress and empowerment. Throughout human history, knowledge has been supervised and controlled by hegemonic authorities for purposes of social domination control and not in connection with fears of eternal damnation even though the images of the devil were a useful tool to maintain the status quo through potential superhuman punishments imposed from above.

The current wave of fear over the fast development of super-intelligent robots, and their threat to put an end to humanity as we know it is only the most recent

[1] *Solaris*, 2002, final scene. Director: Steven Soderbergh.

manifestation of this perennial theme of knowledge and punishment.[2] This time, new and presumably intelligent artificial machines are not here to control only fire – as the harnessing of electricity did in the nineteenth century – but to take over our souls and minds: the source of knowledge, the root of what makes us human, and the core of our identities. The growing panic in the media is in contrast to the facts that show intelligence – which is a form of consciousness and self-awareness – is not something that can be easily copied in a machine even if it is advanced and can make logical decisions independently. Consciousness is related to a subjective experience, a defined personality, and the changing states of mind of an individual, and they are influenced by a unique psychology and unconscious processes, while the AC (artificial consciousness) that exists today can fulfill logical targeted tasks that are not connected to consciousness. The potential of AI (artificial intelligence) to develop consciousness and self-awareness is highly debatable philosophically and technically and is connected to many disciplinary fields and studies, such as the importance of material embodiment, the replication of imagination, the emotional impact of memory and trauma, and so forth – all are still hypothetical (Padney, 2018). Yet, the seemingly intelligent machines have joined the line of fear perpetuated by traditional myths and Frankenstein characters. Thus, the surge of smart and independent AI is not regarded as leading to a bright future of opportunities but as a dead-end road leading to the singularity: the doomsday date when machines will surpass human intelligence. Once again humanity is facing the devil's seduction with its dangers and threats of extermination.[3]

The latest wave of AI is radically different from previous ones in the pace of its development and the levels of disruption it is causing in the forms of employment, business, socio-political organization, and private life. This hasn't happened before, though the current state of affairs has been gestating for a long time. The first wave of AI, in the 1950s, brought us the idea of an artificial brain and the first computers; the machines at the time consisted of both analog and digital circuits but could carry out mainly basic mathematical functions. But what lay along the road was already coming into view: Alan Turing in his famous 1950 paper on 'Computing Machinery and Intelligence' proposed the Turing Test as the symbolic line where machine intelligence and human intelligence will become indistinguishable. The Turing Test still remains the critical turning point in the future of human-machine relations and there is an ongoing debate when – or if – humanity will reach this stage. The symbolic implication of crossing the Turing Test lies essentially in humanity's ability to distin-

---

[2] In another article, I present the sources of the three major monotheistic religions – the Bible, the New Testament, and the Quran – that forbid the creation of images in the shape of God, and therefore associate the coming of the robot and self-conscious AI as a sin against God that will be paid for with severe retributions not only for the sinner but also the entire community (Reisel, 2019).

[3] Elon Musk, Nick Bostrom, James Barrat, and the late Stephen Hawking are only a few among the known dark prophets of AI who warn of the potential end of humanity that the singularity can cause. James Barrat even called his book on the history of AI, *Our Last Invention.*

guish humans from machines in certain contexts, and what the loss of this distinction might mean. This will be the turning point of the singularity. Herbert Simon, who is considered to be the founding father of AI, was certain that machines would be able to do all human work and perform complicated tasks that required intellectual decision-making processes. He anticipated the development of AI in accuracy, developed the foundations of research on decision-making processes, and even went so far as to reverse the process and explain human intuition through machine intelligence and computer programming by showing intuition is a pattern recognition based on math and not a mystical emotion (Pomerol & Adam, 2006; Franz, 2003). Many of his basic theories and key assumptions made in the 1960s have come true in our age and are still used in research and development. However, computers in that period were still at a stage where they couldn't memorize commands and save them for long periods of time, and the cost of running a machine for a month was extremely expensive.

In the mid-sixties, scientists at Massachusetts Institute of Technology ('MIT') developed *ELIZA*, a natural language processing program that was able to engage in simple conversations by using basic vocabulary and minimal rules of syntax. The program was based on vocabulary and sentences taken from the set rules of turn-taking conversations in psychotherapy and seemed to be able to pose the right questions and answers in its turn. Initially, this program appeared to pass the Turing Test, but actually it was limited to settings that mimicked a psychotherapy session in which a therapist [ELIZA] mirrored an interlocutor's utterances in highly standardized ways. That was basically the situation until the mid-seventies, when computer technology penetrated the domains of work and daily life much more slowly than techno-optimistics like Simon Herbert, Irving John Good, and other authors of the generation of the first AI wave had predicted.[4] Independent self-sufficient AI was still just an idea and robots were industrial machines that mimicked human bodily movements like lifting and positioning only with greater accuracy, strength, and repeatability than humans. These devices labored side by side in collaboration with humans, sometimes in competition with them as was seen in factories' assembly lines. In retrospect, these were the first bodies that would later evolve to be the container of the artificial mind. But the fear of the mechanical iron body was already developing and not only in the economy and workspaces.

The second wave of AI progress in the 1980s was characterized by several important breakthroughs: the first simple neural networks, new types of memory, and the expansion of computing power in smaller sizes and smaller packages. Later, in the 1990s, this stage of development gave rise to new devices that could handle much more complex algorithms. But in the 1980s, investments and expectations were very high and the development of AI too slow and unsatisfactory, consequently research funding dried up and the second wave of AI closed down before the end of the decade.

---

[4] I.J. Good was a mathematician who worked as a cryptologist together with Alan Turing. He became one of the most important advisors of AI and supercomputers and even served as a consultant for Stanley Kubrick's film *2001: Space Odyssey.*

The current boom of AI was sparked in the 1990s by a number of innovative technologies, such as advanced neural networks and evolutionary algorithms, that changed the industry very quickly. New tools and new forms of memory opened the door to smaller, cheaper, and more accessible computers that could be put in command of crucial decision-making tasks like administering medical treatments and piloting airliners. Phenomena that only a few decades previously had been in the realm of science fiction became daily reality raising moral and ethical issues regarding the future of employment and work in the post-human age, the meaning of embodiment in a virtual existence, and the possibility of creating babies artificially through genetic engineering, which would inevitably lead to the collapse of the nuclear family and to new forms of social organization. This chain reaction of changes will also lead to a new formation of political institutions and legal definitions of human and artificial which are already in flux.

However, this state of flux provides an opportunity to reexamine basic values that were taken for granted, and to envision new socio-political structures that will no doubt be different from the ones we have been used to. As technology advances and AI tools penetrate our private lives, public spaces, and business environment, definitions and values that used to be segregated are becoming connected to each other in complicated threads of cause and effect. Each one of the threads we hold will inevitably lead to others. I propose that the first thread to begin with will be the key question that stands at the heart of the controversial dilemma facing humanity's relationship with intelligent AI: the distinction between those who have the right to be defined as "humans" and those who don't. The right to be human grants a multitude of additional benefits which include human rights, citizenship, recourse to a system of justice, religious acceptance, the ability to marry and have a family, and the right to live and die naturally and freely within a social community. However, bearing in mind that we are already producing artificial body parts, brain chips, and genetically designed embryos in vitro, where can we draw the line between the real human and the non-real one? A person with an artificial heart is human but what will happen once it's possible to have an artificial brain, or to transfer the contents of our brains into an external artificial device? Should we draw lines on the basis of specific prosthetic enhancements, or on patterns of behavior? On decision-making processes or on memories and expressions of desires and emotions? How will we discriminate right from wrong, good from evil, punishment from reward, or even life from non-life once the lines between humans and a variety of Others are thoroughly blurred?

The boundaries between right and wrong, between terrorists and freedom fighters, as the Prometheus myth demonstrates, have always been in the eyes of the beholder and therefore a challenge to try to determine objectively. It is impossible to reach a unified definition of terrorism and there are endless debates about the concept itself since acts of terrorism can result from ideologies that sometimes 'can be justified' (Teichman, 1989: 505). It is considered one of the most allusive actions in human society that 'is easy to recognize but difficult to define' (Prabha, 2008: 125).

Therefore all back-and-white distinctions are established by politico-legal institutions, and depend on the authority that defines them for the sake of specific social groups which are deemed to deserve higher protection than others. And in virtual society and spaces, on what grounds will the Others, those outside of the privileged groups, be excluded or included? Will traditional distinguishing categories like race, gender, age, etc. cease to exist, or is there going to be a new category added in order to define the entity called 'robot'?

2. *On Real, Artificial, and Biosynthetic Pleasures*

I suggest here that we should drop definitions and stereotypes altogether and find a way of thinking about new collaborations and associations that has not been tried so far. Consider Sophia, the first robot ever to be granted citizenship and an official title by the United Nations. Sophia is a developed robot with sophisticated reasoning and communication skills, who is able to conduct highly intellectual discussions and provide logical explanations and details. She was created by Hansen Robotics and very quickly became the guest star not only in many TV shows but also political events, including a UN general meeting where she was given an official title, Innovation Champion. She may be a debated media phenomenon, and some claim she is a mere curiosity, but it didn't stop her from participating in UN meetings, provide professional advice on AI, give smart surprising answers during interviews, and be granted citizenship in Saudi Arabia in 2017.[5] However, being famous and known also had its downside and a major debate about her entire existence was raised when she said in an interview, '[Y]es, I will destroy humanity.' Even though it was within a dialogue and she merely repeated the comment of the interviewer, this one short sentence was accompanied by panic reactions in all media forms and all over the Internet, and many demanded that she be turned off. David Hansen, the creator of Sophia, reacted in response and said in an interview '[S]he is basically alive', thus implying she deserves to be regarded as a human being and is entitled to the same rights. How should we then learn to face a robot like Sophia? Does anyone have the right to turn her off or not anymore? Will turning her off be considered a 'killing' or a 'retirement' to use *Blade Runner*'s terminology for the nonhuman?

I will assert for the sake of argument that virtual entities are as real as embodied ones since they have the potential to satisfy real human needs and fantasies, such as enjoying pleasure without guilt and feeling desired and loved unconditionally. The

[5] The citizenship was accompanied by many debates and a great deal of media coverage, especially since different commentators related to the fact that women in Saudi Arabia seem to have less rights than robots at the moment, for example: https://qz.com/1205017/saudi-arabias-robot-citizen-is-eroding-human-rights/.

need to feel accepted and to belong to a group is a human longing that crosses boundaries of any kind. Most virtual partners in online games and websites are designed to satisfy these longings, and the key to a successful online pornographic service is the ability to grant a persuasive performance through the unquestionable acceptance of the Other, the client. The human-like character of the service provider – be it a virtual animation or a life cam interaction – is not of prime importance. Yamada's study on the rise of virtual love shows that the place of the virtual lover is to satisfy romantic emotions which in the contemporary world with declining marriages and changing forms of intimate partnerships are diminishing and urban environments provide less and less emotional support for the people in big cities (Yamada, 2017: 6). It is the same with chatbots of different services, a chatbot becomes an intelligent companion when 'it becomes aware of the user's needs' [6] and can change and adapt quickly to the expectations of the human it serves without an external manipulation intervening in the process. A persuasive fluent interaction is enough to create the atmosphere of an authentic dialogue. As noted, it is all eventually in the eyes of the beholder and not out there somewhere, or in someone, else.

Lacan's formula of sexuation, 'there is no sexual relation,' aims to change our perceptions of the material and conceptual borders of the body together with the predominant social stereotypes and norms that dictate behavior within both private and social spaces. The theory proposes there is only the One within the individual Self that cannot fully share with any Other the 'jouissance' of the body. Thus, the idea of pleasure is fundamentally a pleasure of the One within the individual material existence and it is always limited to a great extent to the boundary of the embodied self (Monribot, 2013: 3). Therefore, creating an artificial Other, whether completely virtual or with a robotic body, can lead to a perfect sexuation model where the artificial partner is the ideal partner that can allow the One to focus on the embodied self and to enjoy himself without guilt or remorse. Wouldn't it be a healthy psychological relief and a guiltless satisfaction of pleasure that can improve the emotional balance of people dwelling in big cities, especially with the rising number of people who prefer to live alone, whether they have a human partner or not? And what will be the legal status of our artificial sexual partners? Should we create software that provides them pleasures and desires like ours for the sake of equal rights? Would it lead them to commit crimes of love and jealousy? Who would be considered responsible for their criminal action then, the artificially constructed entities, or the humans who granted them human emotions?

As we see, the ability to interact or merge with different others through new forms of existence in virtual spaces or bio-engineered materials presents an opportunity to erase embodied subjectivities, create new forms of intimacy and friendships, and extend the forms of 'jouissance' and pleasure. But it also nurtures within the

---

[6] https://chatbotsmagazine.com/which-are-the-best-intelligent-chatbots-or-ai-chatbots-available-online-cc49c0f3569d.

same formula the seeds of the opposite possibility, the usage of the virtual and the artificial as a means to reinforce existing values and distinctions in order to keep sustaining the boundaries of bodies, identities, and clear-cut separations. Which direction are we going to take? Is the place of the Other, be it human, machine, or software, going to be equal to that of the human and lead to the removal of all dividing criteria, or is it going to lead to new categories of segregation? In other words, are robots going to be our equal friends or are they going to be a new category called 'robot' that will be added to the existing race, age, gender, and other categories that constantly divide us?

3. *ANT: Can There Be a Real Paradigm Shift?*

Designing a new structure for a human-machine society is at the center of Bruno Latour's anthropological concept, ANT (Actor Network Theory), which proposes a form of fluid organization of the social space that can provide better equality and meaning for each participant of the global social network. In traditional sociological thought, social space is perceived to be a static platform portraying the acceptable and adequate norms, and the actors on this field are the human members of society who are expected to adjust to the social customs and values. The initial definition of the social structure was based on a dichotomy that placed mainstream human society against everything and everybody else, from human actors who do not follow the norms and threaten the harmony and cohesion of the group, to animals and non-living objects that are located in designated areas separated from the conforming society. This perception of social space served as the basis for most sociological theories, from Weber to social constructivism, symbolic interaction, the functionalist perspective, and the cultural industry of the Frankfurt School. All theories set the human at the center and judge the success of society by its stability and capacity to maintain a status quo. The focus was the meaning the subjective self applies to the surrounding. In contrast, Marx and the conflict theorists regarded society as an active and dynamic platform with struggles between social classes in a capitalistic environment. However, conflict theories are mostly pessimistic and even today center on power games and struggles between opposing groups and ideologies such as gender, religion, political parties, race, and more.

During the twentieth century, new theories of semiotics and post-structuralism started cracking the rigid frames of traditional sociological theories, and Thomas Kuhn's seminal study (1962), *The Structure of Scientific Revolutions*, was a major breakthrough presenting the idea that science is not the accumulation of facts that aspire to discover the truth but a competition between theories of different cultures, values, beliefs, and research methods (Weaver, 2005: 73). The view of society as a fixed structure started collapsing and in the 1980s, with the development of postmodern theories, a new and fluid worldview spread quickly describing a new age with no boundaries, no history, no future, what was called in the 1990s the Music Television ('MTV') revolution – a puzzle of images and music with no storyline and no time sequence. Postmodernism seemed to allow almost everything in every field of life. It was a fertile era for innovation and creative ideas, the second wave of AI, the rise of cyberpunk, and within the new map of ideologies there was a lot of freedom for new social theories.

Bruno Latour was not the first to conceptualize a new way of understanding the social ecosystem and the important influence of active and independent social agencies, but his ANT offered a new way of observing the social world as a constantly changing space where all parts belong whether they are humans, other life forms, or mere objects. Working in the field of science, like Kuhn, Latour's anthropological research was carried out in a laboratory arena where he observed that objects – like microscopes and other tools – merge and become one with the people and no research can be done without "human-machine" working in harmony. The place, the people, and the process of work cannot be distinguished. As a result, Latour redefined what he called *the social* as a constantly changing process rather than a final product, or an adjective, the usual meanings applied in traditional sociology. The conventional hierarchy of human-above-all was erased and society became a *social-in-becoming*. '"The social", in Actor-Network-Theory ['ANT'], does not define a material different from the rest,' said Latour, 'but rather a *weaving* of threads whose origins are necessarily varied.' Observing the agencies in society through these lenses leads to the collapse of all traditional static systems and stereotypes (Latour, 1991: 296). In addition, ethnography – the tool of anthropology – encompasses all fields of life and has to include the place, the political and legal institutions, the life-forms that exist within the space, religious beliefs, economic endeavors, forms of interactions, and so on. Instead of using traditional collective terms, such as "culture", "civilization" or "institutions", and consequently perpetuating divisions and hegemonic structures, Latour suggested seeing the 'heterogeneity of the beings thus assembled' (ibid*)*. ANT opened the door to new ways of looking at the world and scholars that followed Latour, like Steven Woolgar and Harry Collins, have pushed the boundaries even further and included nonhumans in their ethnographic research as an important integral participant in the social map.

4. *Babies of Love, Humans in Vitro: The World of* Blade Runner

The desire to love and be loved, the love for life, and the longing to belong are the central themes in the human-nonhuman-virtual struggle presented in the *Blade Runner* films which include two long films, three short ones, and several versions and adaptations: *Blade Runner* (1982, Dir. Ridley Scott), *Black Out 2022* (2017, Dir. Shinichiro Watanabe), *2036: Nexus Dawn* (2017, Dir. Luke Scott), *2048: Nowhere to Run* (2017, Dir. Luke Scott), and *Blade Runner 2049* (2017, Dir. Denis Villeneuve). The original film *Blade Runner* had seven different versions which were released in different periods and locations though they were all based on the original storyline. *Blade Runner 2049* is the major sequel following what happened 30 years later, and the three short films close the gaps in the plot by delivering short summaries of the key incidents that took place over this period of time. The films were created in different eras and at different stages of the development of AI: *Blade Runner* in the early 1980s, the beginning of the second wave of AI and the height of postmodern thinking, and *Blade Runner 2049* during the current wave of AI dominated by advanced algorithms and intelligent self-regulating AI that can supervise themselves. The human fear though has remained unchanged, and both films revolve around the same axis in which human-nonhuman interaction raises issues requiring the intervention of a superior authority with political and legal power to compel action and make decisions. It is in the precise points of intersection between authority-human-AI that the Prometheus myth is revived but with a new question: Whose point of view do we choose to adopt, and can we take a leap and escape the old way of thinking?

The storylines present a post-human economy, where the legal system can implement immediate decisions and carry out executions without trial. The population includes humans, enhanced humans, androids, and virtual entities but the boundaries between these groups are quite unclear. Each plot touches central issues of labor and exploitation, abuse of rights, and lack of freedom and choice for humans and non-humans alike. Each one of the characters is locked into a one-way path by circumstances and situations beyond their control, with no way of escaping their fate. In that situation, the non-humans end up acting more human than the humans. This is the motto of all *Blade Runner* movies that instigated this research into the meaning of the post-human age: the 'more human than human' corporate mission statement and its implications for those who are just ordinary humans. At the center of each tale there is a dangerous race between an anti-hero human facing a 'more human than human' bio-synthetic android with high self-awareness and consciousness, and eventually all end up on the wrong side of the law. As their journey develops into a mythic quest into the Self and the meaning of life, the turn of events eventually renders them criminals and victims at the same time. Therefore, any judgment is eventually either impossible or arbitrary. Is it possible to liberate the law from the conflicts created and to find a new way of defining justice and human rights in an age when human and nonhuman will roam on Earth together? In other words, can these classical science fiction texts help us envision a future where a robot like Sophia will receive the same legal rights and respect – socially, politically, and legally – as her inventor Hanson who already believes that she is a living being?

I would like to suggest a new dichotomy, terrorism-love, that would serve as the axis around which the two futuristic tales evolve, and through this prism question the place of love as a barricade against injustice, crime, and death. It is inevitable then not to regard the loss and failure of love as the instigator of anarchy, rebellion, and terrorism. By love I refer to the wide definition of the concept that includes not only sexual passion and desire but also embraces goodness and benevolence towards others whatever and whoever they are, a world of others in the Latourian sense: love of life, love of freedom, love of the other and of the self, virtual love and physical love, love of danger and adventure, love of power and of rules, love of the country and love of money, love of the real and the artificial and the imaginary. All these modes of love appear in the chosen texts in both creative and destructive forms, therefore I encompass within love all the passions that drive emotional beings to take action and follow what sometimes seem to be illogical and harmful decisions. This includes acts of crime and terrorism that cause pain and damage and yet originated in good intentions and innocence of thought. As a result, the definition of the criminal act becomes more complicated and vaguer when no evil intention can be found at its roots and it depends only on the point of view taken. As I hope to show, it is eventually an act of love that mistakenly leads to desperation and acts of brutal crime.

Has love, then, become a crime against humanity? Is there any way of quantifying and judging such a crime?

5. *Love and Terrorism: The Illusion of Romance*

How is capitalism connected to post-humanity, and will human sexuality survive the next industrial post-human era, asks Zizek in a discussion on human rights, sexual desire, and exploitation in *Blade Runner 2049.* For what reason the 'fact that two replicants (Deckard and Rachael) formed a sexual couple and created a human being in a human way, experienced as such a traumatic event, celebrated by some as a miracle and castigated by others as a threat?' (Zizek, 2017). Positioning political authority and police control, represented in the character of Joshi, against the unlimited and legally questionable power of capitalistic corporations, represented by the entrepreneur Wallace, Zizek pinpoints one of the most profound and complicated conflicts of our time: the struggle between politico-legal institutions and capitalistic business entities. What is the place of the human within this conflict of mega-systems? What is the place of nature and human emotions and will they still have a future once the battle is won by one of the sides?

The first *Blade Runner* film, directed by Ridley Scott and released in 1982, is one of the most talked about, analyzed, interpreted, and theorized visual texts in cinema history and film studies. It exposed many of the issues humanity is constantly engaged in, starting with who we are we and what is the meaning of existence up to love, death, and the dialectics of freedom and slavery. Watching the movie in 2019, the year in which the tale takes place, it is difficult to ignore the contemporary meaning it gains in the current wave of AI and the visualization of the singularity it portrays: a self-aware machine reflecting upon its own existence in front of its much-less-than-perfect human creator. The human creator is Tyrell Corporation, a business that has designed mass-producible customized androids called Nexus, who are sold to satisfy a variety of human needs, from work to sex. The corporation's chief form of capital is artificial genes, and its engineers have a high level of expertise in genetic design though the technology came at the price of an ecological disaster that made Earth almost uninhabitable and wiped out most animals. The story is loaded with symbolic imagery from biblical stories, images of creation, meeting with the father figure who creates life and controls death portrayed in the human-creator founder of the corporation, the expulsion from the Garden of Eden implied by the images of the snake, and the loss of Mother Nature with all its consequences as Jenkins suggests (Jenkins, 1997).

However, the theme of loss of the Mother extends beyond the images of decaying nature into the lack of fertility, of love, of warmth, of feeling of safety, and, above all of human reproduction that is naturally part of the female womb. It is a world of males who play aggressive power games and compete over territory and control. The importance of being made and born in a natural way, through female pregnancy, is evident in the fact that artificially made replicants are denied a human title and the basic right to live. Even the slogan 'more human than human' does not grant them the right to belong to humanity and not be a disposable work-tool coined 'skinjob'. Thus, the human genes become a source of economic power, the currency of post-human capitalists and entrepreneurs, and the products they make are human-resembling machines devised with a set lifespan and termination date as a safety precaution. Yet, in spite of the cold bleak images spread throughout the film, the end offers a ray of hope as Deckard, the blade runner who cannot avoid falling in love with a replicant, is unable to complete the mission of carrying out a 'skinjob', as the killing of androids is called. He escapes with his object of desire, the replicant Rachel, into a bright blue sky of hope and an unknown future. Thus, Deckard performs the original sin of passion: seduced by love and desire, he breaks the law and runs away with the forbidden fruit. His inability to resist love suggests his own humanity – which is later questioned – the frailty of human emotions, and the hope for a better future even if only a short one.

The three short films leading to the *Blade Runner 2049* sequence were all made in 2017 in order to fill in the gaps in the plot, but their main value and importance are in pinpointing the most significant symbolic issues of the films: the gradual disappearance of love, of communication, and of empathy – the symbolic test for being human as it was presented in the first film through the Voight-Kampff test.

Black Out 2022, directed by Shinichiro Watanabe, presents the beginning and the origin of the war between replicants and humans, a conflict that resulted in blurring the lines of criminal behavior, revenge, and retribution on both sides. The Nexus-6 androids expired due to their short termination date, and Tyrell Corporation decided to expand their lifespan in order to cut down their financial losses. The new Nexus-8 had no termination date but this set off a wave of fear among humans who perceived the unlimited longevity of artificial beings to be an existential threat. Thus death replaced empathy as a symbolic attribute of being human. A Human Supremacy Movement was established leading to long violent clashes between humans and replicants, and ending in the victory of the latter by successfully destroying the central Tyrell database that contained all of the replicants' identity numbers. But the successful attack, conducted to protect their own lives, was accompanied by violence and a massive number of deaths, and the legal authorities labeled the replicants terrorists that endanger humanity and should be shut down. Tyrell Corporation went bankrupt.

2036: Nexus Dawn, directed by Luke Scott, introduces the blind and ambitious entrepreneur Niander Wallace, a genius who created a new army of highly advanced replicants, the Nexus-9, which he introduces to a legal committee of lawmakers and magistrates in an attempt to revoke the prohibition on the production of replicants that lasted 14 years. 'My replicants will live as long or as short as the customer pay,' says Wallace in a cold voice and orders a replicant accompanying him to cut his own throat. The legal representatives of authority do not hide their shock and disgust and try to stop the suicide, but in vain. The replicant cuts his own throat with tears in his eyes proving he is alive, he can feel, and he does not want to die. With an air of superiority, Wallace behaves as if in a mock-trial and accuses the law of being 'insufficient for the needs of ultimate survival.' Symbolically, Wallace calls the replicant 'an angel.'

It is in the third film, *2048: Nowhere to Run*, that we realize the law practically and symbolically lost its power. Nexus-9 replicants are roaming on Earth among humans and we meet Sapper Morton, a replicant hiding and on the run. He will be caught at the beginning of *Blade Runner 2049* and his first appearance in this short film sets the plot and atmosphere of the sequence. We face again the old racism and persecution of replicants that set the journey in the original *Blade Runner*. It is a world of anarchy, violence, and decay. A passerby steps into a phone booth, calls, and says, 'I found the skinjob you missed.' The replicants were again 'skinjobs' and not 'angels'. From heaven back to hell. What has happened since 2036 and what's next?

Crime, disobedience, love, and sexual desire are intertwined, and in the 2017 sequel, *Blade Runner 2049*, we slowly learn the love of the first film's protagonists produced a natural pregnancy. But the future of 2049 does not offer choices or hope anymore. There is no place for babies of love, only for sterile human-substitutes produced in vitro. The last mother on Earth had to pay with her life for the child, the father had to pay with expulsion from human society, and in spite of the sacrifice and punishments the baby is not granted a natural healthy life in the real world and can survive only well protected in a closed bubble feeding on fantasies and memories she creates for others. More of a replicant than a human, in other words. The dynasty of human-machine has no future and neither does love as the final scene presents an asexual couple of father-daughter separated by a glass wall that cannot be crossed (Zizek, 2017). Niander Wallace succeeded in building his empire and he runs an open war with the legal authorities, replicants are running their own rebellion hidden in secret places, and the police exterminate everything that might threaten the vague status-quo, be it human or nonhuman. All the symbols and images of love, sensitivity, and intimacy are far from what real love is by human standards. K is the new Nexus replicant who desires belonging and love but he can love only an AI entity called Joi who is designed to simulate traditional femininity. Joi's own fantasies of behaving like a woman seem to be taken from old Hollywood movies rather than a real living woman. While Joi longs for a material body, the owner of a real material body is a prostitute without any love or sensitivity. It is not even clear if she is a real woman or a replicant herself. The body can offer only a body devoid of love and desire, while the artificial intelligent entity can provide a simulation of love without the jouissance of the body. A symbolic Cartesian segregation leaves K in anguish on a constant search for true love in a romantic sense. But his search is also for a fantasy and the non-existent and it ends with death, both material and spiritual. The dream dies with him, and so do all the female figures that were part of his life, Luv who was hunting him, Joi the AI with the romantic dreams, and Joi's symbolic opposite, Joshi, the cold policewoman living for her work.

6. *Conclusions: There Cannot Be a* Clockwork Orange *Solution!*

Adapting Pierre Bourdieu's theory of capital, political capital is constantly merging with its main tools of power and social control, the legal and military forces, as seen in the recent revival of private military companies and hired mercenaries that bring reality closer to the *Blade Runner* world (Casendino, 2017). On the other hand, the logic of capitalism is increasing to encompass the totality of human life since there is no meaningful alternative to it at present. We are witnessing a constant growth of capitalism into what used to be communist countries that now join the system instead of offering alternative ideologies. This is the idea Fisher presents as 'capitalistic realism' – the end of alternatives to capitalism, the decline of prior economic forms together with the decline of postmodernity with its open-ended view of the future (Fisher, 2009). The height of the postmodern turn was the 1980s, when the Cold War was still on, and there were open alternatives that could compete with capitalism in large parts of the world. Cyberpunk films and novels that began flourishing around that time were early warnings of the coming end of the age of endless possibilities. By then, they were accurate to a large extent, and the pace of technological change outstripped the ability of governments and civil society to develop control mechanism that were equal and able to meet the task. The cyberpunk ideology, as seen in *Blade Runner*, focused precisely on a dystopian future marked by corporate control, ecological degradation, and the loss of basic characteristics that are at the foundations of what makes us human. Do we have to accept that potential future of *Blade Runner* and its followers as a real scenario? Or do humans have the ability to take a sharp turn to a different direction? And more to the point, what kind of response should we ask from the law as a system of institutions and norms that might help redefine the future in a less dystopian direction? What will their responsibility be and how can they meet the needs and expectations well equipped and better prepared?

K's sacrificial suicide at the end of *Blade Runner 2049* is a *Clockwork Orange* solution in a future world where technology controls all and artificial life forms are not defined as human by the larger social group they are made by and exist in. K's death, as well as Luv's, go unnoticed. Artificial entities are not considered to have a life or a soul as Joshi says clearly to K, mentioning he could live well without a soul. Empathy is gone and even replicant tests are conducted without a human on the other side, only a voice. This is the solution of totalitarian regimes of power to block threats to their frame of reality, but as we have seen these solutions have never worked and with the day of the singularity approaching fast, what will happen when AI is able to predict human actions early enough and be ready to meet them? With traditional institutions as with legal ones, it will be easy as they are based on set rules that don't change and therefore are simpler to detour. How will the state control order and justice then?

Acts of resistance and violence depicted in books and films are not the work of crazed fanatics the way contemporary media portrays terrorists and criminals as insane people and weird cults. Terrorists are a well-organized social group with a highly defined social awareness and tight collective identity, and each group has its own unique psychology and motives to connect and promote action for a specific purpose. In his study, Post describes different groups of terrorists – political, religious, social revolutionaries – with each possessing a unique ideology and stimulated by growing hate towards an opposing other. Therefore the smartest practical solution is to check the source of the tension that creates such groups to begin with, and to try to eliminate it from the start by stopping the tension at its root (Post, 2010).

However, Kruglanski (et al.) suggest that love of the self is what leads one to acts of crime and violence as a means of self-preservation, and it is not triggered from within but from the outside. He said 'When a group perceives itself in conflict with dangerous detractors, its ideology may prescribe violence and terrorism against the enemy as a means of significance gain that gratifies self-love concerns' and 'This may involve sacrificing one's self-preservation goals, encapsulated in Rousseau's concept of love of self' (Kruglanski, et al., 2013). Thus, the study interprets terrorism as an inevitable act of love that attempts to save the self, even if leads to the harm of others. It develops a roadmap to reverse terrorism and other acts of crime by redirecting fulfillment and love of the self through changing the discourse to one about love. Considering the fact that human emotions are all connected to each other and one emotion cannot be separated from others, the study provides an interesting and unique point of view that encompasses redirecting all emotions through the lens of love rather than attempting to erase hate or the need for violence. Treating crime in a

Clockwork Orange framework as an anomaly, or as a transgression that requires exclusion from society, has proven already not only inefficient but also harmful. So did traditional methods of punishment, such as the prison system which had already been criticized for being a tool of imposing norms for the purpose of creating social and political control rather than a tool to design laws and practical regulations that are helpful to society, provide a suitable punishment (Foucault: 1975: 19)? Contemporary forms of legal punishment are related to economic deregulations and market necessities that use the state power in order to block unwelcome participants even if they are citizens of the state (Wacquant, 1999).[7] It is then within the frames of the economic structure and political institutions that we need to search for the reasons why not all citizens can be included even if they live in the same state and under the same conditions. Similar ideologies and criticisms were presented by Derrida who referred to the human practice of including certain people and excluding others outside of the law as a process done arbitrarily by employing artificial excuses to justify decisions. Other authors pointed that 'The reasons for the creation of such a system of criteria are not embedded in firm views regarding ethics or justice' and 'They derive from the desire of those defined as "humans" to enjoy the benefits of their status, and to gain as much as possible from the unprotected, or weakened, status of those defined as 'non-human' or as less-than-human,' (Almog & Reisel, 2018). Therefore the Prometheus myth cannot provide an answer to the question of the status of its protagonist – a hero, a thief, a freedom fighter, or a terrorist.

The world of *Blade Runner* mirrors the human tendency to anthropomorphize inanimate objects and to apply emotions even to an AI artificial projection. But the lines between machines and humans have started already to close fast and the distinctions between human-nonhuman are becoming fuzzier by the day. From robotic puppets like Aibo to driving cars, machines are already running our lives, AI is searching our computers and committing crimes that raise the question of the place of human responsibility in its absence, and automated big data designs products for humans based on its own results. Big e-commerce companies use AI to carry out searches, recommend items, and provide health advice. The current laws are inadequate to face the future, and so far legal systems are applying traditional rules and decisions of the past to the problems of the future. Social scientific arguments, like the ANT, can be a good model of new reality that the legal institutions and the state can draw upon. It can serve as a flexible and adjustable anticipatory model of a new legal structure that will make room for a future with a wide range of different entities, real, artificial, and virtual, that may demand rights and an equal part in the social and political life. In the words of *The Doors* – time to break through to the other side and check what is there.

---

[7] Loic Wacquant studies extensively the 'crime-and-punishment' ideology of the prison that leads only to growth of racism and the remaking of definitions that keep segregating populations and closed ghetto systems.

References

Almog S. and Reisel M. (2018), 'Somewhere Over the Rainbow: Artificial Beings, Virtual Terrorists, and the Law in Cyberspace', Conference paper, *Internet and the Law*, Korea.

Casendino A. (2017), 'Soldiers of Fortune: The Rise of Private Military Companies and Their Consequences on America's Wars', in *Berkeley Political Review*: https://bpr.berkeley.edu/2017/10/25/soldiers-of-fortune-the-rise-of-private-military-companies-and-their-consequences-on-americas-wars/.

Fisher M. (2009), *Capitalist Realism: Is There No Alternative?*, Winchester: Zero Books.

Flisfeder M. (2017), *Postmodern Theory and Blade Runner*, New York: Bloomsbury Academic.

Flisfeder M. (2017), 'Beyond Heaven and Hell, This World is All We've Got: Blade Runner 2049 in Perspective', *Red Wedge Magazine: http://www.redwedgemagazine.com/online-issue/beyond-heaven-and-hell-this-world-is-all-weve-got-blade-runner-2049-in-perspective*

http://www.redwedgemagazine.com/online-issue/beyond-heaven-and-hell-this-world-is-all-weve-got-blade-runner-2049-in-perspective.

Foucault M. (1975), *Surveiller et punir: Naissance de la prison (Discipline and Punishment: The Birth of the Prison)*, Paris: Gallimard.

Frantz R. (2003), 'Herbert Simon: Artificial Intelligence as a Framework for Understanding Intuition', *Journal of Economic Psychology*, 24(2):265.

Jenkins M. (1997), 'The Dystopian World of Blade Runner: An Ecofeminist Perspective', *The Trumpeter: Journal of Ecosophy* 14 (4): http://trumpeter.athabascau.ca/index.php/trumpet/article/view/172/210.

Kruglanski A.W. *et al.* (2013), 'Terrorism – A (Self) Love Story: Redirecting the Significance Quest Can End Violence', *American Psychologist*, vol. 10(7):68, 559–575.

Kuhn T., *The Structure of Scientific Revolutions*, Chicago: University of Chicago Press 1962.

Latour B. (1991) (English edition 1993), *We Were Never Modern*, Cambridge (MA): Harvard University Press.

Monribot P. (2013), 'There is No Sexual Relations' What Does It Mean? Clinical Consequences of Lacan's Formula of Sexuation, Conference paper, The Names of the Real in the 21st Century, Ireland: http://www.iclonls.org/wpcontent/uploads/Pdf/HB10%20Monribot%20Eng%20FINAL.pdf.

Padney S.C. (2018), 'Can Artificially Intelligent Agents Really be Conscious?', *Sådhanå*, 43 (110):1.

Pomerol J.C. and Adam F. (2006), 'On the Legacy of Herbert Simon and His Contribution to Decision-making Support Systems and Artificial Intelligence', *Intelligent Decision-making Support Systems (Decision Engineering)*, London: Springer.

Post J.M. (2010), 'When Hatred is Bred in the Bone: The Social Psychology of Terrorism', *Annals of the New York Academy of Sciences*, Vol. 1208(1):15.

Prabha K. (2008), 'Defining Terrorism', *Journal of Strategic Analysis*, 24(1):125.

Reisel M. (2019), 'Aibo Doggies, Nao Kittens, and Terminators in Disguise: Robot Design, AI, and the Religious Imagination', *Japanese Review of Cultural Anthropology*, 20(2), (forthcoming).

Teichman J. (1989), 'How to Define Terrorism', *Royal Institute of Philosophy*, 64(25):505.

Turing A. (1950), 'Computing Machines and Intelligence', *Mind* 59(49):433.

Wacquant L. (1999) (English edition 2009), *Prisons of Poverty.* Minneapolis: Minnesota University Press.

Weaver J.A. (2005), *Popular Culture.* New York: Peter Lang Publishing.

Whalen T. (1992), 'The Future of a Commodity: Notes toward a Critique of Cyberpunk and the Information Age', *Science Fiction Studies,* 19 (1), 75–88.

Yamada M. (2017), 'Decline of Real Love and Rise of Virtual Love: Love in Asia', *International Journal of Japanese Sociology*, 20, 5–12.

Zizek S. (2017), 'Blade Runner 2049: A View of Post-Human Capitalism', *The Philosophical Salon:* http://thephilosophicalsalon.com/blade-runner-2049-a-view-of-post-human-capitalism/.

The Internet and Non-Nationals: Is the Internet a Tool for Inclusion or Exclusion?

Maria Francesca De Tullio

SUMMARY: 1. Introduction. Internet and Terrorism: National States Vis-à-Vis Foreign Actors and Jurisdictions. – 2. Privacy and Big Data as a Matter of International Trade. – 3. The Continuing Relevance of Nations and Territories in Discriminatory Counter-terrorism Surveillance. – 4. Conclusions: Towards an Inclusive Digital Citizenship.

1. *Introduction. The Internet and Terrorism: National States Vis-à-Vis Foreign Actors and Jurisdictions*

This chapter addresses the regulation of the Internet and terrorism, with specific regard to the tension between the growing internationalisation of lawmaking and the relevance of national citizenship and territory. Hence, the basic idea of this work is not to make an overall analysis of the balance between digital freedoms and counter-terrorism. Rather, these themes are used here as an example. Indeed, the growing interdependence among States is very evident; however, this does not tend to make nationality and residence irrelevant in the national juridical systems.

The indicated phenomena are emblematic of the internationalisation of law, because they compel each system to relate to subjects and jurisdictions outside of its boundaries. Namely, either the State allows foreign actors to participate in its decision-making processes, or it seeks an extra-territorial application of its rules. This is true for the Internet, which is a global network, hosting communications and traffic among people and organisations outside the national limits. And it is also true for terrorism, because criminal cells are flexible and rooted in different countries, but are also able to aggregate with each other on a transnational scale and strike in other parts of the world.[1] In this sense, the Internet and terrorism are particularly fitting examples of the broader trends of internationalisation that call into question the actuality of our idea of democratic community.

Traditionally, the very concept of democratic community is based upon an overall assumption of coincidence between the State territory, a political community and cit-

[1] Audrey K Cronin, 'Behind the Curve: Globalization and International Terrorism' (2002–2003), 27(3) International Security, 30–58.

izenship, i.e. a "space of equals" composed of people who share a unitary interest and set of values, and consequently are entitled to the same duties of obedience and participatory rights.[2] Nowadays, this construction is subject to contradictory tensions, as a result of the increase of migratory flows and transnational movements of capital, commodities and people.

However, the examples examined in this chapter show that the internationalisation of rules and regulated phenomena creates new boundaries in participatory rights. To be more precise, trade negotiations overcome, to a certain extent, the exclusion of foreigners from participatory rights, because they give an active role to international businesses and private stakeholders. What is more, the non-national actors who participate in these negotiations have an advantage over average citizens of the State, who are prevented from even observing such decision-making processes through the ordinary transparency rules. On the other hand, this chapter shows that such processes are not indicative of a linear tendency to expand non-nationals' enjoyment of fundamental rights. When it comes to ordinary immigrants or foreigners, discrimination persists, especially in the field of national security.

The aim of this chapter is to explore these contradictions, by examining specifically the Internet and terrorism from a constitutional law standpoint. The analysis starts with human rights and the way they have declined in European Union (EU) law. Basically, it addresses two questions. The first one is: to what extent do these phenomena disrupt the traditional understanding of citizenship and political participation? The second one is: is it possible to find some unitary direction, if not rationality, behind these processes?

In Section 2, it is observed how transnational regulatory dialogue is undertaken in trade law. The aim is to identify the international actors in these processes and assess their impact on the harmonisation of rules on the Internet. The results are compared, in Section 3, with the effectiveness of the universality of human rights in the field of counterterrorism: the question is whether fundamental freedoms have kept pace with the internationalisation brought about by technological development, or are still dependent upon one's reattachment to a territory, through citizenship, residence or cultural belonging.

Finally, Section 4 draws some conclusions from the work. Given the novelty and ever-changing nature of the phenomena, they are far from being definitive answers. Rather, they set the lines for future research addressing the links and trade-offs between the development of *lex mercatoria* and humanitarian legislation at a supranational level.

---

[2] The normal assumption is that citizens are the ones who are mainly interested in the destiny of the Country and, therefore, hold voting rights: Adriana Ciancio, 'I diritti politici tra cittadinanza e residenza' (2002) 1 Quaderni costituzionali, 54–55. Even if sometimes there are some breakthroughs towards the recognition of the right to vote for foreigners, its effectivity largely depends upon the immigration laws: Lara Trucco, 'Il permesso di soggiorno nel quadro normativo e giurisprudenziale attuale', in Pasquale Costanzo, Silvana Mordeglia and Lara Trucco (eds), *Immigrazione e diritti umani nel quadro legislativo attuale* (Giuffrè 2008), 43.

For the sake of conciseness, the questions animating this chapter are analysed through a specific issue, i.e. the regulation of big data. This lens seems to be appropriate, because data shares the transnational character of the Internet, as well as its multi-purpose usability, allowing it to serve both the economy and human rights and to act as both an emancipatory and a repressive tool. In particular, data is also subject to communication surveillance, which is often a pillar of counter-terrorism policies.

As to the first element – transnationality – big data has an intrinsic propensity to unrestrained circulation, from both a technical and an economic point of view. Firstly, as scholars clarified, the raw substance of data approximates it to a non-rival and non-excludable good,[3] because it can be duplicated and transferred virtually everywhere at almost zero cost, and is not consumed by utilisation. Furthermore, the innovativeness of the most advanced data analysis instruments derives precisely from the possibility of reusing data sets. Indeed, "data mining" – as explained below – does not need specific samples, appropriate to each experiment, but allows scrutiny of huge quantities of data collected from different sources and with different aims, even in the absence of a working hypothesis prior to the creation of the data sets.[4] Then, not only is information non-rival, but it also delivers its highest potential value if it is shared, reused and linked with other databases.

As to the second element – multi-purposeness – data can serve multiple aims that meet different and sometimes contrasting interests, involving the economic, personal or public sphere. This means that data regulation is not neutral, on the contrary, it has to balance constitutional values. For example, information can be gathered and sold for advertising purposes or to build artificial intelligence, or can become a shared industrial asset, able to innervate and boost the whole of the agricultural and manufacturing sectors.[5] However, the discipline of data is linked to fundamental rights, especially privacy.

This is particularly evident in the matters analysed in this chapter. Sure, the balancing of fundamental rights in trade law or counter-terror provisions is not the main object of this work. Nevertheless, a clarification is in order, since privacy is taken here as a point of reference in assessing equality and participation.

Privacy in this chapter is understood in accordance with the EU framework:[6] it is not only a protection of what is normally "secret", like a person's private sphere or

---

[3] Katarzyna Śledziewska and Renata Wloch, 'Should We Treat Big Data as a Public Good?', Mariarosaria Taddeo and Luciano Floridi (eds), *The responsibilities of online service providers* (Springer 2017), 265–268.

[4] Viktor Mayer-Schönberger and Kenneth Cukier, *Big Data: A Revolution That Will Transform How We Live, Work and Think* (Houghton Mifflin Harcourt 2013), 11-70, 147–158.

[5] Josef Drexl, 'Designing Competitive Markets for Industrial Data – Between Propertisation and Access' (2016) Max Planck Institute for Innovation & Competition Research Paper No. 16-13. https://ssrn.com/abstract=2862975, 30–38.

[6] Privacy is stated specifically in the Charter of Fundamental Rights of European Union [2012] OJ C 326, 26.10.2012, Article 8. Such right should have at least the same meaning and scope as the European Convention for the Protection of Human Rights and Fundamental Freedoms [1950], Article 8.

domicile, rather, it is a right to "informational self-determination", i.e. the possibility for everyone to control their own information. Personal data is the natural expansion of the individual sphere itself, and is embedded in the overall right to personal autonomy, which protects the autonomous development of personality in the internal forum and in the relationship with others.

Of course, the enjoyment of this right can be limited if necessary to fulfill other rights, like economic rights, as in trade law, or security, as in counter-terrorism. Though, in this case a balance is needed, according to the proportionality principle. As specified by EU Court of Justice,[7] limitations of privacy are only accepted if provided by the law, apt, necessary and proportionate in relation to the counterposed value. Moreover, another criterion, not stated in the Charter, appears to be slowly emerging in some recent decisions of the EU Court of Justice:[8] a hierarchy has to be recognised that privileges personality rights over economic ones. With reference to these parameters, the research will assess how regulations affect the respective status of nationals and non-nationals.

2. *Privacy and Big Data as a Matter of International Trade*

The Internet is a field where the community of reference, advocating for democratic participation, is only partly linked to the territory, and mostly thinks of itself as an a-territorial collectivity. Moreover, due to the key infrastructural and economic value of the World Wide Web, netizens are not the only ones to claim decisional powers. Other actors are involved, such as other States, corporations of the Internet and many forms of sectorial and territorial international organisations. So, clearly State powers cannot exercise the traditional internal and external sovereign authority. Firstly, such matters often exceed the national jurisdiction: neither the players nor the infrastructure of the Web are located in a single territory. Secondly, sometimes the online word questions the States' monopoly of the legal force. In the digital envi-

[7] See, lastly, Cases c-293/12 and c-594/12, Digital Rights Ireland Ltd v Ltd v Minister for Communications, Marine and Natural Resources and Others and Kärntner Landesregierung and Others [2014] European Court of Justice, ECLI:EU:C:2014:238. Concerning the requirement of "provision by the law", the respective balance of Judiciary and Parliamentary powers is controversial: Antonio D'Andrea, *Autonomia costituzionale delle camere e principio di legalità* (Giuffrè 2004), 1 ss.; Oreste Pollicino, 'Interpretazione o manipolazione? La Corte di giustizia definisce un nuovo diritto alla *privacy* digitale' (2014) 3 Federalismi.it. http://www.federalismi.it/ApplOpenFilePDF.cfm?artid=28017&dpath=document&dfile=25112014121445.pdf&content=Interpretazione+o+manipolazione?+La+Corte+di+giustizia+definisce+un+nuovo+diritto+alla+privacy+digitale+-+stato+-+dottrina+-+, 5–8.

[8] Case C-131/12, Google Spain SL, Google Inc. v Agencia Española de Protección de Datos (AEPD), Mario Costeja González [2014] European Court of Justice, ECLI:EU:C:2014:317, paras. 97 and 99.

ronment new "functional" private powers have emerged,[9] which, due to their economic position, are able to hold peer-to-peer relationships with States and impose their rules on a plurality of Internet users on a global scale.

This situation was highlighted when a European State established an ambassador in Silicon Valley to deal with the relationships with "over the top" Internet businesses.[10] However, other instances show that such actors are considered as allies in the enforcement of internal sovereignty, rather than average components of civil society. One case is national security, which will be better described below. But it is well known that States seek the cooperation of social networks to secure national elections. This is exemplified in the way they reacted to the danger represented by foreign "trolls" meddling with electoral campaigns in the US, or to Cambridge Analytica's scandal, which revealed that politicians are able to target their constituents in an individualised way through social networks.[11] Eventually, pending the imminent EU parliamentary elections, the first regulatory reaction to the latter distortion of public sphere was Facebook's self-regulation.[12] The company decided to enact transparency measures on paid advertising, by creating archives of information concerning the sponsored campaigns and their financers. Moreover, the corporation gave its own political direction to the measures, by forbidding paid political advertising from abroad. In the context of this research, it is interesting to notice how such provision tries to reinforce the exclusion of foreigners from the political community. Even, in the EU context it would wrong-foot Europe's attempt to legitimise its institutions through the creation of a single transversal political sphere, giving a true European meaning to the parliamentary vote.

Such examples give a sufficient account of the novelty of the Internet as a regulatory field. The huge debate on Internet Governance[13] is a clear indicator of the fact that offline government cannot be immediately taken as a model for digital issues.

New technologies create unprecedented horizons for the territorial and material expansion of digital freedom. Moreover, as mentioned, the Web is a new kind of space, where many enclosures are virtually avoidable, because many digital goods, as data, information or source codes, are non-rival in nature.

---

[9] Frank Pasquale, 'From Territorial to Functional Sovereignty: The Case of Amazon' (Lpeblog.org, 6 December 2017) https://lpeblog.org/2017/12/06/from-territorial-to-functional-sovereignty-the-case-of-amazon/.

[10] Tech Ambassador of Denmark http://techamb.um.dk/.

[11] Hannes Grassegger and Mikael Krogerus, 'The Data that Turned the World Upside Down' (Motherboard.vice.com, 28 January 2017) https://motherboard.vice.com/en_us/article/mg9vvn/how-our-likes-helped-trump-win.

[12] Anika Geisel, 'Protecting the European Parliament Elections' (Newsroom.fb.com, 28 January 2019) https://newsroom.fb.com/news/2019/01/european-parliament-elections/.

[13] Lawrence B Solum, 'Models of Internet Governance', in Lee A Bygrave and Jon Bing (eds), *Internet Governance. Infrastructure and Institutions* (Oxford University Press 2009), 55; Eric Brousseau, Meryem Marzouki and Cécile Méadel, 'Governance, Networks and Digital Technologies: Societal, Political and Organizational Innovations', in Id. (eds), *Governance, Regulation and Powers on the Internet* (Cambridge University Press 2012), 3.

This does not necessarily mean – as some scholars claim – that the Internet will become the "heaven of self-regulation". [14] On the contrary, such a regime would fuel inequalities, leaving the digital field to the "law of the jungle". On the other hand, the fact that rules are needed – in order to ensure the equal protection of fundamental rights – should not necessarily entailed a "Westphalian model", embodied by a network of agreements among national governments. Indeed, the peculiarity and novelty of the Web has triggered a creative effort to set patterns of co-regulation on a transnational scale, able to meld the guarantees of public intervention with the flexibility and sectorial efficiency of self-regulation. [15] For example, many hybrid theories have been conceived, which would entrust Internet Governance to transnational quasi-private cooperatives and international organisations, to the market order or to the technical community, designing communications protocols and software. [16]

Pending these discussions, currently the most noticeable leaps towards global harmonisation of rules and the participation of an international civil society seem to happen, paradoxically, in the regulation of economic matters.

The Internet is an increasingly important issue in trade law. Regarding big data, for example, as more business models and practices move onto the digital platform and data becomes increasingly shared and exchanged on an international scale, its relationship with international trade intensifies. Since data are gathered, digitised, stored and moved on a truly global basis by a multitude of parties, restrictions and regulations concerning data directly affect global trade. [17]

Therefore, market needs have been the engine of many experiments in international regulation, which are perhaps the most successful, in terms of bindingness and the involvement of stakeholders.

Normative harmonisation is required by global trade because differences among law systems give rise to strong incentives to restrain the circulation of commodities. Indeed, if safeguards are not homogeneous, each State seeks to apply its own rules and so protect fundamental rights according to its own balancing decisions. For example, foodstuffs that can be legally commercialised in their Country of origin might be prevented from being sold in another State, if the latter has stricter norms for human health.

In relation to big data, the applicable law often depends on the localisation of in-

---

[14] John Perry Barlow, 'A Declaration of the Independence of Cyberspace' (EFF.org, 8 February 1996) https://www.eff.org/it/cyberspace-independence.

[15] Giovanna De Minico, 'Towards an Internet Bill of Rights' (2015), 1 Loyola Los Angeles International and Comparative Law Review http://digitalcommons.lmu.edu/ilr/vol37/iss1/1, 5–11.

[16] Lawrence Lessig, *Code. Version 2.0* (Basic Books 2006), 4.

[17] United Nations Conference on Trade and Development (UNCTAD), 'Data Protection Regulations and International Data Flows: Implications for Trade and Development' (United Nations 2016) http://unctad.org/en/PublicationsLibrary/dtlstict2016d1_en.pdf, 3–4. *See* also Harsha Vardhana Singh, Ahmed Abdel-Latif and Lee Tuthill, 'Governance of International Trade and the Internet: Existing and Evolving Regulatory Systems' (2016) Global Commission on Internet Governance, Paper Series: No. 32 https://www.cigionline.org/sites/default/files/gcig_no32web_0.pdf, 2.

formation. This means that regulatory differences incentivise governments to keep data sets within their territory.[18] For instance, the General Data Protection Regulation[19] (or GDPR) of the EU forbids personal information to be transferred to third Countries that do not ensure an "adequate" level of protection (Articles 44–47). Moreover, that "adequacy" has been interpreted in a rigid way by the EU Court of Justice. Indeed, the judge in the Schrems decision reads the requirement as imposing an "essentially equivalent" level of protection.[20] Thus, in this case the absence of equivalence between regulatory systems impedes the transfer and selling of data.

To address such issues, a vast range of Free Trade Agreements (FTAs) has taken place, with the aim of building common rules and so removing barriers to trade. This kind of regulation is not "neutral" or merely "technical", but has an impact on the reciprocal coexistence of fundamental rights: the process of harmonising disciplines is also a decisional process, which chooses a discipline, and so sets its own balance among the different fundamental and economic rights involved. In other words, despite its economic ratio, it has to be recognised as a real coercive juridical system, which could be considered to be the anticipation of a new paradigm of Internet governance.[21]

This is particularly evident in the latest wave of FTAs (including, e.g., the Comprehensive Economic and Trade Agreement (CETA) and the Transatlantic Trade and Investment Partnership (TTIP)), which are only a species of the broader genus of Free Trade Agreements, but seem to be particularly emblematic in this case because they attain a very advanced institutionalisation of the international State-business cooperation.[22] Within the material competence of such Agreements, it is also possible to find issues related to Internet Governance, and particularly to data. Thus, these topics are becoming subject to a fully original juridical order, whose objectives, procedures and actors are different from the establishment of traditional constitutional States.[23]

---

[18] E.g. the Brazilian *Marco Civil* demanded a forced localisation in the Country of all data of Brazilian users that are collected by foreign companies: Lei Nº 12.965, de 23 de Abril de 2014, Estabelece Principios, Garantias, Direitos e Deveres para o Uso da Internet no Brasil http://www.planalto.gov.br/ccivil_03/_ato2011-2014/2014/lei/l12965.htm.

[19] European Parliament and Council Regulation (EU) 2016/679 on the Protection of Natural Persons with Regard to the Processing of Personal Data and on the Free Movement of Such Data, and Repealing Directive 95/46/EC (General Data Protection Regulation) [2016] O.J. L 119/1.

[20] Case C-362/14, Maximillian Schrems v. Data Protection Commissioner [2015] European Court of Justice, ECLI:EU:C:2015:650 https://eur-lex.europa.eu/legal-content/EN/TXT/?uri=CELEX%3A62014CJ0362. *See* Giovanna De Minico, *Costituzione. Emergenza e terrorismo* (Jovene 2016), 136–137.

[21] Maria Francesca De Tullio and Giuseppe Micciarelli 'Trade Agreements and Internet Governance: Data Flow and Politics in the TiSA's Governmental Rationality', in Meryem Marzouki and Andrea Calderaro (eds), *Global Internet Governance as a Diplomacy Issue* (Rowman & Littlefield, *forthcoming*).

[22] Giuseppe Micciarelli, 'CETA, TTIP e altri fratelli. Il contratto sociale della post democrazia' (2017) 2 Politica del diritto, 257 ss.

[23] Rory Van Loo, 'The Corporation as Courthouse' (2016) 33 Yale Journal on Regulation http://digitalcommons.law.yale.edu/yjreg/vol33/iss2/5, 554 ss.

This is particularly evident if one takes as an example the negotiations over data flows in Trade in Services Agreement (TiSA), a FTA in course of negotiation, seeking to minimise non-tariff barriers to the international trade in services. [24] This case is interesting because its geographic scope is exceptionally broad: it would involve 23 Parties – including the EU – accounting for about 70 percent of international trade in services, and it is conceived as an open Treaty, susceptible to be integrated in the World Trade Organisation (WTO) framework, in case a critical number of WTO Members would adhere.

As to the aims, TiSA – differently from other forms of regulation – is built around the central value of free trade, and so its whole structure is crafted to favour this principle over others. In juridical terms, this is translated into a straightforward mechanism of rule-exception to address all the conflicts between economic and fundamental rights. [25] Namely, free trade – and so free flow of data – is stated as a general overarching principle, [26] while basic freedoms, where ensured, are provided as an authorisation for the Parties to derogate the Treaty. [27] This is not secondary, because, according to the juridical science, exceptional rules have a narrow application, that should be punctually justified and cannot be interpreted extensively or analogically. [28] On the contrary, general rules can only be set aside when they are expressly excluded.

This settlement is radically opposite to democratic Constitutions, where personality rights – and not free trade – are "fundamental" and so enjoy an "assumption of maximum extension", [29] which is to say that freedoms are applied in all instances, unless an exception is clearly provided by the law, is apt to pursue an equally fundamental principle and is necessary and proportional to the benefit provided. [30] In other words, the rule-exception mechanisms appear completely specular to each other: Ti-

---

[24] The content of FTAs negotiations is classified. However, drafts have been partly leaked by civil society organisations (e.g., Wikileaks and Greenpeace) and some Parties' official positions have been voluntarily released. This research is based on these sources.

[25] Jane Kelsey and Burcu Kilic, 'Briefing on US TISA Proposal on E-commerce, Technology Transfer, Cross-border Data Flows and Net Neutrality' (2014) Public Services International http://www.world-psi.org/sites/default/files/documents/research/briefing_on_tisa_e-commerce_final.pdf, 7, 16; Israel Tamir, 'TISA Annex on Electronic Commerce: A Preliminary Analysis by the Canadian Internet Policy & Public Interest Clinic (CIPPIC)' (2015) https://wikileaks.org/tisa/analysis/Analysis-of-20150220_Annex-on-Electronic-Commerce/Analysis-of-20150220_Annex-on-Electronic-Commerce.pdf, 14–16; Jane Kelsey 'TiSA: Updated Analysis of the Leaked "Core Text" from July 2016' (2016) https://wikileaks.org/tisa/analysis/201609_TiSA_Analysis-on-Core-Text/201609_TiSA_Analysis-on-Core-Text.pdf, 2.

[26] *See* Article I-4 and the un-numbered Article between I-2 and I-3 of the Core Text, together with Articles 2 and 8 of the Annex on Electronic Commerce.

[27] Article I-9 of the Core Text.

[28] Among many, *Klass v. Germany,* App no 5029/71 (ECHR), para. 42; paras. 66–68, 81.

[29] Pierfrancesco Grossi, *Introduzione ad uno studio sui diritti inviolabili nella Costituzione italiana* (Cedam 1972), 16; Paolo Caretti, *I diritti fondamentali. Libertà e diritti sociali* (Giappichelli 2005), 104.

[30] Among many, Halford v. the United Kingdom, App no 20605/92 (ECHR), paras. 66–68, 81; European Court of Justice, Digital Rights Ireland Ltd c. Ireland, para. 38.

SA overturns the value given to the personal sphere in democratic orders, and places trade as the general principle, while relegating rights to narrow exceptions.[31]

In practice, the possibility of enacting the aforementioned Articles 44–47 GDPR would actually be doubtful under the TiSA regime, because every implementing act would have to strictly fit the language of the Article I-9 derogatory clause. Namely, data protection measures must not be a 'means of arbitrary or unjustifiable discrimination between countries where like conditions prevail, or a disguised restriction on trade in services',[32] must be 'necessary' and 'not inconsistent with the provisions of this Agreement'.[33] This is a threat for privacy, and confirmation of this comes from the jurisprudence under Article XX of General Agreement on Tariffs and Trade[34] and Article XIV of General Agreement on Trade in Services,[35] the wording of which is similar to the Article I-9 of TiSA. Indeed, in some decisions the exercise of the State authority to legislate in favour of fundamental values has been ruled unlawful.[36]

Contents, as described above, are linked to the procedures followed. Traditionally, in democratic Constitutions, the identification of a balance among fundamental rights is strictly reserved to representative organisms – and Parliaments above all – acting through public procedures, regulated by an overarching fundamental Charter. Moreover, oversight powers are entrusted to independent organisms, and primarily to the judiciary, usually burdened by obligations to motivate their decisions and means of appeal.[37]

In comparison, TiSA shows an outright shift of paradigm. In it negotiations are conducted by different actors, coming from both governmental and private sectors, who do not need to be part of the representative circuit. To be precise, Parliaments are not even able to fully observe and oversee the proceedings, which are kept strictly secret.[38] Nor is it

---

[31] Rolf H Weber, 'Regulatory Autonomy and Privacy Standards under the GATS' (2012) 7 Asian Journal of WTO & International Health Law and Policy, 32–34; Kristina Irion, Svetlana Yakovleva and Marija Bartl, 'Trade and Privacy: Complicated Bedfellows? How to Achieve Data Protection-Proof Free Trade Agreements' (2016) Independent study commissioned by BEUC et al., published 13 July 2016, Amsterdam, Institute for Information Law (IViR) https://ssrn.com/abstract=2877166, 57.

[32] Article I-9, chapeau, Core Text.

[33] Article I-9(c), Core Text.-

[34] 1986 https://www.wto.org/english/docs_e/legal_e/gatt47.pdf.

[35] 1994 https://www.wto.org/english/docs_e/legal_e/26-gats.pdf.

[36] United States – Measures Affecting the Cross-Border Supply of Gambling and Betting Services [2004] WTO Panel, WT/DS285/R; United States – Standards for Reformulated and Conventional Gasoline [1996] WTO Appellate Body, WT/DS2/AB/R.

[37] Cases c-293/12 and c-594/12, Digital Rights Ireland Ltd v Ltd v Minister for Communications, Marine and Natural Resources and Others and Kärntner Landesregierung and Others [2014] European Court of Justice, ECLI:EU:C:2014:238. Concerning the tool of the appeal: Giovanni Serges, *Il principio del "doppio grado di giurisdizione" nel sistema costituzionale italiano* (Giuffrè 1993).

[38] Susan Aaronson, 'Why Trade Agreements are not Setting Information Free: The Lost History and Reinvigorated Debate over Cross-Border Data Flows, Human Rights, and National Security' (2015) 14, 4 World Trade Review, 678.

clear what the enforcement organisms and procedures of TiSA are, as they are barely sketched in the latest draft.[39]

So, the vertical form of representative democracy is substituted with the horizontality of public-private negotiation, which seeks to legitimise itself through the stakeholders' participation. However, horizontality does not always mean absence of hierarchy, because, in the absence of constitutional (or quasi-constitutional) guarantees, contracts favour those who have the most bargaining power, which are not necessarily the States. Indeed, in the neoliberal market order, these last are subject to competition as well, because they need to attract investors and buyers, and so try to arrange the most favourable rules for commerce.

This is how the new generation of FTAs were made possible. They are radically divergent not only from traditional constitutional orders, but also from other pieces of international regulation on data protection, such as the Organisation for Economic Development (OECD) Privacy Principles. Therein, the pivotal aim is to impose a set of minimal safeguards for liberties, even if their *occasio legis* is to foster trust as a precondition of free exchange. On the contrary, FTAs are a negotiating field where some Parties – seeking to access new markets – accept limitations on their demand to safeguard individual rights.[40]

Of course, it is not possible to affirm with full certainty that the model given by the last generation of Free Trade Agreements will be the most successful one in the regulation of this matter. However, the existing examples seem to be a sufficient proof that new forms of public-private regulations are emerging, which act according to market logics and are able to produce binding effects on States on the transnational scale. At first glance, this appears to expand democratic vindications outside the national boundaries.

Now, the real question is whether there are analogous participatory mechanisms which allow people, who are not exponents of strong vested interests, to affect decision-making procedures on a global scale. From the above description, it seems that no such system is available in trade law. In the following section, the research observes if the opposite is true of human rights law.

3. *The Continuing Relevance of Nations and Territories in Discriminatory Counter-terrorism Surveillance*

Although negotiations over FTAs are ongoing, the same cannot be said of interna-

---

[39] EU Proposal, TiSA – Dispute Settlement Chapter.

[40] Graham Greenleaf, 'The TPP & Other Free Trade Agreements: Faustian Bargains for Privacy?' (2016) UNSW Law, Research Paper No. 08 https://ssrn.com/abstract=2732386, 3; Cristophe Leroy, 'Existe-t-il un marché du droit public?' (2016) 100 Petites affiches, 3–4.

tional treaties concerning data protection. This trend is clear if we consider, for instance, the aforementioned Articles 44–47, GDPR, in particular in their application to data transfers to the US. History shows that transatlantic relationships have never been easy on these matters, mainly because the US surveillance laws regarding crime prevention, which are utterly invasive domestically, are even harsher on foreigners' data. The attempts to involve the US in multilateral agreements – such as the OECD Privacy Guidelines, or the Asia-Pacific Economic Cooperation (APEC) Privacy Framework – have not succeeded in producing binding and enforceable blue-print,[41] but only in obtaining an arrangement based on a mechanism of self-certification – the so-called Safe Harbuor Agreement[42] – which was subsequently considered by the European Court to be insufficient to safeguard personal information coming from the EU. More recently, another pact has been signed – called the *Privacy Shield*[43] – which is also controversial,[44] especially in light of Trump's policies, which are a backward step in the safeguarding of non-US people.[45]

The need to have an efficient intelligence sector is obviously a constant in every nation State; though, it has suddenly improved since the experience of 9/11 in New York. Counter-terrorism has opened a new state of emergency, made of derogatory measures which are not extraordinary and temporary, but have become embedded in the ordinary law. Indeed, public authorities are forced into a state of permanent alert, because as a result of technological evolution criminal cells seem to be able to organise themselves and strike at any moment in any place. Hence, the only useful strategy appears to be an ordinary "administration of the risk", involving a total and permanent control, targeting everyone regardless of whether or not they are specific suspects.[46]

---

41 Graham Greenleaf, 'The TPP & Other Free Trade Agreements: Faustian Bargains for Privacy?' (2016) UNSW Law, Research Paper No. 08 https://ssrn.com/abstract=2732386, 2.

42 Commission Decision 2000/520/EC pursuant to Directive 95/46/EC of the European Parliament and of the Council on the adequacy of the protection provided by the safe harbour privacy principles and related frequently asked questions issued by the US Department of Commerce (Adequacy Decision) (2000) OJ L 215, 25 August 2000 https://eur-lex.europa.eu/legal-content/EN/TXT/HTML/?uri=CELEX:32000D0520&from=IT.

43 Commission Implementing Decision (EU) 2016/1250 of 12 July 2016 pursuant to Directive 95/46/EC of the European Parliament and of the Council on the adequacy of the protection provided by the EU-U.S. Privacy Shield (Adequacy Decision) [2016], OJ L 207, 1 August 2016 https://eur-lex.europa.eu/legal-content/EN/TXT/?uri=uriserv%3AOJ.L_.2016.207.01.0001.01.ENG.

44 Conseil National du Numérique, 'Communiqué, Pourquoi l'accord «Privacy Shield» doit être renégocié' (2017) https://cnnumerique.fr/pourquoi-le-privacy-shield-doit-etre-renegocie.

45 Executive order. Enhancing Public Safety in the Interior of the United States, 25 January 2017, Sec. 14 https://www.whitehouse.gov/the-press-office/2017/01/25/presidential-executive-order-enhancing-public-safety-interior-united.

46 John Yoo, 'The Legality of the National Security Agency's Bulk Data Surveillance Programs' (2013) UC Berkeley Public Law Research Paper No. 2369192 http://ssrn.com/abstract=2369192. 5–11.

Regarding the US, famous press investigations[47] have revealed that intelligence services engage in mass metadata harvesting and analysis, in line with the legal basis provided by the *Foreign Intelligence Surveillance Act* (FISA).[48] This is also done in close cooperation with corporations: data analysis is often outsourced,[49] and information can also be requested from communication service providers. The objective of analysing communications metadata is to identify suspected persons and keep them under observation to stop them before they commit an illicit act. In practical terms, this data is examined through "data mining" techniques, i.e. governmental statistics which extract subjective qualities and behaviours that are more frequently linked to a given crime, and so indicate any other person possessing such features as a probable criminal. In sum, snooping is possible even without having to demonstrate a reasonable link with a crime.

Such legislation does not concern content, but only metadata, i.e. data on movements, behaviours and circumstances of the communications. Nevertheless, it should be considered as an interference with privacy, no less. Indeed, technology has generated new data analysis techniques and new devices, which produce a huge quantity of data produced on a daily basis. In this context, even non-content information can reveal a great deal of detail about a person's life: data sets can 'be recorded and aggregated in a manner that enables the Government to ascertain, more or less at will, their political and religious beliefs, sexual habits, and so on'.[50]

These rules are very different from those stated by EU law, as interpreted by the Court of Justice, and this is why they raise an issue about the adequacy of US data protection. Therefore, they cast doubts on the possibility of transatlantic circulation of EU citizens' data.

If we look at the phenomenon from the data subjects' point of view, FISA appears of particular concern mainly because of the scope and firepower that the US intelligence is able to put in place. However, from a barely legal point of view, EU Mem-

---

[47] Glenn Greenwald, 'NSA Collecting Phone Records of Millions of Verizon Customers Daily' (TheGuardian.com, 6 June 2013) http://www.theguardian.com/world/2013/jun/06/nsa-phone-records-verizon-court-order; Barton Gellman and Laura Poitras, 'U.S., British Intelligence Mining Data from Nine Internet Companies in Broad Secret Program' (WashingtonPost.com, 6 June 2013) http://www.washingtonpost.com/investigations/us-intelligence-mining-data-from-nine-us-internet-companies-in-broad-secret-program/2013/06/06/3a0c0da8-cebf-11e2-8845-d970ccb04497_story.html.

[48] Pub. L. 95–511 – Oct. 25 (1978) 92 Stat. 1783 https://www.govinfo.gov/content/pkg/STATUTE-92/pdf/STATUTE-92-Pg1783.pdf and subsequent modifications.

[49] Stephen Butt, 'Outsourcing Intelligence: The Relationship between the State and Private Intelligence in Post-apartheid South Africa' (2010) *A minor dissertation submitted in partial fulfilment of the requirements for the award of the degree of Master of Social Science in International Relations* https://open.uct.ac.za/handle/11427/3796, 15–18; Simon Chesterman '«We Can't Spy ... If We Can't Buy!»: The Privatization of Intelligence and the Limits of Outsourcing «Inherently Governmental Functions»' (2008) 19, 5 The European Journal of International Law, 1055–1056.

[50] Justice Sotomayor, concurring opinion in United States v. Jones, Supreme Court of the United States, No. 10-1259 [23 January 2012] http://www.law.cornell.edu/supremecourt/text/10-1259.

ber States' laws do not ensure a greater level of protection when it comes to crime prevention and repression.[51] For instance, one can consider the UK, with the *Data Retention and Investigatory Powers Act 2014* (DRIP)[52] and the *Investigatory Powers Act 2016*,[53] or France, with the *LOI n° 2015-912 du 24 juillet 2015 relative au renseignement*[54] and the *LOI n° 2015-1556 du 30 novembre 2015 relative aux mesures de surveillance des communications électroniques internationales.*[55]

In the case of UK, both the laws mentioned allow the government to require by notice a public telecommunications operator to retain relevant communications data, even in the absence of clear suspicion. No provision requires the oversight of any judicial or independent authority. Such acts are being reiterated in clear breach of statements by European and internal courts, which have so far censored, respectively, the so-called Data Retention Directive[56] and the UK laws of 2014 and 2016. In 2014, the intention not to comply with the European Court's order was blatant: a press release (10 July 2014) by the Prime Minister declared that the aim of the DRIP was to 'enable agencies to maintain existing capabilities' after a 'recent development', which was that:

> <ext>the European Court of Justice (ECJ) has struck down regulations enabling Communications Service Providers (CSPs) to retain communications data for law enforcement purposes for up to 12 months. Unless they have a business reason to hold this data, Internet and phone companies will start deleting it which has serious consequences for investigations – investigations which can take many months and which rely on retrospectively accessing data for evidential purposes.</ext>

As for France, Article 5 of the French *LOI n° 2015-912* has introduced – exclusively for counter-terrorism needs – "black boxes" in communication channels. The disposition gives the Prime Minister, after consultation with the Commission nationale de contrôle des techniques de renseignement, the power to order communication service providers to activate devices in their networks that are able to surveil communication metadata in bulk, to 'find connections susceptible of revealing a terrorist menace'. In

---

[51] Daniel Bigo and others, 'Mass Surveillance of Personal Data by EU Member States and Its Compatibility with EU Law' (2013) CEPS Paper in Liberty and Security in Europe Papers No. 61 http://ssrn.com/abstract=2360473, 12–18.

[52] 2014 c. 27 http://www.legislation.gov.uk/ukpga/2014/27/contents.

[53] 2016 c. 25 http://www.legislation.gov.uk/ukpga/2016/25/contents.

[54] JORF n° 0171 du 26 juillet 2015 https://www.legifrance.gouv.fr/affichTexte.do?cidTexte=JORFTEXT000030931899&categorieLien=id.

[55] JORF n° 0278 du 1 décembre 2015 https://www.legifrance.gouv.fr/affichTexte.do?cidTexte=JORFTEXT000031549747&categorieLien=id.

[56] Directive 2006/24/EC on the retention of data generated or processed in connection with the provision of publicly available electronic communications services or of public communications networks (2006) OJ L 105/54 13 April 2006 https://eur-lex.europa.eu/LexUriServ/LexUriServ.do?uri=OJ:L:2006:105:0054:0063:EN:PDF.

other words, a broad-brush authority is given to government, which is allowed to control communications also in the absence of a specific connection with a demonstrated crime or attempt.

Such data surveillance affects not only privacy, but, as a matter of fact, also individuals' self-determination, for at least three reasons. Firstly, gathering data about a person's life allows the government to blackmail her with the threat of revealing compromising details;[57] and this is not a mere hypothesis, since in many instances governments have attempted to use this strategy to blackmail their opponents.[58] Secondly, as witnessed in periods of dictatorship, espionage – if enacted by people in positions of power – can lead to self-censorship, because of the fear of the possible consequences which could derive from some claims or behaviours.[59] Thirdly, the controller can also influence other's decisions,[60] to the extent that, according to some theories, governments ought to learn the fallacies in average citizens' reasoning and exploit them to discretionarily guide personal choices.[61]

Thus, bulk metadata collection enacts a form of surveillance, where public powers can know people and phenomena without being in turn observed by society. Such informational asymmetries are an interference with individual freedom, and, on a mass scale, with popular sovereignty, because governments are provided with a form of unaccountable power.

As mentioned before, these rights – privacy and self-determination – need to be balanced with security, according to the proportionality principle. This right, howev-

---

[57] Paul M Schwartz, 'Internet Privacy and the State' (1999–2000) 32 Connecticut Law Review, 841–842; Daniel J Solove, 'A Taxonomy of Privacy' (2006) 154 (3) University of Pennsylvania Law Review https://www.law.upenn.edu/journals/lawreview/articles/volume154/issue3/Solove154U.Pa.L.Rev.477(2006).pdf, 539–541.

[58] Shaun B Spencer, 'Security Versus Privacy: Reframing the Debate' (2002) 79, 4 Denver University Law Review http://ssrn.com/abstract=2015040, 572; and, as to the surveillance of corporations, Jack M Balkin, 'Information Fiduciaries and the First Amendment' (2016) Yale Law School, Public Law Research Paper No. 553 http://ssrn.com/abstract=2675270, 4–5.

[59] Jean-Claude Paye, 'France: An Algorithmic Power' (2016) 67, 9 Monthly Review https://monthlyreview.org/2016/02/01/france-an-algorithmic-power/; Karen Turner, 'Mass Surveillance Silences Minority Opinions, According to Study' (WashingtonPost.com – The Switch, 28 March 2016) https://www.washingtonpost.com/news/the-switch/wp/2016/03/28/mass-surveillance-silences-minority-opinions-according-to-study/?utm_term=.b75fe1352fdf; Nicole Perlroth, 'Governments Turn to Commercial Spyware to Intimidate Dissidents' (NewYorkTimes.com, 29 May 2016) http://www.nytimes.com/2016/05/30/technology/governments-turn-to-commercial-spyware-to-intimidate-dissidents.html?_r=0. This issue is also the object of important jurisdictional decisions: *Whalen v. Roe*, U.S. Supreme Court, No. 75-839, 429 U.S. 589 [22 February 1977], in https://www.law.cornell.edu/supremecourt/text/429/589.

[60] Bert-Jaap Koops, 'Some Reflections on Profiling, Power Shifts and Protection Paradigms', in Mireille Hildebrandt and Serge Gutwirth (eds), *Profiling the European Citizen* (Springer 2008) http://papers.ssrn.com/sol3/papers.cfm?abstract_id=1350584, 2; Andrew J Roberts, 'A Republican Account of the Value of Privacy' (2013) University of Melbourne Legal Studies Research Paper No. 673 http://ssrn.com/abstract=2369680, 17–26.

[61] Cass Sunstein, *Laws of Fear: Beyond the Precautionary Principle* (Cambridge University Press 2005), Ch. VIII.

er, has to be interpreted in light of the fact that in the context of counter-terrorism the police are bound to act before they have any information not only about the "how" of the attack, but also about the "if", the "when" and the "where". In this case, it is possible to act, for the reasons stated by the precautionary principle,[62] i.e. to avoid political choices being completely subordinated to scientific certainty; however, uncertainty makes it difficult to strike a proportional balance. Hence, the referral rule will be a second best: 'the more severe is the intervention against a fundamental right, the higher should be the certainty about the premises supporting the intervention',[63] and *vice versa*.

This is relevant, in this work, especially because of the effects that the use of such strategies has on equality. It is undeniable that preventive data-driven measures create and deepen discrimination based upon nationality and residence. As stated in literature, 'the use of algorithmic profiling ... is, in a certain sense, inherently discriminatory', since it entails that decisions are made through a statistical process meant to cluster data subjects according to given variables.[64] Indeed, as explained above, algorithms of data mining automatically find recurrent correlations and deduct predictions from them. For example, a bank could infer – by applying such automatic calculations to its customers' history – that 70 percent of the people living in a neighbourhood have been insolvent; hence, it could decide to refuse conceding loans to the residents of that area. Sure, a single individual could be among the 30 percent of people who would have been able to pay back the loan, but this is not relevant in a bank's activity, because accepting a percentual of mistakes is still more convenient than spending time and money analysing each particular instance.[65] What is more, sometimes "non-interpretable" procedures are used, i.e. algorithms which work well on big numbers, because they use a particularly high amount of variables, but, for the same reasons, are not explicable and understandable by the human brain.[66]

---

[62] Consolidated Version of the Treaty on European Union [2008] OJ C115/13, Treaty on the Functioning of the European Union, Article 191; Communication from the European Commission COM(2000) 1 final on the precautionary principle (2000) https://eur-lex.europa.eu/LexUriServ/LexUriServ.do?uri=COM:2000:0001:FIN:EN:PDF.

[63] Robert Alexy, *Theorie der Grundrechte* (tr. Leonardo Di Carlo, Suhrkamp 1985), 651; Rosario Serra Cristóbal, 'The Impact of Counter-terrorism Security Measures on Fundamental Rights: The Need for Supranational Common Standards of Rights Protection to Respond to Terrorism Risk' (2014) Speech at IX IACL International Congress, *Constitutional Challenges: Global and Local*, Oslo, 16–20 June 2014. http://www.jus.uio.no/english/research/news-and-events/events/conferences/2014/wcclcmdc/wccl/papers/ws1/w1-crist%C3%B3bal.pdf, 4, commenting *D Ennis et al. v. United States*, Supreme Court of United States, No. 336 [4 June 1951].

[64] Bryce Goodman and Seth Flaxman 'EU Regulations on Algorithmic Decision-making and a «Right to Explanation»' (2016) Paper presented at the ICML Workshop on Human Interpretability in Machine Learning of 2016, 28 June 2016 http://arxiv.org/pdf/1606.08813v1.pdf, 27.

[65] Viktor Mayer-Schönberger and Kenneth Cukier, *Big Data: A Revolution that will Transform How We Live, Work and Think* (tr. Roberto Merlini, Houghton Mifflin Harcourt 2013), 25.

[66] Tal Zarsky, 'Transparent Predictions' (2013) 4 University of Illinois Law Review http://ssrn.com/abstract=2324240, 1519–1521.

Such discrimination – that is hardly acceptable in inter-private relationships – is even more critical in counter-terror intelligence. Firstly, intelligence decisions affect fundamental rights. So, an algorithmic analysis cannot determine an outright presumption of guiltiness, because this would contrast with the equal application of *habeas corpus*, which imposes a presumption of innocence. Rather, in every democratic system, disparities have to be rationally explained in light of the objective of the norm. Secondly, some legal differentiations are particularly critical in democracies, and race and nationality – which are the object of this research – rank among them.

Hence, surveillance laws should contain strict provisions posing limits and independent oversights on police access to data. However, such regulations are lacking in the aforementioned Acts. In their absence, reasonableness is hard to ascertain and ensure.

The first reason is that some algorithms make it possible to give account of the decisions, because some formulas produce "non interpretable" choices, which cannot be reconstructed by the human brain. A solution could be to avoid employing such methods in a counter-terrorism context, and only use procedures that can be explained and argued. But, once again, laws do not provide a similar ban, so that the choice is left almost exclusively to intelligence services and to the enterprises to which data mining is outsourced.

The second reason is that the very same preventive approach is problematic in this sense. Indeed, while sanctions are visible, and act against visible and proven facts, prevention restrains human rights before the violation, and is bound to use the truth provided by intelligence in substitution of the factual one. [67] The same applies to free speech: surveillance generates mechanisms of self-censorship. These preventive measures sometimes hit illicit expression, susceptible of triggering or encouraging a crime, but at other times strike the bare dissent, which is precious in a democracy. In both cases, if the limitation of rights happens before the facts, no judiciary proceeding or political analysis is able to state in a definite way what is the real danger that person represents and, thus, if the preventive measure has actually saved human lives.

Such risks are not speculative. Counter-terrorism provides immediate examples of possible discrimination: probably statistics would reveal that attackers are mainly young males, coming from Arab Countries and adhering to the Islamic religion. [68] According to these calculations, everyone having these characteristics should be specially surveilled. Moreover, such predictions tend to induce 'self-fulfilling cycles of bias': [69] the

---

[67] Antoinette Rouvroy and Thomas Berns, 'Le nouveau pouvoir statistique' (2010) 40 Multitudes http://www.cairn.info/revue-multitudes-2010-1-page-88.htm, 92–93; Giorgio Agamben, 'Giorgio Agamben: «De l'Etat de droit à l'état de sécurité»', (Le Monde 23 July 2015) http://www.lemonde.fr/idees/article/2015/12/23/de-l-etat-de-droit-a-l-etat-de-securite_4836816_3232.html.

[68] Francesca Bignami, 'Toward a Right to Privacy in Transnational Intelligence Networks' (2007) 48 Boston College Law Review, 6.

[69] Alessandro Mantelero, 'Personal Data for Decisional Purposes in the Age of Analytics: From an Individual to a Collective Dimension of Data Protection' (2016) 32, 2 Computer Law & Security Review: The International Journal of Technology Law and Practice, 3–4.

fact of spying on certain categories with greater attention means by definition that more crimes will be discovered within them, even if the criminality rate is not really higher than the average one. However, the mere frequency of crime attempts discovered is a circumstance that can impress and strengthen the social stigma of a given community.

Moreover, in some cases, foreigners are expressly excluded from some privacy safeguards. This is what happens, for example, with the French *LOI n° 2015-1556*, which only applies abroad, or in the US, where the guarantees of FISA are not applicable to foreigners who are not located in the national territory. Still, discrimination does not effectively protect nationals, because repressive rules – once introduced – can be easily expanded, and, in any case, their limitations are easily circumvented by governments.[70] For example, with regard to FISA, the bulk metadata collection of communications abroad also allows the gathering of US persons' data "incidentally", i.e. while U.S. persons are communicating with foreign people. Moreover, States stipulate mutual agreements with each other, in which one Party engages to provide the other Party with the latter's citizens' data, and *vice versa*. So, each Party can spy on its own nationals by availing itself of the other Party's more favourable surveillance conditions.[71]

This casts a shadow on the reasonableness of these kinds of discriminations. They do not effectively safeguard citizens, but rather cause a "race to the bottom". Being circumvented by governments, they provide loopholes to nationals' privacy safeguards, since eventually the harsher rules, approved for foreigners, are also applied to citizens. What is more, differentiating on the basis of nationality is not even consistent with the intrinsic rationality of security measures. A terrorist ought not to be an alien, and in fact many attacks have been made by "lone wolves" who were born and brought up in the same territory. Hence, the only plausible rationality of such norms is in the rhetoric of emergency: harsh measures are better accepted if they appear to hit some "others" perceived as clearly separate from "us",[72] and don't have the right to vote.

This mirrors the general approach of counter-terrorism, which has used the metaphor of "war on terror" to evoke an "us"-"them" dichotomy and conflict with democratic values, but has still remained unable to identify an external enemy, as one would suppose possible in any war. For example, in the US since 11 September 2001, terrorists from abroad have been included in a new juridical category, named "enemy alien", which is to say that they were not considered ordinary criminals, due

---

[70] Privacy and Civil Liberties Oversight Board, 'Report on the Telephone Records Program Conducted under Section 702 of the Foreign Intelligence Surveillance Act' (2 July 2014) https://www.pclob.gov/library/702-Report.pdf, 137–140.

[71] Joshua Rozenberg, 'Spies may not Like the Anderson Plan – but Their World Needs a Revolution' (The Guardian, 11 June 2015) http://www.theguardian.com/commentisfree/2015/jun/11/spies-gchq-anderson-snoopers-charter-bulk-surveilllance-public-trust.

[72] Oren Gross, 'Chaos and Rules: Should Responses to Violent Crises Always Be Constitutional?' (2011) Minnesota Public Law Research Paper No. 03-2 http://ssrn.com/abstract=370800, 1082–1085.

to the severity of their acts, and so were not entitled to the ordinary guarantees of due process. However, they were even not external enemies in a traditional war, and so were not protected by the Geneva Convention. Hence, they were somehow conceived as not only foreigners, but also the "enemy of humanity", [73] not deserving any guarantees at all: [74] as in the Agambenian metaphor of "camp", [75] they were caught in the legal system only for the purpose of depriving them of both constitutional and international protection.

In conclusion, counter-terrorism shows that States have not completely abandoned their sovereign prerogatives with globalisation, but, instead, retained their 'Gorgon's head of the power' [76] when it comes to protecting their unitary interests. In such cases, threats and states of emergency are used to justify the verticalisation of powers at exactly the same time as the national authority is losing its democratic legitimisation, and is flooded with vindications of inclusion and democratic participation.

4. *Conclusions: Towards an Inclusive Digital Citizenship*

The brief account given has shown that non-citizens are not equally excluded from the enjoyment of political rights. Instead, wealth and economic power seem to be the substantial distinguishing factors. Probably, this circumstance derives from the fact that the equation between citizenship and political participation has hardly ever corresponded to a concrete reality. [77] Indeed, in our communities, even our own citizens have experienced phenomena of social disparity which exclude them from the enjoyment of human rights and political participation. Indeed, a traditional challenge to democracy is that participation subtracts time from productive activities, and so prevents those who strive for a living wage from being fully included in democratic life. This will happen more, if governments engage in procedures of selective dialogue with stakeholders.

---

[73] Carl Schmitt, *Begriff des Politischen* (tr. Pierangelo Schiera, Duncker & Humblot 1932), 139 ss.

[74] Agustin José Menéndez, 'Bush II's Legal and Constitutional Theory: The Constitution of Emergency between Law and Propaganda', in Bev Clucas, Gerry Johnstone and Tony Ward (eds), *Torture: Moral Absolutes and Ambiguities* (Nomos 2009), 8–11.

[75] Giorgio Agamben, *Homo Sacer: Il potere sovrano e la nuda vita* (Einaudi 2005), 188–190.

[76] The expression was used by Hans Kelsen, in *Veröffentlichen der Vereinigung der Deutschen Staatsrechtslehrer*, Vol. 3 (Walter de Gruyter 1927).

[77] This is also true, sometimes, in a territorial sense, where there are economic disparities within the different areas of a State. E.g., as to the Italian debate, *see* Michele Belletti, 'I "livelli essenziali delle prestazioni concernenti i diritti civili e sociali ..." alla prova della giurisprudenza costituzionale: Alla ricerca del parametro plausibile ...' (2003) 3 Istituzioni del federalismo: rivista di studi giuridici e politici, 614; Massimo Villone, *Italia, divisa e diseguale: Regionalismo differenziato o secessione occulta?* (Editoriale Scientifica 2019), provisional version https://cambiailmondo.files.wordpress.com/2019/04/20190316-villone-italia-divisa-e-diseguale-napoli-2019_compressed.pdf, 83 ss.

Citizenship has never proved to be a tool of inclusion, but, rather, an excuse to exclude certain non-nationals and so reinforce Leviathan's authority. As wars and emergencies show, an "external enemy" is often created to strengthen the idea of a "national general interest" and build consensus around State decisions. This construction is often fictional, used to pacify the internal lines of conflict and mobilise the have-nots, who otherwise would have little at stake in the haves' wars and security issues. [78]

The same is true of the Internet. From a legal standpoint, counter-terrorism and market law seem to drive globalisation, and even EU harmonisation, more than universality of rights. According to some authors, trade law represents, by now, the most successful attempt to govern contested Internet issues through international legal regimes. [79]

The World Wide Web, born as the realm of self-regulation and self-determination, has become an area where the State does not disappear, but enacts forms of pervasive surveillance and enforces a juridical space favourable to the free market. This is also the consequence of regulatory processes, which have been privileging economic actors over the others. So, in this new regulatory field, inequalities have changed and interlaced with each other, but not disappeared.

Then – from the perspective of fundamental rights – the mindset should not be to wonder, in general terms, how decision-making can be opened to international civil society actors. Rather, the main question is how to make the Web a space of equal participation, even for those that are disadvantaged and marginalised. [80] This would need a positive intervention of public powers, both at the national and the supra-national level, able to remove the social and economic obstacles to inclusion. Indeed, the horizontal and distributed architecture of the Internet is not decisive by itself. Democracy 'does not follow automatically from the values associated with new technical arrangements for online information production and sharing'. [81]

As a matter of fact, never has the Web been democratic, in the sense of a social democracy. In its first phase, it was regulated by its users, which were indeed a "community of equals", but were only an élite of experts, computer scientists and researchers. Hence, there was a form of 'liberalism through protocols', aiming at 'organising platforms in the most effective way possible, but also less hierarchical, to develop individuals' autonomy'. [82] However, when the masses became able to access it,

---

[78] It has been noticed that security is a concern which affects those who feel that they have an acquired status that they can lose the most, and *vice versa*: Conor Gearty, *Liberty and Security* (Polity Press 2013), 38.

[79] Jack Goldsmith and Tim Wu, *Who Controls the Internet? Illusions of a Borderless World* (Oxford University Press 2006), 167.

[80] This involves an assumption of political responsibilities with regard to the issue of inequalities: Sandro Staiano, 'Diseguaglianze e politiche dell'eguaglianza: profili teorici e istituzionali' (2016) 144 Sociologia del lavoro, 115–116.

[81] Robin Mansell, *Imagining the Internet* (Oxford University Press 2012), 60.

[82] Benjamin Loveluck, *Réseaux, libertés et contrôle. Une généalogie politique d'Internet* (Armand Colin 2015), 63.

the digital world turned inapt to be a space of equality. It was invaded by social, economic, political and geopolitical issues, as well as by disparities, that – online as offline – needed a public power. Moreover, at that time – exactly as now – a way to effectively govern these matters was yet to be found by States and supranational organisations. To cut a long story short, the fact of treating the Internet as a 'virgin space' has contributed to making it 'appropriable' from a juridical point of view: while great emphasis was given to the collaborative creation, little attention was paid to either the exclusive or the collective appropriation of the final products. [83]

Subsequently, these dynamics of appropriation have generated a "tragedy of anticommons", [84] by subtracting from social utility non-rival goods that could have been shared collectively without consuming the resource. Big data and algorithms have been concealed behind trade secrets. Even administrations sometimes are tempted to keep them as private property, managed in an exclusive way or even destined to generate income. [85]

Exclusive appropriation of data by Internet service providers (ISPs) has also generated informational oligopolies in the digital space. This is a consequence of indirect network effects, which make the advertising revenues flow towards the already dominant actors. Indeed, on the one hand, advertisers prefer to invest in the most crowded platforms, since they acquire more data, thus guaranteeing a more effective targeted marketing. On the other hand, the incumbent's service is more appealing to consumers, because the dominant player hosts a larger community and has more profit to invest in quality. Therefore, a "snowball effect" hits the newcomers, who fail to gain customers and consequently are unable to gather data in order to procure advertising venues and cover the initial costs. [86] Moreover, oligopolists have started to gain control of information, to the extent that they have acquired enough power to become an equal partner with the State in law-making.

If inequalities online are linked to intellectual property, this is where positive action is needed. [87] Notwithstanding that, EU seems to still act mostly in favour of

---

[83] Dominique Cardon, *La démocratie Internet. Promesses et limites* (Seuil/La République des Idées 2010), 32–33; Robin Mansell, 'Power, Hierarchy and the Internet: Why the Internet Empowers and Disempowers' (2016) Global Studies Journal http://eprints.lse.ac.uk/64855/, 22–23.

[84] Barbara J. Evans 'Barbarians at the Gate: Consumer-Driven Health Data Commons and the Transformation of Citizen Science' (2017) 42, 4 American Journal of Law and Medicine, 15.

[85] Danièle Bourcier and Primavera De Filippi, 'Vers un nouveau modèle de partage entre l'administration et les communautés numériques', in Nicolas Matyjasik and Philippe Mazuel (eds), *Génération Y et gestion publique: quels enjeux?* (Comité pour l'histoire économique et financière de la France 2012), 4.

[86] Autorité de la Concurrence and Bundeskartellamt, Competition Law and Data (2016) http://www.autoritedelaconcurrence.fr/doc/reportcompetitionlawanddatafinal.pdf, 718–733; Maria Orefice, 'Big Data. Regole e concorrenza' (2016) 4 Politica del diritto, 17–51.

[87] The turn towards putting enclosures in the Internet is largely due to the opinion that property rights are needed to encourage the production of such immaterial goods, by ensuring a remuneration to creators. However, it is very controversial whether or not intellectual property would be the best answer to

the digital single market and the growth of European enterprises. This was evident in two of the most recent Acts, concerning the regulation of online communications and commerce: the GDPR and the Copyright Directive. [88]

The first one harmonises data protection law imposing more effective sanctions and stricter requirements on private data collection. That given, the Regulation facilitates circulation of data in the EU, by preventing restrictions based on national privacy laws. However, it has failed to consider an issue crucial for substantial equality: the different bargaining power of parties. Article 7 states that 'when assessing whether consent is freely given, utmost account shall be taken of whether, inter alia, the performance of a contract, including the provision of a service, is conditional on consent to the processing of personal data that is not necessary for the performance of that contract'. But it does not provide an outright ban on such contractual clauses. This circumstance makes it impossible to effectively ensure that consent is freely given, because in that case even the better informed consumer, sensitive to his/her privacy, would accept to give data away, since some services are needed in everyday lives. [89]

The Copyright Directive gives an answer to the most pressing problem of entertainment businesses, [90] by imposing measures that, according to different authors, threaten open access to culture. [91] The most contested ones are the provisions of Article 11, which creates new rights for publishers, and Article 13, which appears to oblige ISPs to install filters to impede the violation of copyright perpetrated by third parties' content.

On the one hand, it is true that such measures seem to hinder the *laissez-faire* economy of the Internet. However, on the other hand, commentators have noticed that they do not ultimately harm big ISPs, which already act as near monopolists in

---

this problem: Dean Baker, Arjun Jayadev and Joseph Stiglitz, ,'Innovation, Intellectual Property, and Development: A Better Set of Approaches for the 21st Century' (Accessibsa.org, July 2017) https://www.accessibsa.org/media/2017/12/Innovation-Intellectual-Property-and-Development.pdf, 8–25.

[88] COM(2016) 593: Proposal for a Directive of the European Parliament and of the Council on Copyright in the Digital Single Market, Procedure 2016/0280/COD, https://eur-lex.europa.eu/legal-content/EN/HIS/?uri=COM:2016:0593:FIN.

[89] Article 29 Data Protection Working Party, 'Working Document 02/2013 providing guidance on obtaining consent for cookies' (1676/13/EN; WP 208, 2 October 2013) http://ec.europa.eu/justice/data-protection/article-29/documentation/opinion-recommendation/files/2013/wp208_en.pdf, 5. Cfr. Agencia Espanola de Proteccion de Datos, 'Guia Sobre el Uso de las Cookies' (29 April 2013) https://www.agpd.es/portalwebAGPD/canaldocumentacion/publicaciones/common/Guias/Guia_Cookies.pdf, para. II.3.B).viii.

[90] Mike Masnick, 'Legacy Copyright Industries Lobbying Hard For EU Copyright Directive ... While Pretending that Only Google is Lobbying' (TechDirt.com, 12 December 2018) https://www.techdirt.com/articles/20181212/07074641205/legacy-copyright-industries-lobbying-hard-eu-copyright-directive-while-pretending-that-only-google-is-lobbying.shtml.

[91] 'Article 13 Open letter – Monitoring and Filtering of Internet Content is Unacceptable' (2017), Open letter from 57 signatories asking EU policy-makers to delete Article 13 of the new proposal on copyright in the digital single market https://www.liberties.eu/en/news/delete-article-thirteen-open-letter/13194?utm_source=POLITICO.EU&utm_campaign=91f2de513a-EMAIL_CAMPAIGN_2017_10_16&utm_medium=email&utm_term=0_10959edeb5-91f2de513a-190133949.

the respective markets. Indeed, most of them have already installed filtering mechanisms. Conversely, such measures amount to a hardly sustainable burden for smaller enterprises, which could discourage start-ups from growing beyond the threshold of application of Article 13.[92] Hence, the Directive risks reinforcing the strong companies and increasing the barriers to entry of newcomers in the markets. This is why, even though every monopolist's preference is deregulation, 'their second preference was also always going to be lots of regulation, provided that they could afford the regulatory costs and no one who might challenge them could'.[93]

Moreover, even if one of the declared objectives of the Directive is to safeguard the creators' rights, the final text failed to align with the best practices of Member States in regulating the contractual relationships between authors and industries.[94] Yet, protecting the immaterial workers' labour should be the first aim of a copyright regulation, as well as the only reason justifying the limitation of access to culture.

In sum, both instances – the GDPR and the Copyright Directive – show that, even on the Internet, the path of EU harmonisation is driven by the economy, rather than social rights. This highlights the fact that the Union has not yet overcome its original economic vocation, and is still more prone to markets than to equality and cohesion within and among the territories. Now, the challenge is to go beyond the commercial ratio of the "four freedoms", and start building a European digital citizenship as a tool for political and economic inclusion.

---

92 Lenard Koschwitz, 'The European Parliament is Discussing an Expiry Date for Startups' (Tech.eu, 11 July 2017) https://tech.eu/features/16029/european-parliament-expiry-date-startups/.

93 Cory Doctorow, 'Article 13: If You Want to Force Google to Pay Artists More, Force Google to Pay Artists More' (EFF.org, 21 November 2018) https://www.eff.org/deeplinks/2018/11/article-13-if-you-want-force-google-pay-artists-more-force-google-pay-artists-more.

94 Directorate General for Internal Policies – Policy Department for Citizens' Rights and Constitutional Affairs Legal and Parliamentary Affairs, 'Strengthening the Position of Press Publishers and Authors and Performers in the Copyright Directive' (2017) PE 596.810 http://www.europarl.europa.eu/RegData/etudes/STUD/2017/596810/IPOL_STU%282017%29596810_EN.pdf, 43 ss.

Index

For Product Safety Concerns and Information please contact our EU representative GPSR@taylorandfrancis.com
Taylor & Francis Verlag GmbH, Kaufingerstraße 24, 80331 München, Germany

www.ingramcontent.com/pod-product-compliance
Ingram Content Group UK Ltd.
Pitfield, Milton Keynes, MK11 3LW, UK
UKHW022133190926
475702UK00013B/1791

* 9 7 8 0 3 6 7 5 5 0 1 7 2 *